RAINBOW'S END

California Series on Social Choice and Political Economy
Edited by Brian Barry, Robert H. Bates, and Samuel L. Popkin

RAINBOW'S END

*Irish-Americans and the Dilemmas of
Urban Machine Politics, 1840–1985*

STEVEN P. ERIE

UNIVERSITY OF CALIFORNIA PRESS
BERKELEY   LOS ANGELES   LONDON

University of California Press
Berkeley and Los Angeles, California

University of California Press, Ltd.
London, England

© 1988 by
The Regents of the University of California

First Paperback Printing 1990

Library of Congress Cataloging-in-Publication Data

Erie, Steven P.
    Rainbow's end: Irish-Americans and the dilemmas of urban
machine politics, 1840–1985 / Steven P. Erie.
    p. cm—(California series on social choice and political
economy)
    Bibliography: p.
    Includes index.
    ISBN 0-520-07183-2
    1. Irish Americans—Political activity.   2. Politics, Prac-
tical—United States—History.   3. Municipal government—
United States—History.   4. Metropolitan government—
United States—History.
I. Title. II. Series.
E184.I6E75   1989
352'.000899162—dc19
                                                87-35488
                                                CIP

Printed in the United States of America
    2   3   4   5   6   7   8   9

To My Grandparents
Delbert Vincent and Idamae Elizabeth O'Brien
and
To My Cousin Scott

List of Tables

Contents

Preface

San Diego, California, may strike the reader as a strange place to complete a book on the legendary Irish-American big-city political machines such as New York's Tammany Hall or the Daley organization in Chicago. Yet America's Finest City (as the local news commentators are so fond of saying) may not be so inappropriate a locale after all. Despite a reputation as a WASP bastion, the city has Irish political bloodlines. Mayor Maureen O'Connor is as Irish as they come. Former Mayor (and current U.S. Senator) Pete Wilson reportedly inherited his political talent from an Irish grandfather on the Chicago police force.

Underneath the veneer of nonpartisan reform, San Diego is also no stranger to the political corruption associated with the big-city eastern machines. In recent years a mayor, a city councilman, and a registrar of voters have resigned from office under shadow of an indictment or conviction.

In actuality, San Diego is but the final way station on a project that has enjoyed a long gestation period. My initial interest in Irish-American politics is a product of my own bloodlines. On my mother's side of the family are O'Briens, O'Neills, McGinleys, and Tobins—public payrollers all. Grandfather O'Brien was an assistant county assessor; Great Grandfather O'Brien, a county sheriff. Great Uncle Billy O'Neill was an "expediter" for the Daley machine, smoothing relations between North Side businesses and the party organization. In a literal sense, this book was "in the blood."

There have been other way stations and helpers. At UCLA, a dissertation on San Francisco ethnic and working-class politics in the late nineteenth century introduced me to Chris Buckley, an early West Coast Irish-American political boss, and to the methodological possibilities and pitfalls posed by the historical study of urban politics. I wish to thank Stephan Thernstrom, Francine Rabinovitz, Leo Snowiss, and Chuck Ries for encouraging (or at least acquiescing in) my interest in ethnic political history.

In a more immediate sense, this book is the outgrowth of a collaborative study of big-city political machines begun in the late 1970s with John Petrocik and Paul Sacks. John, Paul, and I spent a profitable year debating the nature of machine politics and how to study it. By their nature, triads are unstable, and ours was no exception. Tired of being on the perpetual short end of a two-to-one voting split and eager to study a political machine up close, I journeyed to Albany, New York.

There I found the powerful Irish-American Democratic organization of which an awed James McGregor Burns wrote a few years ago that "it is so well preserved that it should be put into the Smithsonian before we forget what a political machine looks like." I wish to thank the late Erastus Corning II, former mayor of Albany, William Kennedy, and my colleagues and friends at SUNY Albany for sharing their thoughts about the "house that Dan O'Connell built."

Next came a year's tour of duty with the U.S. Department of Health and Human Services in Washington, D.C. This sensitized me to the importance of the welfare state—critical for understanding the fate of the big-city machines in the twentieth century—and to the importance of intergovernmental politics.

San Diego, home of the largest St. Patrick's Day parade west of Chicago, has been a marvelous place to complete the work on this project. I would like to bestow honorary Celtic status on my colleagues, graduate students, and friends at UC San Diego for all the support they have shown. Vanessa Cunningham, Pete Irons, Sandy Lakoff, Tracy Strong, Sam Kernell, David Laitin, Neal Beck, Gary Jacobson, Priscilla Long, John Gilmour, Jim Ingram, Kathy Underwood, Mike Coste, Judy Johnson, Marilyn Wilson, and Nicole Moran read—and improved—innumerable drafts. Anita Schiller and Sue Galloway deserve special thanks for mobilizing the entire University of California library system to track down fugitive references. From afar, Clarence Stone, Stephan Thernstrom, David

Greenstone, Amy Bridges, Marty Rein, Norton E. Long, and Michael P. Smith have lent encouragement and constructive criticism. Michele Moran and Kelly Charter are to be thanked for their word-processing assistance. I owe to Michael K. Brown an example of how to pay professional and personal debts. He shall receive repayment in kind.

My most profound intellectual debt is owed to my friend Harold Brackman. Harold's sage and incisive comments on an early version of the manuscript enabled me to deepen the argument and to shape a flawed manuscript into a readable book. A free copy from the author is hardly adequate payment for his labors.

Del Mar, California
June 1987

Chapter One

The Irish and the
Big-City Machines

Rainbow's End is a study of Irish-American machine politics from the mid-nineteenth century to the present in eight once heavily Irish cities: New York, Philadelphia, Chicago, Boston, San Francisco, Pittsburgh, Jersey City, and Albany. Daniel Patrick Moynihan has observed that the Irish-American genius has been organizational rather than entrepreneurial or intellectual.[1] Displaying a "distaste for commerce" and ideas, the Irish labored to build the American Catholic church and the big-city Democratic machines. Arguably the largest section in the pantheon of Irish-American heroes is reserved for the big-city party bosses, from Tammany Hall's "Honest John" Kelly in the 1870s to Chicago's Richard Daley in the 1970s.

Notwithstanding the demise of the old-time big-city machines, Irish-American politicos are still larger-than-life figures. The departed Celtic party bosses continue to cast a long shadow over contemporary urban minority groups, particularly blacks and Hispanics, who search for routes of group economic advancement. The Irish are reputed to have used a political route to travel from rags to riches, capturing the patronage-laden machines and turning public employment into an Irish preserve. Before today's ethnic groups emulate the Irish, however, they would do well to carefully examine the Irish experience with the big-city machines, separating historical fact from fiction. This study attempts such a task.

The machine emerged as the major urban political institution in the late nineteenth century; the Irish were among its leading architects and practitioners. A form of clientele politics, the party machine organized the electorate in order to control the tangible benefits of public office—patronage, services, contracts, and franchises. The machine employed these resources to maintain power. Bosses purchased voter support with offers of public jobs and services rather than by appeals to traditional loyalties or to class interests.

With roots in the second or Jacksonian party system of the 1820s and 1830s, the full-fledged or mature urban machine did not emerge until the third party system entered an advanced stage in the 1870s and 1880s. By 1890 centralized machines controlled one-half of the nation's twenty largest cities. Tammany Hall finally had consolidated its hold over Manhattan. Hugh McLaughlin's Democratic organization ruled neighboring Brooklyn. In Philadelphia, the McManes's Republican machine, which had governed the city since the end of the Civil War, was about to give way to the Durham and Vare GOP machines. Chris Magee ruled Republican Pittsburgh, and George Cox controlled Republican Cincinnati. Edward Butler had created a bipartisan machine to run St. Louis. San Francisco was controlled by the Democratic "Blind Boss" Christopher Buckley and the fire department, his political praetorian guard. Robert "Little Bob" Davis controlled Jersey City and surrounding Hudson County. Boss William F. Sheehan ran politics in Republican Buffalo. An entrenched Democratic machine, successor to Martin Van Buren's Regency, ruled Albany.[2]

Although the Irish did not control all of the big-city machines by 1890, they had captured most of the Democratic party organizations in the northern and midwestern cities. Lamenting the "Irish conquest of our cities," Yankee John Paul Bobcock furnished in 1894 a roll call of the late-nineteenth-century Celtic party bosses: John Kelly and Richard Croker in New York City, Hugh McLaughlin in Brooklyn, Mike McDonald in Chicago, Pat Maguire in Boston, Christopher Buckley in San Francisco, William Sheehan in Buffalo, and "Little Bob" Davis in Jersey City. In the twentieth century, more names would be added to the list: Charles Francis Murphy in New York City; Ed Kelly, Pat Nash, and Richard Daley in Chicago; James Michael Curley and Martin Lomasney in Boston; David Lawrence in Pittsburgh; Frank Hague in Jersey City; Dan O'Connell in Albany; and Tom and Jim Pendergast in Kansas City.[3]

The Irish, as Edward Levine argues, were "given to politics."[4] No other ethnic group made the same contribution to the building of the urban machines. Germans migrated to the United States in as large numbers as the Irish. The Germans were also nearly as urbanized as the Irish, settling in midwestern rather than eastern cities. Yet there were few German bosses or machines. Jews embraced reform and labor rather than machine politics. San Francisco's Abe Ruef and Chicago's Jake Arvey were among the few Jewish bosses. A few black bosses such as William Dawson in Chicago and Homer Brown in Pittsburgh ran sub-machines of white-controlled organizations. To the extent that the Irish-American bosses designated an ethnic heir apparent, it was the Italians. Italian bosses such as Carmine De Sapio of Tammany Hall took over many of the aging Irish machines in the late 1940s and 1950s. Yet the Italians were usually called on to preside over the machine's demise, not its rebirth. In more than one sense, the Italians were left "holding the bag."

Not only did the Irish predominate among urban ethnic party bosses, but they were also the architects of the strongest and most long-lived big-city machines. Compared with their Republican counterparts, Irish-run Democratic machines proved to be mobilizing and welfarist organizations. Republican machines, in Lincoln Steffens's phrase, were constructed "in the air."[5] As urban offshoots of state-level GOP machines, Republican big-city machines relied on the Yankee middle-class vote and did little to mobilize immigrant voters. With a middle-class constituency demanding low taxes, big-city GOP machines had little incentive to incorporate working-class immigrant groups and reward them with costly welfare services.

Big-city Democratic political machines, in contrast, were built "from the bottom up." Rooted in the institutional life of working-class ethnic neighborhoods—saloons, clubhouses, volunteer fire departments—Democratic organizations did a better job than their Republican counterparts of naturalizing and registering immigrants and rewarding them with patronage jobs and social services. The resulting longevity of Irish Democratic machines is re-

markable. Under Celtic tutelage, Tammany Hall ran New York
(with minor exceptions) from 1874 to 1933. The Hague machine
controlled Jersey City from 1917 to 1949. Dan O'Connell built the
Albany machine in 1922; it has yet to lose a city election. The Chicago machine ruled the Windy City from 1931 until Harold Washington's mayoral victory in 1983.

Yet the once mighty Irish machines are now in eclipse. Government bureaucracies and labor unions have assumed the welfare
and employment functions once fulfilled by the machines. Civil
service reform has limited their supply of patronage jobs. Their
ethnic constituents have moved to the suburbs. Of the legion of
Irish machines, only those of Chicago and Albany remain as relics
of the past. In all likelihood, these two vestiges will soon pass from
the scene. The powerful Chicago machine has been progressively
weakened since 1976, losing the mayoral elections of 1979 and
1983. The Albany machine entered an interregnum phase with the
death of Erastus Corning, O'Connell's successor, in 1983.

The Rainbow Theory of the Machine

Paradoxically, the demise of the Irish machine has been accompanied by a metamorphosis in our understanding of its achieve-
ments. During its heyday, it was castigated by progressives as
corrupt and undemocratic. For muckraker Lincoln Steffens, the
shame of machine politics was the "triumph of the commercial
spirit" in public life.[6] Political reformer Frederick Howe scored the
city boss for serving as a "majordomo" for large transportation
and utility firms while ignoring the welfare of the working class.[7]
For M. Ostrogorski, machine politics marked the triumph of
"party formalism," the elevation of office over political principle.[8]

In the machine's twilight era, social scientists such as Robert
Merton and Robert Dahl offered a much different understanding
of its performance. The new view may be termed the "rainbow"
theory of the old-style urban machine. The theory refers to both
the *players* and the *prizes* of urban politics. In this view, urban machines, though corrupt and undemocratic, actively worked to incorporate working-class immigrant groups such as the Irish, Jews,
and Italians. Machines supposedly fashioned multiethnic "rain-

bow" electoral coalitions, rewarding each group with jobs and services drawn from a sizable pot of municipal gold.[9]

The prizes awaiting ethnic capture in city politics appeared substantial. Urban machines controlled thousands of official and unofficial patronage jobs, the latter with firms franchised by or doing business with the city. More than 40,000 New York municipal jobs, for example, were at Tammany Hall's disposal in the late 1880s. Machines also controlled the awarding of public contracts, especially important in an era when cities were making their major capital improvements. Between 1900 and 1910, for example, San Francisco embarked on an ambitious program to make the city the "Paris of North America." Municipal expenditures rose threefold, from $5.6 to $17.4 million, to pay for new schools, hospitals, parks, playgrounds, sewers, and utilities. Local newspapers estimated that more than 6,000 contract jobs had been created by the program, considerably exceeding the combined city-county payroll.[10]

According to the rainbow theory, the Irish were the main beneficiaries of machine politics. Robert Dahl, for example, argues that the Irish used a political strategy to move from the working class into the middle class in the late nineteenth and early twentieth centuries. Celtic political activity—voter mobilization, participation in party politics, and municipal office holding—supposedly led to a disproportionate share of public sector resources, thereby accelerating the development of an Irish middle class. First- and second-generation Irish displayed a singular talent for electoral politics. In San Francisco, the proportion of adult Irish males registered to vote in 1900 was nearly double that of the city's other foreign-born adult males—70 percent versus 37 percent—and equaled that of the native-born.[11]

Group political mobilization seemingly brought economic results. Controlling such cities as New York, Chicago, Boston, and San Francisco by the 1880s, Irish bosses helped "Hibernianize" the public payroll. In the nation's fourteen largest cities between 1870 and 1900, the proportion of public employees of Irish parentage climbed from 11 percent to 30 percent while the proportion of the labor force of Irish parentage in these cities remained at 20 percent. Using public sector job opportunities, the Irish appeared to move into the urban middle class with surprising rapidity considering their meager job skills and the employment discrimination they encountered. Between 1870 and 1900 the proportion of first- and second-generation Irish in white-collar jobs in cities of more than 100,000 population, where over 40 percent of the nation's Irish-Americans lived, rose from 12 percent to 27 percent, while among the non-Irish in the big cities, the increase in white-collar ranks was relatively smaller, from 27 percent to 34 percent.[12]

The rainbow theory figured prominently in the ethnic revival movement of the 1960s and 1970s. Blacks and "unmeltable" whites drew on—and further embellished—the legend of Irish power. In particular, the legend served as a yardstick in the black power debates because it supposedly demonstrated the efficacy of local electoral strategies for capturing public sector resources, enabling significant numbers of an ethnic group to escape poverty. Blacks found the Irish model increasingly compelling as their political demands shifted from obtaining legal rights in the South to remedying economic conditions in the urban North. Black political leaders were called on to exchange nonelectoral skills—mass protest and constitutional litigation—for the electoral and organizational skills practiced by the Irish. As Charles Hamilton argues, "While other racial and ethnic leaders could spend time exploring the process of machine politics—learning how to recruit and deliver voters, and how to reward, punish and bargain for benefits— blacks had to spend time checking legal precedents and filing lawsuits. . . . Blacks, in other words, developed plaintiffs rather than precinct captains. . . . There were no black success models in the manner of Tammany Hall, Boss Crump, or the Cook County Democratic political machine."[13]

Notwithstanding its popularity, it is time to lay the rainbow theory of the urban machine to rest. In this study I argue that throughout most of their history, urban machines did *not* incorporate immigrants other than the Irish. The machine's arsenal of resources was far more modest than it sometimes appeared. Owing to the scarce nature of the machine's benefits, the Irish could not readily translate political power into group economic advancement. Limited as these prizes were, the Irish jealously guarded them, parsimoniously accommodating the later-arriving Southern and Eastern Europeans and blacks. The newcomers struggled constantly with their Irish political overlords. Their anti-Irish insurgency took varied forms: third parties, reform movements, and revolts within the machines. For the later ethnic arrivals, integration into the urban machines was a hard-won, delayed, and ultimately limited accomplishment.

My critique of the rainbow theory is based on a reassessment of both the machine's electoral strategies and its resource supply. In brief, the entrenched Irish machines were one-party regimes with few opponents. Having already constructed a minimal winning coalition among "old" immigrant—that is, Western European—voters, the established machines had little need to naturalize, register, and vote later ethnic arrivals. Moreover, machine bosses did not control an unlimited cornucopia of benefits. In particular, there was a limited supply of patronage with which to reward various ethnic claimants. So that the Irish could control the machine's scarce core resources of power and patronage, the Celtic bosses gave the slowly mobilizing "new" immigrants from Southern and Eastern Europe less valuable benefits—services, symbolic recognition, and collective benefits such as labor and social welfare legislation.

If power represented the "approved Irish secular value," as Edward Levine argues, there were limits to its use.[14] In this study, I address two interrelated dilemmas of the Irish machine, one economic, the other political. The first dilemma is that it was a poor mechanism for Irish economic advancement. Individual Irish bosses, contractors, and lawyers made fortunes off the machine. Tammany boss Richard Croker, for example, born penniless, retired from political life to enjoy the pleasures of raising horses on his baronial estate in Ireland. Yet I would argue that political machines could not serve as a route from rags to riches for the Irish working class. The first generation of machines built in the late nineteenth century controlled too little patronage to affect appreciably the life chances of the Irish. The twentieth-century machines created a much greater supply of patronage, and the Irish crowded into the public sector. On the eve of the Depression, more than one-third of the Irish workforce in machine cities depended on patronage for their livelihood. Yet the patronage created was blue-collar rather than white-collar, the wrong sort for group social mobility. As policemen, firemen, and city laborers, the Irish remained solidly lower-middle-class. Only with the machine's decline, forcing the Irish into higher education and private sector jobs, have the Irish been able to build a solid middle class rooted in business and the professions.[15] There were good political reasons for machines to prefer creating blue-collar jobs even though this hindered Irish economic advancement. Blue-collar jobs were cheaper, and more could be created for a given outlay. More jobs meant more votes for the machine.

The second dilemma of the Irish machine was political. The machine's organizational maintenance needs—building citywide electoral pluralities, securing necessary party financing, placating the business community—introduced a conservative strain into Irish-American urban leadership, resulting in lost opportunities to represent working-class political interests more fully. As they learned to manipulate the levers of urban power, Irish bosses turned their backs on more radical forms of working-class politics. The machine ultimately tamed Irish voters as well as leaders. The Irish working class was in the forefront of the labor insurgency against the machines in the 1870s and 1880s. Yet Irish enthusiasm for labor politics dimmed as ever-larger numbers were brought into the patronage system. The failure of labor parties in the big cities can thus partly be understood in terms of the threat they posed to the entrenched Irish machines and their ethnic beneficiaries.

The Life Cycle of the Urban Machine

Rainbow's End is a study of big-city machine politics as well as of ethnic politics. A second purpose of this study is to offer a new theory of the life cycle of the urban machine—its origins, longevity, and decline. Regarding the machine's origins, I offer a revision of the two leading theories. A "mass" theory, found in the work of Edward Banfield, James Q. Wilson, and Daniel Patrick Moynihan, argues that machines emerge as a reflection of an ethnic group's values and social structure. For Banfield and Wilson, the machine's trafficking in divisible benefits is a response to the "private-regarding" ethos of the European immigrants. For Moynihan, Celtic machines such as Tammany Hall are a reproduction of Irish village life.[16]

An "elite" theory, such as that found in the work of Martin Shefter, views the machine as an elite- rather than mass-created institution. Immigrant voters may demand divisible material benefits, but this demand pattern does not inevitably produce a centralized political machine. Party bosses build centralized machines by successfully resolving the organization's maintenance needs—a winning supply of votes, reward and discipline of the party's precinct and ward captains, control of public officials, and adequate party financing.[17]

This study poses a question that neither of these theories adequately answers: Why did cities such as New York produce powerful long-lasting machines whereas cities such as Boston, America's Dublin, never rose above factional ward politics? Mass and elite theories would predict that centralized machines would emerge in each city. Both cities had large Irish populations. Both cities had talented and ambitious Irish party leaders—John Kelly, Richard Croker, and Charles Francis Murphy in New York and James Michael Curley and Martin Lomasney in Boston.

I answer this question with an *intergovernmental* theory of big-city machines that highlights the pivotal role of local alliances with party leaders at the state and federal levels during the machine's fragile incubation period. In New York, unlike Massachusetts, Democratic governors friendly to Tammany Hall in the 1880s directed state patronage to the fledgling machine, seriously weakening Tammany's factional opponents by freezing them out of state assistance. Machine-building alliances extended to the federal level as well. During the 1930s, Irish party bosses such as Ed Kelly and Pat Nash in Chicago and David Lawrence in Pittsburgh used federal job programs such as the WPA to build a new generation of Democratic machines.

Once centralized machines emerged, how did they maintain themselves in power? The rainbow theory suggests they built multiethnic coalitions, enticing each group with the organization's apparent arsenal of jobs, services, and other tangible benefits. In this study I offer a different theory of the machine's longevity. Contrary to the rainbow theory, the political mobilization of ethnic groups entailed substantial risks. Newly enfranchised voters could demand more than the machine could offer. Moreover, throughout most of its history, there were sharp limits on the machine's supply of material inducements. For example, the willingness of voters and taxpayers to support an increase in city tax rates or indebtedness limited the number of municipal patronage jobs. The specter of middle-class tax revolts haunted Irish party bosses from John Kelly in the 1870s to Richard Daley in the 1970s. To these political constraints on the machine's patronage stock must be added legal constraints. State Republican machines and even a few reform Democratic governors fashioned constitutional straitjackets on the machine's ability to raise and spend public money.

Whereas the rainbow theory *assumes* a cornucopia of machine resources and concentrates on the question how machines distributed benefits to different claimants, I start with the premise that party bosses had to husband *scarce* resources. The demands of ethnic groups and the working class for jobs and services nearly always exceeded the machine's available supply. The secret of machine longevity, then, was bringing electoral demand into balance with resource supply.

How did machines manage electoral demand? I distinguish between two distinct stages of machine building: an embryonic stage, where fledgling machines face strong competitive electoral pressures from the opposition party and from rival factions within their own party; and a consolidation stage, where machines have triumphed over their opponents and have built minimal winning voter coalitions. Embryonic machines are mobilizers. They face competitive pressures to increase the number of partisan voters. Entrenched machines, in contrast, are selective mobilizers. Having defeated the other party's machine and rival factions, consolidated machines need only bring out their traditional supporters. There is little electoral incentive to mobilize newer ethnic arrivals.

Embryonic machines actively courted nonvoters. Tammany Hall's record naturalization of 41,000 immigrants in the 1868 gubernatorial campaign is testimony to the budding machine's weakness, not its strength. Similarly, late nineteenth-century Irish Democratic machines in San Francisco, Boston, Jersey City, and Albany naturalized and registered the "old," that is, Western European, immigrants. In cities controlled by fledgling machines, there was a dramatic increase in the size of the urban electorate and in voter participation rates.

The problem with the mobilization approach to managing electoral demand is that newly enfranchised voters must in some fashion be rewarded. Otherwise, their grievances against the machine mount and they are ripe for capture by the machine's opponents. Embryonic machines, however, often did not have the resources to pay off their new constituents. The mobilizing Irish machines of the late nineteenth century were forced by political and legal constraints to pursue conservative fiscal and patronage policies. The price of mobilizing the "old" ethnics was the continued threat of working-class insurgency. In the 1886 New York mayoral election, for example, Tammany Hall lacked the resources to buy off the ethnic working class and barely beat back the challenge of Henry George and the United Labor party.

Electoral mobilization without reward forced fledgling machines to develop a second set of voter management techniques. Electoral fraud and repression represented the major secondary techniques. In New York City's crucial 1886 mayoral election, Tammany Hall countered massive Irish and German working-class support for Henry George with thorough control of the city's police and thus of the ballot box. Uncounted ballots, nearly all for George, were seen floating down the Hudson for days after the election. In the twentieth century, the Chicago and Albany machines confounded the census takers by registering and voting the dead, the departed, and even the unborn. O'Connell's organization in Albany, for example, claimed the votes of 61 percent of the city's entire *population* of 131,000 in the 1940s.

Besides voter fraud, emerging machines used repression to weaken their opponents. Irish party bosses were famous for the ingenuity with which they systematically weakened labor and socialist parties. Machine-controlled bureaucrats and judges denied parade and meeting permits. The party's plug-uglies armed with brass knuckles waded into peaceful assemblies. Opposition leaders were frequently arrested on trumped-up charges. For insurgent Jews and Italians, the Irish machines specialized in rigorous enforcement of Sunday closing laws and in punitive denial of business permits.

Entrenched machines, in contrast, managed electoral demand in different ways. With little competitive electoral challenge, these machines turned a deaf ear to the pleas of newcomers for help with naturalization, registration, and voting. For example, what accounts for Tammany Hall's about-face in its treatment of immigrants between the 1860s and the early 1900s? The massive party-sponsored naturalization of the Irish and the Germans gave way to a not-so-benign electoral neglect of later-arriving Jews and Italians. Tammany's Yankee party chieftains in the 1860s had as much revulsion toward the Irish as Irish bosses after the turn of the century would have against the Southern and Eastern Europeans. The difference is that Tammany needed the immigrant vote in the 1860s and 1870s to fend off both a strong state Republican party and rival local Democratic organizations such as Irving Hall and the County Democracy. Having finally banished its opponents, except for an occasional reform mayor, the Tammany Hall of Charles Francis Murphy in 1910 no longer needed the new immigrant vote. Chicago's Irish Democratic party bosses Roger Sullivan and George Brennan worked far harder than their Tammany counterparts in the teens and twenties to naturalize and register the city's Poles, Czechs, Jews, and Italians. They had to, for Republican boss and mayor "Big Bill" Thompson was successfully mobilizing and wooing the same new ethnic voters.

The voter management strategy of the entrenched Irish machines—to mobilize the old but not the new immigrants—contributed to their short-term longevity. The machine's limited stock of patronage jobs and services would suffice to reward a smaller electorate of old but not new immigrants. This electoral strategy, however, had long-term costs. One of the chief reasons that the established Irish machines fell was that enterprising opposition leaders finally succeeded in mobilizing the new ethnics. For example, the Irish machines of New York and Jersey City fell in the 1930s and 1940s as reform leaders such as Fiorello La Guardia actively worked to naturalize, register, and win the votes of Italians, Jews, and Poles. In the 1980s, the Chicago machine staggered when finally challenged by the black community.

Electoral management is only half the story of the Irish machine's longevity. Machines also had to manage resources. The rainbow theory addresses the distributional strategies of the machines: how the Irish got police and fire jobs, the Jews teaching jobs, and the Italians lowly places in sanitation. Yet machines concentrated as much on *creating* resources as distributing them. Far too little attention has been given to what I would term a "supply-side" theory of the machine. What were the primary means machines used to enlarge the supply of tangible benefits, particularly new patronage jobs? What were the attendant political benefits *and* risks of different ways of enlarging the pie?

This study offers the beginnings of a "supply-side" theory of the machine. I consider such resource-enhancement strategies as tax increases, increases in public debt, annexation and incorporation, reliance on private sector patronage, and alliances with county, state, and federal bosses to capture additional public sector patronage. But each expansionary strategy had risks as well as benefits. For example, tax increases prompted middle-class tax revolts. Annexation enlarged the city's boundaries without increasing the tax rate. Yet annexation also enlarged the big-city electorate by including the outward-migrating and antimachine middle class.

Rainbow's End also presents a more complicated picture of the Irish machine's distributional decisions than that offered by conventional theory. The rainbow theorists posit an electorally "rational" distributional process: Machines allocate jobs and services to ethnic groups in proportion to their anticipated vote for the organization's candidates. This study argues that machine allocational decisions were more retrospective than prospective. Machines overrewarded previously incorporated groups and underrewarded newly incorporated groups. The Irish machine's supply of patronage jobs, for example, dramatically increased during the Progressive era. Remembering the old immigrants' antimachine insurgency in the 1870s and 1880s, the Celtic bosses gave the bulk of the new public sector jobs to the Irish rather than to Jews or Italians.

Rainbow theorists miss another dimension of the machine's allocational processes. The Irish machines developed elaborate ethnically differentiated benefit systems. The machine's core resources of power and patronage were reserved for the Irish, with minor shares given to the most serious challengers among the new ethnics, for example, Jews rather than Italians. Irish bosses preferred to give newcomers less valuable resources: services such as business licenses, symbolic recognition such as nomination to minor offices or machine observance of ethnic holidays such as Columbus Day, and labor and social welfare legislation.

Rainbow theorists also posit that machines trafficked primarily if not exclusively in divisible benefits rather than collective benefits. Divisible benefits such as patronage jobs could be rewarded or withheld from individuals in exchange for support for the machine. Collective benefits like Social Security checks, however, were distributed to program rather than political eligibles. Machines supposedly opposed collective benefits because they reduced the machine's monopoly over jobs and services for the working class. Machines could not control the allocation of collective benefits as readily as they could for divisible benefits.

This study, however, argues that machines actually supported collective benefit programs, ranging from the labor legislation of the Progressive era to the social welfare legislation of the New Deal and Great Society eras. The Irish machines lobbied for collective benefits in order to pay off junior ethnic coalitional partners at minimal cost to continued Irish control over the machine's divisible benefits of power and patronage. The machine's collective benefit strategy worked with Jews and Italians during the Progressive and New Deal eras and with blacks during the Great Society era.

The allocation of less valuable benefits to later ethnic groups represented a short-term machine distributional strategy. What happened when the new ethnics finally mobilized? In the long run, successful machines had to be more accommodating of the new ethnics' political demands. For working-class voters, demanding a great share of patronage jobs and welfare services, successful machines had to fashion a favorable exchange ratio between claimants and resources. Machines were in trouble when the ratio broke down because of rising numbers of voters or declining numbers of patronage jobs. Many of the established Irish machines fell precisely because they were unable to increase their resources as the big-city electorate grew.

The Depression and New Deal represented a watershed for big-city Irish machines. The machines' limited political incorporation of Southern and Eastern Europeans finally failed. Democratic presidential candidates Al Smith and Franklin D. Roosevelt brought

Jews, Italians, and Poles into the voting booth in record numbers. In cities such as New York and Chicago, the number of voters *doubled* between 1928 and 1936. What would happen if these new ethnic voters turned on the aging machines? Because of the Depression, the Irish machines found their resource base depleted at precisely the time they needed additional resources in order to court the new ethnics. The frenetic machine pursuit of federal patronage, particularly the WPA, can be understood as a strategy to increase the supply of machine benefits for the new voters.

To secure middle-class votes, however, machines had to devise a much different menu of policies. Middle-class voters were homeowners, sensitive to tax increases and less desirous of patronage jobs and welfare services. Middle-class voters demanded low taxes and homeowner services such as garbage collection and street repair. The longevity of the Irish machines of Chicago, Albany, and Pittsburgh well into the post—World War II era is attributable to their ability to shift from working-class to middle-class policies for white ethnics while piggybacking welfare-state programs for blacks and Hispanics.

This new theory of the machine's longevity in terms of an equilibrium between claimants and resources, particularly for working-class ethnic groups, is also a theory of the machine's demise. Middle-class reformers rarely destroyed machines. As Tammany sachem George Washington Plunkitt once observed, reformers were "shortlived morning glories."[18] Tammany Hall, for example, easily survived the reform administrations of Seth Low and John Purroy Mitchel. Machines were in trouble both when reformers increased the number of political participants by mobilizing the newer ethnic arrivals *and* when the machines lacked the resources to outbid them. Machines were in serious trouble when reformers rewarded as well as mobilized the newcomers. In New York City, Fiorello La Guardia permanently weakened Tammany Hall between 1933 and 1945 by mobilizing the city's Jews and Italians *and* by rewarding them. La Guardia tightened the city's civil service system in order to recruit Jews and Italians at the expense of the Irish while dramatically increasing the size of the city's human services bureaucracies. A new cohort of ethnic working-class voters had been politically indoctrinated and rewarded by Tammany's opponents. The Wigwam (as Tammany was called) would never be the same.

This study is particularly critical of one leading theory of the machine's demise. Rexford Tugwell in *The Brains Trust* and Edwin O'Connor in his magnificent *The Last Hurrah,* a barely fictionalized account of Boston's James Michael Curley, argue that New Deal social welfare programs destroyed the machines by breaking the organization's monopoly over the jobs and services distributed to urban working-class voters. With the advent of Social Security, Aid to Families with Dependent Children (AFDC), and unemployment compensation, urban voters no longer had to go to the machines for help.[19]

In some ways the New Deal did weaken local machines. FDR's mobilization of the urban ethnic vote destroyed or permanently weakened the established Republican machines in cities such as Pittsburgh and Philadelphia. The New Deal electoral coalition also turned on the entrenched Irish Democratic machines in cities such as New York and Jersey City. With many of the big-city machines reduced to rubble, New Deal labor legislation and social programs appeared to make it harder to build a *new* generation of machines. The Wagner Act, for example, strengthened labor as a political actor—in local as well as in national politics. In cities like Detroit with a strong reform rather than machine tradition, unions stepped into the political vacuum created by weak parties. The United Auto Workers' Committee on Political Education performed such party functions as getting out the vote. Union collective bargaining agreements took the place of the machine's patronage and welfare services. With unions performing traditional party functions, machines were harder to rebuild in the post–New Deal era. New Deal social programs, particularly Social Security, reduced the machine's control over the stream of government benefits going to voters and thus enabled some voters to be more politically independent.[20]

Yet for machines that survived the twin shoals of the New Deal electoral coalition and the Depression, the social programs of the New Deal and the Great Society represented potent tools for machine strengthening. In the postwar era, a third set of migrants came to northern cities. Poor blacks and Hispanics demanded the machine's traditional menu of patronage jobs and welfare services.

Yet machines could no longer supply these working-class benefits. Eroding tax bases and civil service reform cut deeply into the supply of patronage. Newly prosperous white middle-class voters demanded low taxes. Machines catered to the newer migrants with welfare-state programs, particularly public housing and AFDC, at minimal cost to the city treasury and to white taxpayers. Machine control of the black and Hispanic vote, however, now depended on a steady stream of social program benefits. With cutbacks in federal and state social programs in the Reagan era, this flow of benefits to the minority community was interrupted. The black revolt in the 1980s against the last of the machines was in large part fueled by welfare-state retrenchment. Social program retrenchment, not growth, has destabilized the few remaining big-city machines.

Overview of the Study

This interpretation of the machine's performance and beneficiaries is based on a comparative study of machine dynamics in eight once heavily Irish-American cities—New York, Philadelphia, Chicago, Boston, San Francisco, Pittsburgh, Jersey City, and Albany—from the mid-nineteenth century to the mid-1980s. As Table 1 shows, in 1870 these cities were among the eleven most heavily Irish of the twenty-five cities with more than 50,000 population. They ranged from Boston, with nearly one-quarter of its population born in Ireland, to Chicago, with almost one-eighth of its residents from the Emerald Isle. Of the ten most heavily Irish cities, only New Haven and Providence have been excluded from this study because of the paucity of data about their formative political histories. The existing studies of New Haven and Providence politics, however, suggest a replication of the patterns of machine and ethnic politics uncovered in the eight cities studied.[21]

This study is not based solely on a case study of a single machine. Nor is it based on case studies of only those cities where mature machines developed. Instead, I compare two sets of big cities with large Irish-American populations: those where Irish-controlled machines emerged and those cities where no strong citywide machine appeared or where a machine not controlled by

TABLE 1. *The Irish in the Cities, 1870*

	Irish-Born as Percentage of Total Population	Foreign-Born as Percentage of Total Population	Total Population	Rank (by Total Population)	Number of Irish-Born	Number of Foreign-Born
Boston	22.7	35.1	250,526	7	56,900	87,986
Jersey City	21.5	38.6	82,546	17	17,665	31,835
New York	21.4	44.5	942,292	1	201,199	419,094
Albany	19.1	32.0	69,422	20	13,276	22,207
New Haven	18.9	28.2	50,840	25	9,601	14,356
Brooklyn	18.7	36.5	396,099	3	73,985	144,718
Providence	17.5	24.9	68,904	21	12,085	17,177
San Francisco	17.3	49.3	149,473	10	25,864	73,719
Pittsburgh	15.2	32.3	86,076	16	13,119	27,822
Philadelphia	14.3	27.2	674,022	2	96,698	183,624
Chicago	13.4	48.4	298,977	5	39,988	144,557
Newark	11.9	34.2	105,059	13	12,481	35,884
Cleveland	10.7	41.8	92,829	15	9,964	38,815
St. Louis	10.4	36.1	310,864	4	32,329	112,249
Rochester	9.7	34.0	62,386	22	6,078	21,184
Buffalo	9.6	39.3	117,714	11	11,264	46,237
Detroit	8.8	44.5	79,577	18	6,970	35,381
Cincinnati	8.6	36.8	216,239	8	18,624	79,612
New Orleans	7.7	25.3	191,418	9	14,693	48,475
Louisville	7.6	25.5	100,755	14	7,626	25,668
Allegheny	7.6	28.8	53,180	23	4,034	15,308
Washington, D.C.	6.4	12.6	109,199	12	6,948	13,757
Baltimore	5.7	21.1	267,354	6	15,223	56,484
Milwaukee	5.3	47.3	71,440	19	3,784	33,773
Richmond	2.4	7.4	51,038	24	1,239	3,778

Source: U.S. Census Office, *Ninth Census, 1870* (Washington, D.C.: Government Printing Office, 1872), vol. 1, Table 8, pp. 386–391.
Note: This table includes the twenty-five cities with a population greater than 50,000 in 1870.

the Irish emerged. Table 2 shows that strong Irish-led Democratic machines were built in New York, Chicago, San Francisco, Pittsburgh, Jersey City, and Albany. In Philadelphia, as Dennis Clark argues, the Irish were handmaidens to a long-lived Republican machine they did not control.[22] Boston, the most Irish of the big cities, never rose above factional ward politics.

Mature machines exhibited certain characteristics. First, power was centralized in the hands of a single party boss. Second, the machine's power extended citywide. Despite pockets of opposition, mature machines commanded large electoral majorities. Consolidated machines also controlled most local offices and agencies and the patronage they commanded. Third, they exhibited staying power, winning several consecutive municipal elections and remaining in power for at least a decade. Fourth, machines trafficked primarily (but not exclusively) in divisible material benefits such as patronage jobs and welfare services. Political ideologies were foreign to the operation of the big-city machines. As a big-city machine politician remarked to James Bryce in 1880, "What are we here for except the offices?"[23]

Not only were there variations across cities in whether mature machines emerged, but there were also variations over time *within* machine cities in terms of the strength and longevity of the local party organization. In the late nineteenth century, Irish bosses built a first generation of Democratic machines in New York, San Francisco, Albany, and Jersey City. Of these four early machines, only Tammany Hall survived the debacle of 1896. During the Progressive era the Irish constructed a second generation of "reformed" machines in Albany and Jersey City. The New Deal realignment destabilized most of the entrenched Irish machines while spawning a third generation of more ethnically diverse Democratic machines in Chicago and Pittsburgh.

The temporal dimension of the Irish machines is of crucial importance. Each generation of machines embraced a distinct electoral coalition and set of policies. The four stages of Irish machine development considered in this study are as follows.

1840–1896. The Irish famine migration landed in the eastern cities in the late 1840s and early 1850s. By the late 1870s and early 1880s a first generation of Irish-run Democratic machines had emerged in New York (including Brooklyn, a separate city until

TABLE 2. *Machine Building in the Eight Cities, 1840–1985*

Political Regimes

City	1840	1850	1860	1870	1880	1890	1900	1910	1920	1930	1940	1950	1960	1970	1980	1985
New York[a]	Competitive Parties			Democratic Factionalism		Irish Democratic Machine (S) (Bosses Kelly, Croker, Murphy, Olvaney)					Fusion Reform	Italian Democratic Machine (W) (De Sapio)		Democratic & Fusion Reform		
Philadelphia						Yankee Republican Machine (S)						Democratic Reform				
Chicago			Democratic Factionalism						Yankee Republican Machine (W)	Irish Democratic Machine (S) (Kelly, Nash, Daley)				Democratic Factions		
Boston					Irish Democratic Factionalism								Democratic Reform			

	Nonpartisan Reform	Democratic and Labor Factions	Irish Democratic Machine (S) (Buckley)	Competitive Parties	Labor Machine (Ruef) (W)	Republican Reform		Democratic Reform
San Francisco	Nonpartisan Reform	Democratic and Labor Factions	Irish Democratic Machine (S) (Buckley)	Competitive Parties	Labor Machine (Ruef) (W)	Republican Reform		Democratic Reform
Pittsburgh	Yankee Republican Machine (S)						Irish Democratic Machine (S) (Lawrence, Barr)	Democratic Reform
Jersey City	Irish Democratic Machine (W) (Davis)			Republican Reform		Irish Democratic Machine (S) (Hague)	Irish Democratic Machine (W) (Kenney)	Democratic Reform
Albany	Yankee-Irish Democratic Machine (W) (Herrick, McCabe)			Yankee Republican Machine (S)		Irish Democratic Machine (S) (O'Connell, Corning)		Democratic Reform

Sources: Harold Zink, *City Bosses in the United States* (Durham, N.C.: Duke University Press, 1930); and Terry Nichols Clark, "The Irish Ethic and the Spirit of Patronage," *Ethnicity* 2 (1975): 327–343; as well as various sources cited in chapters 2–5.

Note: Regime typology based on (a) political structure; (b) dominant party; and (c) dominant ethnic group. Political structures: reform; competitive parties; one-party factionalism; weak machines (W); and strong machines (S).

[a] Manhattan until 1898; includes Brooklyn and the outer boroughs after 1898.

1898), San Francisco, Albany, and Jersey City. These cities featured large Irish voting populations *and* were in states with friendly Democratic governors. These early laissez-faire machines actively mobilized the Yankee and "old" immigrant—Irish, German, and English—working class. Because of the strength of their Republican opponents at both the local and state levels, these early machines pursued conservative fiscal, patronage, and labor policies. Lacking adequate patronage with which to co-opt the militant Irish working class, the early machines were plagued with working-class and immigrant insurgency.

1896–1928. A second generation of more long-lived Irish machines emerged during the Progressive era in Jersey City and Albany. The new machines differed from their nineteenth-century counterparts in key respects. First, they selectively mobilized the "old" but not the "new" immigrants, for example, the Irish but not the Jews or Italians. Second, they supported collective benefit programs such as Progressive-sponsored labor and social welfare legislation. Third, with the movement of the property-owning Yankee middle class to the suburbs, the ranks of the machine's opponents were reduced. The Irish machines could now pursue more expansionary fiscal policies with lessened risk of electoral reprisal. Expansionary fiscal policies increased the supply of patronage with which to reward restive working-class Irish voters. As ever-larger proportions of the Irish working class were drawn into the machine's patronage system, Irish enthusiasm for more radical labor politics diminished. The slowly mobilizing "new" ethnics were given services and symbolic recognition rather than patronage and power. However, the stability of the second-generation machines depended on restricting the newly arriving Southern and Eastern Europeans from electorally participating and making claims on the machine's resources.

1928–1950. The entrenched Irish machines became vulnerable to overthrow as the Depression depleted the patronage supply and as the New Deal party realignment finally mobilized the resentful Southern and Eastern Europeans. Yet the New Deal represented a machine-building as well as destabilizing force. In cities with weaker Democratic party organizations such as Chicago and Pittsburgh, the intraparty ethnic succession wars had been fought before the 1930s. In these cities, Irish bosses built a more ethnically diverse third generation of machines by capturing federal work relief patronage and by mobilizing and rewarding the new ethnics with power and jobs.

1950–1985. The postwar era marks a fourth and presumably final stage of machine development. Surviving Irish machines in Chicago, Pittsburgh, and Albany selectively mobilized middle-class white ethnics but not the newly arriving blacks and Hispanics. The postwar Irish machines offered a new set of locally financed policies: low taxes and homeowner services rather than the high taxes, massive patronage, and welfare services characteristic of earlier machines. As whites left the cities and the number of minorities grew, the postwar machines piggybacked federal welfare-state programs to appeal to the newer migrants. Welfare-state cutbacks politically galvanized blacks and threatened the remaining machines.

This study uses a wide variety of untapped data sources to study the electoral base, resources, and policies of big-city Irish machines. In terms of primary sources, I rely heavily on municipal reports, state blue books, federal census reports and program statistics, city directories, and newspaper almanacs. Municipal reports furnish valuable information on city revenue, spending and indebtedness patterns, patronage lists, voter registration, and election returns. State blue books yield lists of local public officials, public employees, and election returns. The dicennial federal census reports are a veritable gold mine of information on the big cities, particularly regarding ethnicity. They tell us about the ethnic composition of the big-city population, voting-age electorate, and specific groups of urban public employees such as policemen, firemen, teachers, and public officials. Federal program reports, such as those for AFDC and the WPA, furnish program expenditures and the number of recipients for various cities. Privately printed city directories provide rosters of local public officials and city employees. Finally, newspaper almanacs such as the New York World–Telegram *Almanac* and the Chicago Daily News *Almanac* yield big-city budgetary and electoral data in addition to lists of local party officials.

There are major reliability problems with many of these sources. The big-city machines were adept at their own version of double-entry bookkeeping: one set for the party bosses and one set for the public. Voter registration figures and election returns were padded for public consumption. City finances were systematically under-reported. Given these problems with primary sources, I have also used the massive secondary literature of books, articles, and dissertations on the politics of these machines, cities, and states.

The study is divided into two parts. The first part, consisting of Chapters 2 through 5, examines the four distinct stages of Irish-American machine politics: 1840–1896, 1896–1928, 1928–1950, and 1950–1985. The second part, consisting of Chapters 6 and 7, is theoretical. Chapter 6 examines machine building and the relation of party machines to the state. It focuses on the machine's life cycle: why centralized party organizations emerged in some cities and not in others, how machines maintained themselves, and what caused the machines' decline. The analysis also considers the clientelist perspective on the machine, placing the American big-city party organizations in broader comparative perspective. Chapter 7 addresses representational issues: the ways in which machines affected ethnic group political and economic life, and how machines shaped working-class politics. In particular, the chapter examines the machine's supposed "redistributional" function and the role of machines in producing America's muted version of working-class politics.

Chapter Two

Building the Nineteenth-Century Machines, 1840–1896

Introduction

Between 1846 and 1855 1.4 million Irish famine immigrants came to the United States. Though nearly all were rural cotters and laborers, more than 90 percent of the migrants would settle in the cities. The immigrants were field laborers, not farmers, in a single-crop economy. Only 6 percent of them would resettle on the land.

Because of the trans-Atlantic packet boat routes, most of the immigrants landed in the eastern port cities of Boston, New York, and Philadelphia. Lacking cash and the physical stamina to move inland, more than one-quarter of the famine immigrants would remain in these three cities. Parish priests encouraged them to stay in the eastern cities, where a network of Catholic churches already existed. Slowly, however, the uprooted followed canal and railroad projects, fanning out to the growing cities of New England, upstate New York, and the Great Lakes—New Haven, Providence, Albany, Buffalo, Cleveland, Detroit, and Chicago. Other port cities, particularly San Francisco, would also draw Irish immigrants. Not only had a rural people become overwhelmingly urban, they also settled in the largest cities. By 1870, 42 percent of the nation's 1.8 million Irish-born lived in the twenty-five cities with populations greater than 50,000. In contrast, only 10 percent of the country's 29 million native-born whites lived in the big cities.[1]

The Irish diaspora dramatically altered the complexion of the northern cities. In 1845, the Irish-born accounted for 2 percent of Boston's population; by 1855, 20 percent. By 1850 there were 133,730 Irish-born inhabitants of New York City, 26 percent of the total population. As of 1870, first-generation Irish constituted one-eighth of the population of the twenty-five largest cities. In 1870 the cities with the largest proportion of Irish-born residents included Boston, New York, Jersey City, Albany, New Haven, Brooklyn, Providence, San Francisco, Pittsburgh, and Philadelphia (see Table 1). If we add the American-born sons and daughters of Irish parents, the magnitude of the Celtic urban invasion becomes even more dramatic. In 1880, for example, an estimated one-third of New York City's residents were of Irish parentage.

The Irish migration to the cities soon took political form. The machine represented the dominant urban political institution of the late nineteenth century; the Irish were among its leading architects. The centralized big-city machines organized and linked the "input" and "output" dimensions of the local political system. On the input side, precinct captains mobilized the electorate. Local bosses controlled party caucuses and conventions and thus nominations to local office. By controlling voters and officeholders, the machine could control the output side of politics—patronage jobs, contracts, franchises, and services.

The machine maintained itself in power by skillfully deploying these resources. Bosses purchased voter support with individual economic inducements such as offers of public jobs or services rather than by appeals to traditional loyalties or to class-based interests. Tangible divisible benefits also disciplined the party's rank and file. Minor party officials were themselves municipal employees. Powerful ward chieftains were often rewarded with a share of the patronage commensurate with their district's share of the total party vote. Thus the machine sustained itself by exchanging material benefits for political support.[2]

The roots of the early big-city machines can be traced to the second or Jacksonian party system of the 1820s and 1830s. By the 1830s property requirements for voting in local elections had been relaxed. At the same time, the patronage or spoils system came to be perfected as an instrument of party discipline. By the 1840s party organization had taken on its modern geographical and hierarchical form. Battalions of precinct workers organized urban neighborhoods, reporting to precinct and ward captains, who in turn reported to the downtown bosses. In the 1840s party managers perfected new devices to swell the ranks of party loyalists. To capture the votes of the burgeoning immigrant population, Tammany Hall opened its famous Naturalization Bureau in 1840. An instant success, the department naturalized 11,000 foreigners by 1844.

In the 1850s embryonic and short-lived machines appeared in cities such as San Francisco and New York. In San Francisco, David Broderick, of Irish descent and recently arrived from Tammany Hall, briefly organized the city's Irish and German working class. Recognizing that voter loyalty could be purchased with a system of material payoffs, Broderick quickly tripled municipal expenditures and indebtedness. Broderick's tactics were emulated in New York City by Mayor Fernando Wood, the native-born darling of the city's foreign-born. During his administration, city outlays also tripled, from $3.2 to $9.8 million. Between 1855 and 1865, the number of naturalized voters in the city nearly doubled, from 43,000 to 78,000, while the number of native-born voters barely increased from 46,000 to 52,000. These embryonic machines dissolved in the party realignment and protean intraparty factionalism of the late 1850s. The mature long-lived machine would be a product of the third rather than the second party system.[3]

The Irish Role in Building the Early Machines: Four Questions

By 1890 Irish bosses ran most of the big-city Democratic machines constructed in the 1870s and 1880s. The Celtic bosses included Tammany Hall's Kelly and Croker, Brooklyn's McLaughlin, the Bay Area's Buckley, Buffalo's Sheenan, Jersey City's Davis, and Albany's Patrick McCabe. The Irish had also taken over the Democratic party in cities where centralized machines had not been built. For example, Mike McDonald led the Democrats in the Windy City, and Pat Maguire led them in the Hub. The Irish dominated the lower echelons of the urban Democratic party as well. By 1886, the Irish held 58 percent of the seats on the San Francisco Democratic party central committee. Sixty-nine percent of the members of Chicago's Democratic committee were Irish in 1890.

By 1892, the brogue had replaced Tammany's secret Indian hand-shake; 61 percent of the Tammany Society officers were Irish.[4]

Notwithstanding the prominence of the Irish in the early big-city machines, four issues can be raised regarding their role in machine building. First, what accounts for their unusually high group political participation rates? The Irish capture of the urban Democratic party depended on a large Irish voting bloc. In city after city the Irish mobilized politically much more quickly than other ethnic groups. Irish naturalization and voter registration rates were the highest of the immigrant groups. The Irish talent for electoral politics extended to high turnout rates and bloc voting for machine candidates. Some of the differences between ethnic groups in levels of group electoral participation can be attributed to the later arrival of the Southern and Eastern Europeans. By the 1880s most Irish-born adult males were voting; the "new" ethnics were barely getting off the boat. Yet even ethnic groups such as the Germans, who arrived at the same time as the Irish, had lower voter participation rates. To the extent that Irish power initially rested on group mobilization (and perhaps on the nonmobilization of other ethnic groups), what explains the differences in ethnic voter participation rates, particularly among the first wave of "old" European immigrants?

Second, although the Irish quickly mobilized in most cities, there was no one-to-one relationship between cities with large Irish-American populations (and thus numbers of voters) and cities in which Irish-run machines emerged in the late nineteenth century. In contrast with New York, Brooklyn, San Francisco, Jersey City, and Albany, where Irish machines were created, other cities with large Celtic populations did not produce centralized machines, or, if they emerged, they were controlled by other groups. Boston, the most Irish of the American cities, never produced a centralized machine. In Philadelphia and Pittsburgh, the state Republican machine built local Yankee-run GOP machines in the aftermath of the Civil War. In both of these cities, the Irish-American vote was split, the most enterprising shifting into the Republican camp. Save for a few contractors, Irish political influence was limited. In Chicago, another city with a large Irish population, competitive two-party politics and intraparty factionalism were the characteristic forms of politics in the late nineteenth century. In the twentieth century, it would take non-Irishman Anton Cermak to unite the various Irish factions in the Windy City and construct a citywide machine. Why did centralized Irish machines emerge in some of the cities with large numbers of Irish voters and not in others?

Third, why did the Irish urban machines of the late nineteenth century pursue politically risky conservative fiscal and patronage policies? In the Irish cities, the sharpest increases in city expenditures occurred in the 1860s and 1870s, *before* centralized machines were created and before the Irish controlled them. Once in power, the first generation of Irish bosses were guardians of Yankee fiscal orthodoxy. Yet conservative fiscal policies made the fledgling Irish machines extremely vulnerable to revolts from below. In cities such as New York and San Francisco, the early Irish machines had little patronage to dispense to immigrant working-class voters. With few rewards, working-class grievances against the machines mounted. As a consequence, the urban working class, the core constituency of the Democratic party, often revolted against the early machines, supporting local labor parties instead. Given the rainbow theory's account of substantial machine resources, their allocation to impoverished voters, and the supposed ensuing support of working-class voters for machine candidates, what accounts for the paucity of early machine resources and for the machine's inability to fully win the allegiance of the urban ethnic working class?

Fourth, notwithstanding the folklore about the ability of large numbers of Irish to use political routes of economic advancement, it appears that the early machine's fiscal conservatism limited the number of patronage jobs available for distribution. What were the resources of the early Irish-run machines? How much patronage was there and what share went to the Irish? In the absence of patronage, what kinds of appeals did the early Irish bosses make to working-class Irish voters? How successful were nonmaterial appeals?

Students of machine politics have grappled with these intertwined issues of ethnic political behavior and early machine building. "Mass" or group theorists trace the distinctive big-city political style of groups such as the Irish to their European background. Daniel Patrick Moynihan, for example, argues that early nineteenth-century Irish village life laid the foundations for later urban machines such as Tammany Hall.[5]

If Moynihan is correct about the Old World roots of the Irish machines, then how do we account for the fact that the same social conditions gave birth to much different patterns of Irish political participation in late nineteenth-century Ireland? In the context of an agrarian economy, Ireland produced a nationalist politics organized around the causes of land reform and home rule. In the context of an industrializing urban economy, Irish-Americans produced a mass politics of party, organization, and patronage. To understand Irish-*American* politics, one must look to New World as well as Old World roots.[6]

Likewise, group theorists would explain the fiscal conservatism of the first generation of Irish machines in terms of traditional Catholic values imported from Ireland. In subsequent pages I argue that there are weaknesses in this account of early machine fiscal behavior. The Irish-American community of the late nineteenth century was not monolithically conservative, as the group model would imply. In particular, the urban Irish working class grew increasingly militant and alienated from the early machines in the 1870s and 1880s. The conservatism of the Irish party bosses was as much a *consequence* as a cause of machine politics. I argue that the machine's maintenance needs, not a Catholic view of a static social order, introduced a cautious strain into early Irish political leadership.

Elite theorists have also addressed these questions. Martin Shefter, for example, has argued that machines emerged in some cities and not in others because of differences in local political alliances. Successful machine builders forged alliances with the conservative business community. I will argue that political alliances had to be developed vertically as well as horizontally, to the state capital as well as to the downtown business club. Machine fortunes heavily depended on which party or faction controlled the statehouse. State election laws affected the machine's ability to naturalize, register, and win the votes of the immigrants. State laws affected the machine's capacity to increase local taxes and indebtedness. State patronage significantly increased the machine's supply of public jobs.[7]

Irish-American Politics:
Old and New World Roots

For the Irish, there were Old World roots to their political skills, intense group solidarity, and the high value they placed on the economic rewards of politics. In Ireland, English Ascendancy produced the Penal Laws, a series of parliamentary acts passed between 1695 and 1746, which were designed to weaken Catholicism, the religion of 90 percent of Ireland's population, by reducing Catholics to a position of economic and political inferiority relative to Protestants. The Penal Laws restricted Catholic ownership and inheritance of land. Catholics were denied the privileges of voting, of holding public office, and of practicing law. The combined effect of these impositions was to forge a common bond of solidarity as Irish Catholics were reduced to penury and powerlessness.[8]

The struggle to repeal the Penal Laws, culminating in Catholic Emancipation in 1829, brought the Irish experience with mass political organization and with local electoral manipulation. In the early nineteenth century, Daniel O'Connell built the first Irish mass political organization. His Catholic Association sought religious and political emancipation, using parish priests to collect a "Catholic rent" from their parishioners to finance the organization's political activities. The association also pressured the recently enfranchised Catholic freehold voters to support the association's candidates in municipal elections. The Penal Laws' restrictions on Catholic voting and office holding had been somewhat relaxed in the 1790s. In 1793, the vote was given to Catholic tenants whose holdings yielded an annual interest of at least 40 shillings. Similar to English extraparliamentary organizations of the time, O'Connell's association secured votes and offices with promises of patronage. As Emmet Larkin has argued, by the late 1820s O'Connell's "unified national phalanx" of mobilized clergy and tenant farmers represented an "embryo Irish national state."[9]

The Irish would also benefit politically from the spread of the national educational system in the early nineteenth century. Although some argue that this nondenominational system was primarily designed to weaken its informal Catholic counterpart, the hedge schools, it is clear that the national system soon gained popularity with both the peasantry and the clergy. The Gaelic-speaking peasants wanted the economic and social advantages that speaking English might bring. The clergy wanted control of the financial and job patronage available from the system. With the increasing popularity of the educational system, the proportion of the population that spoke English rose dramatically, from an estimated 50 percent in 1800 to 95 percent in 1851. Literacy rates also rose. At least one-half of the famine emigrants were literate in English.[10]

Thus the Irish came to the New World with political advantages that other groups, such as the Germans, did not possess. German political unification would be achieved only in 1870. Class, regional, and religious differences divided the migrating Germans. Religion, especially, would split the German-American vote; German Catholics would gravitate to the Democratic party while German Lutherans would vote Republican. Language barriers would lengthen the process of naturalization and thus retard the development of potential voting strength. Finally, by arriving with farming, mercantile, and technical skills, the Germans, unlike the unskilled Irish, would not be as attracted by the economic payoffs of political participation.[11]

It would be a mistake, however, to view growing Irish-American involvement in urban politics, compared with groups such as the Germans, as solely the product of political values and skills imported from the struggle against the English. The development of the American party system also shaped the character of Irish-American political participation. The famine Irish arrived as the parties were entering their modern or mobilization phase. Urban Irish immigrants served as electoral cannon fodder in the competitive bidding wars among Democrats, Whigs, and Republicans. By the 1830s, internal improvements had become a "bipartisan obsession." The parties vigorously solicited Irish voters by offering them jobs on canal and highway projects.[12]

In the 1850s, after the Irish had been introduced to the electoral process and the patronage system, the party system buckled under the combined weight of sectionalism and nativism. The Irish migration was the largest Catholic migration to date. As Robert Kelley notes, "Few issues caused such continuing turbulence in the transatlantic Anglo-American community as the 'Irish Question.' . . . The Irish, in short, were the people who played the role of 'blacks' in British life, and in the United States, the same attitudes toward them persisted. . . . The arrival of the Catholic Irish, therefore, immediately shifted all political equations in America."[13] With the nativist reaction to Irish Catholics in the 1850s, signified by the rise of the Know-Nothing party and by the subsequent shift of many Protestant groups into the Republican party, Irish Catholic identification with the Democratic party was further solidified. In the years after 1860, the Irish Catholic vote would be heavily Democratic.

The Irish quickly mobilized in the big cities. Coming in the late 1840s, large numbers of Irish were soon naturalized and voting. By 1855, for example, more than one-fifth of New York's and Boston's voters were Irish, their numbers tripling since 1850. In the late nineteenth century, Irish naturalization, registration, and turnout rates regularly exceeded those of other groups, even the early-arriving Germans. Table 3 displays ethnic group voter registration rates for San Francisco in 1900. In the Bay Area, the proportion of Irish-born registered voters was nearly double that of the city's other foreign-born—70 percent versus 37 percent—and nearly equaled the rate for the native-born. In contrast, only 57 percent of the Germans were registered. The Irish also had higher turnout and bloc voting rates in San Francisco, further increasing their electoral leverage. In the five local and state elections held between 1894 and 1902, Democratic candidates received more than 60 percent of the total vote in the four most heavily Irish Assembly Districts (ADs 29–32) compared with less than 50 percent of the vote in the three heavily German districts (ADs 37, 39–40).[14]

The other Irish cities also featured higher rates of Irish electoral participation. In Boston, for example, 60 percent of the Irish-born males were registered voters in 1885 compared with 37 percent of the non-Irish. The midwestern cities, with alien suffrage laws allowing immigrants filing their first naturalization papers to vote, had higher immigrant voter registration rates than the eastern cities. Sixty-two percent of Chicago's foreign-born were registered to vote in 1892 compared with 39 percent of Boston's immigrants. Yet even in the Windy City the Irish were more politically active than other ethnic groups. Seventy-seven percent of the city's Irish-born were registered to vote in the 1892 presidential election compared with 64 percent of the Germans. Second-generation Irish

TABLE 3. *Gaining Political Leverage: Naturalizing and Registering the Immigrants, San Francisco, 1900*

Ethnic Group[a]	Citizens as Percentage of Voting-Age Males	Registered Voters as Percentage of Voting-Age Males	Total Number of Voting-Age Males	Total Number of Adult Male Citizens	Total Number of Registered Voters
Irish	95.3	69.6	11,871	11,310	8,261
Yankee[b]	100.0	72.6	62,251	62,251	45,189
Non-Irish immigrants	66.0	36.8	54,863	36,219	20,183
German	90.7	56.5	14,297	12,966	8,082
British	83.6	51.5	6,947	5,806	3,581
Scandinavian	85.0	37.9	6,311	5,367	2,390
Canadian	86.7	60.9	2,248	2,223	1,561
Italian	51.0	19.7	4,128	2,107	814
French	62.4	28.9	2,256	1,596	738
Chinese	4.3	0.1	9,601	414	7
Other immigrants	67.8	34.3	8,775	5,740	3,010
All voting-age males	71.2	57.1	128,985	109,780	73,633

Sources: U.S. Census Office, *Twelfth Census of the United States, 1900* (Washington, D.C.: Government Printing Office, 1901), vol. 1, Tables 82, 83, pp. 936–945; San Francisco Board of Supervisors, *San Francisco Municipal Reports, 1900–1901* (San Francisco: W. H. Hinton, 1901), pp. 373–374.
[a]By country of birth.
[b]Includes all native-born.

were even more politically active than their fathers, further augmenting Celtic voting strength. In New York City, for example, first- and second-generation Irish constituted one-quarter of the population but one-third of the registered voters in 1890.[15]

State Politics and the Building of the Early Irish Machines

A large Irish voting bloc was a necessary but not a sufficient condition for building the Irish machines. Irish voter registration and turnout rates were high throughout *all* eight cities surveyed. Irish machines, however, were built in the 1880s in some of these big cities and not in others. Irish bosses constructed strong centralized machines in New York (and soon-to-be-annexed Brooklyn), San Francisco, Jersey City, and Albany, but *not* in Boston, Philadelphia, Pittsburgh, or Chicago.

What accounts for machines emerging in some cities with large numbers of Irish voters and not in others? Two post–Civil War state party developments shaped urban machine building. First, in states such as New York and New Jersey, the Republicans unintentionally strengthened fledgling urban Democratic party organizations. In the late 1860s Radical Republicans embarked on a program of "urban reconstruction." Yet reconstruction backfired, further driving the immigrants into the Democratic party and enabling the Democrats to strengthen their formal party apparatus at the precinct and ward levels. Second, in New York, New Jersey, and California, pro-machine Democratic governors were elected in the 1870s and 1880s. Pro-machine governors strengthened the big-city party organizations in a variety of ways, particularly by channeling state patronage to them and by denying state resources to the machine's reform opponents. In other states, however, unfriendly Republican *and* Democratic governors and legislatures hindered the building of big-city machines.

The Radical Republican Attack

Near the end of the Civil War, Radical Republicans captured control of the New England and Middle Atlantic states. Their program of "reconstruction at home" attempted to weaken the emerging Democratic urban machines in two key ways: by making it harder for the Democrats to register immigrant voters and by loosening Democratic control over the saloons, the police, and the fire departments.

The Radicals tightened state suffrage laws in order to reduce the number of immigrant Democratic voters. In New York, the Radical-controlled state legislature passed a stringent voter registration law that applied only to New York City. At the 1867 state constitutional convention, Radicals such as Governor Reuben E. Fenton dominated the proceedings. The Radicals championed black suffrage but proposed lengthening the time period before naturalized immigrants would be eligible to vote. In New Jersey, the Republican-controlled state legislature passed a "sunset" act that closed the polls at dusk, making it more difficult for workers to vote. Adding insult to injury, the Garden State Republicans passed a voter registration law that applied only to the Democratic strongholds of Jersey City and Newark.[16]

At the national level, Radicals in Congress passed legislation designed to reduce fraudulent naturalization, registration, and voting by the urban Democrats. The Enforcement Act of 1870, passed to protect the constitutional rights of newly freed blacks, contained two sections designed to weaken the Democratic city organizations. Election frauds such as false registration and repeat voting were made federal offenses if perpetrated in federal elections. Furthermore, federal marshals were authorized to supervise these elections and to use federal troops if necessary to promote honest elections.

The Naturalization Act, also passed by Congress in 1870, posed an even greater threat to the Democratic city machines. The act tightened federal controls over the issuance of naturalization papers by *state* courts and extended to six months the period before which newly naturalized citizens were eligible to vote. The act also gave U.S. circuit court judges extraordinary powers over the conduct of national *and* state elections in cities with populations greater than 20,000. Federal judges were authorized to appoint commissioners to oversee voter registration, challenge voters, and count ballots in the cities.[17]

Suffrage restrictions and federal control over the electoral process were not the only means the Radicals employed to weaken the Democrats' ability to mobilize urban voters. In the nineteenth century, the cities did not have home rule charters and thus could be ruled by whichever party controlled the state. The Radicals used their control of the state executive and legislative branches to implement a program of urban institutional reform. State-controlled boards and commissions would supplant city agencies in performing such critical functions as public safety, health, and the licensing of saloons. The Radical program was largely designed to weaken the Democratic-controlled local institutions—the police and fire departments and saloons—responsible for organizing immigrant voters.

In New York there were prewar precedents for state interference in New York City's governance. In 1857, state Republicans had stripped the New York City police department, an important Tammany tool for revenue raising and for controlling the ballot box, from Democratic Mayor Fernando Wood's control and had placed the department under state control. The Republicans created the New York Board of Supervisors strictly as a state institution. Unlike similar boards in other counties of the state, the city board had no independent taxation authority. The board could levy only those taxes decreed by the Republican-controlled state legislature. The state legislature, in turn, was required yearly to pass a special act declaring the amount needed for the city's budget.[18]

New York's Radical Republican politicians adopted other measures to weaken the institutional base of the Democratic party in cities such as New York, Albany, and Buffalo. The Metropolitan Fire Department Act of 1865 created a state-controlled paid fire department in New York City, weakening the volunteer fire departments. As James Mohr notes, the local fire companies by the mid-1850s had become de facto Tammany ward organizations, particularly in Irish neighborhoods as the Irish had begun to man the fire lines. The Metropolitan Health Law of 1866 created a state-controlled metropolitan sanitary district to enforce health regulations and the city's excise laws. Besides stripping Tammany of street-cleaning contracts, the new law gave the health board liquor licensing power over the city's saloons, the heart of Tammany's ward organizations.[19]

Radicals in New York sought as well to neutralize upstate urban sources of Democratic strength with state boards and commissions. The Radical-dominated legislature created the Albany Capital Police District in 1865 and Buffalo's Niagara Police District shortly thereafter. Rochester, a more Republican city, received no state police commission.

Radical Republicans in other eastern states with big-city Democratic strongholds pursued similar programs of "urban reconstruction." To quell growing Irish influence in Jersey City, the Garden State's Republicans abolished the city's elected police chief and replaced the position with a state-appointed police commission. In 1871, the Republican-dominated state legislature abolished the city's government, replacing it with a series of state-appointed commissions. In Massachusetts, Radicals created state police and health boards, stripping the cities of their authority.[20]

Besides threatening the ability of the Democrats to mobilize urban voters, state-run commissions significantly reduced the number of patronage jobs controlled by local machines. In New York, for example, the Radicals succeeded in drying up most locally controlled patronage. By 1868 the Democratic-run city council controlled less than one-sixth of the city's expenditures.

Yet the Radical Republican attack on the Democratic machines backfired. Arguing that they were being treated like surrogate southerners, Tammany's leaders "work[ed] the naturalization mill full blast" and perfected their party organization. With its informal institutional base in the police department, volunteer fire departments, and saloons weakened, Tammany turned to strengthening the formal party organization. By the late 1860s representatives of the Wigwam manned all 230 election districts, linked by a strong chain of command.[21]

The Radical plan to institute black suffrage while tightening voter qualifications for foreign-born whites solidified immigrant support for the Democratic machines. In New York City, Irish support for Tammany had waned during the Civil War because the Irish felt they had not received a fair share of patronage in exchange for their votes. Tammany defused the incipient Irish rebellion by attacking the Radicals' new voter registration law. In Jersey City, the Republican attack forced the Irish to close ranks behind Robert Davis, ending middle-class Irish insurgency against the Democratic party leadership.

The Election of Pro-Machine Governors

A second and more important state party development affected urban machine building. With the waning of Radical Republican strength in the 1870s and the resurgence of the northern Democratic party, the embryonic city machines needed a prolonged gestation period protected by a sympathetic Democratic state administration. Friendly Democratic governors could strengthen machines in various ways. By channeling state patronage through the emerging machines, governors withheld vital resources from the machine's reform opponents. Pro-machine governors also minimized the harm done by Republican-controlled legislatures. But unsympathetic Democratic governors could seriously retard machine building. Antimachine governors could fuel the ambitions of local reformers by giving them state jobs.

The role of state Democratic politicians in successively promoting urban factionalism and then machine consolidation is illustrated in New York City politics in the 1870s and 1880s. Determined to resurrect Tammany Hall in the wake of Boss William Marcy Tweed's downfall in 1871, Irishman John Kelly invited Samuel Tilden and other respectable Democratic businessmen and lawyers into the Wigwam. Once Tammany was made respectable, Boss Kelly attempted to oust the so-called Swallow-tails, Tilden's wealthy entourage whom Kelly had brought in as window dressing. After supporting Tilden for governor in 1874, Kelly split with him after the election over matters of patronage. Tilden aligned himself with Irving Hall, an anti-Tammany Democratic club, and directed state patronage in that direction. Tilden's successor and friend, Lucius Robinson, also aligned himself with the anti-Kelly forces in the party. In a move reminiscent of his break with Tilden, Kelly later broke with newly elected Democratic Governor Grover Cleveland over state patronage allocations. Cleveland then aligned himself (and delivered state jobs) to the County Democracy, Tammany's most powerful rival club in the 1880s.

Thus a succession of anti-Tammany Democratic governors were elected in the 1870s and 1880s. They underwrote the anti-Tammany party factions, particularly Irving Hall and the County Democracy, with generous allocations of state patronage. Only with the election in 1885 of a more pro-Tammany governor, David B. Hill, was state assistance redirected. Governor Hill was originally intent on placating all factions in the city—the Tammany, Irving, County, and Brooklyn party organizations. Beset with leadership scandals and the defection of key supporters to Tammany, and weakened by attempted fusion with the Republicans, the County Democracy began to collapse in the late 1880s. Governor Hill immediately built an implicit alliance with Tammany by opposing state ballot reform—the replacement of party-printed and distributed ballots—and began redirecting state patronage to Tammany. By similar tactics, Hill also strengthened the Democratic machine being built upstate in Albany.[22]

Pro-machine governors were also elected in New Jersey and California in the 1880s, aiding Irish urban bosses in these states in consolidating their rule. In New Jersey, Democratic Governor Leon Abbett formed an alliance with the Irish boss of Jersey City, Robert Davis. Abbett gave state patronage to Davis rather than to his Yankee reform opponents and in other ways protected Davis and his organization from hostile action by the Republican-controlled state legislature.[23]

In California, San Francisco's Boss Chris Buckley strengthened his organization by adroit alignment with the ascendant wings of the state Democratic party. In 1882, Buckley joined the antimonopolist wing in electing George Stoneman as governor. As public support for Stoneman waned, Buckley switched to the conservative wing. In 1886, Buckley succeeded in securing the Democratic gubernatorial nomination for Washington Bartlett, the conservative mayor of San Francisco. With Bartlett's narrow victory, Buckley maintained his influence over the allocation of state patronage.[24]

Unfriendly State Administrations

In Massachusetts, Pennsylvania, and Illinois, however, the state party system hindered the building of Irish Democratic machines in Boston, Philadelphia, Pittsburgh, and Chicago in the late nineteenth century. In Massachusetts, Irish-born Pat Maguire had emerged by the mid-1870s as the "first among equals" in Boston's Democratic party. In 1885, under Maguire's tutelage, the city elected Hugh O'Brien as its first Irish Catholic mayor.[25]

The Radical Republicans unwittingly aided Maguire's machine-building efforts. As the Irish began to demand political power in the Hub after the Civil War, Radical Republicans such as Frank Bird and Governors Alexander Bullock and William Claflin pursued a program of urban reconstruction. The governor was given the power to appoint the Boston police commission and liquor licensing board. The Republican-controlled legislature established a taxation limit for Boston, the only city in the country where such a state-imposed limit existed. The state also strictly regulated the city's debt. Boston could not raise its debt above 2.5 percent of assessed valuation without permission from the state legislature.

Despite supporting legislation removing civil and political liabilities for blacks and Indians, the Radicals stalled on removing constitutional restrictions for white immigrants. In 1857, Republicans and Know-Nothings had joined to impose a literacy test on voting. In 1859, naturalized immigrants were barred from voting or holding office until they had been citizens for two years. Fearful of growing Irish voting strength in Boston, the Radicals refused to extend their antidiscriminatory campaign to the white immigrants.[26]

The Republican program to weaken Irish Democratic control of Boston succeeded in solidifying Irish support for the Democratic party. Yet Maguire's efforts to build a Boston Tammany were frustrated in the 1870s and 1880s by weaknesses in the state Democratic party. The state's Democrats entered the 1880s with a reputation that made the party a "byword for incapacity." In 1882, profiting from an economic downturn and from Republican factionalism at the state and national levels, Ben Butler, a born-again Democrat, was elected as only the second Democratic governor since the Civil War. Butler was unable to centralize the city's politics. Having campaigned primarily on the issue of retrenchment (accusing the Republicans of fiscal extravagance) and facing a hostile Republican-controlled legislature, Butler's short-lived administration was a negative and divisive one characterized by "government by veto." With little state patronage to reward the Boston Irish in return for their support, Butler was defeated by the Republicans in 1883. The Republicans, in turn, controlled the state for the rest of this crucial machine-building decade.[27]

Pat Maguire's only opportunity to use state patronage from a friendly Democratic administration to centralize the city's politics was briefly presented in 1890. Yankee Democrat William E.

"Billy" Russell was elected governor in that year. State patronage became the litmus test of Russell's relationship with the Boston Irish "saloon Democrats." Writing to Russell, Congressman Joseph H. O'Neill, a Maguire political ally, warned: "I hope you will not make the mistake of F. O. Prince [a Yankee who was elected Boston's mayor in the 1870s] who believed that there were [only] a half dozen men with Irish blood who had brains but that the balance was fit only to fill places with less than a thousand a year. You can well afford to divide even." Though handicapped by a Republican-controlled state legislature, Governor Russell gave as much state patronage as he could to the Boston Irish during his three one-year terms in office.[28]

Maguire's ability to construct a durable city machine with state patronage and to halt what one observer termed the "growing feudalization of the party" was interrupted by the depression of 1893 and the resulting loss of city hall and the statehouse. With Maguire's death in 1896, the process of feudalization accelerated. The remnants of the Maguire machine were liquidated, and the party was drawn and quartered by feuding Irish political chieftains. As early as 1892, John F. "Honey Fitz" Fitzgerald defeated Maguire ally O'Neill and seized control of the North End. Martin Lomasney was installed as the ward boss of the West End, and Patrick J. Kennedy (father of Joseph P.) took control of the East End. Soon James Michael Curley, later mayor and governor, emerged to control the South End. The Hub's Irish Democratic politics would be faction-ridden from this time onward.[29]

With the Boston Irish divided, Yankees from the western part of Massachusetts solidified control over the state party. When Democratic governors were occasionally elected, as was Yankee William Douglas in 1904, they did little to centralize Irish power in Boston. Governor Douglas actually worked to *reduce* the influence of the Irish in the state party and directed state patronage away from the Hub's contentious Irish ward bosses.[30]

A different set of state political forces hindered Irish machine building in the Middle Atlantic and North Central states that skirted the Mason-Dixon line, particularly in Pennsylvania and Illinois. In the post–Civil War era, the GOP normally controlled these states. Yet GOP state hegemony was threatened by a possible urban-rural Democratic alliance. There were large numbers of immigrants in cities such as Philadelphia, Pittsburgh, and Chicago. Large numbers of ex-southern Democrats lived in the rural southernmost counties of these states. In order to prevent an alliance between the urban foreign-born and the downstate native-born Democrats, the Republicans built their own machines in cities such as Philadelphia and Pittsburgh as offshoots of the state machine.[31]

In Philadelphia, Democratic factionalism in the 1850s encouraged a Republican machine to develop. The prewar Democracy (as the early Democratic party was called) was split between an American (i.e., native-born Protestant) and an Irish Catholic wing. As the Republicans rose to power, Irish Democrats were isolated in the First Congressional District in South Philadelphia. With the consolidation of a Republican urban machine in the 1870s, David Martin, the local protégé of Republican state boss Matthew Quay, began encouraging the recruitment of the Irish into the GOP machine. In particular, Martin wooed Irish contractors with public works contracts. The Irish contractors, in turn, delivered the votes of their Irish laborers to the machine.[32] In Pittsburgh, the state GOP also created a strong local machine during the Civil War. In the postwar era, the Steel City machine would serve as an integral part of the powerful state Republican machine run by Simon Cameron. As in Philadelphia, the large Irish vote was split as the politically ambitious joined the Republican party.

Even in cities with large Irish populations, late nineteenth-century Republican urban machines were decidedly different from their Democratic counterparts. Democratic machines were constructed from the bottom up. Rooted in the institutional life of ethnic neighborhoods—saloons, clubhouses, volunteer fire departments—Democratic machines extended upward to the city, county, and state levels. Republican machines were constructed, in Lincoln Steffens's phrase, "in the air," that is, from the top down. As adjuncts to state machines, GOP urban machines relied heavily on federal and state rather than local patronage. Designed to prevent Democratic control of the cities and a possible challenge to GOP state hegemony, Republican organizations encouraged political passivity and nonparticipation on the part of the immigrant working class.[33]

In Illinois, the state party system inhibited both Republicans and Democrats from constructing a Chicago machine in the nineteenth century. The Windy City's Mike McDonald, the Irish Democratic party leader, attempted to build a local machine in the 1870s. But McDonald's efforts were frustrated by Republican predominance in the state, which lasted from the Civil War to World War I. In the postbellum era, General John A. "Black Jack" Logan fashioned a Republican state machine by monopolizing federal patronage. Yet Chicago-downstate tensions plagued Republican state politics, and Logan was unable to construct a Republican machine in Chicago.[34]

Even with the state Republicans weakened by factionalism, the Windy City's Democrats were unable to use their occasional control of state government to construct a citywide machine. By the early 1890s, two major factions had emerged in the Chicago Democratic party. Mayors Carter Henry Harrison I and II both campaigned on a "personal liberty" (Sunday drinking) platform. Both developed a broad base of ethnic political support, including Germans, Slavs, and Irish saloonkeeper-politicians such as "Bathhouse John" Coughlin and "Hinky Dink" Kenna, bosses of the downtown First Ward. Yet the Harrisons' party leadership was challenged by John Hopkins and Roger Sullivan, leaders of the so-called gas crowd faction, because of Sullivan's presidency of the Ogden Gas Company. The Hopkins-Sullivan faction drew the support of most of the remaining Irish ward leaders.[35]

In the political upheavals of the early 1890s, radical Democrat John Altgeld was elected governor of Illinois. Rather than reducing party factionalism in Chicago through the adroit use of state patronage, Altgeld succeeded in further inflaming the factional divisions. The governor alienated the more conservative Sullivan faction by vetoing utility give-away legislation. He alienated the Harrison faction by opposing the younger Harrison's mayoral reelection bid in 1899. Lacking a friendly Democratic state administration, neither faction was able to consolidate its control over party and city. Chicago's Irish-controlled Democratic machine would emerge only in the twentieth century.[36]

Thus we have seen the importance of the state party system in shaping the fortunes of the early Irish machines. Radical Republicans pursued a program of electoral and institutional reform in the eastern states with urban Democratic (and Irish) strongholds. Rather than weakening the embryonic Democratic city organizations, the Radical attack succeeded in strengthening these machines. The election of pro-machine Democratic governors in states such as New York, New Jersey, and California further aided Irish machine building.

The Radical program of urban reconstruction was less necessary in the Middle Atlantic and North Central states where big-city GOP organizations were stronger. Yet in the northern states along the Mason-Dixon line, a possible alliance of city and country Democrats could have upset the consolidating Republican state machines. To prevent such an alliance, the Pennsylvania state GOP organization, for example, constructed adjunct urban machines in Philadelphia and Pittsburgh. In Illinois, however, where the Republican state organization was increasingly faction-ridden and where an antimachine Democrat was elected governor, neither party was able to build a centralized machine in the Windy City in the late nineteenth century.

Conservative Machine Policies and Revolts from Below

Once we understand how (to borrow Lincoln Steffens's phrase again) the early Irish machines were built both from the bottom up—by group mobilization—*and* from the top down—by state party alliances—a third question presents itself. Why did the new machines immediately embark on a program of retrenchment, thereby alienating working-class voters?

Table 4 examines changes in per capita spending for the big cities between 1880 and 1902. The Irish cities were far heavier spenders under Yankee than Irish rule. In 1880, before the Irish political conquest, outlays in the Irish machine cities of New York, San Francisco, Jersey City, and Albany averaged $30 per capita. In Boston, soon to be Irish-run but faction-ridden, the per capita outlay of $51 was among the highest in the country. Republican machines spent less, even where there were large numbers of Irish to feed. Per capita spending in the GOP strongholds of Philadelphia and Pittsburgh averaged $22. In competitive-party Chicago, where numerous boards and commissions performed traditional municipal functions, per capita outlays were significantly smaller ($12) than in Democratic or Republican machine cities. In the fourteen

TABLE 4. *Machine Retrenchment, 1880–1902*

Cities and Regimes	Average Per Capita City Outlays ($)		Percentage Change from 1880 to 1902
	1880	*1902*	
Irish cities (8)	29	18	−37.9
Irish Democratic machine (New York, San Francisco, Jersey City, Albany)	30	17	−43.3
Irish Democratic nonmachine (Boston)	51	35	−31.4
Non-Irish Republican machine (Philadelphia, Pittsburgh)	22	16	−27.3
Non-Irish nonmachine (Chicago)	12	11	−8.3
Non-Irish cities (14)[a]	15	15	0

Sources: U.S. Census Office, *Report on Valuation, Taxation, and Public Indebtedness: 1880* (Washington, D.C.: Government Printing Office, 1884), Table 4, pp. 218–247; U.S. Bureau of the Census, *Special Reports: Statistics of Cities, 1902* (Washington, D.C.: Government Printing Office, 1902), Table 21, pp. 252–299.

[a] Includes all cities with more than 50,000 population *and* less than 13 percent Irish. See Table 1, p. 18.

remaining cities with populations of more than 50,000 (see Table 1), with smaller Irish populations and fewer machines, per capita municipal spending averaged only $15.[37]

The fledgling Irish machines soon performed a fiscal about-face. Between 1880 and 1902, average per capita outlays in the four Irish machine cities plummeted 43 percent, from $30 to $17. Public spending in politically fragmented Boston fell 31 percent, from $51 to $35. Even the Republican machines were not immune to retrenchment. Per capita outlays in Philadelphia and Pittsburgh dropped 27 percent, from $22 to $16. In the remaining cities, including Chicago, per capita spending remained relatively constant over this twenty-two-year period.

Spending *rose* during the machines' formative phase, in the 1860s and 1870s, when the immigrants were being mobilized, and fell as the machines consolidated power. Wary of tax revolts, Irish party bosses quickly built alliances with the Yankee middle class and business community. The propertied classes demanded cutbacks, after the excesses of the 1860s and early 1870s, and the early Irish bosses acquiesced. The early Irish machines, then, had all the trappings of Yankee reform administrations, complete with calls for municipal taxation limitations. Yet retrenchment posed severe hardship for the machine's natural constituency, the immigrant working class. The secret to the longevity of the early Irish machines was their ability to balance the contradictory demands of the middle class and the working class, for retrenchment and for patronage.[38]

The Irish bosses first heeded conservative Yankee businessmen, imposing retrenchment on the Irish working class as the price of assuming power. In New York City, anti-Tammany conservative William F. Havemeyer was elected mayor in 1872 in the wake of Tweed's downfall. Havemeyer quickly reduced the city budget from $36 million to $32 million. Notwithstanding the economic suffering caused by the panic of 1873, Havemeyer cut back on public works spending. Boss Kelly, dependent on the reformers to resurrect the Wigwam after Tweed's downfall, did little to moderate Havemeyer's fiscal policies. Kelly would soon demonstrate his own Irish brand of fiscal (and political) prudence. As city controller between 1876 and 1880, Kelly substantially reduced the city's massive Tweed-induced debt. As one close observer noted approvingly of Kelly's fiscal stewardship: "It requires a great man to stand between the City Treasury and this most dangerous mass."[39]

In San Francisco, Boss Chris Buckley also embarked on a program of fiscal retrenchment in the 1880s. In the 1882 municipal election, Buckley promised a "dollar limit" on the municipal taxation rate, that is, one dollar for each one hundred dollars of assessed valuation. Between 1882 and 1886 the Buckley-controlled Board of Supervisors succeeded in reducing the city tax rate from $1.50 to $1.05 while reducing inflated property values by one half, from $400 million to $200 million. With the machine's revenue sources drying up with fiscal reform, Buckley turned to ways of holding the line on public spending. Salaries were reduced and some positions were abolished. Between 1880 and 1890 San Francisco's population grew by 50 percent; public spending remained constant at $4.8 million.[40]

Conservative fiscal policies made the first generation of Irish

machines susceptible to revolts from below. In 1875 Tammany reduced city wages from $2.00 to $1.60 a day. As a result, John
Morrissey and the "short-hair" or lower-class faction in Tammany
broke with Kelley in 1875, claiming that Kelly was no longer sensitive to the needs of the working class, particularly the Irish. Tammany lost the 1875 mayoral election in part because of erosion in
its working-class support. In the 1886 New York mayoral election,
many working-class Irish and Germans deserted Tammany and
supported Henry George, the United Labor party candidate, nearly
toppling Tammany.[41]

In San Francisco, Chris Buckley experienced a critical loss of
working-class and ethnic support in the late 1880s. Retrenchment
angered the working class because it meant little patronage and
poor services. As labor revitalized in the 1880s—the number of
trade unions increasing from eighteen in 1878 to forty-five in
1883—Buckley failed to appeal to the growing labor movement.
The late 1880s brought worsening economic conditions to the city.
As the machine was unable to meet the needs of the working class,
estimated to account for one-third of the electorate, many workers
shifted their allegiance from the machine. Blue-collar workers
turned their energies to building the trade union movement, either
supporting antimachine candidates or withdrawing from party
politics. In the 1888 mayoral contest, Buckley's nominee, Edward
B. Pond, polled only 38 percent of the vote in a three-way contest
with Republican Charles R. Story and independent Democrat
C. C. O'Donnell. Though Pond barely won the election, thanks to
a split in the antimachine vote, he captured only 40 percent of the
Irish vote. Two years later, Buckley's candidate would lose the Irish
vote and the election, ending the "Blind Boss"'s control over Bay
Area politics.[42]

What accounts for the fiscal conservatism of the first generation
of Irish machines and for their inability to control their working-
class and immigrant constituency? Nathan Glazer and Daniel Patrick Moynihan have stressed the causal role of Irish Catholic political and social conservatism. They argue that "the Irish just
didn't know what to do with their [political] opportunity. They
never thought of politics as an instrument of social change—their
kind of politics involved the processes of a society that was not
changing."[43]

There are weaknesses, however, in the "group" interpretation of machine fiscal conservatism. The Irish-American community in the late nineteenth century was not monolithically conservative. Although critical political, economic, and social elites—machine politicians, the emerging "lace curtain" middle class, and the Catholic church hierarchy—were conservative on fiscal and labor issues, the rank and file was not. In fact, the urban Irish working class grew increasingly militant in the 1870s and 1880s. The working class formed the largest element in the Irish-American community, and its political support was essential to the urban Democratic machines. In cities such as New York, Jersey City, San Francisco, and Boston, more than 60 percent of the Irish-born workforce in 1870 was in unskilled and semiskilled occupations.

The depression of the 1870s brought a surge of Irish working-class support for local labor parties. In San Francisco, deteriorating economic conditions and increasing job competition between white and Chinese workers led in 1877 to the formation of the Workingmen's party of California. Led by Irish-born Denis Kearney, the labor party captured the city government and successfully pressured for a new state constitution. James Bryce argued that "the chief cause that made the new party grow, for grow it did, . . . was the support given their countrymen (Kearney and other WPC leaders) by the Irish, here a discontented and turbulent part of the population."[44] Most unskilled and semiskilled Irish workers deserted the Democratic party and formed the backbone of the new labor party, as they would again after the turn of the century with the Union Labor party. In Chicago, Irish working-class voters helped elect aldermen and state representatives of the socialist-backed Workingmen's party.[45]

The trade union movement also helped shape the growing class consciousness of urban Irish-American workers. In the late 1870s and early 1880s, the Knights of Labor drew strong support from Irish workers in the coal industry. The Knights spearheaded the national movement to create an independent labor party of trade unionists, socialists, and Greenbackers. The Irish were actively involved in the campaign to unionize the building trades, by 1900 the most highly unionized group of occupations in the country. Although the Irish did not predominate in the building trades rank and file, they quickly took over union leadership. By the turn of the century, nearly one-half of the presidents of the unions comprising the American Federation of Labor were Irish. Craft union leaders were committed to bread-and-butter or business unionism, entering local politics for such limited purposes as ensuring that city contracts involved union personnel. Cautious and conservative in local politics, the Irish-controlled building trades set a record for industrial conflict, generating nearly three times as many strikes, boycotts, and sympathy strikes as other industries such as mining.[46]

The Irish-American nationalist movement also helped shape the class consciousness of the Irish working class. The Fenian Brotherhood, organized in 1858, and the Clan na Gael, successor to the Fenians in the 1870s, represented working-class movements. Their republicanism, however, lacked a social program. Local leaders of the Land League, organized in 1880, sought reform of the American as well as Irish land systems. Radical Land League branches were concentrated in the anthracite coal region of Pennsylvania (where they functioned as surrogates for the Knights of Labor) and in the industrial cities of New England and the Middle Atlantic states. Even in cities such as New York and San Francisco, where moderates dominated the leadership of the local leagues, there was a strong connection between the local branches and the local labor movement. In New York, the Central Labor Union came into existence as a consequence of trade union rallies in support of tenant farmers' rights in Ireland. The Central Labor Union would challenge Tammany Hall's political hegemony in 1886 by nominating Henry George on a labor party ticket.[47]

With rising Irish working-class militancy, Irish party bosses frequently were more conservative than Irish voters on fiscal, labor, and social issues. The conservatism of Irish political leaders may have been as much a *consequence* as a cause of machine politics. In power, the machine's maintenance needs—building cross-class voting coalitions, placating the business community—introduced a conservative strain in early Irish machine leadership, resulting in lost political opportunities. As they learned to manipulate the levers of urban power, Irish politicians turned their backs on more radical working-class political ventures. As former Fenian revolutionary Jeremiah O'Donovan Rossa sadly observed: "We Irish of New York are American politicians before we are Irish, or anything else."[48]

Martin Shefter has suggested a second explanation of machine fiscal conservatism. Rather than drawing on Irish political culture as the explanatory factor, Shefter's "elite" model focuses on the nature of the local business groups supporting the machine. In New York, the speculators who supported Tweed and demanded expansionary fiscal policies gave way to the bankers, corporate lawyers, and independent businessmen who demanded that Kelly pursue "tight-fisted" economic policies.[49]

In order to understand why early Irish bosses sought alliances with business groups demanding retrenchment, one must distinguish between two distinct stages of machine building: a formative phase and a consolidation phase. In the machine's formative stage, which extended from the 1840s to the 1880s, party bosses expanded both the size of the electorate *and* the public sector. In New York City, Tammany Hall bosses Fernando Wood and William Marcy Tweed naturalized 9,207 immigrants per year between 1856 and 1867. The pace of naturalization soon quickened. In 1868, Tammany naturalized 41,112 foreign-born in order to swell the ranks of Democratic loyalists and to win the crucial gubernatorial contest in that year, freeing the city of state Republican control. The Wigwam hired the New York Printing Company, which Tweed owned, to print 105,000 blank naturalization applications and 69,000 certificates of naturalization. Immigrants fresh off the boat were given red tickets, allowing them to get their citizenship papers free. Tammany paid the required court fees and provided false witnesses to testify that the immigrants had been in the country the necessary five years.[50]

Running its naturalization mill "full blast," Tammany succeeded in dramatically increasing the number of voters. Table 5 traces the growth of the electorate and Tammany's electoral fortunes under four political bosses between 1855 and 1897: Fernando Wood, William Marcy Tweed, "Honest John" Kelly, and Richard Croker. During the Wood era, from the late 1840s to 1863, Tammany Hall worked its citizenship factory at "half blast," relying more on purchased and repeat voters than on the newly enfranchised. Voter fraud met with surprisingly little success. Between 1855 and 1863, as the city's electorate grew by one-fifth, Tammany managed to win only one of five mayoral elections as the artful Wood shuttled his army of fraudulent voters between the Wigwam and Mozart

TABLE 5. *The Tiger Lays Claim to New York: Voting and Turnout Under Four Tammany Bosses, 1855–1897*

| | | Mayoral Elections | | | Turnout | | |
| | | Number of Contests | Tammany Victories | Tammany Percentage of Total Vote | First Election | Last Election | Percentage Increase |
Tammany Boss	Years						
Fernando Wood	1855–1863	5	1	38.6	59,643	71,101	19.2
William Marcy Tweed	1865–1872	3	2	51.8	71,101	134,878	89.7
"Honest John" Kelly	1874–1884	5	4 [a]	53.1	134,878	226,035	67.6
Richard Croker	1886–1897	6	5	49.4 [b]	226,035	300,939	33.1

Sources: For 1855–1886: New York Tribune, *Tribune Almanac and Political Register* (New York: G. Dearborn); for 1887–1897: New York State Legislature, *Red Book, State of New York.*

[a] Three Tammany victories were shared with its rivals, Irving Hall and the County Democracy.
[b] Includes three plurality victories in three-way contests with Republican, reform, or labor candidates.

Hall, Tammany's arch organizational rival in that era for control of the Democratic party.

Boss Tweed cranked up Tammany's naturalization mill. During Tweed's short tenure, the city's electorate nearly doubled, from 71,000 to close to 135,000 voters. A. Oakey Hall, Tweed's handpicked candidate for mayor in 1868, received 75,000 votes, more than triple the number received five years earlier by Tammany nominee Francis I. A. "Boodle" Boole. Starting in the early 1870s, "Honest John" Kelly took up where Tweed had left off. Tammany's citizenship factory continued to churn out new voters. By Kelly's death in 1886, the Wigwam had naturalized nearly 80 percent of the city's Irish, German, and other "old" (Western European) immigrants. These new citizens swelled the ranks of the Tammany Tiger's voters, consolidating the machine's hold over party and city. Under Kelly, Tammany won (or shared victory with Democratic rivals Irving Hall and the County Democracy) in four of five mayoral contests, averaging 53 percent of the vote. However, an entrenched Tammany would no longer have to turn out newly minted voters. Under Kelly successor Richard Croker, the triumphant Tiger won five of six elections between 1886 and 1897 as the city's electorate grew at one-half the rate it had under Kelly— 33 percent as opposed to 68 percent.

During this formative stage, the early Irish machines did more than mobilize immigrant voters. They also increased the size of the public sector in order to *reward* the new voters. In cities such as New York, per capita expenditures and debts soared from the 1850s to the early 1870s as *some* of the newly enfranchised voters were rewarded with newly created public jobs. Boss Tweed, for example, embarked on a program of massive deficit financing in the late 1860s in part to enlarge the city payroll. A contemporary observer estimated that there were 12,000 to 15,000 members of Tweed's "Shiny Hat Brigade," the holders of newly created municipal sinecures. Under Tweed the city's debt tripled, rising from $36 million in 1868 to $136 million at the end of 1870.[51]

But there were political limits on the fledgling machine's ability to expand its resource base. The nineteenth-century machine harnessed a system of municipal government organized primarily to promote economic growth and heavily dependent on local property taxes for revenue—the source of over two-thirds of city revenue in this era—in the context of fierce competition between cities for business location and capital investment.

In the machine's formative stage, soaring property tax rates and indebtedness resulted in a competitive disadvantage for business location and investment and in a political backlash by businessmen and middle-class property owners. As C. K. Yearley argues, the property-owning urban middle class was peculiarly affected by the machine's expansionary fiscal policies. The poor did not own property and thus escaped direct taxation. The rich shifted their wealth to more intangible forms of personal property—savings, securities, and credits—to escape taxation. Thus the machine's taxation burden largely fell on the property-owning middle class, which supplied the backbone of support for the antimachine municipal reform movements of the period from 1870 to 1910.[52]

In the nineteenth-century machine's mature or consolidation phase, extending from the mid-1870s to the turn of the century, a conservative fiscal strategy more acceptable to business and the middle class evolved. Tax rates and expenditures in machine cities such as New York and San Francisco stabilized as bosses such as Kelly and Buckley made peace with the business community. In the 1880s and 1890s population increases outpaced city expenditures, and per capita outlays in the Irish machine cities plummeted (see Table 4). Bosses had to find new ways of raising revenue and buying off the machine's rapacious working-class followers.

The Irish bosses first turned to indebtedness. Debt-financed public works projects finessed the conflicting political demands of the working class and middle class. Public works projects represented a valuable patronage source, particularly for the Irish-run building trades. At the same time, debt costs could be more easily hidden in the city budget, thereby placating the middle class, as long as the property tax rate remained constant.[53]

Yet the Irish bosses found their ability to borrow money severely hampered. Table 6 shows changes in the debt burden for the big cities between 1880 and 1902. The eight Irish cities were heavy borrowers in 1880. Per capita debts in these cities averaged $66 compared with $55 in the fourteen big cities with smaller Irish populations. After 1880, however, the Irish bosses were unable to borrow in order to pay for (and pay off) the "New Democracy" of

TABLE 6. *Going into Debt, 1880–1902*

Cities and Regimes	Average Per Capita City Debt ($)		Percentage Change from 1880 to 1902
	1880	*1902*	
Irish cities (8)	66	72	9.1
Irish Democratic machine (New York, San Francisco, Jersey City, Albany)	68	70	2.9
Irish Democratic nonmachine (Boston)	78	148	89.7
Non-Irish Republican machine (Philadelphia, Pittsburgh)	77	60	−22.1
Non-Irish nonmachine (Chicago)	25	29	13.8
Non-Irish cities (14)[a]	55	58	5.5

Sources: U.S. Census Office, *Report on Valuation, Taxation, and Public Indebtedness: 1880* (Washington, D.C.: Government Printing Office, 1884), Table 22, pp. 883–890; U.S. Bureau of the Census, *Special Reports: Statistics of Cities, 1902* (Washington, D.C.: Government Printing Office, 1902), Table 38, pp. 443–449.

[a] Includes all cities with more than 50,000 population *and* less than 13 percent Irish. See Table 1.

immigrant working-class voters. In the machine cities of New York, San Francisco, Jersey City, and Albany, the average debt burden increased by only 3 percent between 1880 and 1902. Boston's Irish ward bosses, in contrast, borrowed freely as the Hub's debt soared by nearly 90 percent. Compared with Boston's free spenders, the Republican bosses of Philadelphia and Pittsburgh succumbed to pay-as-you-go financing; their debt burden dropped by 22 percent.

The Irish Democratic machines wanted to borrow but could not. In the 1870s and 1880s their opponents succeeded in imposing constitutional restrictions on their ability to borrow money. Following the panic of 1873, which brought many cities to the verge of bankruptcy, conservative governors and state legislatures— Republican *and* Democratic—sought legal restrictions on the indebtedness powers of machine-controlled local governments. In New York, for example, anti-Tammany Democrat Governor Lucius Robinson accused the cities of a "disposition to play with debt and court taxation as if for a pastime." At Robinson's behest, the legislature proposed and voters approved a constitutional amendment that limited the borrowing power of local governments to 10 percent of their assessed valuation. Other constitutional restrictions on city borrowing powers included the requirement of local voter approval for municipal debts and the provision of a special tax or sinking fund for payment of city debts.[54]

With mounting constitutional limits on debt-financed capital improvement programs, machines turned to expanding the city as a whole rather than the relative size of the public sector. In particular, machine politicians pursued an aggressive annexation program to enlarge the city's boundaries and revenue base. Between 1880 and 1900, the twenty largest cities increased their territory by nearly one-third, with New York, Boston, and Chicago leading the way.[55]

Republican state governors and legislators also endorsed big-city annexation—but as a means of weakening the Democratic machines. In 1897, the Republican-controlled legislature of New York passed the Consolidation Act, uniting the five boroughs into the City of Greater New York. State GOP boss Thomas Platt proposed the act, believing that the city Republicans could win in 1898. In 1894 the GOP state ticket had carried the five boroughs. The Consolidation Act doubled the city's revenue base (and swelled the ranks of the patronage army to 60,000) without increasing the tax rate. The Republican stratagem backfired. Tammany won a resounding victory in the first consolidated election, capturing new patronage with which to cement working-class political allegiances.[56]

Annexation represented a double-edged sword for the Irish machines. On the one hand, annexation increased the machine's supply of jobs, always appealing to the working class, without necessarily increasing the property tax rate, of prime concern to the middle class. On the other hand, this strategy increased the number of nominally antimachine voters as it captured the outward-migrating Yankee middle class.

The fiscally starved Irish machines of the late nineteenth century also relied on a "vice tax" as a way of raising revenue. With the constant threat of middle-class tax revolts and the drying up of government revenue, machines offered police protection for gambling and prostitution in exchange for badly needed cash. In New

York City, for example, Richard Croker developed a police graft system in the late 1880s, substantially filling Tammany's coffers with the payoffs from gambling, drinking, and prostitution. Croker would soon learn the political risks as well as the benefits of a vice tax. In the early 1890s the Lexow Committee conducted a damaging investigation of the graft ring in the Tammany-controlled New York police department. Reformers capitalized on middle-class outrage to win the 1894 city elections.[57]

The fiscal conservatism of the first generation of Irish party bosses can thus be traced to the fragile machine's maintenance needs. Expansionary fiscal policies invited middle-class and business tax revolts. Conservative fiscal policies, in contrast, invited working-class insurgency. To temper the conflicting demands of the two classes for retrenchment and patronage, the Irish bosses chose conservative tax policies, were forced to adopt cautious borrowing programs, vigorously promoted annexation, and cashed in on vice.

Rewarding the Irish: The Limits of Early Machine Patronage

As Tammany boss Richard Croker candidly admitted, the machine needed to bribe the masses with spoils—"Here they take the shape of offices."[58] The lowly economic status of the Irish made them unusually susceptible to this form of machine flattery. In the late nineteenth century, the Irish lagged far behind other groups economically. In the eight cities surveyed, 67 percent of the Irish were unskilled or semiskilled laborers in 1870, compared with 28 percent of the Yankees and Germans. Few Irish were middle-class. In 1870 only 10 percent of the Irish in these eight cities held white-collar jobs, compared with 37 percent of the Yankees and 28 percent of the Germans.[59]

Did the Irish takeover of the Democratic machines dramatically improve their economic lot? A fourth question about the early machines involves the amount of patronage they actually controlled and how much they gave to the Irish. As I argue in Chapter 1, the prizes awaiting capture in city politics *appeared* substantial. Urban machines controlled thousands of public sector and private sector patronage jobs, the latter with firms franchised by or doing business with the city. Tammany Hall, for example, controlled 40,000 municipal jobs during Boss Kelly's rule. Machines also controlled the awarding of public works contracts, important in an era when cities were shifting their function from caretaking to providing amenities. For the Irish-controlled building trades, capital improvement projects were prizes indeed. Furthermore, the city payroll seemed to offer relatively greater advancement opportunities than did the private sector. In San Francisco, for example, 63 percent of all city workers in 1870 were in white-collar jobs compared with only 28 percent of those privately employed. Given the machine's apparent cornucopia of resources, it is small wonder that, as E. L. Godkin so acidly observed, the Irish undertook politics in a "predatory state of mind."[60]

Relative to the number of immigrant and working-class voters, however, the early machine's patronage supply was limited. Public jobs were the most important machine resource. How many of these political loaves and fishes were available to feed the party faithful? By today's standards, the public sector in the era of the nightwatchman state was quite small. Political constraints on increasing the property tax rate coupled with legal constraints on city borrowing powers restricted the nineteenth-century machine's ability to create patronage for the Irish. In 1870, the public sector accounted for only 3 percent of the big-city workforce, slowly climbing to 5 percent by 1900. Even Tammany's vaunted patronage army of more than 40,000 in the late 1880s was no more than platoon size in a labor force of nearly 1 million. In contrast, the public sector today comprises nearly 20 percent of the big-city labor force. The Irish would have to wait until the era of big government to use the public sector as a *group* route from rags to riches.[61]

Despite the limited amount of early machine patronage, the Irish grabbed what prizes there were. Table 7 traces Irish public employment gains in the big cities between 1870 and 1900. The four Irish machines successfully "Hibernianized" the public payroll. Despite falling per capita outlays, city employment in New York, San Francisco, Jersey City, and Albany rose from 10,950 in 1870 to 66,505 in 1900 as the number of Irish payrollers ballooned from 1,966 to 24,324. The Irish bosses had the Republicans to thank for much of their patronage coup. New York GOP boss Thomas Platt's miscalculation with the 1897 Consolidation

Act handed Tammany Hall 20,000 new patronage jobs—representing nearly 40 percent of the overall increase in the machine cities—on a silver platter. Aided by their foes, the Irish bosses could achieve both patronage and retrenchment.

Demonstrating an early and effective ethnic affirmative action policy, the four machines gave the Irish more than 40 percent of the newly created patronage. Yet the Irish did not always need friendly machines to place them on the city payroll. In Irish-controlled but nonmachine Boston, for example, the proportion of city workers of Irish descent rose from a paltry 5 percent in 1870 to 32 percent in 1900. In Chicago under Democratic party bosses Mike McDonald, Carter Harrison I, and Carter Harrison II, the Irish claim on the city payroll soared from 14 percent to 31 percent. Not to be outdone, the Republican machines of Philadelphia and Pittsburgh politically rebaptized the Irish and put them on the GOP payroll, though in smaller numbers.

Even with these dramatic public job gains, most Irish officeseekers in the late nineteenth century were bound to be disappointed. Because machines presided over governments of limited size and function, there were too few patronage plums for too many Irish jobseekers. As Table 7 shows, in 1900 only 6 percent of first- and second-generation Irish in New York, San Francisco, Jersey City, and Albany worked directly for government. In these four machine cities, 295,000 Irish entered the labor force between 1870 and 1900. The private sector, not the machine, generated up to 90 percent of the new urban job opportunities for these workers.

For the same reason, few middle-class gains were achieved by the Irish in the public sector during this period. San Francisco's Irish, for example, received one-third of the 2,500 white-collar public jobs created between 1870 and 1900. At the turn of the century, however, government employed fewer than 10 percent of all Irish white-collar workers. Here, too, the private sector was responsible for the vast majority of Irish middle-class job gains.[62]

Upwardly bound Irish had entered the public sector at the wrong time. Machines specialized in padding blue-collar payrolls in the police, fire, and public works departments. At the same time, the Irish machines deliberately limited white-collar job opportunities, particularly in the school system. More blue-collar than white-collar jobs could be created for a given financial outlay, an impor-

TABLE 7. *How Many Plums? The Irish and Big-City Patronage, 1870–1900*

Cities and Regimes	Municipal Employment, 1870[a]			Municipal Employment, 1900[a]			Percentage of Irish Workforce Employed by City Government	
	Irish[b]	All	Percentage Irish	Irish[b]	All	Percentage Irish	1870	1900
Irish cities (8)	2,994	21,697	13.8	42,841	129,463	33.1	1.3	5.6
Irish Democratic machine (New York, San Francisco, Jersey City, Albany)	1,966	10,950	17.9	24,324	66,505	36.6	1.4	5.8
Irish Democratic nonmachine (Boston)	132	2,660	5.0	3,227	10,143	31.8	0.5	3.8
Non-Irish Republican machine (Philadelphia, Pittsburgh)	535	5,566	9.6	6,516	24,750	26.3	1.2	4.5
Non-Irish nonmachine (Chicago)	361	2,521	14.3	8,774	28,065	31.3	1.8	8.7
Non-Irish cities (14)[c]	1,723	20,323	8.5	13,801	69,694	19.8	2.6	7.5

Sources: U.S. Census Office, *Ninth Census, 1870* (Washington, D.C.: Government Printing Office, 1872), vol. 1, Table 32; U.S. Bureau of the Census, *Special Reports: Occupations at the Twelfth Census* (Washington, D.C.: Government Printing Office, 1904), Tables 41, 43.

[a] Based on more complete public employment information for the nation and for San Francisco, the 1870 figures have been increased by 20 percent; the 1900 figures, by 50 percent.

[b] For 1870, municipal employees born in Ireland; for 1900, municipal employees of Irish parentage.

[c] Includes all cities with more than 50,000 population *and* less than 13 percent Irish. See Table 1.

tant consideration for the vote-seeking Irish party bosses. White-collar patronage, in addition, did not have the same vote yield. Teachers represented the largest single source of white-collar public jobs, and most teachers were women, unable to vote in this era. Furthermore, middle-class political pressures limited machine influence over the hiring and firing of teachers. As a consequence, the heavily Catholic Democratic machines reached a concordance between church and state on limiting public school financing. A poorly financed public school system made the church-run parochial school system—where most Irish bosses had themselves been educated—all the more attractive. Given the machine's proletarianization of the public sector, greater job opportunities now loomed in the private sector, where growth in the white-collar service sector outpaced gains in blue-collar manufacturing. In the Bay Area, for example, the white-collar share of public employment dropped from 63 percent to 48 percent between 1870 and 1900; in the private sector, the white-collar share rose from 28 percent to 37 percent.[63]

Ironically, the relative security of blue-collar jobs in police, fire, and public works departments may have actually hindered the *early* development of an Irish-American middle class by encouraging long tenure in low-status positions. In San Francisco, the Irish garnered one-half of all blue-collar public jobs created between 1870 and 1900. However, compared with privately employed blue-collar workers— Irish and non-Irish—Celtic blue-collar civil servants were twice as likely to hold the same poor-paying job for twenty years.[64]

Perhaps the nineteenth-century machine's economic benefits for the Irish were more indirect than the public payroll. Bosses also controlled private sector patronage, particularly through the award of public works contracts or through control of "unofficial" patronage with firms dependent on the party organization for contracts and franchises. How did the Irish fare with the machine's stock of private sector jobs?

Some Irish clearly benefited from public works projects. The main beneficiaries were contractors, workers in the building trades, and the army of casual laborers. The Irish quickly gravitated into the urban contracting business. As early as 1870 nearly one-fifth of the nation's big-city contractors were Irish-born. As David Mont-

gomery notes, the characteristics of the construction industry—
low capital requirements, the important role of governmental action, and the complex social network of subcontracting—were
ideal for the Irish. Irish workers in the building trades particularly
benefited from public works projects because Irish contractors
preferred to hire Irish employees. But as unskilled and semiskilled
"new" immigrants flooded into the cities, they too began to demand employment on public works projects. By the turn of the
century, the organizationally blessed Irish dominated the union
leadership of the building trades but not the rank-and-file membership. Only in a few trades—such as plumbing and steamfitting—
did the Irish predominate. The majority of the Irish-American beneficiaries of public works projects were unskilled laborers. In cities
such as New York and San Francisco at the turn of the century,
fully 40 percent of the city's unskilled laborers were Irish. For this
sizable pool of Irish unskilled laborers, contract labor jobs represented poor-paying irregular employment, not a channel for ethnic
group economic progress.[65]

How did the Irish fare with the machine's supply of "unofficial"
patronage, that is, jobs in firms doing business with the machine
and filled by party workers in exchange for favorable governmental action? Financially starved machines had strong incentives to
expand the number of these positions, especially as civil service reforms protected increasing numbers of municipal employees. Yet
there were countervailing economic incentives encouraging businesses to resist machine encroachment on their payrolls. As Robert
Brooks observed, businesses preferred paying cash for political
favors rather than hiring inefficient party workers.[66] The lowly
character of private sector political jobs further limited advancement opportunities. Most utility jobs involved unskilled or semiskilled work. Although it is virtually impossible to estimate the
amount and ethnic distribution of this form of patronage, a survey
of the payrolls of private utilities and street railroads in San Francisco is revealing. In 1900, after twenty years of Irish rule, the Irish
were *not* overrepresented on these payrolls, contrary to what one
would expect had these jobs been machine-controlled and of economic value.[67]

Private sector patronage generated substantial economic opportunities for *individual* Irishmen. Irish contractors, in particular,

grew rich on padded public works contracts. It is questionable, however, whether these forms of patronage afforded economic advancement for large numbers of Irish workers. Regarding city capital improvement programs, the public payroll dwarfed the capital budget in size in late nineteenth-century municipal budgets. In Buckley's San Francisco, for example, more than one-half of the city budget of nearly $5 million in 1880 went for salaries. The remainder was divided evenly between capital improvements and expenses. In this era, public works projects generated only one-third to one-half the job opportunities of the public payroll. If the Irish had been employed on big-city public works projects at roughly the same rate as they were on the city payroll, then the machine's private sector jobs could have absorbed only an additional 3 to 4 percent of the Irish labor force. The early machine's combined public and private patronage could provide employment—much of it temporary or blue-collar—for only one out of ten Irish workers.[68]

Given this tale of machine parsimony, how do we account for the apparent rapid development of a sizable Irish middle class in the big cities? Between 1870 and 1900 the proportion of Irish in white-collar jobs in the eight cities surveyed rose from 10 percent to 24 percent. Could machines have improved the lot of the Irish in more indirect ways than patronage? If machines opened the private sector labor market to the Irish, the best they could do was provide entry-level positions. For the 90 percent of the Irish middle class in the private sector, economic progress was slow and uneven. As Stephan Thernstrom has carefully shown for Boston, most privately employed white-collar Irish were marginally middle class, having entered clerical and sales work rather than business and the professions. The Irish in America, as Daniel Patrick Moynihan accurately observed, would prove to be functionaries rather than entrepreneurs.[69]

In taking over the northern urban Democratic party and crowding into the machine's patronage enclave in the late nineteenth century, did the Irish significantly limit opportunities for *other* immigrant groups to seek fame and fortune—such as it was—in the public sector? At first glance, there appears to be little evidence for a so-called crowding effect. In the four Irish machine cities, non-Irish immigrants received one-third of the public jobs generated between 1870 and 1900. Before complimenting the Irish bosses on their political foresight in using patronage to reduce non-Irish discontent with Irish rule, it should be noted that these cities were steadily filling with the non-Irish during this period. By the turn of the century, the other immigrant groups constituted nearly 60 percent of the workforce in cities such as New York and San Francisco, yet they held only 36 percent of the public jobs. In the Irish machine cities, the non-Irish patronage "quota," that is, the share of public jobs allotted to non-Irish workers relative to their numbers in the labor force, rose from 39 percent in 1870 to 61 percent in 1900. By running the machines, the Irish bagged more than their fair share of patronage. In New York, San Francisco, Jersey City, and Albany, the ratio of public to overall employment for the Irish more than doubled from 64 percent in 1870 to 135 percent at century's end.[70]

What caused these early differences between Irish and non-Irish in the relative receipt of machine patronage? One obvious explanation lies in the different job skills ethnic groups brought to the New World. The largely unskilled Irish *needed* public employment; the skilled Germans generally did not. Even among the Germans, though, there were large numbers eager to do menial work. In the big cities, one-quarter of the German workforce in 1870 toiled as unskilled or semiskilled laborers.

A second explanation focuses on group voting strength rather than job demand. As Table 3 shows, the Irish had high naturalization, registration, and voting rates; other ethnic groups did not. Public employment allocations were highly sensitive to group electoral strength. In San Francisco between 1870 and 1900, differences in electoral mobilization rates (consisting of voter registration, turnout, and bloc voting) for the city's eight major ethnic groups accounted for 60 percent of the variance in group patronage shares.[71]

Yet more was involved than group muscle at the polls. Even when the non-Irish were naturalized, registered, and voting, they rarely received their fair share of public jobs. The Irish regarded politics and public employment as their secular calling. They hoarded as much patronage as they could, fending off other groups whether these groups voted or not. Thus in the Irish-run machine cities, the patronage yield of Irish votes far outstripped non-Irish votes. San

Francisco's machine, for example, added 15,172 new Irish voters and 2,286 new Irish payrollers between 1870 and 1900. During the same period, 13,238 Germans were added to the city's voter registration rolls, but only 611 found their way onto the public payroll. Irish votes in the Bay Area had more than three times the patronage yield of German votes. The ratio of new voters to new public jobs was seven to one for the Irish; for the Germans, twenty-two to one.[72]

Even by hoarding patronage from other ethnic groups, however, the first generation of Irish machines controlled too little gravy to fully satisfy the Irish working class. Unable to increase the machine's patronage supply any faster, Irish politicos chose two less costly ways of calming the Irish working class: heavy doses of labor rhetoric and recreational clubs.

In New York, fiscally conservative Tammany boss "Honest John" Kelly employed anticapitalist and antimonopolist rhetoric in the early 1880s to appeal to the city's increasingly restive working class. According to Eric Foner, the shift in Kelly's political rhetoric reflected the success of the Land League in propagating radical ideas among the Irish working class.[73] In San Francisco in the mid-1880s, conservative Boss Buckley belatedly realized the growing power of labor. Decrying the "cursed monopolists," the "Blind Boss" called for reduced transportation and utility rates for the city's working class.[74]

The Celtic machines also tried "circuses"—recreational clubs—in lieu of "bread"—patronage. As Shefter notes, in the close 1886 New York mayoral contest, pitting Tammany against organized labor, Henry George's United Labor party skillfully employed a popular network of labor recreational clubs affiliated with trade union locals to solicit working-class support. Tammany got the message and soon developed an equivalent with its year-round district recreational clubs. In San Francisco, the Buckley machine also opened district clubhouses in working-class and immigrant neighborhoods.[75]

Yet the symbolic and social appeals of the early budget-conscious Irish party bosses were never fully adequate to cement working-class and immigrant loyalties to the big-city machines. Social inducements such as district clubs were never as attractive to the working class as were economic benefits, whether patronage, welfare services, or labor legislation. In the late nineteenth century, revolts from below were the price paid for the machine's conservative fiscal policies. Under a new generation of Irish bosses in the twentieth century, machines would be constructed from sturdier materials. The second generation of Irish machines would figure out how to supply bread as well as circuses to the masses.

Chapter Three

Guardians of Power:
The Irish Versus
the New Immigrants,
1896—1928

Death, Transfiguration,
and Machine Rebirth

The fragile penny-pinching Irish Democratic machines collapsed in the depression-ridden 1890s. As the panic of 1893 lengthened into depression, voters blamed the Democrats. The Democracy controlled the presidency, many governorships of northern states, and most of the big-city machines. Democratic politicians did little to alleviate the suffering of the growing army of unemployed. As leader of the Bourbon, or conservative, wing of the party, President Grover Cleveland remained committed to a balanced budget, laissez-faire economics, and federal nonintervention. Democrat Cleveland's nonintervention policy, however, did not extend to the Irish big-city bosses, his nominal allies. Ever the reformer, Cleveland joined forces with the Republicans as the economy worsened to attack the Democratic machines by denying them badly needed federal patronage.[1]

Fending off presidential attack from above and facing growing discontent from below, the Irish machines sought to soothe the masses on the cheap. Forced to choose the low-cost alternative, machines championed the workers' social—but not economic—demands: racetracks, gambling, and drinking. The Republicans, in contrast, promised bread rather than circuses. Campaigning on the issue of economic discontent, the GOP proposed government programs to put the jobless to work.

Capitalizing on the economic grievances of the urban working class, Republicans and reformers dethroned the reigning Irish Democratic bosses. In San Francisco, Republican boss Gavin Mc-Nab defeated "Blind Boss" Buckley in 1891 with substantial Irish and working-class support. During the turbulent 1890s, leadership of the Bay Area oscillated among Republicans, populists, and reform Democrats but not Democratic machine politicians. In Jersey City, the Davis machine succumbed to Republican reformer Mark Fagin in 1901. Reformers—Democratic as well as Republican—controlled Jersey City politics until World War I. In Albany, a reform fusion ticket triumphed over the Irish machine in the 1894 city election. Though the Democrats temporarily recaptured city hall, Republican boss William E. "Billy" Barnes took advantage of Democratic factionalism in 1899 to topple the incumbent machine. Wooing patronage-hungry Democratic politicians into his own organization, Billy Barnes would run Albany until 1921. Even Tammany did not emerge unscathed from the 1890s. The Wigwam lost the city elections of 1894 and 1902, prompting Boss Croker's resignation.

Despite the debacle of the 1890s, the Irish machines reemerged in strengthened form after the turn of the century. Following Boss Croker's resignation, Charles Francis Murphy took over Tammany Hall. Under Murphy and his successors, a revitalized Tiger ran the city (with minor exceptions) from 1903 to 1933. In 1917 Democrat Frank "I Am the Law" Hague was elected mayor of Jersey City. Hague built one of the most powerful—and repressive—machines in the country. Controlling the city, the county, and even the state, Hague ran Jersey City with an iron hand until 1949. Not to be outdone, Albany Democratic boss Dan O'Connell set the record for machine longevity. In the 1921 city elections, O'Connell capitalized on a rift between the Barnes machine and the Irish working class over an unsettled transit strike. Wooing the Irish back into the Democratic party, O'Connell routed Barnes at the polls and quickly consolidated power. As of 1987, the Albany Democratic machine had yet to lose a city election.

The second-generation Irish machines little resembled their

predecessors. Their strength lay in the provision of bread—lots of it—rather than circuses. Under the new machines, spending, borrowing, and patronage soared in the early twentieth century. Lavished on a single ethnic group, patronage tamed the restless Irish working class. With jobs and money, the new machines built a reliable electoral following. To win elections, machines merely mobilized the sizable Irish payroll army, Irish families, jobseekers, and, when needed, purchasable voters. With the machine's opponents reduced to a corporal's guard, the party bosses needed only a manageable rather than a large vote.

The electoral incentives of the new big-city party organizations differed considerably from their predecessors. Facing strong opposition, the late nineteenth-century machines had been mobilizers of the immigrant vote. With token opposition, the twentieth-century machines selectively brought out the vote. Having already fashioned a minimal winning electoral coalition among the earlier-arriving immigrants with the sturdiest of materials—jobs and money—the new machines turned their backs on later-arriving immigrants. Thus the second-generation party organizations did not naturalize, register, and vote the Southern and Eastern Europeans, who arrived from the late 1880s onward, at anything approaching the rate at which the Irish had been politically incorporated in the mid-nineteenth century.

Given the slowdown in immigrant assimilation, the twentieth-century Irish machines had little need to share power and jobs with the non-Irish. Instead, the newcomers were given less valuable rewards—social services, symbolic recognition, and collective benefits such as state labor and social welfare legislation. The strategy of parsimonious reward, however, would ultimately backfire. In the 1930s and 1940s, Southern and Eastern Europeans entered the voting booths in record numbers. Mobilizing the newcomers and seizing on their discontent with the machine's limited rewards, reformers succeeded in toppling many of the entrenched Irish machines.

There were important variations between cities in machine rebirth and policy transformation, raising several questions for analysis. First, as with the earlier machines, there was no one-to-one relationship between cities with large numbers of Irish-American voters and cities where Irish machines reemerged. The new machines did not invariably arise phoenix-like from the ashes of earlier organizations. In some machine cities, the ashes were hot; in others, not. While New York, Jersey City, and Albany produced both first- and second-generation machines, San Francisco did not. The Bay Area's Democratic party remained moribund from the turn of the century to the early 1960s. In New York, reformers briefly interrupted Tammany's reign, enough to topple Boss Croker, but not the party organization. In Jersey City and Albany, a generation would pass between the old and new Irish machines.

In the other four Irish cities, where first-generation Irish Democratic machines had not been built, the early twentieth century would also prove inhospitable to rule by Irish Democratic bosses. Irish-run Boston remained faction-ridden throughout this period. Neither John F. "Honey Fitz" Fitzgerald, Martin Lomasney, nor, later, James Michael Curley could centralize power in the heavily Democratic Hub. Chicago's competitive and factional politics carried well into the twentieth century. Despite alternating periods of Democratic and Republican rule in the Windy City, neither party could consolidate power until the 1930s. And in a Republican era bracketed by McKinley and Hoover, Yankee GOP machines would run Philadelphia and Pittsburgh.

What explains the emergence of a new cohort of Irish machines in some of the cities with large numbers of Irish voters and not in others? Can the intergovernmental theory advanced to explain late nineteenth-century machine building be extended into the twentieth century? Can the rebirth of some of the Irish machines be explained by alliances with pro-machine Democratic governors? Alternatively, can the failure to rebuild the San Francisco machine or centralize power in Boston and Chicago be explained by hostile state administrations?

Second, what explains the revolution in the machine's fiscal policies? Nineteenth-century urban party bosses had not been able to expand dramatically the size of the public sector and patronage supply. Property tax increases invited middle-class tax revolts. State constitutional restrictions hamstrung the machine's ability to borrow money for public works projects. But twentieth-century machines taxed and borrowed with political impunity. In the face of mounting tax burdens, why did middle-class protest fizzle? In the face of growing debt burdens, what remained of state financial safeguards?

Third, what kind of patronage did the new machines control and what share went to the Irish? The nineteenth-century machine's limited and largely blue-collar patronage afforded the Irish opportunities for individual but not group social mobility. The twentieth-century machine's patronage policies, in contrast, appear to support the rainbow theory that politics served as an important route of group advancement for the Irish. As the new machine's prizes grew, ever larger numbers of Irishmen crowded into the public sector. Yet what accounts for the sluggish economic progress of the Irish well into the twentieth century? As Andrew Greeley has shown, the Irish, compared with the Jews, were slow to build a middle class anchored in business and the professions. The Irish middle class was just emerging on the eve of the Depression; its arrival would not occur until after World War II. In light of their political success, why was middle-class status so slow in coming for the Irish? Was there an *inverse* relationship between Irish political success and economic advancement? Did the second-generation Irish machines create white-collar job opportunities or did they continue to pad—with Paddys—blue-collar city payrolls?[2]

Fourth, why did the second-generation Irish machines do so little to assimilate and reward the Southern and Eastern Europeans? In the short run, this represented a rational electoral and allocational strategy. The fortunes of entrenched machines depended on the payroll and purchased vote, not the newcomers. Compared with the Irish, moreover, the Jews, Italians, Poles, and Czechs were slow to become citizens and exercise the franchise. With little muscle at the polls, they did not threaten—and thus could not bargain with—the Irish bosses. In the long run, however, the machine's strategy of minimal accommodation was self-defeating. As the newcomers slowly became citizens and voted, Irish prominence in urban public life rested on an increasingly fragile electoral base. Ultimately dealt a losing hand by demographic changes, the Irish bosses fought a brilliant rearguard action against the new ethnics. Yet the Celtic bosses could only delay—not prevent—the challenge of the newer arrivals to the continued Irish monopoly over power and patronage. With a sizable patronage infusion, the new machines could have afforded to incorporate and reward the Southern and Eastern Europeans. Why did the second generation of Irish-American party bosses fail to share the machine's now ample resources and thus risk another round of antimachine revolts from below? To these four questions about the early twentieth-century Irish machines we now turn.

State Politics and Machine Rebirth

The big-city Irish machines resurfaced during the brief period of national Democratic hegemony after 1912. The dominant Republican party had split between Regular and Bull Moose factions, allowing the Democrats to score victories at the national, state, and local levels. At the federal level, the Democrats effectively controlled the presidency and Congress for the first time in twenty years. At the state level, the Democrats won gubernatorial elections in major urban-industrial states such as New York, New Jersey, Massachusetts, and Illinois. Newly elected Democratic governors could assist machines in a variety of ways. Needing patronage to reward their followers, fledgling machines gratefully accepted state jobs. Friendly Democratic governors could also use their veto powers to prevent GOP-controlled state legislatures from interfering in urban affairs.[3]

Pro-Machine States

New Jersey and New York elected pro-machine Democratic governors between 1912 and 1921, allowing the reborn Jersey City and Albany machines to consolidate power. In Jersey City, would-be boss Frank Hague aligned himself in 1913 with Democratic Governor James F. Fielder. Serving as a city commissioner, Hague initially built his organization with Fielder's aid and protection, needed against Democratic Mayor Otto Wittpenn, Hague's rival and Fielder's gubernatorial opponent in 1913. Elected mayor of Jersey City in 1917, Hague moved immediately to control the governorship. Hague needed a pliable Democratic governor to shield his machine from the Republican-controlled state legislature, to increase his resources with state jobs, and, finally, to control the state Civil Service Commission and state Board of Taxes and Assessments in Trenton. A friendly civil service board would allow Hague to hire and fire city workers at will. A sympathetic state tax board, in turn, would permit Hague to expand his patronage army by increasing local property tax assessments for the city's railroads, oil companies, and public service corporations. In 1919, Hague succeeded in placing his friend Edward I. Edwards in the governor's chair. The Hague then gave the gubernatorial nomination to George Silzer as Edwards was moved to the U.S. Senate. Replacing Silzer, Hague protégé A. Harry Moore was elected in 1925 to the first of three terms as governor of the Garden State. Controlling state patronage, civil service, and taxing authority, Hague consolidated his rule.[4]

In Albany, would-be boss Dan O'Connell launched his political career in 1919 by running for assessor on a reform platform, accusing GOP boss Barnes of high taxes and excessive public spending. Once elected, O'Connell forged ties with Democratic Governor Al Smith. Though Smith lost his gubernatorial rebid in the 1920 Republican landslide, the Albany Democrats were instrumental in his political comeback. At the 1921 state Democratic convention held in Syracuse, the Albany county delegation supported Smith. The 1921 election installed Smith in the statehouse and O'Connell across the street in city hall. Throughout the 1920s a grateful Smith would assist "Uncle Dan's" fledgling organization. Smith gave O'Connell 160 state jobs, particularly needed in light of the machine's low tax policies. O'Connell systematically padded the voter registration rolls to turn a two-to-one Republican advantage in 1921 into a two-to-one Democratic advantage by 1927. What O'Connell could not pad, he bought. Precinct captains purchased the flophouse vote on North Pearl Street on election day. The state did not intervene. O'Connell's tax policies, as Frank Robinson has observed, were "played like a violin." The machine sold lowered tax assessments to homeowners and deliberately overassessed businesses relative to residences. Again the state did not intervene. State noninterference in Albany affairs continued under Democratic governors Roosevelt and Lehman in the late 1920s and 1930s. Only with the election of Republican Thomas E. Dewey as governor in 1942 would the state finally investigate the city's voter registration and tax records. It was too late. O'Connell had fully consolidated power and easily derailed the former district attorney's antimachine crusade.[5]

Established machines such as Tammany Hall were less affected by state party politics than were the embryonic Hague and O'Connell organizations. After consolidating power in the late 1880s, the

Wigwam merely required the existence of a stable state political structure, regardless of the controlling party. Tammany bosses Croker and Murphy worked closely with state Republican boss Thomas Platt and his successor, Billy Barnes, to protect their respective political organizations. Murphy and Platt joined forces to defeat the direct primary bill sponsored by progressive GOP Governor Charles Evans Hughes. Even federal assault did not necessarily harm entrenched machines. Democratic President Woodrow Wilson's anti-Tammany federal patronage policies failed to weaken the Wigwam.[6]

Even though they were less buffeted by state politics, established machines still worked to control the governorship and state legislature. The governorship meant state patronage, the legislature, greater local autonomy and welfare legislation. With Tammany's help, Democrat John A. Dix was elected governor of New York in 1910, the first Democratic governor in years. A grateful Dix reciprocated by enlarging Tammany's patronage army with 300 state jobs. Dix's Democratic successor was William Sulzer, a protégé of Tammany boss Croker and a member of the Wigwam for twenty-five years, who became a born-again reformer in office. Tammany then worked as hard disposing of the turncoat Sulzer as it had in initially electing him. The Tiger also labored to control the state legislature. Tammany controlled the 1911 and 1913 sessions, the first controlled by the Democrats in twenty-five years. The machine helped pass important state social welfare legislation popular with the city's working class, particularly the Jews, who showed signs of political independence by supporting Socialist and Progressive candidates.[7]

Antimachine States

In contrast to New Jersey and New York, other state party systems were hostile to machine incubation. In the period 1896 to 1928, Republicans dominated California and Pennsylvania, preventing the rebirth of the Bay Area machine and any serious challenge to the GOP machines of Philadelphia and Pittsburgh. In Massachusetts and Illinois, however, Democratic governors were elected between 1910 and 1917. Yet these governors actively opposed the

Irish party bosses of Boston and Chicago as the bosses sought to consolidate power.

In San Francisco, an Irish successor to the Buckley machine did not emerge. The Democrats returned to power in 1897 as Irish reform Democrat James D. Phelan was elected mayor. Faced with a lockout and strike by the city's Irish teamsters in 1901, the conservative Phelan dispatched the Irish police force to convoy strikebreakers, break up picket lines, and disperse gatherings of strikers. Phelan's antilabor policies infuriated working-class Irish and contributed to the precipitous decline in Democratic party fortunes. In the 1901 city election, working-class Irish turned their backs on the Democrats and supported the newly organized Union Labor party. Skillfully using labor rhetoric, Abraham Reuf, a minor Republican party official, built a labor "machine" that ran San Francisco from 1901 to 1907. By 1907, however, the labor party's fortunes had fallen sharply as Reuf and other ULP leaders were indicted for graft. Patrick H. "Pinhead" McCarthy, the Irish-born head of the powerful Building Trades Council, breathed new life into the labor party, serving as mayor of the city between 1910 and 1912. Reuf and McCarthy relied heavily on the Irish vote. Having defected from the antilabor Democrats, the city's Irish gave the labor party nearly two-thirds of their votes in the six city elections held between 1901 and 1911. Yankees and Germans, in contrast, gave the ULP only one-third of their votes.[8]

Neither McCarthy nor the Irish leaders of the Democratic party could rebuild an Irish working-class machine, in part because they were outbid by the state Republicans. The Republicans controlled the Golden State from the late 1890s to the early 1930s. Elected governor in 1910, progressive Republican Hiram Johnson proposed state legislation significantly broadening the GOP's appeal to San Francisco's working-class Irish. Under Johnson's leadership, the state legislature passed far-reaching labor and social welfare legislation. As a result, Johnson brought many Bay Area working-class and Irish voters into the Republican party. The progressive platform also included such machine-weakening measures as the direct primary, nonpartisan local elections, and the initiative, referendum, and recall. The Bay Area's Irish Democratic politicians were stymied. Their constituents had first deserted them for labor candidates in city elections. Now Johnson was wooing the Irish working class into Republican politics at the state level. Electoral reforms, particularly nonpartisanship in city elections, made the task of machine building even more difficult. Republican politician James "Sunny Jim" Rolph quickly stepped into the political breach. Elected mayor in 1913, Rolph was a local version of Hiram Johnson. The progressive Rolph fashioned a broad-based bipartisan coalition of workers and businessmen that ruled the city into the 1930s. As in Philadelphia and Pittsburgh, the more politically ambitious Irish Democrats gravitated into the ruling camp.[9]

In contrast to GOP-controlled California, Massachusetts and Illinois elected Democratic governors during the Wilson era. But these governors did little to centralize Democratic or Irish power in Boston and Chicago. In Boston, Democrats John F. "Honey Fitz" Fitzgerald, elected mayor in 1905, and James Michael Curley, elected mayor in 1913, both tried their hand at building citywide machines. Growing Irish-Yankee friction in the state Democratic party, however, prevented Fitzgerald and Curley from eliminating each other and the remaining Irish ward bosses. Following Pat Maguire's death in 1896, Yankees from western Massachusetts consolidated their control over the state Democratic party organization as the contentious Boston Irish fought among themselves. The westerners would do little to relinquish control of the party.

In the early twentieth century, the Democrats finally broke the Republican stranglehold on the Bay State, electing three governors: William Douglas in 1904, Eugene Foss in 1910, and David A. Walsh in 1913. All three, however, came from the party's western wing and did little to centralize Boston's Irish politics. In 1905 Fitzgerald began building a citywide machine. The number of city employees multiplied as he hired temporary workers not covered by civil service. Governor Douglas did everything in his power to frustrate Fitzgerald, including giving state patronage to Fitzgerald's opponents. James Michael Curley would also use the powers of the mayor's office to try building a machine. Curley, like Fitzgerald before him, failed as relations between city hall and the statehouse soured. Even though Irishman Walsh had been elected governor, his primary allegiance was to the westerners. Walsh did little to help Curley in his quest to be a city boss.[10]

The Illinois Democratic party also experienced a resurgence during the Wilson years. Democrat Edward R. Dunne was elected governor in 1912. Elected on a reform platform, Dunne actually worked to *increase* rather than decrease Democratic factionalism in Chicago. A nominal protégé of Carter Harrison II, Dunne played the Harrison and Hopkins-Sullivan factions against each other, using state patronage to build an independent reform wing within the local party. Without state patronage, Mayor Harrison never moved beyond a personal following. When Hopkins and Sullivan began building a machine with county patronage, they found their efforts frustrated by Dunne's state patronage-based organization.[11]

In states such as Massachusetts and Illinois, *weak* state Republican machines paradoxically hurt Irish Democratic bosses trying to consolidate power in the cities. In the aftermath of the Civil War, the concerted Radical Republican attack on the emerging big-city Democratic machines had backfired. The urban Democratic party had been strengthened, not weakened. The Republican resurgence of the 1890s brought a new round of state attacks on the big-city Irish machines, directed by younger Republican bosses—Thomas Platt in New York, Murray Winthrop Crane in Massachusetts, and William Lorimer in Illinois. In contrast to Pennsylvania, the new state Republican machines were too faction-ridden to wrest control of the cities from the Democrats.

Weak state GOP bosses bolstered their position vis-à-vis Republican rivals by cutting deals with local Democratic politicians. GOP rivals, in turn, built alliances with other factions in the urban Democratic party. In the post-1896 era, Republican state dominance combined with factionalism meant that no machine, Republican or Democratic, could easily emerge in the cities. Interparty collusion reinforced intraparty factionalism.[12]

Republican state factionalism and collusion with the big-city Democrats were most advanced in Illinois. By 1900, the Republicans were split between a state faction headed by "Blond Boss" Lorimer, successor to "Black Jack" Logan, and an opposing federal faction fueled by patronage from the McKinley administration. Lorimer's strength lay in his control of the Cook County Republican organization, in ties to downstate Republican governors such as John R. Tanner, and in legislative henchmen such as Eddie Dwyer and "Fire Escape" Gus Nohe who controlled the General Assembly.

After the turn of the century, however, Lorimer's control of both state and county Republican organizations was seriously weakened. At the state level, the federal faction denied renomination to Lorimer ally Governor Tanner and forced Lorimer to accept downstate politician Richard C. Yates as the gubernatorial nominee. A limited alliance of convenience between Lorimer and Governor Yates broke down over Yates's renomination, and the Lorimer organization was denied state patronage. Lorimer's Cook County organization was then captured by States Attorney Charles S. Dineen, a former Lorimer protégé responsible for organizing the Swedes of southwest Chicago, who launched his own candidacy for the governorship. In a bitter contest in 1904, Dineen was elected governor.

Lorimer made deals with various Democratic city politicians to weaken his Republican opponents. In the 1908 gubernatorial election, Lorimer "knifed" Governor Dineen in Cook County, throwing his organization's votes to the Democratic nominee Adlai Stevenson. Still intent on revenge, Lorimer enlisted the aid of Hopkins and Sullivan to bolster his campaign in the state legislature for a U.S. Senate seat. Collusion between Lorimer and Hopkins-Sullivan reinforced factionalism among both the state Republicans and Chicago Democrats.[13]

Paradoxically, the *strengthening* of the Lorimer machine in the 1920s aided Democratic machine building in Chicago. In 1920, Lorimer's candidate, Len Small, won the governorship. In Cook County, Lorimer duplicated the feat by directing Republican "Big Bill" Thompson's victorious mayoral campaign. Lorimer and Thompson specifically targeted the city's newly arrived Southern and Eastern European immigrants. To remain competitive with Lorimer and Thompson, Democratic chieftain Roger Sullivan and his successor, George Brennan, broadened the base of the city's Democratic party by actively assimilating the new ethnics as citizens, voters, precinct captains, party committeemen, and public officeholders.

State politics thus continued to shape the destinies of the Irish machines and would-be Irish bosses well into the twentieth century. In New Jersey and New York, friendly Democratic governors nurtured the Hague and O'Connell machines during their fragile incubation period. In California and Pennsylvania, however, strong state Republican leaders or machines frustrated the urban Irish Democrats. The big-city Irish politicos missed their greatest opportunities in Massachusetts and Illinois during the Wilson years. Democratic governors in these two states did everything in their power to prevent the consolidation of urban and Irish power.

It is also important to note how state Republican machines shaped the fortunes of the urban Democracy. On the one hand, weak state GOP machines institutionalized interparty collusion and factionalism among the big-city Democrats. On the other hand, strong state Republican machines encouraged a political dialectic of challenge and response, forcing the big-city Democrats to strengthen their organizational apparatus and broaden the party's ethnic electoral base. Yet too much state Republican strength, as in Pennsylvania or California, relegated the urban Democrats to minority party status.

The Liberal Fiscal Policies
of the New Machines

Unlike their predecessors, the new Irish machines went on a spending spree. Between 1880 and 1902, a period of generally stable prices, per capita spending in the four Irish machine cities had dropped from $30 to $17 (see Table 4). After the turn of the century, machines jettisoned their fiscal diet and went on a spree. Between 1902 and 1932, a period of rising prices until 1929, per capita outlays in New York, Jersey City, and Albany rose from $17 to $78. A portion of this increase was illusory, for the cost-of-living index doubled. Yet not all of the municipal spending increase was eaten by inflation. Table 8 compares big-city spending patterns from 1902 to 1932 in constant (1902) dollars. The Irish machines led the way on a big-city spending splurge. In New York, Jersey City, and Albany, real, that is, inflation-adjusted, per capita outlays rose by 112 percent after having dropped by 43 percent in the late nineteenth century.[14]

The reborn machines also went on a borrowing binge. In the nineteenth century, bosses Kelly, Croker, Buckley, Davis, and Mc-

TABLE 8. *Cities on a Spending Spree, 1902–1932*

	Average Per Capita City Outlays ($)		Percentage Change from 1902
Cities and Regimes	*1902*	*1932*ᵃ	to 1932
Irish cities (8)	18	33	83.3
Irish Democratic machines (New York, Jersey City, Albany)	17	36	111.8
Irish Democratic nonmachine (Boston)	35	44	25.7
Non-Irish Republican machine (Philadelphia, Pittsburgh)	16	28	75.0
Non-Irish nonmachine (Chicago, San Francisco)	14	27	92.9
Non-Irish cities (13)ᵇ	15	29	93.3

Sources: U.S. Bureau of the Census, *Special Reports: Statistics of Cities, 1902* (Washington, D.C.: Government Printing Office, 1902), Table 21, pp. 252–299; U.S. Bureau of the Census, *Financial Statistics of Cities Having a Population over 100,000, 1932* (Washington, D.C.: Government Printing Office, 1934), Table 4, pp. 72–74.

ᵃ In 1902 dollars. For the cost-of-living measures used to adjust city spending and indebtedness for the period 1880 to 1932, see U.S. Bureau of the Census, *Historical Statistics of the United States: Colonial Times to 1957* (Washington, D.C.: Government Printing Office, 1960), series E 157–160, p. 127.

ᵇ Includes all cities with more than 50,000 population in 1870 *and* less than 13 percent Irish. See Table 1. (Allegheny annexed by Pittsburgh in 1907.)

Cabe had either been unwilling or unable to borrow. As Table 6 shows, the early machines' debt burden barely grew between 1880 and 1902. Bosses Murphy, Hague, and O'Connell, however, discovered that public debt was a many-splendored thing. Between 1902 and 1932, real per capita debt in New York, Jersey City, and Albany rose by 50 percent, from $93 to $140. The Irish bosses easily outpaced other big-city politicians in their early and enthusiastic commitment to Keynesian municipal financing. By the early 1930s, the three Irish machines' average debt burden was 41 percent higher—$140 versus $99 per capita—than that for the other nineteen big cities.[15]

Murphy, Hague, and O'Connell could spend and spend and borrow and borrow because members of the Yankee middle class were voting with their feet and leaving the cities, and because a financial modus vivendi had been reached with the state Republican bosses.

The Yankee middle class had formed the backbone of opposition to the taxing and spending schemes of the early Celtic machines. By the late nineteenth century, however, changes in urban transportation allowed the middle class to move to the streetcar suburbs.[16] Machine politicians used annexation and consolidation to enhance the organization's resources and to enlarge city boundaries by capturing the affluent migrants and their pocketbooks.

As the social and economic disparity between the suburbs and the cities grew, the affluent fought back. Continuing its suburban exodus, the middle class successfully pressured the state GOP bosses to lead it to the promised land. In response, Republican-controlled state legislatures made big-city annexation more difficult by imposing the requirement of dual voter approval in the city and to-be-annexed area. At the same time, the GOP made suburban incorporation easier. Machines could no longer swallow the suburbs. In the 1890s, the twenty largest cities had increased their territorial boundaries by 32 percent. Between 1900 and 1910, however, the big cities could increase their borders by only 11 percent.[17]

With middle-class suburbanization, the threat of big-city tax revolts evaporated. As impoverished Southern and Eastern Europeans replaced the Yankee middle class in the cities, bosses appealed to renters rather than homeowners. By 1920, more than three-quarters of all homes in New York, Jersey City, and Albany were rented.[18] Facing lower-class renters, bosses Murphy, Hague, and O'Connell could raise property taxes, the source of over two-thirds of municipal revenue, or pass bond referenda with little voter opposition. The machine's spending and borrowing spree would be paid for by nonvoting absentee landlords.

Disenfranchised urban landlords fought back at the state level. No longer able to stop the torrent of tax increases and bond elections with their votes, big-city property owners appealed to the state to limit the machine's fiscal appetite. Yet many of the state financial safeguards of the late nineteenth century had been torn down in order to heal divisions within the GOP's ranks. After 1896, the new Republican majority had quickly fractured into two camps. State Republican bosses such as New York's Platt confronted urban independents such as Theodore Roosevelt, who demanded an end to state interference in city affairs. To reduce the rift between independents and regular Republicans, GOP bosses reluctantly supported "home rule" for the cities. Finally recognizing the legal and financial independence of the cities, state machines removed many of the old constitutional barriers on local taxing, spending, and borrowing.[19]

Reform Republicans soothed the fears of urban property owners with *state* rather than local tax reform. Progressive GOP governors such as New York's Benjamin J. Odell, Jr., demonstrated their sympathy with property by lifting the double tax burden on real estate. In the late nineteenth century, both state and local governments relied heavily on property taxes. In 1890, for example, real property taxes accounted for 82 percent of local revenue and 64 percent of state revenue. This double burden heightened middle-class sensitivity to tax increases. After the turn of the century, tax reformers reduced the middle-class burden by separating local and state revenue sources. Local governments would continue to rely on the property tax. State revenues, however, were significantly diversified to include corporation, personal income, and gasoline taxes. By 1932 property taxes accounted for only 14 percent of state revenue compared with 72 percent of local revenue.[20]

Freed of the burden of financing both state and local government, the urban middle class jumped on the machine's spending bandwagon, demanding more public spending for parks, recreation, health, and education. In municipal bond elections, middle-class voters supported outlays for new parks, hospitals, and schools. Enthusiasm for capital improvements united the middle class and the working class. In ten bond elections held in San Francisco between 1899 and 1910, for example, middle-class and working-class voters approved by identical three-to-one margins an aggregate $151 million increase in the city's debt to pay for schools, hospitals, parks, sewers, and city-owned railroad and water systems.[21]

To Tax or To Borrow:
A Tale of Jersey City and Albany

Irish bosses could capitalize up to a point on the new middle-class enthusiasm for public spending. The pain threshold had been raised. But homeowners would still balk at massive property tax increases to pay for public projects employing the machine's patronage army. Debt financing concealed machine financing from middle-class view: machines could absorb some public debts without necessarily increasing taxes. Nevertheless, machines had strong *organizational* incentives to tax rather than borrow. Taxing enlarged the permanent city payroll—the machine's primary reward to the cadre of party officials and voters. Borrowing, in contrast, generated temporary patronage on public works projects for construction workers. For obvious reasons, bosses preferred permanent public sector patronage to temporary private sector jobs.

Some machines taxed; others borrowed. Machines taxed when voters rented and property was absentee-owned. They borrowed when large numbers of tax-conscious homeowners voted. Different property-owning patterns in Jersey City and Albany propelled the Hague and O'Connell machines along different expansionary fiscal routes. Boss Hague taxed. In the first ten years of his rule, real per capita spending in Jersey City tripled, from $15 to $47. By 1930 Jersey City had the dubious honor of having the highest municipal tax rate in the country. O'Connell borrowed. During the first ten years of Uncle Dan's rule, per capita spending in Albany only rose from $14 to $28. Yet between 1902 and 1932, Albany's per capita debt nearly tripled, from $45 to $118. By the early 1930s, nearly one-third of the entire city budget was devoted to servicing the massive debt. In Jersey City, in contrast, the debt burden rose by a modest 50 percent.

Jersey City's economy of large absentee-owned corporations shaped Hague's taxation policies. Serving as a major terminus for railway traffic into New York City, the city had fourteen railroads by 1875. The railroads soon owned one-third of the land in the city. City politicians had cast covetous eyes on the railways. Railroad property taxes could fill city coffers, and their payrolls could provide steady employment for the machine's precinct workers and voters. To elude the grasp of rapacious local politicians, the railroads successfully lobbied the state in 1884 for passage of the Railroad Tax Act. The act forced the city to tax most railroad property at substantially lower rates relative to other taxable property.[22]

Hague succeeded where other politicians had failed. He built his party organization by boldly taxing the city's railroads, public service, and oil companies in order to pay for the largest per capita city payroll in the country. Under Hague, the assessed evaluation of railroad property ballooned from $67 million to $167 million. For public service corporations, property values were raised from $3 million to $30 million. Unintimidated by the Rockefellers, Hague reassessed the city's Standard Oil property from $1.5 million to $14 million. Claiming that Hague was a modern-day Robin Hood, the big companies fought back, appealing the city's reassessments to the pro-railroad state Board of Taxes and Assessments. Predictably, the state board ruled against Hague, forcing the Jersey City boss to consider how he planned to maintain his massive patronage army. Hague decided to take over the state. A pro-Hague governor would appoint a sympathetic tax board, and the dramatic reassessments would stick.[23]

Grooming and electing a succession of Garden State Democratic governors, who obliged Hague by appointing his men to the tax and civil service boards, Hague passed the cost of the swollen city payroll to the big corporations rather than to the city's voters, 80 percent of whom were renters and thus immune to the machine's attack on property. Conceding defeat, the corporations passed the Hague tax bill on to their customers as a cost of doing business in Hudson County. With his windfall profits, Hague padded the city's payroll from 1,745 in 1917 to 7,297 in 1930.[24]

Uncle Dan chose to borrow rather than tax. Compared with Jersey City, Albany's revenue base was more diversified and smaller. Instead of national corporations, the city's economy consisted of small family-owned retail businesses. Large parcels of tax-exempt state property limited the upstate machine's opportunity for plunder. Most important, however, the city was fast becoming a haven for homeowners rather than renters. Between 1920 and 1940, as the machine discouraged apartment building, the city's home-ownership rate rose from 28 percent to 41 percent.

As the ranks of tax-conscious homeowners grew, O'Connell's fiscal policies became more circumspect. In the 1920s, the city's public spending grew slowly, more comparable to the rates of non-Irish or nonmachine cities than to New York and Jersey City. To raise revenue, the machine sold low tax assessments to homeowners, a practice that continued into the 1970s. To further favor homeowners, the machine created a two-tier system of assessments. The O'Connell organization assessed commercial property at 64 percent of market value and residential property at 28 percent. Low taxes did not necessarily mean few patronage jobs. The Albany machine preferred quantity to quality, creating a welter of poor-paying blue-collar jobs in the parks and public works departments. Forced to keep the tax rate down, O'Connell keenly appreciated the ways public debt could be put to political use. The city's heavy borrowing created private sector patronage and helped finance the organization's tax auction scheme.[25]

Rewarding the Irish: The Patronage Possibilities of the New Machines

The taxing and borrowing policies of the second generation of Irish machines generated an enormous cache of patronage with which to reward the Irish and reduce working-class discontent. Between 1900 and 1930 the public sector nearly tripled in size in the three machine cities. Local government employment in New York City, for example, mushroomed from 54,386 to 148,421. The machines' primitive Keynesianism allowed the bosses to tighten their grip on the urban labor market as the public sector expanded more quickly than the private sector. Between 1900 and 1930 the booming public sector absorbed 10 percent of all job growth in New York, Jersey City, and Albany compared with only 5 percent between 1870 and 1900.[26]

Reformers fought the bosses with civil service plans designed to shield public personnel decisions from party influence. Yet the merit system did not appreciably affect the bosses' ability to staff the public payroll with the politically and ethnically deserving. The New York state constitution created civil service boards in New York and Albany as early as 1884 when Tammany and the McCabe machines were consolidating power. By state law in 1911, the New Jersey Civil Service Commission began administering the merit system in Jersey City. Bosses Murphy, O'Connell, and Hague easily circumvented these restraints. In New York City, for example, the Tammany-controlled civil service board rarely posted public notices of city job openings. Jobseekers were advised to visit their local ward boss instead. Irish civil service examiners gave essay rather than objective examinations to jobseekers in order to

enhance their discretion over the choice of applicants. Exam scores
were rarely posted. The city's antiquated merit system covered only
a limited number of permanent positions, and Tammany hired,
fired, and rehired an army of temporary workers exempt from civil
service coverage. Before there were Kelly Girls, there were Tammany's "Kelly Boys."[27]

Twentieth-century machines soon uncovered other stores of
public sector patronage. Urban machines particularly coveted
county government. Machines needed to control the county prose-
cutor's office and court system as a buffer against attack by Democratic rivals and state Republicans. Control of the county tax assessor's office allowed bosses like O'Connell to manipulate and sell
low assessments. Above all, the county represented a lucrative
source of patronage. After passage of the 1897 Consolidation Act
in New York, Manhattan-based Tammany quickly moved to capture county as well as city patronage, in part to weaken rival
Democratic organizations in the outer boroughs, such as Brooklyn's McLaughlin machine. By 1930 Tammany controlled nearly
13,000 county jobs. In the tradition of "Little Bob" Davis, Boss
Hague ruled Hudson County as well as Jersey City, adding 1,700
county positions to the machine's arsenal of 5,600 city jobs. O'Connell emulated Murphy and Hague by moving to control Albany
County and its 346 patronage positions. As the number of urban
voters grew relative to rural voters, big-city bosses moved to take
over state politics and patronage as well. Pro-machine Democratic
governors in New York and New Jersey gave the Irish bosses hundreds of state jobs.[28]

The machines' private sector patronage also ballooned, both in
the construction industry and with firms doing business with the
city. The machines' mounting debt generated sizable employment
on public works projects. In San Francisco, for example, Boss
Reuf's labor "machine" embarked on an ambitious program of
capital improvements. Between 1900 and 1910 city outlays tripled
as the proportion of the budget devoted to public works rose from
20 percent to nearly 40 percent. Local observers estimated that
public projects had created more than 6,000 construction jobs,
rivaling in size the combined city-county payroll.[29]

Murphy, Hague, and O'Connell also turned to large corporations as another source of jobs and profit. Tammany's Murphy

called it his "businessmen's plan" to diversify the machine's resources as a hedge against fickle voters. Besides contractors, Murphy tithed city-regulated transportation and utility firms for patronage jobs and campaign contributions. Ironically, Tammany's reform opponents had significantly contributed to the machine's stock of private sector patronage by enlarging local government's regulatory responsibilities over privately owned street railways and utilities. Tammany quickly discovered the political uses of the regulatory state. In exchange for favorable franchise terms, public service corporations would make campaign donations and employ some of the machine's henchmen. Murphy's hedge paid off handsomely. In 1914, Tammany faced political disaster. Reformer John Purroy Mitchel was elected mayor, and the Wigwam lost city and county patronage. Martin Glynn, the Democratic gubernatorial nominee, was defeated. Claiming that he owed the organization nothing, President Wilson refused to give Murphy federal patronage. Even without public offices, Tammany prospered as campaign coffers remained filled with corporate contributions, and party workers were shuttled into the private sector.[30]

The second-generation Irish machines controlled patronage indeed. The expanding city and county payroll accounted for 10 percent of all urban job growth between 1900 and 1930; debt-financed public works projects added another 6 to 8 percent. State jobs and "unofficial" patronage further supplemented the machine's job roster. In all, the Irish machines created or controlled more than 20 percent of post-1900 job growth compared with less than 10 percent in the pre-1900 era.

Could the Irish now use the machines as a *group* route from rags to riches? Second-generation machines disappointed few Irish jobseekers. Table 9 estimates Irish employment gains in city and county government in New York, Jersey City, and Albany between 1900 and 1930. The Celtic surge into the public sector continued. Local government employment in the three machine cities rose from 59,202 in 1900 to 158,453 as the number of Irish payrollers increased from 21,749 to 82,116. Hiring their own, the Celtic bosses gave the Irish more than 60 percent of the new public jobs. Given the slow increase in the number of Irish workers and their continued ascent in public employment, the proportion of the Irish workforce employed by local government increased dramatically.

TABLE 9. The Patronage Tree Bears Fruit: Machines Reward the Irish, 1900–1930

Machine Cities	Local Government Employment, 1900[a]			Local Government Employment, 1930[a]			Percentage of Irish Workforce Employed by Local Government	
	Irish[b]	All	Percentage Irish	Irish[c]	All	Percentage Irish	1900[b]	1930[c]
New York	19,926	54,386	36.6	76,734	148,421	51.7	5.8	23.6
Jersey City	1,293	3,052	42.4	4,254	7,297	58.3	5.1	20.8
Albany	530	1,764	30.0	1,128	2,735	41.0	4.6	14.8

Sources: U.S. Bureau of the Census, Special Reports: Occupations at the Twelfth Census (Washington, D.C.: Government Printing Office, 1904), Tables 41, 43; U.S. Bureau of the Census, Fifteenth Census of the United States, 1930 (Washington, D.C.: Government Printing Office, 1933), vol. 2, Table 11, vol. 4, Table 12; U.S. Bureau of the Census, Statistical Abstract of the United States, 1938 (Washington, D.C.: Government Printing Office, 1938), Table 234, p. 229; New York World, World Almanac, 1931 (New York: New York World, 1931), pp. 210, 545–549 (New York and Jersey City); Terry Nichols Clark, "The Irish Ethic and the Spirit of Patronage," Ethnicity 2 (1975): Fig. 3, p. 342 (Albany); and Table 7, above.

[a] Includes city and county employment.

[b] First- and second-generation Irish Americans.

[c] Estimated for first-, second-, and third-generation Irish. See Chapter 3, n. 31, p. 277, for estimating procedure.

In New York City, for example, the public sector employed nearly one-quarter of all first-, second-, and third-generation Irish workers in 1930, up from 6 percent in 1900.[31]

Machines also created private sector job opportunities for the Irish with their expanded menu of public works projects and their regulatory leverage over corporations. Although it is impossible to estimate precisely the machine's private sector patronage and the share received by the Irish, it is fair to assume that the construction industry and public service corporations employed at least half as many Irish as did local government. On the eve of the Depression, then, Tammany Hall and the Hague organization directly or indirectly employed at least one-third (and perhaps more) of the Irish workforce in the two cities.

The twentieth-century machines' patronage policies appear to support the contention that politics served as an important conduit of Irish economic advancement. Yet compared with Jews, the Irish were slow to build a professional and business class. The "lace curtain" Irish middle class, tied to civil service and the building trades, was just emerging by the late 1920s. With the coming of the Depression, Irish middle-class aspirations were set back until after World War II.

Paradoxically, Irish political success and economic failure were intimately related. Contrary to the conventional wisdom, machine patronage *reinforced* the lowly status of the Irish. In their endless quest to stretch the vote-getting value of patronage, bosses continued to proletarianize the public sector. In New York City, the blue-collar proportion of the public payroll rose from 54 percent in 1900 to 60 percent in 1930 as thousands of unskilled and semi-skilled Irish took jobs in municipally owned subways, street railways, waterworks, and port facilities. Municipally owned utilities accounted for over one-half of Irish public sector job gains in New York in this era. Employment in the city's expanding police and fire departments accounted for another 21 percent of Irish government gains. In all, three-quarters of the Irish using Tammany's employment agency were shuttled into a blue-collar cul-de-sac.[32]

Nearly monopolizing blue-collar patronage, the Irish were forced to share white-collar patronage with other ethnic groups. The school system represented the largest and fastest growing source of white-collar public employment as Southern and Eastern

Europeans entered the classroom. Yet Jews soon displaced the Irish as teachers. In New York, Jews represented 11 percent of entering teachers in 1900 and 40 percent in 1930. The judicial and legal departments represented a prime source of white-collar patronage for Irish lawyers. After the turn of the century the Irish crowded onto the local bench and into the city and county corporation counsels' offices. Yet by the late 1920s Jews were also making an appearance as government attorneys and judges. Squeezed by the Jewish advance, upwardly mobile Irish filled low-paying clerkships.[33]

Thus the Irish in the early twentieth century crowded into the middling ranks of the public sector—in police and fire departments, utilities, and government clerkships. Yet as poorly paid policemen, firemen, and municipal clerks, the Irish were solidly lower-middle rather than middle class. By channeling so much economic energy into the public sector, the Irish forsook opportunities in the private sector, save for industries such as construction that depended on political connections. Ironically, as the public sector grew more blue-collar and Irish, the private sector grew more white-collar and non-Irish. In New York City, for example, the white-collar proportion of the private sector workforce rose from 34 percent in 1900 to 45 percent in 1930 as the Irish share of private employment dropped from 23 percent to 9 percent.[34]

Yet patronage and more patronage tamed the once wild Irish as city sinecures dampened the Celtic enthusiasm for labor politics. In New York, the last serious threat of working-class Irish insurgency against Tammany occurred in the 1905 mayoral election. Portraying himself as an urban populist, mayoral candidate William Randolph Hearst of the Municipal Ownership League attacked the unholy alliance between Tammany and private utility firms seeking public franchises. Irish-American labor leaders supported Hearst and his program of public ownership of the city's utilities. Hearst targeted the Irish vote, attacking George B. McClellan, Tammany's "silk-stocking" mayoral candidate, as an Anglophile—anathema to the Irish—and accusing Boss Murphy of "aristocratic habits." McClellan barely beat Hearst, 228,000 to 225,000, as the self-styled populist ran even with Tammany in working-class Irish districts. Tammany took the hint. After the election, the machine sponsored city ownership of utilities, creating thousands of sinecures for the Irish and bringing them securely into the organization's fold. Running on the Civic Alliance ticket in 1909, Hearst was badly trounced by Tammany's Gaynor as the Irish stayed in the Wigwam. Thereafter, Tammany would receive more than 75 percent of the working-class Irish vote. Celtic discontent with Tammany would now come from the reform-minded middle class rather than from labor.[35]

In Jersey City, Hague's pro-Irish patronage policies also paid off at the polls. As in other locales, the Jersey City Irish had grown militant in the late nineteenth century, experimenting with nationalism and unionism as alternatives to machine politics. In particular, the Irish Land League and Irish-run Central Labor Union led strikes and boycotts against the railroads, the major employers of the city's Irish working class. The League and labor forced the Davis machine leftward as Irish cops were sent to protect Irish strikers. The Irish reembraced the machine as Davis's policies earned corporate enmity. What Davis did with labor policies, Hague did with public jobs. Believing his fellow Irish had an innate political ability lacking in other groups, Hague gave the Irish a virtual franchise on public employment. The payroll Irish and their families returned the favor, treating their vote for Hague as a "religious obligation." In the Horseshoe district, a gerrymandered ward lumping most of the city's Irish together, the Hague organization regularly rolled up forty-to-one majorities.[36]

The New Immigrants: Old and New World Obstacles to Mobilization

Just as Bosses Murphy, Hague, and O'Connell learned how to subdue the Irish with patronage, they were confronted with the problem of how to incorporate the millions of "new" immigrants from Southern and Eastern Europe. Fleeing political and economic oppression, the new migrants began arriving in the cities in large numbers in the 1880s. Jews, Italians, and Poles predominated. For the Jews and Italians, New York City, the port of entry for three-quarters of all immigrants arriving between 1880 and 1914, would represent the urban mecca. New York counted 55,000 Russian and Polish Jews and 40,000 Italians among its residents in 1890, representing 5 percent of the overall population. By 1930, Gotham

would be home to more than 2.5 million Jews and Italians, now
representing 36 percent of the population. For the Poles, Chicago
would be home. A trickle of Polish émigrés became a torrent as the
number of Chicago Poles swelled from 24,086 in 1890 to 401,316
in 1930, constituting 12 percent of the city's population.

The second-wave immigrants arrived with none of the political
advantages brought by the Irish from the Old World. Few Southern and Eastern Europeans spoke or read English. Most arrived
with local and family rather than national identities, formed in the
village and shtetl. In southern Italy and Sicily, for example, geographical and language barriers reinforced a web of local loyalties
and identities known as *campanilismo*. Even residents of nearby
villages were viewed as foreigners.

Return migration would also politically handicap the new immigrants, particularly the Italians. Coming to the United States primarily for economic reasons, single working-age males constituted
80 percent of all Italian immigrants arriving before 1914. Working
for a *padrone* as casual labor on construction projects, the Italians
scrimped and saved to return to their homeland. In all, 42 percent
of all Italian immigrants arriving in America before World War I
would return to Italy. Of the second-wave immigrants, Jews would
stay. Fleeing the pogroms carried out after the assassination of Czar
Alexander in 1881, Jews sought permanent refuge and brought
their families with them. In contrast with the Italians, only 7 percent of the Jews would return to Europe.[37]

Fearful that the Irish bosses would claim the votes of the Southern and Eastern Europeans and threaten GOP control of state and
federal government, Republicans hastily erected a series of legal
barriers to citizenship and voting. At the federal level, the Republican majority passed the Naturalization Law of 1906 to tighten and
lengthen the citizenship process. Radicals were disqualified. Naturalization courts began demanding literacy in English as a condition of citizenship. The act required more stringent proof of both
lawful entry into the country and five years' continuous residence.
Under the new law, the denial rate on naturalization petitions rose
from an estimated 3 percent to 15 percent. Italians, in particular,
were affected by the literacy test. On the eve of World War I, naturalization courts turned down nearly one out of every five Italians
seeking citizenship. Under the 1906 act, the naturalization process

doubled in average length—to eleven years—as would-be citizens were forced to provide witnesses testifying to the character of their entry into the United States and to the length of their residence.[38]

At the state level, Republican legislators were simultaneously tightening state voter qualifications to hamper the ability of the big-city Democratic machines to capitalize on the new supply of European votes. The state suffrage restriction movement took various forms. In the Midwest alien suffrage was abolished. In the mid-nineteenth century, thirteen predominately midwestern states had enticed settlers by permitting aliens who had filed their first naturalization papers to vote. Alien suffrage was an early casualty of the new immigration and the GOP resurgence in the 1890s. As early as 1894, Michigan's Republicans sponsored a constitutional amendment disenfranchising aliens. With the GOP surge, other states followed Michigan's lead; by 1910 alien suffrage was no more.[39]

Literacy tests represented a second way of restricting the vote, particularly in the Northeast. The literacy test movement began in Connecticut in the early 1890s as the state's GOP passed a constitutional amendment requiring that voters be able to read the Constitution. The reading requirement particularly affected the state's Italian-Americans. Literacy tests soon spread to nearly half the states, including Massachusetts. In New York, the GOP created a de facto literacy test by combining the secret ballot with voting machines or the "office" type of paper ballot. Secret voting by machine or office ballot required voters themselves to read the ballot.[40]

The ascendant Republicans also handicapped the new ethnics with personal registration laws applied only to urban voters. In the wake of charges of extensive ballot box stuffing leveled against the urban Democratic bosses, the New York Republicans in 1890 mandated that big-city voters register and reregister in person. While not directly aimed at the Southern and Eastern Europeans, the new registration requirements discouraged participation by making voting more difficult.[41]

The Republicans had small cause for worry. The entrenched Irish big-city bosses had no intention of churning out new citizens and voters. Although the Irish bosses did not support restrictions on citizenship and voting, once they had consolidated power they had little incentive to mobilize the newcomers. In the absence of competitive party pressures, machines relied on already constructed—and rewarded—electoral coalitions. Political assimilation of the new ethnics on the scale of the earlier machine-sponsored incorporation of the Irish would inevitably generate demands for an ethnic redistribution of power and patronage. With the middle class leaving the cities, state GOP bosses offering home rule and tax reform to stave off insurgency by urban progressives, and the new ethnics not participating, the Irish bosses faced the best of all political worlds: fewer potential opponents and more resources to reward the already mobilized.

The GOP had greater headaches where Irish machines had *not* consolidated power. Competitive electoral pressures, whether from the Republicans or from Democratic rivals, would force would-be Irish bosses to court the newcomers more actively. In order to outbid their opponents at the polls, fledgling machines would need to operate their citizenship and voting factories at full blast.

Table 10 shows the sensitivity of the citizenship process to local politics for the eight cities surveyed between 1900 and 1930. Contrary to the conventional wisdom that Irish politicos served as the most active brokers for the new immigrants, citizenship came slowest under entrenched Irish Democratic rule. In New York and Boston, barely one-half of the foreign-born had become citizens by 1930. In contrast, competitive party pressures hastened both Irish Democrats and Republicans to turn out new citizens in Jersey City, Albany, and Chicago. In Jersey City, Boss Hague's fledgling organization in the 1920s assisted the foreign-born in overcoming the hurdles to citizenship. The Barnes GOP machine in Albany had done the same between 1900 and 1920 to stave off a Democratic resurgence. In Chicago, Thompson's Republicans and Sullivan's and Brennan's Democrats engaged in the Great Naturalization Wars. In his pathbreaking study of the early Chicago Democratic machine, Harold Gosnell observed that more than 70 percent of Democratic precinct captains in 1928 reported assisting their constituents with naturalization. By 1930 the Windy City's politicians had secured citizenship for nearly two-thirds of the city's foreign-born. Even Yankee GOP bosses appeared to be better friends of the citizenship-seeking immigrants than did their Irish counterparts in New York and Boston. Reversing their nineteenth-century exclusionary habits, the Republican machines of Philadelphia and Pittsburgh by 1920 had registered more than two-thirds of the foreign-born.[42]

Yet not all of the intercity differences in naturalization rates can be traced to differences in ethnic and party hegemony. Ports of entry, whether New York, Boston, or San Francisco, had the lowest citizenship rates, in part because they had greater numbers of newly arrived immigrants. As Table 10 shows, New York was the great ethnic entrepôt; nearly half of the city's immigrants arrived after 1910. With the fewest new arrivals, Republican machines faced the lightest naturalization burden. In Pittsburgh, for example, two-thirds of the foreign-born had arrived before 1910.

Internal group dynamics also affected the rates at which the Southern and Eastern Europeans became citizens. Arriving with their families, Russian and Polish Jews were quickest to put down roots. Italians, however, were "birds of passage." Intending to return to their homeland, Italian laborers did not become citizens. With Tammany's naturalization mill working at half blast, 39 percent of New York's Russian-born—more than three-quarters Jewish—had become citizens by 1920 compared with only 27 percent of the Italian-born. In competitive Chicago, the two parties turned out new citizens at faster rates. Forty-five percent of the city's Russian-born and 35 percent of the Italian-born were citizens by 1920, even though larger numbers were newer arrivals compared with those in New York.[43]

Registration represented a second hurdle facing the new immigrants on the road to the ballot box. Here too the second-wave immigrants in cities such as New York and Boston suffered from the inertia of one-party and one-group rule. The Celtic party bosses registered the Irish en masse and the Southern and Eastern Europeans en individuel. Machine politicians sponsored the naturalization and registration of small numbers of "reliable" Southern and Eastern Europeans, for example, those on the public payroll and their families, those on public works projects, and the holders of machine-granted business licenses and contracts. This policy of not-so-benign electoral neglect became evident as the Irish consolidated power. In Boston, for example, an estimated 25 percent of the naturalized Italians and 39 percent of Russian-born citizens were registered to vote in the critical 1896 presidential election,

TABLE 10. *At Half Blast: Naturalizing the New Immigrants, 1900–1930*

	Percentage of Voting-Age White Immigrants Naturalized				Number of Voting-Age White Immigrants				Percentage Arriving Before 1910
	1900	1910	1920	1930	1900	1910	1920	1930	
New York	55.6	38.4	42.6	54.4	539,746	828,793	1,797,882	2,147,979	53.3
Jersey City	61.5	43.9	50.0	64.6	27,104	37,707	70,677	66,662	61.8
Albany	70.1	58.9	61.8	65.4	7,768	8,192	16,348	16,980	61.0
Boston	53.3	46.3	46.5	52.8	81,058	103,160	221,036	216,349	60.5
Chicago	68.6	50.2	54.8	64.2	271,962	379,850	743,803	800,515	60.1
San Francisco	68.4	48.0	52.3	55.3	56,102	75,768	128,791	145,606	57.3
Philadelphia	51.0	41.6	49.4	66.7	127,915	167,072	361,456	349,555	62.2
Pittsburgh	54.3	41.1	53.3	70.5	55,958	70,148	111,907	104,013	66.6

Sources: U.S. Census Office, *Twelfth Census of the United States, 1900* (Washington, D.C.: Government Printing Office, 1901), vol. 1, Tables 82, 83; U.S. Bureau of the Census, *Thirteenth Census of Population, 1910* (Washington, D.C.: Government Printing Office, 1913), vol. 3, Table 5; U.S. Bureau of the Census, *Census of Population, 1920* (Washington, D.C.: Government Printing Office, 1923), vol. 3, Table 10; U.S. Bureau of the Census, *Fifteenth Census of the United States, 1930* (Washington, D.C.: Government Printing Office, 1933), vol. 2, Tables 18, 19, 24, 25.

Note: Figures fo: 1900 and 1910 include males only; for 1920 and 1930, males and females are included.

compared with 88 percent of the naturalized Irish. Adding ethnic insult to injury, Irish bosses inflated the number of Southern and Eastern European voters by registering and voting newly arrived Irish under assumed names. "Big Tim" Sullivan, the Tammany district boss of the Lower East Side, regularly rounded up fresh Irish immigrants in saloons and had them vote under Jewish names.[44]

Heightened citizenship and registration requirements coupled with limited machine sponsorship meant that the new immigrants' actual voting strength lagged far behind potential influence. Between 1890 and 1920 the Jewish and Italian proportion of New York's voting-age population ballooned from 10 percent to 30 percent, whereas their share of the city's voters only rose from 2 percent to 13 percent.[45]

The growing potential vote of the Southern and Eastern Europeans should have been of some concern to the Irish bosses. Yet until the new immigrants began voting and displaying political independence from the machines, the party bosses concentrated on building a large-scale patronage-for-votes system in the Irish-American community. The first-generation machines did not have enough patronage to easily swing elections. In New York, for example, Boss Tweed's temporarily bloated patronage army of 12,000 to 15,000 in the late 1860s represented 16 to 20 percent of the Tammany vote. Bosses Kelly and Croker were forced to economize *and* naturalize and register the old immigrants in record numbers in order to beat back the strong challenge posed by reformers and rival Democrats. Between 1870 and 1890 the number of voters climbed from 132,000 to 274,000, growing at a rate one-third faster than the number of adult males. As the turnout rate rose from 53 percent of the voting-age males in 1870 to 62 percent in 1890, the payroll vote grew smaller. By 1892 the public retinue represented only 13 percent of the Wigwam's vote.[46]

After 1897 the "New Tammany" consolidated power by letting the Naturalization Bureau languish while expanding the vote-rich public payroll. Table 11 shows the changing shape of the New York City voting universe under Bosses Croker and Murphy between 1897 and 1925. Tammany reversed the relationship between the growth in the actual and potential electorates. Between 1897 and 1925 the actual electorate grew at *one-third* the rate of the potential electorate. Voter participation rates nose-dived as naturalization

TABLE 11. *The Tiger Conquers New York: Voting and Turnout Under Bosses Croker and Murphy, 1897–1925*

Tammany At The Polls

Mayoral Election	Outcome	Vote Share (%)	Payroll Share of Tammany Vote (%)	Voter Participation Rates		Total Adults[a] (thousands)	Total Citizens[a] (thousands)	Total Voters (thousands)	Tammany Voters (thousands)	Public Employees (thousands)
				Adults (%)	Citizens (%)					
1897	Win	44.7	19.5	61.2	81.2	855	645	524	234	46
1901	Loss	45.8	22.1	53.4	73.2	1,086	791	579	265	59
1903	Win	53.4	19.8	50.7	71.9	1,163	821	590	315	63
1905	Win	37.8	29.5	48.8	71.2	1,240	850	605	228	67
1909	Win	42.1	30.3	42.6	65.4	1,395	908	594	250	76
1913	Loss	37.3	36.0	40.6	60.6	1,544	1,035	627	234	84
1917	Win	46.8	28.8	40.5	60.5	1,654	1,108	671	314	91
1921	Win	64.2	14.0	31.6	44.4	3,696	2,633	1,168	750	105
1925	Win	65.8	16.6	28.0	37.8	4,058	3,010	1,138	750	124

Sources: U.S. Census Office, *Eleventh Census of the United States, 1890* (Washington, D.C.: Government Printing Office, 1895), vol. 1, pt. 1, Tables 34, 78, vol. 2, pt. 2, Tables 72, 74; U.S. Census Office, *Twelfth Census of the United States, 1900* (Washington, D.C.: Government Printing Office, 1901), vol. 1, pt. 1, Tables 80, 82, 83; U.S. Bureau of the Census, *Population at the Thirteenth Census, 1910* (Washington, D.C.: Government Printing Office, 1913), vol. 1, Tables 16, 34; U.S. Bureau of the Census, *Census of Population, 1920* (Washington, D.C.: Government Printing Office, 1923), vol. 3, Table 10; U.S. Bureau of the Census, *Fifteenth Census of the United States, 1930* (Washington, D.C.: Government Printing Office, 1933), vol. 2, Tables 24, 25, vol. 3, Table 15; New York World-Telegram, *World Almanac, 1940* (New York: World-Telegram, 1940), p. 795.
[a]Estimated for years between censuses.

and registration atrophied. Only 28 percent of New York's adults voted in the 1925 mayoral election compared with 61 percent in Greater New York's first mayoral election held in 1897.

As the electorate shrank in relative size, Tammany's share of the vote increased, testimony to the entrenched machine's interest in managing the *size* of the voting universe. In the seven mayoral contests held between 1897 and 1917, Tammany's candidates averaged only 44 percent of the total vote. Capitalizing on a large third party vote to split the opposition—Seth Low's Citizen Union in 1897, William Randolph Hearst's Municipal Ownership League in 1905 and Citizens' Alliance in 1909, and Morris Hillquit's Socialist party in 1917—Tammany won five of the seven elections. In the mayoral elections of 1921 and 1925, as women's suffrage doubled the size of the potential electorate, the Wigwam's "Red Mike" Hylan and Jimmy Walker averaged 65 percent of a still shrinking—in relative terms—voting universe.

Completing the shift from circuses to bread, Boss Murphy used the patronage vote to win city elections as the Consolidation Act and city-owned utilities handed Tammany fresh supplies of sinecures. On the eve of World War I, the 91,000 city payrollers represented nearly one-third of Democrat Hylan's overall vote. The Wigwam's private sector patronage further swelled the ranks of machine voters. To voters, patronage represented a more reliable material inducement than bribery. With their jobs at stake, city employees could be trusted to vote and to mobilize their relatives and friends. The number of bribed voters, however, depended on the machine's campaign fund, the funds available to the machine's opponents for counteroffers, and the amount of reform surveillance of the registration and voting processes. As reformers purged the number of venal voters in New York City, Tammany's electoral calculations increasingly hinged on the payroll vote. Across the Hudson, Boss Hague relied even more than Murphy on the patronage vote, while the leaner O'Connell organization upstate could not dispense with corruption as a vital tool for winning elections. With bread—jobs and money—now winning elections, the Irish machines reserved their circuses for the slowly mobilizing new ethnics.[47]

For the Southern and Eastern Europeans, the entrenched machine's limited assimilation accentuated the forms of political and

communal life brought over from the Old World. For Catholic sub-
jects of European monarchies, machine exclusion reinforced political apathy and alienation. For the Jews, exclusion reinforced radical
and reform politics. Excluded as well from the Irish-controlled big-
city labor movement, Jews would turn to the needle trades as a
template for radical political organization. In New York City, Jewish trade unionism was intertwined with socialist politics. Socialist
Labor party leaders such as Morris Hillquit formed the United He-
brew Trades, the first Jewish union, in 1888. Jewish socialists organized the needle trades, which employed one-half of the city's
Yiddish-speaking immigrants by 1910, as the Irish leadership of the
skilled trades largely ignored less skilled workers. Between 1909
and 1913 union membership in the garment industry exploded
from 30,000 to 250,000. The United Garment Workers, the Amal-
gamated Clothing Workers, and the International Ladies' Garment
Workers were militant in the workplace, winning higher wages,
shorter hours, and safer working conditions. Under socialist and
union auspices, Jewish garment workers began thinking of themselves in terms of class and occupation rather than nationality and
religion.[48]

Machine exclusion encouraged the Southern and Eastern Europeans to strengthen their communal institutions. Jewish political
energies were channeled into the building of the *landsmann,* or
mutual aid societies, providing social activities, medical insurance,
and death benefits for their members. These ethnic social welfare
organizations were provincial, however, further isolating participants from the larger urban political system. *Landsmann* members, for example, came from the same town or shtetl. The subsequent development of nationality-based *landsmannshaften*
federations did little to break down the barriers between the ghetto
and the machine. As the new immigrants turned inward, the Irish
party bosses breathed easier.

Guarding the Spoils: Machines "Reward" the New Immigrants

Parsimonious machine accommodation of the new ethnics extended beyond the naturalization court and the ballot box. The
potential power of the newcomers threatened the economic well-

being and psychological security of the payroll Irish. In order to protect the interests of this core machine constituency, Celtic party bosses did little to share top party and governmental positions with the Southern and Eastern Europeans. In New York, Tammany leader "Big Tim" Sullivan ruled the Lower East Side, where the new immigrants congregated. As early as 1910, Sullivan's district was 85 percent Jewish and Italian and only 5 percent Irish. Yet the Irish maintained firm control over the party apparatus. As late as 1932, three-quarters of Tammany's district leaders on the Lower East Side were Irish while less than one-fifth were Jewish. The first Italian leader, Al Marinelli, was not selected until 1931. With a lock on the party organization, the Irish monopolized nomination to elective office. Between 1908 and 1933 every Tammany candidate for the Board of Aldermen, the State Assembly, and the Senate from the Lower East Side was Irish.[49]

Party and ethnic hegemony, not machines per se, encouraged parsimonious accommodation. Boston politics, for example, remained Irish, Democratic, and faction-ridden into the twentieth century. Yet the new immigrants fared little better in Boston than in New York in securing important party and government posts. By 1920, Italians constituted 95 percent of the residents of Boston's crowded North End. In the words of one observer, Honey Fitz's Jefferson Club ran the North End like an "Irish rotten borough." As the Italians joined the Jews in migrating to the city's West End, they were welcomed into Boss Martin Lomasney's Hendricks Club. Although Lomasney carefully recruited promising Italian and Jewish politicos as minor club functionaries, the key posts in the Hendricks Club remained in Celtic hands. Controlling the party apparatus, Boston's Irish Democratic ward bosses kept elective office an Irish preserve. Not a single Italian was elected to the city council or to the state legislature before 1930. As for the city's Jews, only in Dorchester's Fourteenth Ward were they able to control the ward committee and elect members to the city council.[50]

Competitive party pressures forced the Irish Democratic chieftains to more quickly share power and authority with the newcomers. In Chicago, the Southern and Eastern Europeans were partially incorporated into the embryonic Democratic machine during the period of intense party competition and factionalism. The factional cleavages among the Windy City Democrats slowly coalesced along Irish and non-Irish lines. Carter Harrison II pioneered the ethnically balanced ticket in the 1912 Democratic primary. For the nine major county offices, Harrison slated two Germans (one Jewish), two Bohemians, one Pole, an Englishman, and three Irish. Roger Sullivan, leader of the other faction, fielded a predominantly Irish ticket. With Harrison's defeat in the 1915 mayoral primary, Sullivan moved to reimpose Irish hegemony over the Cook County Democratic Central Committee. Purging the Southern and Eastern Europeans, the Irish restoration was soon completed. By 1916 more than 70 percent of the county committee members were Irish. Given the competitive nature of the city's politics, however, Sullivan's restoration of Irish power was short-lived. Aided by William Lorimer, Republican Mayor William Hale "Big Bill" Thompson began building a rival GOP machine during World War I. The Thompson machine incorporated Southern and Eastern Europeans, particularly Jews and Italians. Sullivan and his successor, George Brennan, took the hint and began sharing party posts with the newcomers. Between 1922 and 1930 the non-Irish share of the city's Democratic ward leadership rose from 39 to 50 percent.[51]

The sharing of power and patronage by the Irish Democratic bosses with the Southern and Eastern Europeans was not without risk. In Chicago, Brennan's parceling out of party power to the non-Irish provoked an intraparty revolt by rank-and-file Irish functionaries. The Celtic bosses were trapped between the conflicting demands of party and ethnicity. Incorporation of the new immigrants enhanced the machine's prospects but threatened the Irish. Any move to share the machine's core resources of power and patronage with the non-Irish threatened Irish party functionaries and the legion of working-class Irish dependent on the organization's largesse.

Deference to the machine's core ethnic constituency dictated that entrenched machines offer less valuable benefits such as services, "circuses," and symbolism to the newer arrivals. Tammany's "Big Tim" Sullivan perfected this minimal reward strategy. He and his Irish lieutenants distributed coal, food, and rent money to needy Jews and Italians on the Lower East Side. Tammany's police department opened up station houses as temporary shelters for the homeless. Sullivan expedited business licenses for ethnic shopkeepers and pushcart peddlers. He shamelessly "recognized" the new immigrants with symbolic gestures and donned a yarmulke to solicit Jewish votes. Sullivan solicited Italian votes by sponsoring legislation to make Columbus Day a holiday. Jews and Italians were accorded token nominations to minor party posts and judgeships.[52]

Not to be outdone, Boston's feudal—and feuding—Irish chieftains raised minimalist politics to a high art. Honey Fitz's Jefferson Club and Lomasney's Hendricks Club dispensed food, loans, and licenses to the newcomers but not city jobs, nominations to office, or major party posts. James Michael Curley inaugurated a new era in symbolic politics. Elected to Congress in 1911, Curley crusaded against literacy tests, immigration restriction, and commercial agreements with Russia, where pogroms were raging. Elected mayor in 1913, Curley made symbolic "League of Nations" politics a regular feature at flag-bedecked city hall.[53]

Yet social services and symbolic recognition failed as the slowly mobilizing Southern and Eastern Europeans experimented with alternatives to the Irish ward bosses and machines. Jews particularly resisted the limited blandishments of the Irish politicos. Writing in 1903, social worker Robert Woods observed that "the Jew is a thorn in the flesh of the Irish politician."[54] In New York, Jews actively supported Tammany opponents Henry George, William Randolph Hearst, and Seth Low. Jews were the chief supporters of the city's powerful Socialist party. In 1914, for example, the predominately Jewish Lower East Side sent a Socialist to Congress and several others to the state assembly. Whereas Jews embraced labor and reform politics, Italians went into the Republican camp. New York's GOP made strong inroads into the still-small Italian vote with candidates such as Fiorello La Guardia while the Hub's Yankee Republicans wooed Italians with minor state offices and their advocacy of sound money and high tariffs.[55]

Unwilling to share the core resources of power and patronage, yet recognizing the limited appeal of welfare services and "recognition," Irish bosses turned to collective benefits as a way both of securing the new immigrant vote and of maintaining the Irish monopoly over divisible benefits. In New York, Tammany was responsible for securing the passage of important state labor and social welfare legislation. The Wigwam's representatives controlled the state's Factory Investigating Commission, established in the wake of the disastrous Triangle Shirtwaist Company fire of 1911. The commission proposed fifty new laws affecting the wages and working and safety conditions of women and children. The Tammany-controlled state legislature enacted nearly all of the commission's proposals. The Wigwam's Al Smith, the Assembly's majority leader, and Robert Wagner, the Senate's majority leader, also secured passage of workmen's compensation, stricter tenement laws, a widows' pension plan, state utility and insurance regulation, and educational scholarships for the poor. In Jersey City, Frank Hague converted the city's public hospital into the nation's second largest medical center, providing free health care for the city's residents.[56]

The machine's embrace of the nascent welfare state produced a temporary cessation of hostilities between the Irish bosses and the new immigrants. Tammany's Al Smith, leader in the fight for progressive legislation, ran for governor of the Empire State in 1919 and 1921, cutting heavily into the Jewish Socialist vote in New York City. As Table 11 suggests, Tammany's progressive coattails extended to local office as Hylan and Walker received a majority vote from the city's Jews and Italians in the 1920s.

The growing weakness of the machine's opponents also contributed to the newcomers' belated support of the Irish bosses. In New York, New Jersey, and Massachusetts, the once-dominant state Republican party, originally intent on offering minor offices and patronage to the new ethnics, faltered in its ethnic recognition policies. In New York, for example, the GOP soured into nativism and conservatism, particularly alienating the city's Italians. The massive Tammany vote in the 1920s cut across ethnic and class lines, much as did Hearst's populist campaign of 1905, reflecting the weakness of the opposition as much as the effectiveness of the Wigwam's policies.[57]

The Irish machines played a much more active role in weakening working-class opponents, particularly the Socialists. As the Socialists gained strength among New York's Jews, Tammany struck back. In the 1917 mayoral election, Socialist Morris Hillquit ran a strong race against Tammany's "Red Mike" Hylan. Tammany dispatched wrecking crews to disrupt Hillquit's street rallies, closed public meeting halls to the Socialists, and even stuffed the ballot box to defeat Hillquit. When the Socialists still showed strength at the polls, electing four aldermen and four assemblymen, the machine retaliated by enforcing Sunday closing laws against Jewish businesses on the Lower East Side. The machine's antipathy to the Socialists was more political than cultural, a jurisdictional battle for working-class loyalties rather than a Catholic predilection for social stability and order.[58]

As the Jews, Italians, and Poles slowly mobilized in the 1920s, they finally demanded a greater share of the machine's core resources of power and patronage. Yet with so much of Irish economic well-being and group identity dependent on continued control of the machines and their resources, the Irish bosses were understandably loath to share. To preserve their hegemony, the Irish consciously pursued a divide-and-conquer strategy, pitting one ethnic group and leader against another. At critical moments, the Irish formed strategic alliances with some groups and not with others. As Jews and Italians began flexing their political muscle in New York in the 1920s, the Tammany Irish were forced to choose which group would become a junior coalitional partner, and thus eligible for a greater share of power and patronage. In New York, the Jews became Tammany's chosen people. The Wigwam offered Jews party posts on the Lower East Side, nomination to minor offices, and a greater share of municipal employment, particularly in the legal department and the rapidly expanding school system. Boss Murphy and his successors worked just as actively to reduce Italian influence by adroitly gerrymandering Italian neighborhoods. For all their new-found Tammany support, Italians received few party posts or political nominations and only the most menial jobs as garbagemen, street cleaners, and laborers on the politically sensitive docks.[59]

The failure of the Irish to share the machine's power and patronage with the newcomers ultimately encouraged anti-Irish insurgency. The machine's Achilles' heel would soon be revealed as Irish prominence in public life rested on an ever more fragile base. As Irish representation in the ranks of city employees, public works contractors, and construction workers grew in the twentieth century, Irish representation in the electorate declined. In New York City, first- and second-generation Irish constituted less than 10 percent of the eligible voters in 1930, down from one-third in 1900. In the late 1920s the tempo of naturalization and voting accelerated for the Southern and Eastern Europeans. By 1930 Jews and Italians constituted nearly one-third of New York's eligible voters. The day of reckoning would soon be at hand. In machine cities such as New York and Jersey City, an anti-Irish revolt would take the form of an independent reform movement against machine politics.

Even the greater sharing of power and patronage with the new immigrants in competitive-party cities would not prevent a challenge to Irish rule. Compared with their brethren in the Northeast, Chicago's Irish Democrats had incorporated the Southern and Eastern Europeans in the 1920s. Because the new ethnic party leaders had been given the requisite power and patronage with which to mount an intraparty challenge, the new immigrants' insurgency was channeled *within* the embryonic Democratic machine rather than into reform politics. Czech Anton Cermak was the leader of the anti-Irish dissidents in the city's Democratic party. As a member of the Cook County Board of Supervisors and later the city council, "Pushcart Tony" became a key patronage dispenser. Cermak skillfully employed patronage to factionalize the Irish, drawing important politicians such as Pat Nash into his camp, and to woo the Czechs, Jews, and Poles, all resentful of Irish rule. In the late 1920s, Cermak mounted his anti-Irish putsch and took over the Democratic County Central Committee.[60]

But the real challenge to the second-generation Irish machines would occur in the 1930s in response to national as well as local forces. The Depression and New Deal party realignment threatened the established machines by upsetting the equilibrium between the party's management of patronage and voters. The Depression depleted the machine's patronage stock while the national party realignment dramatically increased the number of new ethnic voters. The national mobilization of the Southern and Eastern Europeans presented a potential electoral challenge to the entrenched Irish Democratic bosses to the extent that the voter turnout surge in presidential elections spilled over into local contests and was captured by reformers. In order to survive the tandem economic and political crises, the Irish bosses would ransack the New Deal in search of more patronage.

Chapter Four

The Crisis of the 1930s: The Depression, the New Deal, and Changing Machine Fortunes, 1928–1950

Economic Crisis/Political Crisis

The 1920s represented the Irish machine's heyday. Freed from state interference, controlling a growing patronage supply, and temporarily shielded from electoral pressures from the new immigrants for a greater sharing of power and jobs, the Irish bosses could meet the demands of both party and ethnicity. Bread had replaced circuses in the machine's repertoire of electoral appeals to already mobilized voters. The swollen ethnic patronage vote now decided local elections. Where job advertisements had once said, "No Irish need apply," the machine's employment agency now proclaimed, "Only Irish need apply." A massive patronage network enveloped the solidly lower-middle-class Irish-American community.

But at the moment the Irish bosses thought they had hit upon a formula guaranteeing both ethnic power and prosperity, its premises unraveled. Starting in the late 1920s, national economic and political forces overtook the machines' destiny. The Depression and the New Deal upset the bosses' management of both patronage and the vote.

As the business slump deepened, entrenched machines faced a mounting fiscal crisis. Declining property tax revenues coupled with growing relief costs created enormous pressures to cut the public payroll and salaries. Yet retrenchment threatened the machine's vote-getting ability and the economic well-being of thousands of Irish payrollers. At the same time, the national political realignment of the 1930s mobilized the new immigrants. In the 1928 presidential election, Al Smith's candidacy brought Italians, Poles, Czechs, and other Catholic groups into the voting booth in record numbers. In 1932 and 1936 Franklin Delano Roosevelt brought Jews into the Democratic camp. With their supply of patronage decreasing rather than increasing, the big-city party bosses viewed the New Deal's voter turnout surge with considerable apprehension.

Nevertheless, the New Deal created *opportunities* for the Irish Democratic bosses. For the entrenched machines of New York, Jersey City, and Albany, the federal emergency jobs programs of the 1930s, particularly the Works Progress Administration (WPA), represented an important source of potential patronage with which to reward the Southern and Eastern Europeans and quell discontent. For Irish Democratic politicians in other cities, the Depression and party realignment had weakened entrenched Republican machines such as the Pittsburgh and Philadelphia organizations and had halted GOP machine building in cities such as Chicago. A new generation of aspiring Irish bosses was eager to fashion New Deal machines by using federal work relief patronage to woo the new immigrants into more broadly based electoral coalitions.

Not all machines responded similarly to the national economic and political upheavals of the 1930s. The twin crises weakened some machines while strengthening others, raising several important questions for analysis. First, why did the Depression represent a destabilizing force for machines in some of the eight cities and not in others? In general, older machines were most weakened by the business slump. Tammany Hall and the Jersey City Hague organization, for example, were forced to slash their public payrolls, angering Irish payrollers and disappointing the new immigrants seeking public jobs as unemployment mounted in the private sector. Retrenchment contributed to Tammany's massive defeat in the 1933 city elections and to Hague's desperate search for federal patronage in order to prevent a similar debacle. Embryonic machines, in contrast, were less politically weakened by the Depression. Although fledgling Irish machines in Chicago and Pittsburgh were forced to cut the city payroll, retrenchment delayed but did not thwart the building of a new generation of Irish-run machines. Why were old machines more politically buffeted by the Depression than were new machines?

Second, why did the national party realignment of 1928–1936 weaken some Irish Democratic machines and strengthen others? Again, the older machines were most destabilized. In New York, Fusion candidate Fiorello La Guardia fashioned a "crazy quilt" coalition of Italians, Jews, and Republicans to overthrow Tammany in 1933. In Jersey City, Hague could delay but not prevent insurgency by the Southern and Eastern Europeans first brought to the polls by Al Smith and Franklin Delano Roosevelt. In 1949 the city's Italians and Poles toppled the once mighty Hague organization. But not all entrenched machines were destabilized. In Albany, the O'Connell organization finessed the challenge of ethnic insurgency set in motion by national political forces. Why were some second-generation machines weakened by national realignment while others were not? Were there differences in the character of the realignment process in New York and Jersey City compared with Albany?

The New Deal coalition also strengthened a new generation of Irish machines being built in cities such as Chicago and Pittsburgh. In Chicago, Democrat Anton Cermak was elected mayor in 1931 with Southern and Eastern European—but not Irish—support. With Cermak's death in 1933, the Irish reasserted control over party and city. Bosses Edward Kelly and Pat Nash harnessed the New Deal's ethnic groups to build one of the country's most powerful and long-lasting machines. In Pittsburgh, the once mighty Republican organization was toppled in the early 1930s, a victim of retrenchment and of the New Deal realignment. Appealing to the Steel City's Southern and Eastern Europeans, Irish boss David Lawrence built a powerful patronage-based Democratic machine that governed the city until 1969. But not all would-be Irish bosses were equally successful. In Boston James Michael Curley could not reduce the long-standing enmity between Irish and non-Irish. Why were some aspiring Irish bosses in cities without entrenched Democratic machines better able than others to woo the Southern and Eastern Europeans?

Third, why were some machines able to capture badly needed

federal patronage, particularly the massive WPA program, while others were not? Of the second-generation machines, the Hague and O'Connell organizations converted the nominally nonpartisan WPA into machine-controlled patronage while in New York Tammany Hall failed to capture the city's 246,000 WPA jobs. In some nonmachine cities, Irish party leaders consolidated power using federal patronage. Kelly and Nash in Chicago and Lawrence in Pittsburgh used WPA jobs to reward the new immigrants and to centralize power. Yet federal patronage eluded other would-be Celtic bosses. In Boston, Mayor and later Governor Curley's machine-building efforts were frustrated by the Roosevelt administration's refusal to turn over control of the Hub's WPA program. Do the dynamics of presidential rather than local politics better explain which machines seized control of federal work relief programs and were thereby strengthened?

The use of federal jobs programs for local machine building raises important questions about the impact of New Deal social programs on the big-city machines. As popularized by Edwin O'Connor in *The Last Hurrah,* the conventional wisdom holds that New Deal programs hastened the demise of the old-time machines. Roosevelt's social programs supposedly weakened the machines because they offered the organization's constituents resources not controlled by the local party boss. National programs enacted in the mid-1930s such as Social Security, Aid to Families with Dependent Children, and federally insured state unemployment compensation featured collective benefits distributed to the categorically—not politically—eligible. In this view, urban machines were weakened because they could not convert collective benefits into divisible benefits—patronage—for which a political quid pro quo—the vote—could be exchanged.[1]

As Lyle Dorsett notes, the New Deal's programmatic effect on the urban machines was far more complex than the conventional wisdom allows. The New Deal's collective benefits *could* be converted into divisible benefits, and political eligibility requirements *could* be reinstated. The big-city bosses viewed the WPA program, ostensibly supplying collective benefits to the welfare-eligible unemployed, as a fresh source of patronage. If bosses controlled the selection of state and local WPA administrators, federal relief jobs could be turned into sub-rosa patronage. Control of the WPA would allow the Hague and O'Connell machines to navigate the shoals of the Depression and national party realignment and permit the Kelly-Nash and Lawrence machines to consolidate power.

Machines were less able to control the New Deal's permanent legacy of welfare and insurance programs than they were the WPA. However, federal social programs such as Aid to Families with Dependent Children and public housing were not beyond the bosses' grasp. In Chicago, for example, the machine's precinct captains expedited welfare applications and threatened recipients with loss of benefits if they voted for the machine's opponents. Thus the welfare state could strengthen as well as weaken local party organizations.[2]

Crisis I: The Depression and Machine Retrenchment

The Depression ended the expansionary fiscal policies of the Irish machines. In New York City, the 1932 municipal budget stood at $631 million, having risen in real terms by 125 percent since 1918, whereas the city's population had climbed by only 15 percent. Gotham's debt stood at $1.9 billion, and more than one-third of the entire budget was devoted to servicing this massive debt.[3]

The budgetary spiral could no longer continue. During the prosperous 1920s, the value of taxable real estate, the source of more than two-thirds of city revenue, had soared. Riding the crest of an inflated real-estate market, machines could increase budgetary outlays substantially without increasing the tax rate. With the economic collapse of 1929, however, city revenues declined precipitously. Nationwide, the value of urban real estate declined by one-quarter between 1929 and 1933. Property tax collections also fell, compounding the cities' revenue shortfall. Between 1929 and 1933 the tax delinquency rate in the big cities rose from 10 percent to 33 percent. New York, Boston, and Chicago were among the hardest hit. In 1933 delinquent property taxes represented 42 percent of all their outstanding taxes.

Demands for greater welfare spending accompanied the revenue collapse as the big-city unemployment rate rose from 5 percent in 1929 to 33 percent in 1933. In New York City alone 1 million workers were in the bread lines during the winter of 1932. Local welfare systems buckled under the burden. New York's Home Relief Bureau enrolled 100,000 families in late 1933 while the city's Emergency Works Bureau placed 110,000 unemployed workers on municipal public works projects. By 1934 New York City's welfare outlays of $121 million represented one-quarter of all general government expenses, up from 3 percent in 1928.[4]

Yet the machine's capacity for economizing was severely limited. In New York, Jersey City, and Albany, one-third of the budget serviced the debt in the early 1930s. The city payroll, accounting for most of the remainder of the budget, represented the backbone of the machine. There were strong organizational pressures to resist cutbacks. A popular verse in New York City in the early 1930s accurately captured the sacrosanct character of the city's budget: "Mayor, may we economize?" "Boys, I won't begrudge it—Hit the depression between the eyes but don't go near the budget."[5]

Faced with the growing imbalance between revenues and outlays, the Irish bosses initially responded by borrowing money to pay for the relief burden, thereby sparing the jobs of thousands of machine payrollers. With large long-term debts, however, the Irish machines quickly ran afoul of state debt limitations. The bosses then entered the short-term money market, offering tax anticipation notes against projected—but not yet collected—tax revenues. In New York, Tammany Mayor John Patrick O'Brien, Jimmy Walker's successor, negotiated a series of short-term bank loans to finance the city's burgeoning home and work relief programs. In Jersey City, saddled with the highest tax rates in the country, the railroads proclaimed a tax strike. Boss Hague hurriedly met with the city's bankers in order to meet the machine's massive payroll and welfare obligations.[6]

With large payrolls and mounting debts, the once free-spending Irish machines began to rely heavily on tax anticipation notes, making them vulnerable to the spending priorities of the banks. By the end of fiscal year (FY) 1933, repayment of short-term notes accounted for more than one-third of all general fund outlays in New York and Jersey City compared with less than 10 percent of the outlays in nonmachine cities. As the fiscal crisis worsened, bankers raised interest rates on short-term municipal loans to reflect the growing risk of default and to force the cities to retrench. New York City paid 5.75 percent interest on short-term loans in 1932, several times the interest rate paid by the banks to their depositors.[7]

In the spring of 1933 the bankers refused to extend additional short-term credit unless the machines substantially reduced city outlays. New York's banks demanded that the O'Brien administration reduce the city's budget by nearly one-fifth as a condition of further loans. In Chicago, a city particularly vulnerable because of a wholesale downward reassessment of real estate, the banks made further loans to the Cermak administration contingent upon a 10 percent reduction in city outlays.

Forced out of the short-term loan market, the Irish bosses turned to state government for financial relief. Tammany's leaders, for example, petitioned the New York Emergency Relief Administration for a state takeover of local relief costs. But assistance was not forthcoming, for the states were beset with a burgeoning fiscal crisis of their own. State income taxes, as well as gasoline and sales taxes, were highly elastic, rising and falling with the state of the economy. As the Depression deepened, state revenues eroded at a faster rate than city revenues. Facing state bankruptcy, Democratic Governor Herbert Lehman turned down Tammany's request.

The city bosses then approached the unsympathetic Hoover administration for federal assistance. Though Hoover opposed a federal bailout, he reluctantly signed the Emergency Relief and Construction Act of 1932. The ERC authorized the federal Reconstruction Finance Corporation to loan up to $300 million to states and localities at 3 percent interest. There was little federal "trickle down" to the cities as most ERC loans went to states as advances on future highway grants. Their hands tied by state borrowing restrictions, the cities received only $3.5 million in federal loans.[8]

As the machines' borrowing opportunities evaporated, the bosses sought new taxing authority. With the Depression's onset, property owners had successfully lobbied the states for tax limits. These restrictions generally took one of two forms. The most common was a rate limitation, expressed as a fixed percentage of the total assessed value of taxable property. States also imposed percentage limits on the maximum annual local budget increase. Unable to squeeze more tax revenue from property, machine politicians petitioned the states for new revenue sources. Tammany, for example, successfully lobbied Governor Lehman and the state legislature for emergency taxing powers to pay for relief. Tammany used its emergency powers to enact a regressive local sales tax—hitting poor families hardest—an inheritance tax, and a levy on public utilities. In New York and other machine cities, the new revenues failed to cover ever-rising welfare costs.[9]

The party was over. Tammany and the Hague organization finally had their backs to the wall as the banks made further loans conditional upon sizable reductions in the machine's twin vertebrae—the payroll and the capital budget. Working with the business community, New York City bankers forced the O'Brien administration to reopen the FY 1933 budget and reduce outlays by 18 percent. The so-called Bankers Agreement of 1933 also created a four-year $429 million ceiling on property taxes, the amount raised in FY 1933, and required a reserve fund against future tax nonpayments. In similar fashion, Jersey City banks made Hague walk the financial plank. The machine's payroll was cut by 10 percent, and city wages were reduced by one-quarter.[10]

Bank-sponsored retrenchment posed severe organizational maintenance problems for the established Irish machines. Payroll and salary reductions thinned the party's cadre of precinct and social service workers and eroded voter support, particularly in the Irish community. A dwindling patronage supply also made it difficult for the machines to reward the now-voting Southern and Eastern Europeans. Faced with bank retrenchment demands and countervailing resistance from the Irish payrollers, the Irish bosses cut back in ways least harmful to the machine and to the payroll Irish. In New York and Jersey City, the most draconian economy measures were directed at the public school system, the hospitals, and the relief agencies. These departments were the least beholden to the bosses, and their employees were increasingly Jewish rather than Irish. By 1934 Tammany had fired 11,000 of the city's 35,000 school teachers.[11]

No matter how cleverly the payroll was pared, retrenchment eroded voter support for the established machines. In New York City, the Wigwam's payroll and salary cutbacks angered municipal employees—Irish as well as Jewish—and paved the way for the breakup of the multiethnic machine coalition fashioned in the 1920s. The firing of Jewish teachers and health and social workers shifted the Jewish middle class away from Tammany and into the La Guardia camp in the crucial 1933 mayoral election that brought the reformers to power for twelve years. The machine's salary reductions also softened the previously monolithic Irish Tammany support. In the 1933 election Irishman John McKee, running for mayor on the Recovery party ticket initially with the combined blessing of FDR, Democratic National Committee Chairman James Farley, and Bronx political boss Ed Flynn, drew a substantial number of Irish voters away from Tammany nominee Mayor O'Brien. With a fractured Irish payroll vote and the new immigrants ripe for revolt, the starving Tiger's days were numbered.[12]

In Jersey City fresh patronage supplies mitigated the immediate effects of retrenchment. Hague shifted some displaced city workers onto the county payroll and quickly moved to control more state and federal patronage, particularly New Jersey's WPA program, in order to appease the city's Poles and Italians. Federal and state resources would soon slip from his grasp. With the coming of World War II, federal emergency jobs programs were terminated. Forced by Roosevelt in 1940 to accept reformer Charles Edison as governor, Hague also found state doors shut. His taxation policies now came back to haunt him. Railroad bankruptcies shifted the machine's onerous tax burden onto homeowners. Unable to create new public jobs and unwilling to fire the payroll Irish and replace them with Poles and Italians, Hague had sown the seeds of ethnic insurgency.[13]

Not all the entrenched machines were weakened by the Depression. In contrast to Tammany and the Hague organizations, the O'Connell machine in Albany was not forced to adopt a politically damaging retrenchment program. Because of the large number of property owners, the upstate machine had pursued cautious taxation and spending policies in the 1920s. Because a significant proportion of the city's labor force was employed by state government, and thus better shielded from the Depression, the city experienced only moderate unemployment levels and welfare demands in the 1930s. With lower taxation and fewer welfare burdens, the O'Connell organization weathered the economic upheaval with its patronage army intact.

As for the new machines, the Depression delayed but did not prevent their consolidation of power. In Chicago, Mayor Cermak succumbed to bankers turning the retrenchment screws. During his short eighteen-month tenure, Cermak reduced the number of city workers by 10 percent—to 18,000—and cut salaries by one-fifth.

The slimming of the public payroll heightened intraparty and inter-ethnic factionalism, particularly between the Irish and the Slavs. When the payroll Irish staged a revolt, Cermak maneuvered Henry Horner into the governor's chair and used state jobs to soften the blow of local retrenchment. Cermak's strained relations with the Irish city workers would also delay the delivery of federal patronage to the struggling Windy City machine. At the 1932 Democratic convention held in Cermak's Chicago, the mayor leaned toward Al Smith rather than FDR in order to placate the city's disaffected Irish Democrats. Unable to claim membership in the FRBC Club ("For Roosevelt Before the Convention") Cermak received little federal patronage. He traveled to Miami in 1933 to meet Roosevelt and plead for more federal aid. An assassin's bullet meant for the president mortally wounded the Chicago mayor instead. Cermak's Irish successors, Mayor Ed Kelly and Democratic County Chairman Pat Nash, expedited the receipt of federal patronage with a massive display of electoral might in the 1935 municipal elections designed to convince Roosevelt that the machine was indispensable to his reelection plans.[14]

The Depression also delayed the consolidation of the Lawrence machine in Pittsburgh. Since the Civil War, the Steel City had been run by a succession of Republican bosses—Squire Tommy Steele, Chris Magee, and William Flinn. With the death in 1921 of state boss Boise Penrose, the Pennsylvania GOP machine split into two factions, weakening the Pittsburgh organization. The Depression and national realignment completed the task of overthrowing Pittsburgh's GOP machine. The Steel City's break with the Republican party began at the national level in 1928 when Al Smith received nearly half of the city's vote. In 1932, the city went Democratic, the first time this had happened in a presidential contest since 1856. Seizing the opportunity, Democratic Party Chairman David Lawrence chose old-line progressive William McNair as the party's nominee in the 1933 mayoral election. McNair won and immediately embarked on an economy program, furloughing hundreds of city employees and reducing city salaries by 20 percent. Estranging Lawrence with his retrenchment program, McNair compounded his difficulties by appointing Republicans to head the patronage-rich departments of public works and public safety. Lawrence would have to force the economy-minded and bipartisan McNair out of office before a machine could be built.[15]

In heavily Democratic Boston, the business slump thwarted Mayor Curley's machine-building efforts. In the 1920s Curley had earned the reputation of being a monumental builder "unintimidated by public debt." In the early 1930s, as the Hub's unemployment rate soared and the welfare caseload increased sixfold, Curley proposed a massive public works program to put the unemployed to work. Curley's countercyclical project died in the Republican-controlled statehouse and in the Democratic-controlled city council. The city treasury's bipartisan guardians were watchful of both the growing fiscal crisis and Curley's political ambitions. The Hub's worsening finances further trimmed the mayor's spending plans. Reluctantly, Curley reduced city salaries by 10 percent and began laying off city workers. By the late 1930s the Boston payroll stood at 12,500, down from 21,000 before the Depression. With local patronage fast disappearing, Curley's machine-building plans would require an infusion of federal gravy.[16]

Yet the Depression's harshest effects were felt by old rather than new machines. For entrenched machines, there were greater organizational, ethnic, and electoral repercussions to payroll cutbacks. For Tammany Hall and the Hague organization, the public payroll employed an army of precinct captains and workers. If party workers were furloughed, established machines were less able to get out their customary vote and deliver expected welfare services. Moreover, the old machines had been most successful in placing the Irish on the city payroll. Cutbacks sent ripples of dissatisfaction through the party's core ethnic constituency. Because the old machines had not yet fought the ethnic wars of succession, unemployed Southern and Eastern Europeans demanded a fair share of public employment at the moment when the Irish bosses were least able to oblige.

Relying less on the public payroll, fledgling machines better survived austerity. In Pittsburgh, only 7 percent of the Democratic committeemen in 1934 were publicly employed. By firing Republican workers, the Lawrence machine could create job opportunities for Democratic workers even as the payroll was trimmed. Despite McNair's austerity program, Lawrence succeeded in placing one-half of the party's precinct captains on the public payroll by 1940. The new machines' retrenchment program produced less ethnic dissatisfaction. The Irish monopoly on public employment had not yet been established. With smaller numbers of Irish working for government, retrenchment did not fall as heavily on the Irish community. Because the Southern and Eastern Europeans had already been integrated into the Democratic party in two-party Chicago and Republican Pittsburgh, the new ethnic leaders had the power to ensure that their countrymen got a fair share of public jobs as the Republicans were purged. For a new generation of Irish bosses, austerity might not produce defeat at the polls as it did for the old bosses. Yet austerity programs rarely allowed nascent machines to consolidate power. For consolidation to occur, new sources of patronage would have to be found.[17]

Crisis II: The National Mobilization of the Southern and Eastern Europeans

Although the national realignment of 1928–1936 improved the Democratic party's prospects nationwide, it represented a destabilizing force for Democratic machines where the ethnic succession wars had not yet been fought. Southern and Eastern Europeans became citizens in record numbers in the late 1920s. Sixty-one percent of New York City's Russian- and Polish-born Jews had received their citizenship papers by 1930, up from 37 percent in 1920. Democratic presidential candidates targeted the new citizens. In the 1928 presidential election, Al Smith's candidacy mobilized nonvoting Italians, Poles, Jews, and other big-city immigrants. In 1932 and 1936 Roosevelt would build on the big-city ethnic coalition initially fashioned by Smith.

The surge in big-city turnout for presidential elections was remarkable. In New York City the number of voters increased by nearly 40 percent between 1924 and 1928—from 1.4 million to over 1.9 million—after having increased by only 15 percent between 1920 and 1924. The number of Gotham voters rose by another 26 percent between 1932 and 1936 as the city's immigrants ratified the New Deal. In all, the national realignment contributed to an effective doubling of the active electorate. Comparable increases in presidential election turnout between 1928 and 1936 occurred in Jersey City, Chicago, and Pittsburgh.

The Irish bosses temporarily breathed easier as the new immigrants embraced the party of Smith and Roosevelt. In New York City, three-quarters of the Italian and Jewish voters pulled the lever for Smith in 1928, up from fewer than one-half supporting Democratic candidate Davis in 1924. More than 70 percent of the Windy City's Poles and Czechs voted Democratic in 1928, up from fewer than 40 percent in 1924. The Southern and Eastern Europeans would line up as solidly for Roosevelt in 1932 and 1936 as they had for Smith in 1928.[18]

Yet the New Deal's electoral coattails did not necessarily extend to the big-city Democratic machines. The new immigrants had gained little from Irish bosses in the teens and twenties. As the Depression deepened, they added the denial of public jobs to their list of grievances against the Irish overlords. Given growing ethnic demands in the early 1930s for a reallocation of patronage and power, the national mobilization of the new immigrants presented a potential electoral challenge to the entrenched Irish machines. The presidential turnout surge could cut quite differently in local contests if captured by the machine's opponents.

Reform leaders in New York and Jersey City mobilized the Southern and Eastern Europeans, capitalizing on their long-standing grievances with Irish rule. In New York City, Fusionist candidate Fiorello La Guardia's strategy in the 1933 mayoral election was to unleash the Jews and the Italians. Jews now constituted one-quarter and the Italians one-sixth of the city's potential electorate. Yet the new immigrants, particularly Catholic women, rarely bothered to register and vote in local elections.

Enlisting fresh ethnic recruits, the Little Flower changed all that. Concentrating on groups such as the Italians with low registration and voting rates, La Guardia's Fusion organization joined other anti-Tammany reform groups in enrolling new voters at a record rate for a municipal election. By election day nearly 800,000 new recruits had been enrolled. The La Guardia organization pioneered the ethnically balanced ticket to woo the new voters. The Fusion "brotherhood" slate featured an Italian for mayor, a Jew for president of the Board of Aldermen, the obligatory Irishman for controller, and a WASP thrown in for good measure for district attorney. Tammany, in contrast, paraded its usual heavily Irish slate before the city's increasingly heterogeneous voters.[19]

La Guardia won in 1933, relegating Tammany to twelve years in the political wilderness, by capitalizing on a split in the traditional Irish machine vote and by mobilizing the new ethnics. Table 12

TABLE 12. The Tiger Turns Tail: Voting and Turnout in New York City, 1925–1937

Mayoral Election	Outcome	Candidate	Tammany At The Polls			Voter Participation Rates		Total Adults[b] (thousands)	Total Citizens[b] (thousands)	Total Voters (thousands)
			Vote Share (%)	Chief Opponent[a]	Opponents' Vote Share (%)	Adults (%)	Citizens (%)			
1925	Win	Walker	65.8	Waterman (R)	30.5	28.0	37.8	4,058	3,010	1,138
1929	Win	Walker	61.0	La Guardia (R)	25.8	31.6	42.1	4,512	3,379	1,424
1932	Win	O'Brien	63.0	Pounds (R)	26.5	35.1	47.5	4,777	3,532	1,676
1933	Loss	O'Brien	27.6	La Guardia (F)	40.9	43.9	58.0	4,837	3,667	2,125
1937	Loss	Mahoney	39.8	La Guardia (R, F, AL)	60.2	44.4	54.2	5,031	4,127	2,236

Sources: U.S. Bureau of the Census, Census of Population, 1920 (Washington, D.C.: Government Printing Office, 1923), vol. 3, Table 10; U.S. Bureau of the Census, Sixteenth Census of the United States, 1940 (Washington, D.C.: Government Printing Office, 1943), vol. 2, Table C–37, p. 157; New York World-Telegram, World Almanac and Book of Facts for 1940 (New York: World-Telegram, 1940), pp. 794–795.

[a] Republican (R), Fusionist (F), American Labor (AL).

[b] Estimated for years between censuses.

shows the changing shape of New York City's voting universe between 1925 and 1937. As late as the 1932 special election to fill Jimmy Walker's unexpired term, Tammany had appeared impregnable, securing 63 percent of the vote. The drop in the Tiger's electoral fortunes was precipitous. In the three-way 1933 regular election, Tammany's share of the vote fell from its customary 60 percent to less than 30 percent as the Recovery party's McKee siphoned off 30 percent. La Guardia's mobilization campaign paid off handsomely. Having edged upward since 1928, voter participation rates took their sharpest jump between 1932 and 1933. Fifty-eight percent of Gotham's citizens voted in the 1933 mayoral election, up from 48 percent the year before.

Yet La Guardia had not fashioned a "Little New Deal" ethnic coalition *sans* Celts. As Arthur Mann notes, La Guardia's "crazy quilt" coalition ranged across the ideological, ethnic, and class spectrum. Old guard Republicans joined Socialists and reform Democrats in supporting Fusion. Eighty percent of the Italian voters cast their ballots for La Guardia, supplying one-quarter of his total vote. The crucial Jewish vote, however, was split along class lines. On the Irish-controlled Lower East Side, La Guardia received only one-third of the working-class Jewish vote. The Fusionists did best among middle-class Jews. As Tammany's economy measures fell heaviest on teachers and health and social workers, the Jewish middle class left the Wigwam. Nearly 60 percent would vote for La Guardia.[20]

La Guardia concentrated his first administration on solidifying new immigrant support to prevent Tammany's resurrection. Since the 1937 city election would be a contest for the Jewish vote, Fiorello immediately embarked on a campaign to increase the number of Jews and other new ethnics on the city's payroll. The city's antiquated civil service system was reformed in order to end job discrimination against the non-Irish. Municipal job openings were publicly advertised. Multiple-choice questions replaced essay examinations, reducing the discretion of Irish civil service examiners. A high school diploma replaced the traditional cursory entrance examination. La Guardia dispensed with the services of Tammany's temporary "Kelly Boys." Under his administration, the proportion of city positions covered by a strengthened civil service system rose from one-half in 1933 to three-quarters in 1940.[21]

The reform mayor also expanded the size of the city's human service agencies (and thus the number of job opportunities for the new ethnic claimants). Forced by the ever-watchful banks to cut the city's payroll by 6 percent in his first year in office, La Guardia subsequently increased employment in the departments of education, health, hospitals, and welfare. Propelled by human services funding as well as by population growth, the city payroll grew by 60 percent during his three terms.[22]

By the tandem tactics of civil service reform and bureaucratic expansion, La Guardia worked a dramatic alteration in the ethnic composition of the city's bureaucracy, particularly in the new human services agencies rather than in the old police, fire, and public works departments where the Irish remained firmly entrenched. The Jews, Tammany's chosen people in the 1920s, were the prime beneficiaries of La Guardia's personnel and social policies in the 1930s. In the city's school system, which the Irish had dominated until World War I, 56 percent of the entering teachers in 1940 were Jewish. The reform mayor's wooing of the new immigrants with the old benefits of patronage politics produced the desired electoral results. As Table 12 shows, La Guardia waltzed to victory in his 1937 reelection bid. A durable reform coalition of Southern and Eastern Europeans had been fashioned that would rule New York until the mid-1940s.[23]

A decaying Tammany remained out of power until 1945. Denied city patronage, it found its payroll reduced to county offices. Then when La Guardia turned to county civil service reform, the Irish Tiger's days were numbered. Denied county jobs in the 1940s, Tammany's aging Irish chieftains turned to the Italian-controlled underworld for desperately needed funding. The "Mafia plan" was not without risk, for the organization's ethnic balance of power soon shifted dramatically. Gangsters such as "Lucky" Luciano and Frank Costello decided to install their own Italian district leaders in Tammany's clubhouses. Led by Carmine De Sapio, an Italian bloc successfully challenged Irish party hegemony in the late 1940s.[24]

Using many of La Guardia's campaign tactics, a similar reform coalition of the new immigrants in Jersey City finally overthrew the Hague machine. Demographics and parsimony had finally caught up with the boss. By 1940 Italians and Poles constituted nearly one-half of Jersey City's eligible voters while the Irish ranks had thinned to one-fifth. Hague had done little to share power and patronage with the now numerous new immigrants. He defused an incipient Italian revolt in the mid-1930s by according greater ethnic representation on the state assembly ticket, the board of education, and the local judiciary. The machine's major patronage-dispensing and policy-making positions remained in Irish hands. Aided by control of the state's WPA and by a moribund Republican party, Hague stalled ethnic insurgency into the 1940s.

Disaster struck in 1949. Dissident Democrat John V. Kenney's mayoral campaign against incumbent Frank Hague Eggers, Hague's nephew and designated heir apparent, was lifted from La Guardia's playbook. Kenney practiced Fusion politics. The Fusionists enrolled a record 12,000 new voters—primarily Poles and Italians. Balanced slates crossed the Hudson as the new immigrants were nominated for major offices. Kenney followed La Guardia in splitting the Irish vote, though on generational lines, as returning Irish war veterans were drawn into the Fusion camp. Kenney's Freedom ticket won a resounding victory, securing 67 percent of the total vote.[25]

Kenney's first administration also drew inspiration from the Little Flower. The mayor quickly increased the payroll by 400—to 8,000—as Poles and Italians drew city paychecks. Unlike La Guardia, however, Kenney's ethnic accommodation policies were directed at machine building rather than reform. The new mayor soon moved to control the Democratic party. Kenney increased the number of ward leaders from sixteen to fifty, appointing loyal Poles and Italians.

Yet not all of the old machines were buffeted by the national political forces set in motion in the late 1920s. Albany's Dan O'Connell was not forced to fight the ethnic wars of succession produced by a rising tide of new immigrant voters. As Kristi Andersen notes, the character of the realigning process differed in Albany compared with New York and Jersey City. Tammany Hall and the Hague organization had faced *mobilization* realignments as the number of new Democratic voters expanded rapidly. In Albany, however, there was no flood of new ethnic voters. The Southern and Eastern Europeans had arrived earlier upstate than downstate. Table 10 shows that 61 percent of Albany's immigrants had arrived before 1910, compared with 53 percent of New York City's. As control of the state capital oscillated between competing machines in the late nineteenth and early twentieth centuries, both parties worked hard to naturalize and register the Southern and Eastern Europeans. As a consequence, Albany's immigrants were voting well before the 1928–1936 realignment. The upstate realignment would be one of *conversion* rather than of mobilization as the electorate grew by only 38 percent over this twelve-year period—only 40 percent of the growth rate in New York City. Uncle Dan assisted Smith and Roosevelt by inviting supporters of the defunct Barnes machine into the Democratic party. By the early 1930s a two-to-one Republican registration advantage had been transformed into a two-to-one Democratic lead.[26]

O'Connell's middle-class "service" machine more easily survived the economic and political upheavals of the 1930s than did the Tammany and Hague working-class "patronage" machines. In the 1920s Uncle Dan faced the task of politically converting a participating, home-owning, and Republican electorate. The Albany machine cultivated homeowners with a low tax rate—thus limiting the supply of patronage—and with the political manipulation of individual property tax assessments. As property changed hands, it was deliberately overassessed. The local ward leader would then graciously reduce the assessment, earning the new homeowner's gratitude *and* vote. For homeowners, the machine specialized in garbage delivery, street and pothole repair, and snow removal. The machine's middle-class menu of lowered taxes and homeowner services brought former GOP voters into the Democratic party in droves. O'Connell's occasional reform opponents would be denied a large pool of nonparticipating and unrewarded immigrant voters.[27]

Tammany Hall and the Hague organization, in contrast, relied more on patronage than on services to bring out the vote. Hague's massive public and private sector patronage army numbered nearly 20,000 in the late 1930s in a voting population of 120,000. The machine instructed each worker on the payroll to secure the votes of family and friends. If each retainer brought in two more votes, the machine was guaranteed victory—as long as the size of the voting population remained the same. Relying on the payroll vote, these machines had little incentive to expand the voting population.[28]

The twin crises of the 1930s fell far harder on machines that relied on jobs than on those relying on services. Because they were more financially extended, high-tax patronage machines were more vulnerable than low-tax service machines to the Depression. Retrenchment weakened the ability of patronage-based machines to mobilize their traditional constituency and to reward the new immigrants. By the early 1930s the neglected Southern and Eastern Europeans were voting in record numbers. Patronage machines were in electoral jeopardy because they had done little to curry favor with the newcomers.

The O'Connell machine learned an important lesson from the travails of the downstate patronage machines. The leaner Albany organization added to its margin of electoral safety in the 1930s and 1940s by systematically padding the lists of registrants and voters, testimony to Uncle Dan's control over the ballot box, the judiciary, and the political opposition. By the early 1940s the machine was defying the actuarial tables, claiming the votes of more than 60 percent of the entire population of men, women, and children.[29]

Although the national realignment played havoc with entrenched—particularly patronage-based—machines, it strengthened the fledgling Democratic organizations of Chicago and Pittsburgh. For the old machines, Irish power had preceded organizational consolidation. For the new machines, however, the ethnic succession wars had been fought *before* both the centralization of machine power and the national realignment. In Chicago Democratic leaders George Brennan and Anton Cermak had actively recruited Czechs, Jews, Poles, and Italians in the 1920s. In his victorious 1931 mayoral campaign, Cermak had carefully exploited national political forces. In presidential politics, the Windy City's realignment was mobilizing. Nearly 40 percent more voters went to the polls in 1928 than in 1924. Al Smith, scion of the Fulton Fish Market, received more than two-thirds of Chicago's new immigrant vote compared with one-third received by Democrat John W. Davis in the three-way 1924 contest. A countervailing local realignment, however, complicated Cermak's election bid. Between 1923 and 1927 the number of local voters had also soared by 40 percent— but into the hands of Republican "Big Bill" Thompson. In the 1927 city election, Thompson received more than one-half of the new ethnic vote. In his 1931 race against Thompson, Cermak wrapped himself in Smith's mantle and captured 65 percent of the new immigrant vote. Earlier than reformer La Guardia, machine politico Cermak had forged a "Little New Deal" coalition without the Celts. Republican Thompson received a sizable vote in normally Democratic wards controlled by disaffected Irish ward bosses.[30]

Although the national realignment was not the destabilizing force in Chicago Democratic politics that it would prove to be in New York and Jersey City, tensions between Irish and non-Irish persisted as Cermak and his successors consolidated power. After Cermak's death the restoration of Irish party leadership by Mayor Edward Kelly and County Chairman Pat Nash particularly rankled the new immigrants. The new Irish bosses avidly courted FDR for federal patronage to placate the ethnic dissidents. To demonstrate the machine's indispensability to Roosevelt, Kelly and Nash defeated the Republicans in the 1935 city election by a record 630,000 votes. The Democratic share of the 1935 local vote—83 percent—doubled the party's 1927 performance. Roosevelt got the message and hand-delivered the state's WPA to Kelly and Nash. The consolidating machine returned the favor. Naturalizing, registering, and voting the new immigrants, the machine's precinct captains pushed the city's presidential turnout rate to an unprecedented 89 percent in 1936, up from 76 percent in 1928.[31]

In Pittsburgh, the Democratic machine's ethnic succession wars were also fought before the new ethnics were mobilized. Though the Irish were the most active and influential group in the Steel City's Democratic party, minority party status encouraged them to share power. By the early 1930s, as the Lawrence machine was consolidating power, the Irish held fewer than one-third of the party's ward committee posts compared with one-fifth for the Germans and one-tenth for the Italians.[32]

Welcoming the newer ethnic arrivals into the revitalized Democratic party, Irish leader David Lawrence hoped to use FDR's coattails to build a Steel City machine. Between 1924 and 1936 Pittsburgh's electorate dramatically grew by 120 percent. The surge in voter turnout benefited the Democrats. In the three-way 1924 presidential election, Democrat Davis had received a paltry 9 percent of the one-quarter million votes cast in Allegheny County. Capitalizing on the 1924 La Follette progressive vote—32 percent—and a rising tide of European Catholic voters, Al Smith in 1928 secured 48 percent of the county's vote. FDR built on Smith's electoral foundations. By 1936 the Democratic standard bearer had captured nearly 70 percent of the county's 562,000 votes. As Bruce Stave has shown in his careful study of the emergence of the modern Pittsburgh Democratic party, the city's polyglot new immigrants—Poles, Italians, Jews, Czechs, Yugoslavians, Hungarians, and Lithuanians—were largely responsible for the resurgence in the fortunes of national Democratic candidates.[33]

Local Democratic fortunes were another matter. Lawrence's ability to harness the New Deal ethnic coalition for local machine building was hampered by Democratic Mayor William McNair. McNair was a progressive rather than a New Dealer. The mayor's constituency, centered in the native-born middle class dissatisfied with the aging and corrupt GOP machine, bore little relationship to FDR's 1932 ethnic vote. Forcing McNair to resign in 1936, Lawrence installed Irish party regular Cornelius Scully in the mayor's chair. Attracting both the Irish and the Southern and Eastern Europeans, Scully's landslide 1937 vote virtually duplicated the 1936 Roosevelt vote.[34]

The full consolidation of the ethnically heterogeneous Chicago and Pittsburgh machines, however, would have to await local capture of federal resources. In both newly Democratic cities, local retrenchment programs had badly depleted the resources needed to cement the allegiance of the new immigrants. Kelly, Nash, and Lawrence would need to devise ways of harnessing the New Deal's relief and recovery programs to their machine-building purposes.

In Boston the potential flood tide of new ethnic voters was not captured by would-be Irish bosses. The city was already Democratic by the late 1920s—67 percent of the registered voters—and heavily Irish. By 1930 more than half of the population was of Celtic descent. Green Power in the Hub did not depend on long-lasting interethnic alliances or a citywide machine. During the Progressive era the city's Irish pols—Fitzgerald, Lomasney, and Curley—had selectively used the new immigrants as a battering ram to challenge Yankee political hegemony. With the arrival of Irish ascendancy in the 1920s, the Irish politicians dispensed with the services of Jews and Italians. The city's swollen bureaucracies—particularly the police and fire departments, water and public works, and the school

system—were turned into an Irish preserve. Frozen out of the solidly Irish Democratic party, many Jews became Republicans. The
nominally Democratic Italians gave their votes grudgingly to Irish
politicians.[35]

With majority party *and* ethnic status, Boston's Celtic politicos
had little incentive to mobilize—or reward—the new immigrants.
Irish hegemony served as the glue holding rampant Democratic
factionalism together. Any bid by one of the feuding Irish ward
bosses to mobilize the new immigrants entailed substantial risks of
challenging Green Power and producing an Irish political backlash.

Hence the New Deal realignment was a curiously incomplete affair in Boston. Well into the 1930s, naturalization rates for the
new immigrants in the Hub lagged (see Table 10). The Irish pols
discovered a temporary use for the new ethnics in their love affair
with Al Smith in 1928. Driven to the polls by the Celtic ward
bosses in 1928, record numbers of new ethnics voted for Smith.
Between 1924 and 1928 the Hub's presidential voters swelled by
40 percent—to 274,000. The Boston politicos never forgot Smith.
With the coming of Roosevelt, however, the Irish spurned the new
ethnics. Presidential turnout in the Hub dropped 6 percent—by
16,000—between 1928 and 1932 compared with a 27 percent increase nationwide. In all, Boston's voter participation rate rose by
only 58 percent between 1928 and 1936—one-half New York
City's increase.

Only one suitor remained—James Michael Curley. Curley was
the beleaguered leader of the pro-Roosevelt forces in the 1932 Massachusetts Democratic primary. Lining up solidly behind Smith, the
other Irish politicos easily carried the day. In the general election,
as most of the city's Celtic politicians took a walk, Mayor Curley
tried to mobilize the Jews and the Italians for Roosevelt—and
himself. He failed. Curley's major voter registration drive netted a
paltry 5,500 new voters. Distrustful of all Irish politicians, the new
ethnics had also taken a walk.[36]

The New Deal Comes to the Cities:
The WPA and Machine Building

The big-city Democratic bosses cast covetous glances at the New
Deal's three major work relief programs. The Public Works Ad-

ministration (PWA), created under the 1933 National Industrial Recovery Act, represented a $3.3 billion program of large-scale public works designed to stimulate recovery of the so-called heavy industries. Nationwide, by mid-1934 the PWA employed 542,000 individuals. The Civil Works Administration (CWA), created in late 1933, was designed to provide temporary employment on small-scale projects for 4.3 million individuals—half of whom were on relief—during the winter of 1933–1934.[37]

The Works Progress Administration (WPA) particularly caught the eye of the urban bosses. Created in 1935, the WPA represented a long-term $7.8 billion program to provide jobs for the welfare-eligible unemployed on small-scale locally initiated public works projects. By mid-1936 the WPA's highway, park, sewer, public building, and social service projects employed more than 3 million individuals nationwide.[38]

Although it was a national program, the WPA had a distinctive urban relief mission. The federal program's urban focus was a product both of jurisdictional battles with the rural-oriented Resettlement Administration and of the agency's decision to target funding in those areas with the highest unemployment rates and largest welfare caseloads—the big cities. As a result, half of all WPA workers nationwide were drawn from cities with populations of more than 100,000. In the cities, WPA expenditures quickly overshadowed all other welfare outlays. By 1936 the WPA accounted for two-thirds of all big-city relief expenditures.[39]

No wonder the big-city bosses coveted the WPA. Federal patronage dwarfed local resources. Table 13 shows the size of the 1936 WPA payroll relative to the municipal workforce and electorate for six of the once Irish cities. In most of the cities, the number of WPA workers more than doubled the municipal workforce. New York City's 246,000 WPA workers, for example, dwarfed the city payroll of 121,000. As Table 13 shows, relief workers and their families also meant a fresh source of machine votes.

This patronage windfall could be used both internally and externally to strengthen the party organization and to appeal to voters. Internally, white-collar supervisory and administrative jobs represented juicy plums for ward and precinct captains. As the Lawrence machine in Pittsburgh consolidated power in the late 1930s, one-third of its ward captains served as WPA project super-

TABLE 13. *Federal Relief for the Bosses: The WPA and the Cities, 1936*

	WPA Workers[a] (thousands)	City Employees[b] (thousands)	Registered Voters (thousands)	WPA Workers as a Percentage of City Employees	WPA Workers as a Percentage of Registered Voters
New York	246.0	121.4	2,324.4	202.6	10.6
Jersey City	5.2	3.7	151.2	140.5	3.4
Albany	3.9	1.9	72.0	205.3	5.4
Chicago	68.4	29.5	1,503.2	231.9	4.6
Pittsburgh	20.8	5.3	246.5	392.5	8.4
Boston	26.0	13.6	305.6	191.2	8.5

Sources: U.S. Works Progress Administration, *Final Report on the WPA Program, 1935–1943* (Washington, D.C.: Government Printing Office, 1946), Table 2, pp. 110–111; U.S. Bureau of the Census, *Sixteenth Census of the United States, 1940* (Washington, D.C.: Government Printing Office, 1943), vol. 3, pts. 1–5, Table 3; International City Managers' Association, *Municipal Year Book, 1937* (Chicago: International City Managers' Association, 1937), Table 2, pp. 183–184, Table 5, pp. 268–269.
[a] Estimated for the cities from state-level data.
[b] Excludes school system employees.

visors. Rank-and-file WPA workers could also be pressed into party service. In Chicago, the Kelly-Nash machine added party workers to the WPA payroll at election time for the sole purpose of canvassing precincts for Democratic candidates. The Jersey City machine found further political profit from relief, demonstrating that Hague could steal from the poor as well as the rich. The city's WPA workers were tithed a portion of their lowly wages for Hague's campaign war chest.[40]

Externally, the WPA meant machine votes as well as jobs. Table 13 shows that the WPA employed up to 10 percent of the big-city electorate. Bosses could extract gratitude from former—as well as current—reliefers. Over the program's life, 1935 to 1943, up to one-quarter of all big-city registered voters were on the WPA payroll at one time or another.[41] Tammany had a taste of federal relief patronage in 1933 with the CWA program. The Tiger's chieftains made party affiliation—not need—the test for employment on federal projects. Most applicants had to be cleared with their district leader. As one Tammany brave boasted, "This is how we make Democrats."[42] Tammany's blatant politicization of the CWA proved an embarrassment in the 1933 city elections. Bosses would have to be more discreet in their wooing of reliefers.

By providing popular neighborhood services, the WPA could win the hearts of other machine voters. For the bosses, the WPA represented a unique public works grant-in-aid—a federally financed, locally picked labor supply for machine-initiated neighborhood projects. WPA project sponsorship lay primarily with state and local governments. By judicious choice of the type, location, and even timing of WPA projects, machines could build neighborhood electoral support. Bosses used WPA funds for such popular projects as street and highway construction and improvements, sewer systems, parks, schools, and libraries. By locating WPA projects in areas of current or potential machine strength and by completing projects before municipal elections, the bosses could appeal for votes on the basis of neighborhood services rendered.[43]

The WPA also helped machines by easing pressure on their twin supports—the capital budget and the municipal payroll. The WPA allowed bosses to trim their capital budgets and keep the city payroll intact. In cities such as New York, the WPA accounted for more than half of all construction activity in the late 1930s.[44]

Yet the partisan conversion of the WPA was not easy. In its early days, the national Works Progress Administration was studiously nonpartisan in its policy-making and personnel decisions. Harry Hopkins, FDR's minister of relief, deliberately drew WPA district boundaries *across* congressional districts and county and city lines in order to minimize congressional and machine influences over the program. The program's initial nonpartisanship could be traceable to the dynamics of New Deal coalition building in Congress. Before his landslide 1936 reelection, Roosevelt needed the support of moderate Republicans and conservative Democrats to enact his domestic relief and recovery program. The president could not alienate these pivotal legislators with a blatant display of the partisan uses of relief.[45]

The WPA was politicized after the 1936 election. Roosevelt now had a solidly pro–New Deal majority in Congress. With less need to placate southern Democrats and moderate Republicans in Congress, Roosevelt could take the nonpartisan wrapping off relief and reward New Deal congressmen—and the men who selected them. Many of the New Deal legislators were beholden to the bosses. Frank Hague, for example, controlled the entire Garden State Democratic congressional delegation. Hague demanded federal patronage in exchange for his hand-picked legislators voting the New Deal line. As for federal relief, the bosses demanded the power to select state and district WPA administrators. Controlling the relief hierarchy, machines could politicize the key processes of project approval and worker eligibility. As federal relief czar Harry Hopkins moved over to become FDR's chief political adviser following the death of Louis Howe, the need to reward the urban New Deal congressmen and the bosses who selected them increasingly influenced WPA decision making.[46]

The puzzling question is why some Democratic bosses and machines and not others were able to control the WPA. Machine longevity does not explain the selective local capture of federal relief patronage. Roosevelt gave relief to some established machines but not to others. The Hague and O'Connell organizations became federal work relief dispensers. In fact, Boss Hague was made de facto relief czar for all of New Jersey. Allocated 18,000 temporary CWA jobs in 1933–1934, Hague was rewarded in 1937 with the state's allocation of 75,000 WPA slots and Hudson County's

10,000 positions. Nearing bankruptcy in the early 1930s when the railroads went on a tax strike, the Hague machine was revitalized by relief. By the late 1930s the organization was a gigantic federal employment and relief agency. More than $64 million in federal WPA and PWA funds poured into the machine's coffers. In upstate New York, the O'Connell machine also acquired valuable WPA patronage. Armed with federal relief, these machines brought the New Deal's newest ethnic recruits securely into the organization's fold.[47]

Roosevelt offered little relief for Tammany, however. By the mid-1930s the Tiger was wounded. After La Guardia's victory, Tammany was reduced to controlling county offices. Democratic Governor Lehman froze the Tiger out of state patronage, supporting Bronx boss Ed Flynn instead. When it came time to dole out federal patronage, Roosevelt also supported Flynn and, covertly, the progressive La Guardia. With New York City's share of national WPA outlays approaching one-seventh, Tammany's hungry braves circled the federal jobs program.[48]

Determined to deny Tammany badly needed WPA patronage, Mayor La Guardia successfully lobbied Washington for an unprecedented separate relief unit for the city, coequal with the forty-eight state agencies. La Guardia then helped select a succession of nonpartisan WPA chiefs for the city, many drawn from the Army Corps of Engineers—General Hugh Johnson, Victor Ridder, Colonel Brehon Somervell, and Oliver Gottschalk. The Wigwam's braves remained hungry.[49]

Some new machines succeeded where Tammany failed. The fledgling Democratic machines of Chicago and Pittsburgh were incubated with federal patronage. In Chicago, factional battles within the state Democratic party initially delayed the delivery of federal work relief. After Mayor Cermak's death, the struggling Kelly-Nash organization vied with Cermak protégé Governor Henry Horner for control of the state party and federal patronage. Roosevelt initially froze out the Chicago machine, remembering its love affair with Al Smith before the 1932 nominating convention. Ever the political realist, though, FDR knew how to count votes. The Kelly-Nash organization brought out the living—and dead—in record numbers for the president in 1936. A grateful FDR responded by delivering 68,000 Cook County WPA positions to the Irish co-bosses.[50]

Kelly and Nash deputized precinct captains as employment brokers for WPA jobseekers. The party's cadres also served as welfare
brokers. To expedite Social Security and AFDC eligibility, the
Windy City's precinct captains initiated client contacts with social
service agencies. By 1936 two-thirds of the machine's lieutenants
reported serving as employment and welfare brokers, up from one-
third in 1928. Kelly and Nash particularly targeted the city's Southern and Eastern Europeans for jobs and relief. The new ethnics
had flirted with the Republicans in the late 1920s and were still
smarting over the Irish counter-putsch following Cermak's death.[51]

Relief patronage also served as the catalyst for building the
Democratic machine in Pittsburgh. Rebuffed by old-line progressive McNair, Lawrence was denied control of the 5,300 city workers. Undaunted, the county chairman found WPA jobs—as supervisors and foremen—for his precinct committeemen. Controlling
the dole, the nascent machine used Allegheny County's 21,000
WPA positions to good political effect. The job-hungry Southern and Eastern Europeans and the vote-hungry machine both
found relief. Between 1930 and 1936 Democratic voter registration jumped from 5 percent to 56 percent. With McNair's long-
awaited resignation and the election of party regular Cornelius
Scully as mayor in 1937, the Lawrence organization captured the
municipal payroll. By 1940 the WPA-based Steel City machine had
consolidated power and would rule the city until shortly after
Lawrence's death in 1966.[52]

The "Purple Shamrock" (as Boston's Curley was called) was not
so lucky. In Massachusetts, Roosevelt appointed an independent
state WPA administrator not beholden to any of the Boston ward
bosses. Curley was outraged. The mayor had been the state's
charter member in the FRBC Club, climbing on FDR's bandwagon
in early 1932. After Roosevelt's election, Curley assumed his early
support would result in his organization's being designated the
clearinghouse for federal patronage in the Bay State.[53]

The president and his state relief administrator assumed otherwise. State WPA czar Arthur G. Rotch vigorously opposed the
Shamrock's schemes for politicizing the WPA. Rotch so micro-
scopically scrutinized Boston's WPA projects for possible signs of
Curleyite influence that work relief in the Hub was nearly brought
to a halt. Elected governor, Curley joined other state Democrats in

forcing Rotch to resign in early 1936. The new relief administrator was no better. Federal WPA chief Hopkins named Paul Edwards, an out-of-state Democrat, to the state post. At Hopkins's urging, Edwards also resisted pressure from Curley and other Boston ward politicians to politicize the program.[54]

No federal relief meant no Curley machine. Yet the New Deal did not weaken Irish power in the Hub. It merely federalized it. In the vacuum created by the lack of a citywide machine, Irish power seeped up from the ward level and coalesced at the federal level. The Hub's New Deal hierarchy included congressmen and U.S. senators—vital to obtaining passage of Roosevelt-backed legislation, and not beholden to any big-city boss. Roosevelt and Hopkins wooed Irish congressmen such as John McCormack with WPA patronage. McCormack put the WPA to good use: a disproportionate number of federal public works projects were targeted in Irish neighborhoods in McCormack's district. McCormack's Irish campaign workers appeared on the WPA payroll. Armed with federal relief programs, the Hub's New Deal political hierarchy weakened the ward bosses and made later machine building more difficult.[55]

The WPA, the Bosses, and Presidential Coalition Building

What explains this puzzling pattern of federal relief going to some of the Irish bosses and not to others? Early support for Roosevelt's presidential ambitions, normally thought to be a key factor in federal patronage allocations, does not explain the pattern. The Hague, O'Connell, and Cermak-Kelly-Nash organizations were not members of the FRBC Club; each had supported Smith in the 1932 Democratic contest. Yet all three pro-Smith machines subsequently took over the local WPA programs. In Boston, however, Mayor Curley had been a Roosevelt loyalist from the beginning. Yet Roosevelt deliberately rebuffed the Shamrock in his efforts to politicize the Bay State relief program.

Much of the answer to the WPA patronage puzzle lies in the dynamics of presidential electoral calculation. By the early 1930s Democratic presidential coalition building depended on winning the Solid South and big northern urban-industrial states—New York, New Jersey, Pennsylvania, Illinois, California, Ohio, Michigan, and Massachusetts. The South furnished 113 electoral college votes while the eight northern states totaled 212 votes. The regional combination provided a winning 325 electoral college votes, well over the magic number of 266.[56]

Yet the Democratic vote harvest in the big northern states was problematic in the early 1930s. Seven of the eight had gone Republican in the presidential elections of 1920 through 1928. Enamored with Smith, Massachusetts had strayed into the Democratic column in 1928. Roosevelt would have to redouble his efforts to woo the northern big-city voters.

Gavin Wright has found empirical support for the argument that FDR's electoral calculations influenced the allocation of WPA jobs. Wright argues that politically targeted New Deal spending could increase voters' personal income, enhancing the likelihood that those rewarded would support Roosevelt. A "rational" Roosevelt should have overallocated federal funding and WPA jobs to pivotal states, defined in terms of their electoral college vote, the uncertainty of the state's vote outcome, and the traditional closeness of the state's Democratic vote to 50 percent of the total. Wright finds these three electoral variables account for nearly 40 percent of the per capita allotment of WPA jobs among the states.[57]

Wright is correct in his conclusion that presidential politics influenced the WPA. But he has misspecified the political and policy processes involved. Regarding state WPA job quotas, there is little evidence of presidential political influence. State job quotas were a function of state relief caseloads. Each state's percentage of the national welfare caseload was multiplied by 3.5 million—the presumed maximum WPA employment—to arrive at its job quota. Big urban-industrial states like New York had the highest per capita WPA job allotments not because of their electoral clout but because of their massive welfare caseloads. Their large relief burdens, in turn, were a function of both the higher unemployment rates in the big cities (relative to elsewhere) and their more developed welfare systems.[58]

Presidential politics intruded *after* state job quotas were determined. The politicization of the WPA was not a public auction where presidential offers of WPA jobs purchased the individual votes of work relief recipients. WPA employment nationwide rarely exceeded 3 million, 4 percent of the country's registered voters in

1936. Most WPA workers were unskilled and unlikely to vote unless mobilized by local machines. A wholesale auction of work relief jobs had enormous political risks as well as a low payoff. Blatant program partisanship could backfire, alienating Congress and the public.

Partisan conversion of the WPA required discreet middlemen—the bosses. Work relief politics was a complicated intraparty bargaining process between FDR, Hopkins, and state and city bosses, not a crude auction with voters. In dealing with the bosses, Roosevelt's patronage policy was prospective, not retrospective. FDR rewarded those bosses and machines best able to enhance his reelection prospects. Because there were substantial costs to politicizing the WPA, FDR and Hopkins could only covertly reward a few bosses. They chose those bosses who could carry the crucial urban-industrial states.[59]

Big-city bosses could help carry their states for FDR in two ways—by the votes they controlled or by alliance with state bosses. The 1928 campaign had mobilized the big-city vote, changing the presidential political equation. Cities could now carry the state. By 1940 New York City's voters represented 51 percent of the Empire State's active voters. Chicago's voters constituted 45 percent of the Illinois electorate. In states where the city vote was smaller, FDR worked more directly with the state than with the city bosses. Urban machine alliances with the state boss or majority faction enhanced the chances of receiving federal relief.

Roosevelt had good reason to reward the city bosses. As Samuel Eldersveld has shown, the big-city vote determined Roosevelt's margin of victory, particularly in 1940 and 1944. In 1932, the nation's twelve largest cities supplied one-quarter of FDR's vote plurality. By 1944 the twelve cities supplied nearly two-thirds of Roosevelt's vote plurality. As for the electoral college vote, Eldersveld argues that Roosevelt would have lost the 1940 and 1944 elections without the votes supplied by the large cities. Roosevelt's 1940 landslide victory resulted in 449 electoral college votes. Had the twelve largest cities gone Republican, FDR would have lost with only 237 electoral votes, well below the minimum 266 needed to win. Without the cities in 1944, FDR's 432 electoral college votes would have been reduced to 239 votes.[60]

Given this electoral incentive, FDR allocated WPA patronage to

big-city bosses meeting the voting bloc or state party alliance criteria. The Kelly-Nash Chicago machine met the voting bloc crite-
rion. The Illinois Democratic party was deeply split between the
Chicago machine and Governor Horner, leader of the downstate
Democrats. FDR initially designated the Horner organization as
the state clearinghouse for federal patronage, remembering the
Chicago machine's opposition to his nomination. After Kelly-Nash
showed itself capable of mobilizing the Windy City's voters and
carrying the state for Roosevelt, the president gave the machine
complete control over the Cook County WPA program.

The Hague and Lawrence machines met the party alliance crite-
rion. Despite the fact that Jersey City represented only 10 percent
of the Garden State's voters, Hague became the chief dispenser of
federal patronage because he was the *state* boss. Pittsburgh's voters counted for even less, making up only 6 percent of the Keystone
State electorate. Yet the Lawrence machine received WPA patronage, in large part because of its initially close alliance with the state
Democratic boss, U.S. Senator Joseph Guffey.[61]

Tammany Hall and the Purple Shamrock flunked both patronage
tests. Though New York City's voters swayed the state, the weakened Wigwam could no longer deliver the big-city vote. Gotham's
vote could be delivered by independent progressives such as La
Guardia, particularly after the American Labor party was created
in 1936 to give the city's reform Democrats a ballot line for Roosevelt and the New Deal independent of the Tammany-controlled
Democratic line. Tammany also fell out of favor with the movers
and shakers in the state Democratic party—Governor Lehman,
U.S. Senator Robert Wagner, and Bronx boss Ed Flynn. With
powerful friends like these, Roosevelt could carry New York without the Tiger.

Boston's Curley also flunked both tests. The Purple Shamrock
could rally less than one-fifth of the state's voters. As for alliances,
the state Democratic party continued to be bitterly divided between a western Yankee and Boston Irish wing. Through the early
1930s the western wing was ascendant, sending David Walsh to the
U.S. Senate in 1927 and Joseph Ely to the governorship in 1930.
Without the western wing's active cooperation, Curley's weak
Boston organization could not deliver the state for Roosevelt. The
Bay State's 1932 Democratic primary demonstrated Curley's weak-

ness to FDR as the Walsh-Ely wing easily carried the primary for Smith. With neither faction able to single-handedly carry the state, the president decided to increase his leverage within a deeply divided party by using federal patronage—including the WPA—to build an independent Roosevelt wing. By the time Curley became governor, the die was already cast.[62]

Roosevelt's patronage treatment of the big-city Irish bosses demonstrated his reluctance to promote an ideological revolution within the Democratic party. Rather than a long-term strategy of turning the states into New Deal bastions, FDR was more interested in short-term electoral results. Far more than the Hudson separated Fiorello La Guardia and Frank Hague. Yet a self-interested Roosevelt could support both.[63]

For machines that successfully navigated the shoals of the Depression and New Deal, rough waters still lay ahead. The postwar era witnessed a new and enduring economic crisis—a structural decline in the economies of the aging northern cities, cutting sharply into the machine's resources. At the same time, the now prosperous white ethnics demanded a new menu of policies: low taxes and homeowner services. Migrating blacks and Hispanics, however, demanded the traditional fare of high taxes, patronage, and welfare services. To finesse contradictory voter demands with minimal resources, the postwar machines would enlist the services of the welfare state's permanent legacy.

Chapter Five

The Last Hurrah?
Machines in the Postwar Era,
1950–1985

The Twilight of Machines?

The Irish machines that marched out of the Great Depression and the New Deal were not the same ones that had marched in. Mighty Tammany was toppled, to be resurrected in weaker and temporary form after World War II. The Hague organization, the Tiger's Siamese twin across the Hudson, succumbed to the same diseases of reform fever, declining resources, and new ethnic insurgency. Only Albany's O'Connell organization smoothly navigated the fiscal crisis and accompanying party realignment. Yet the turbulent 1930s served as more than a graveyard for old-style urban politics. The New Deal also served as a maternity ward for a new breed of ethnically diverse and federally assisted machines in the Windy and Steel cities.

The postwar era, not the 1930s, represented the old-style party organization's Ice Age. The machine's traditional food supply of high taxes, patronage, and welfare services dwindled. The flight of industry and the middle class to the suburbs cut sharply into the tax base of the older Frostbelt cities. The introduction of big-city merit systems in the 1940s and 1950s cut further into the machine's patronage stock, strengthening bureaucracy at the expense of party. In the 1960s, new urban political actors—public sector unions and minorities—mounted a frontal assault on the remnants of the patronage system using the tools of collective bargaining and court-ordered affirmative action plans. By the 1970s, patronage could hardly serve as an instrument of reward and discipline for the party's cadre, let alone as an enticement to voters.

The machine's near-monopoly over welfare services to the urban working class collapsed in the face of competition from new providers—the federal government and labor unions. The New Deal's permanent legacy of social insurance and welfare programs such as Social Security, unemployment compensation, public housing, and Aid to Families with Dependent Children lay beyond the bosses' apparent reach. Guaranteeing union elections and collective bargaining, the Wagner Act underwrote labor's unionization of the big-city industrial labor force. In the competitive bidding wars with capital, labor offered prospective members job security and generous fringe benefits, particularly pensions and health insurance. Not to be outdone, corporations responded with their own lucrative benefit packages. The new social welfare triumvirate of labor, capital, and the federal government drove the big-city bosses with their Thanksgiving turkeys off the block.

Deprived of the leverage of patronage and welfare, machines sought new resources and allies. Growth became the new urban talisman as the machines enlisted business, labor, and the media to revitalize the aging Frostbelt cities. Lavish downtown redevelopment projects in Chicago, Pittsburgh, and Albany were designed to create new jobs and city revenue. Federal programs such as urban renewal, Community Development Block Grants, and Urban Development Action Grants financed the urban—and machine—renaissance. Yet intergovernmental economic aid created new political vulnerabilities. Growth required state enabling legislation and federal financial assistance. When state and national governments were captured in the 1950s by a resurgent GOP or reform Democrats, the big-city Democratic machines found their growth plans challenged.

The most serious dilemma of all for Irish machine builders was the changing character of the big-city electorate. The prewar machine's high-tax, job-creating, and welfare policies had attracted considerable ethnic working-class support. Wartime and postwar prosperity benefited the new ethnics, propelling large numbers into the property-owning middle class with less interest in high taxes and public jobs. Many of the white ethnics joined the suburban exodus. Those who remained in the cities demanded new machine policies: low property taxes and homeowner rather than welfare services, for example, street repairs, garbage collection, and the preservation of white neighborhoods and property values.

Postwar machines also faced the onslaught of a third wave of lower-class ethnic migrants to the cities. Southern blacks came to the northern cities in the largest domestic migration in history. They were soon joined by Hispanics migrating from Puerto Rico, Mexico, and Latin America. The newest migrants dramatically changed the machine cities. In Chicago, for example, blacks and Hispanics constituted 54 percent of the population in 1980, up from one-quarter in 1960. The new migrants demanded the machine's traditional benefits—patronage and welfare services. Without the services of the welfare state, the Irish machines lacked the resources to co-opt blacks and Hispanics and forestall demands for a greater sharing of the organization's lifeblood—power.

Nevertheless, the Chicago, Albany, and Pittsburgh machines showed remarkable resiliency in the face of declining resources and shifts in the big-city electorate. The Chicago and Albany machines reached their zenith in the 1960s—and survived in weakened form into the mid-1980s. The powerful Lawrence organization in Pittsburgh faltered in 1969 only because of a leadership vacuum caused by Lawrence's death and by the retirement of his designated successor, Irish Mayor Joseph Barr..

In a larger sense, though, the postwar era would prove to be an Indian summer for the aging Irish machines. The powerful Chicago machine, progressively weakened since mayor and party boss Richard Daley's death in 1976, lost the mayoral elections of 1979 and 1983. Long dormant in the Windy City's politics, blacks and Hispanics elected Harold Washington mayor in 1983. Retreating to the city council, machine regulars fought a stubborn rearguard action against Washington's rainbow coalition before finally succumbing. In upstate New York, the Albany machine survived Dan O'Connell's death in 1977 but faced a leadership vacuum following O'Connell successor Erastus Corning's death in 1983.

Winter came early for would-be machine builders in the other once-Irish cities. In New York and Jersey City, citywide machines reemerged under new ethnic ownership by the 1950s. Yet these "fourth-generation" machines were weak and porous, unable to crack the whip over an increasingly powerful array of interest groups. By the early 1960s these rebuilt municipal engines overheated as resources declined and as intergovernmental alliances frayed. The new machines also developed a crack in their electoral blocs. Democratic machines historically have depended on ethnic and working-class support. Yet in the 1960s antimachine insurgents were able to enlist blacks and Hispanics in their crusade. As their electoral warranties expired, the new machines fell to reformers.

In Boston, San Francisco, and Philadelphia, where Irish Democratic machines had not been built during the 1930s, the postwar resurgence in local Democratic fortunes produced middle-class reform politics rather than a new generation of machines. In these cities, durable reform coalitions organized around the popular issues of downtown redevelopment, low taxes, civil service reform, and improved municipal service delivery. Patronage eluded the grasp of would-be bosses in these cities as reform tipped the balance of power from party to bureaucracy. Kevin White in Boston and Frank Rizzo and William Green in Philadelphia tried their hands at machine building. All of them failed. None commanded the resources necessary to transform personal campaign organizations into durable party machines.

The postwar era also marked the Ice Age for Irish leadership of the dying big-city Democratic machines. Demographics finally did the Celtic bosses in. Forced to accept the Southern and Eastern Europeans as junior coalitional partners in the 1930s, the aging Irish chieftains staged a brilliant and ever-so-slow retreat into the machine's inner sanctum of patronage-dispensing and policy-making positions. Even there they were not safe from ethnic attack. A new rainbow coalition of blacks and Hispanics challenged white ethnic control of the machine's most coveted, scarcest, and zero-sum resource—power.

This chapter examines the fall, Indian summer, and winter of the big-city Democratic machines and their Irish leaders. We shall proceed seasonally. First, fall. What were the dimensions and causes of the postwar machine crisis of declining resources, unraveling intergovernmental alliances, and changing big-city voter demands? Second, Indian summer. How were the already consolidated Irish machines of Chicago, Albany, and Pittsburgh able to negotiate these changed and inhospitable conditions in the local political marketplace? The late nineteenth-century machine's conservative fiscal and patronage policies had fueled working-class insurgency. In the 1930s and 1940s the Southern and Eastern Europeans revolted against the financially pressed Tammany and Hague machines. In the postwar era, blacks and Hispanics would also demand the machine's traditional fare of patronage jobs and welfare services. Given new ethnic demands for material benefits in an era of declining machine resources, why were the revolts of minorities against the postwar machines so muted and late in coming?

Third, winter. If the entrenched machines found a niche in the barren postwar environment, why didn't a fourth generation of strong and durable machines emerge in the other once-Irish cities? New York and Jersey City both had robust traditions of political machines, for example, centralized party-based governance institutions, and of machine politics, that is, the trading in divisible material benefits.[1] Yet the final yield of the postwar era on both sides of the Hudson was machine politics at the ward or borough level rather than centralized citywide political machines. As for the other cities, Philadelphia had a strong tradition of GOP political machines while Boston and San Francisco traded in divisible benefits. Why did these three cities appear to embrace reform so suddenly and completely in the postwar era?

Finally, spring and the new big-city rainbow coalition. In the 1980s, blacks have infiltrated the walls of the once-Irish municipal Jericho, electing mayors in Chicago and Philadelphia and mounting a serious challenge to Irish rule in Boston. Taking their cue as much from Mayor Daley as from Jesse Jackson, big-city minority politicians such as Harold Washington have tried to build a new generation of black-led urban machines. Black would-be bosses seek to revitalize ward-based electoral systems as machine building blocks. Urban black politicians are also trying to forge cross-ethnic electoral coalitions with Hispanics and Asians. What is the future of political machines and machine politics in the hands of the new big-city minority politicians? Can machines be revitalized to serve the new minority poor, or have they suffered irreversible decline?

Fall: Dimensions of the Postwar Crisis

The Changing Urban Electorate

Two major changes in the big-city electorate threatened the postwar machines—the exodus of working-class white ethnics, the machine's traditional constituency, into the middle class and out of the city; and the massive influx of poor blacks and Hispanics. Machines had little control over these two shifts in the pool of big-city voters. Each had structural origins outside the city—in national and regional economies, in technology, and in federal policy. Yet machines had to respond as the electoral coalitions built in the 1930s and the policies that produced them unraveled.

White ethnics voted with their feet in record numbers in the postwar era. Between 1940 and 1980, 4 million whites, representing more than one-third of the white population, left the eight once-Irish cities for the suburbs and other regions. Many sirens lured them out of the big cities—the automobile, wartime and postwar prosperity, the decentralization of industry, and federal housing and highway policies.

The two-thirds of the white population that remained in these cities shared in postwar prosperity. Blue-collar workers became labor's new unionized aristocracy as collective bargaining agreements in the manufacturing sector guaranteed job security and rising wages. Other sectors of the growing central-city economy—business and financial services, government and nonprofit agencies—generated middle-class jobs for the machine's traditional ethnic constituents.[2]

As white ethnics moved into the middle class, they became homeowners, exchanging tenements in the inner wards for new homes in the outlying wards. Of the Irish machine cities, the process of embourgeoisement was more advanced in Albany with its 25,000 well-paid state employees. By 1940, 42 percent of the state capital's homes were owner-occupied. Postwar prosperity allowed other machine cities to catch up. In Chicago, 46 percent of whites owned their own homes in 1980, up from 30 percent in 1940. In the Steel City, 57 percent of the city's whites were property owners in 1980 compared with 39 percent in 1940.[3]

Rising homeownership rates affected the kinds of taxation and spending policies machines could pursue. Earlier machines had pursued expansionary fiscal policies with little fear of electoral reprisal. Working-class voters were renters, not homeowners; property tax hikes could be passed on to nonvoting absentee landlords. High taxes meant more public jobs, an important inducement to big-city voters.

The electoral risk of high-tax, job-creating policies ballooned during the prosperous 1950s. Middle-class homeowners no longer hungered for the old machine's working-class fare of patronage jobs and welfare services. The white ethnics now hankered for different machine policies—low property taxes, homeowner rather than welfare services, and the preservation of white neighborhoods and local institutions, particularly schools.

White taxpayer revolts were not the only electoral threat facing the postwar machines. The influx of blacks and Hispanics into northern cities represented a second major change in the urban electorate. Before World War II, black life had been rooted in tenant farming and sharecropping arrangements in the poorest southern states. After the war, its focus shifted northward and to the big cities. In the rural South, the mechanization of agriculture disrupted the tenant farming system, contributing to the massive exodus of blacks off the land. In the North, the wartime economy had created an unprecedented demand for labor. The postwar suburbanization of whites further encouraged rural southern blacks to move to the big cities.[4]

The black movement to the big cities was unprecedented in scale. Between 1940 and 1980, 5 million southern blacks packed their bags and moved north. Over 2.5 million of the migrants settled in the eight once-Irish cities. As minorities resettled and whites fled, the black share of these cities mushroomed from 8 percent of the population in 1940 to 30 percent in 1980.

Hispanics joined blacks in the northern cities, particularly in New York and Chicago. New York served as a magnet for Puerto Ricans and, more recently, for immigrants from Latin America. Chicago's diversified industrial base attracted Latinos from Mexico as well as Puerto Rico. By 1980, 1.4 million Hispanics resided in New York City, representing 20 percent of the city's population.

One-half million Latinos crowded into the Windy City, constituting 14 percent of the population.

Compared with white homeowners, poor blacks and Hispanics made different—and potentially conflicting—demands on the big-city machines. White homeowners demanded low taxes and limited public spending for homeowner services rather than patronage and welfare. Impoverished blacks and Hispanics, however, were renters who supported property tax increases to pay for needed city jobs and services. In the eight cities, fully three-quarters of blacks rented in 1980 compared with less than one-half of whites.

Big-city minorities particularly sought public jobs. The postwar suburbanization of private sector jobs contributed to chronically high unemployment rates for blacks. As industry decentralized, blacks were trapped by inner-city residential segregation and the consequent transportation costs imposed.[5] Public employment represented an attractive alternative. In the 1950s and 1960s government represented one of the fastest growing sectors of the central-city economy. City payrolls grew by 44 percent between 1947 and 1970 in the eight once-Irish cities. The heavily white-collar public sector offered higher wages, better fringe benefits, and greater job security than the private sector. Minorities had greater access to government jobs. The public sector pioneered antidiscrimination programs. As their voting strength grew, blacks and Hispanics could politically capture machine patronage.[6]

Minorities also demanded welfare services. Public housing represented a major demand—ironically created by the machine's own policies. Moving to the big cities, blacks confronted an acute housing shortage as machines such as the Daley organization collaborated with real-estate brokers to confine blacks to ghettos. The Chicago machine had a strong political incentive to maintain segregated housing patterns. By reinforcing racial residential patterns with housing, building code, and highway policies, the organization built electoral support in "protected" neighborhoods populated by white ethnics.[7]

Downtown urban renewal also contributed to the minority housing shortage. Machines collaborated with downtown businesses in slum clearance programs designed to revitalize the decaying central city. Uprooting thousands of blacks, urban renewal

TABLE 14. *The Third Wave Arrives: Ethnicity and Race in the Eight Cities, 1980*

	Total Population, 1980	First Wave, as Percentage of 1980 Population		Second Wave, as Percentage of 1980 Population		Third Wave, as Percentage of 1980 Population	
		Irish	Germans	Italians	Poles	Blacks	Hispanics
New York	7,071,639	9.2	6.4	14.2	4.8	25.2	19.9
Chicago	3,005,078	9.2	10.2	4.6	10.0	39.8	14.0
Philadelphia	1,688,210	18.1	13.2	11.4	5.9	37.8	3.8
San Francisco	678,974	12.7	11.0	6.2	1.9	12.7	12.2
Boston	562,994	26.8	5.3	12.3	3.1	22.4	6.4
Pittsburgh	423,938	19.3	24.8	11.6	9.9	24.0	0.7
Jersey City	223,532	15.2	7.1	13.8	8.9	27.7	18.8
Albany	101,727	26.0	15.7	14.8	7.0	16.1	2.0

Sources: U.S. Bureau of the Census, *1980 Census of Population*, vol. 1, ch. C (Washington, D.C.: Government Printing Office, 1983), Table 69; U.S. Bureau of the Census, *Statistical Abstract, 1981* (Washington, D.C.: Government Printing Office, 1981), no. 24, pp. 21–23.
Note: Self-reported ethnic ancestry.

programs substantially contributed to the inner-city housing short-age. As the northern ghettos filled, minorities pressured the big-city machines to build low-income public housing projects.

The dilemma of postwar machine coalition building involved the contradictory character of the demands of minorities and white ethnics. Poor blacks and Hispanics demanded large-scale and costly public investments in jobs and welfare services. Middle-class whites demanded low taxes, public spending for homeowner rather than welfare services, and the maintenance of white con-trol over local institutions such as neighborhood schools and the police.

The changing character of the postwar urban electorate threat-ened not only the longevity of existing machines but also the Irish claim to party leadership. The Irish machines built during the 1930s had integrated the Southern and Eastern Europeans into the party's governing circle and onto the public payroll. Irish accom-modation of the new ethnics, however, remained incomplete. Irish politicians in Chicago, Albany, and Pittsburgh monopolized key policy-making and patronage-dispensing positions well into the postwar era. As a consequence, tensions between Irish and non-Irish persisted. The Daley organization faced Polish insurgency in the early 1960s, and the O'Connell machine in Albany fought re-bellious Italians.

Ironically, white suburban flight may have preserved Irish con-trol over party and government as ethnic insurgents fled the city. In Chicago, the Irish held the mayor's office from 1933 to 1983 (with a three-year hiatus) and held between one-quarter and one-third of the seats on the city council into the 1970s. The Irish also retained effective control of the Cook County Democratic Central Commit-tee into the early 1980s. In Albany, the machine regularly nomi-nated a Protestant for mayor while the party organization and city council firmly remained in Irish hands.[8]

With the migration of blacks and Hispanics, however, Irish leadership both of the existing machines and of party-rebuilding efforts elsewhere rested on an ever-diminishing electoral base. Table 14 shows the ethnic composition in 1980 of the eight once-Irish cities. Residents of Irish ancestry averaged less than one-fifth of the cities' population compared with nearly one-third of Ital-ian, Jewish, and Polish background. Yet the day of ethnic political reckoning would ultimately come from the newest minorities. By 1980, blacks and Hispanics made up more than 40 percent of the population of these cities. Minority leaders joined the ethnic chorus demanding a greater sharing of power and patronage from the entrenched Irish party bosses.

Declining Resources

The postwar era depleted the machine's arsenal of resources to meet this rising chorus of new electoral demands. The stock of patronage jobs dwindled under the combined pressures of civil service reform, union and minority challenge, and a shrinking local revenue base. Where prewar bosses had easily circumvented weak and antiquated civil service protections, postwar bosses found that civil service now had teeth. In New York City, for example, La Guardia tightened the merit system and expanded it to include three-quarters of the city's payroll by the end of his fourth administration, up from 55 percent at his inauguration. The dilemma posed for Carmine De Sapio, Tammany's postwar rebuilder, was substantial. While the city's population had climbed by 11 percent between 1930 and 1960, the number of "exempts"—patronage jobs—had fallen by 22 percent.[9]

Aided by the courts, civil service reformers in other machine cities followed suit. In 1946, the Chicago machine was on the verge of collapse. Party chairman Pat Nash had died in 1943. Mayor Edward Kelly's reputation sagged as city services deteriorated and charges of cronyism in the school board and other agencies mounted. Jacob Arvey took over as party chairman, enlisted the ward bosses to persuade Kelly to retire, and nominated Irish businessman and reformer Martin Kennelly for mayor, outflanking the Republicans who were planning to nominate their own blue-ribbon candidate.

Once elected, "Fartin' Martin" (as Alderman "Paddy" Bauler called him) proved politically inept—except for civil service reform. Uninterested in politics, the reform mayor let the aldermen—the so-called grey wolves—run the city. Yet Kennelly launched an assault on the patronage system, the source of the ward bosses' power. From 1947 to 1955, Kennelly cut the number of patronage jobs held by machine stalwarts by 40 percent, from 30,000 to 18,000.[10]

Reform governors joined reform mayors in attacking the patronage system. In New York, Republican Governor Thomas E. Dewey attacked the O'Connell machine in 1943, extending the stringent state civil service system to include county employment. By the stroke of a pen and several court fights, the Albany machine's public patronage supply was reduced by one-quarter, from 4,300 to 3,100 jobs.[11]

In the 1960s the patronage system came under attack not from reformers but from the machine's nominal allies—unions and minorities. In Chicago, Mayor Richard J. Daley, elected in 1955 as party regulars dumped reformer Kennelly, opposed public employee unionization and collective bargaining as a threat to the patronage system. The Windy City had long been a strong labor town, and the Chicago Federation of Labor was influential in the Democratic machine. Needing organized labor's votes and financial support, the machine returned the favor with massive downtown public works projects, the prevailing wage for craft union members on the city payroll, an elaborate and cost-escalating building code, and the appointment of labor representatives on most of the city's boards and commissions.[12]

Public sector unions were another matter. In the mid-1960s the city's public servants began organizing, posing a direct threat to the machine's cadre of 20,000 political workers masquerading as civil servants. The teachers were the largest of the city employee groups and the first to organize. Because the teachers had been outside the machine's patronage system for thirty years, Daley relented and agreed to collective bargaining. Union recognition meant no loss of party workers.

But the spoils system enveloped most other city employees; here Daley drew the line. Despite the mayor's opposition, public union militancy mushroomed in Chicago in the 1970s. In the hands of militant leaders since 1972, the teachers' union served as the vanguard. Teachers were soon joined by militant transit workers and firefighters, all demanding collective bargaining rights—and an end to patronage.[13]

Albany experienced a similar bitter fight over municipal unionization despite the machine's good relations with the city's traditional labor unions—teamsters, construction workers, and laborers. In the early 1960s the machine had crushed efforts to unionize the police force. By the late 1960s, however, the fire-fighters were unionized, joined by police officers and municipal blue-collar workers in 1973.[14]

Minorities also launched an attack on the patronage system. In Chicago, blacks had served as Daley's margin of electoral victory in the crucial 1955 and 1963 municipal elections when the machine had faced strong challenges. Yet blacks got little in return. The party allocated patronage to ward leaders on the basis of the number of Democratic votes received. Black wards got few patronage jobs because of low voter turnout levels.[15]

Federal civil rights legislation gave minorities another tool besides the vote for claiming their fair share of public jobs from the machines—affirmative action. Title VII of the Civil Rights Act of 1964, prohibiting job discrimination on the basis of race or gender, was extended in 1972 to cover state and local government employment. Blacks in the Windy City quickly brought suit in federal court to end the long-standing discriminatory hiring and promotion practices of Daley's police and fire departments. After a bitter court fight and lengthy negotiations, the machine relented.[16]

Minorities found reform allies in their attack on Chicago's patronage system. In the early 1970s, reformers filed a class action suit in federal court against the machine's political sponsorship system for county jobs. Drawn from the court testimony of the machine's chief patronage job dispensers, Table 15 shows the magnitude of the spoils system in Cook County and Chicago city government in the mid-1970s. More than one-half of the nearly 40,000 city and county jobs were given to party stalwarts. The federal courts upheld the class action suit filed by independent candidates, taxpayers, and voters. The Chicago machine was enjoined from using partisan criteria in government job hiring and firing. More nails had been driven into the patronage coffin.[17]

By the 1970s the machine's patronage system was further buffeted by an eroding local revenue base, the product of population and capital flight. For the prewar machines, growth had been axiomatic. The population of the eight cities surveyed had increased by an average 22 percent per decade between 1900 and 1930, permitting machines to pursue expansionary fiscal policies. The Irish bosses had used the fiscal surplus to modestly redistribute resources from Yankee taxpayers to poor Irish payrollers.

TABLE 15. *"Civil Service" Chicago-Style:*
Public Employment and Machine Patronage, 1976

Public Employer	Total Full-Time Jobs	Percentage of Jobs Politically Sponsored[a]	Estimated Number of Patronage Jobs
City of Chicago	27,000[b]	50	13,500
Chicago Park District	3,869	50	1,935
President, Cook County Board	3,072	50	1,536
Clerk, county circuit court	1,700	75	1,275
Cook County clerk	264	75	198
Cook County sheriff	1,519[c]	—	1,188
Cook County recorder	303	75	228
Forest Preserve District	646	50	323
Cook County treasurer	210	75	158
Cook County assessor	390	50	195
Totals	38,973		21,546

Source: Shakman v. *the Democratic Organization of Cook County et al.,* no. 69 C
2145 (U.S. District Court for the Northern District of Illinois, Eastern Division), "Memorandum in Support of Plaintiffs' Motion for Partial Summary Judgment," p. 24.
[a] Based on court testimony of public officials.
[b] Excludes police and fire personnel.
[c] Excludes police and jail personnel.

In the postwar era urban growth was no longer automatic.
Bosses found their local revenue base shrinking as population and
industry fled from the cities. Aided and abetted by the automobile
and federal housing and highway policies, the suburban exodus of
big-city residents slowly accelerated. In the eight cities, the population dropped by an average 6 percent per decade between 1950
and 1970, the decline accelerating to 12 percent in the 1970s.

Industry followed. Corporate managers in manufacturing firms
chose new suburban branch locations or relocated existing central-
city plants in the suburbs rather than expanding antiquated and
congested big-city production facilities. Federal defense spending

fostered new industries such as aerospace and electronics, which built plants in suburban locations from the beginning.[18]

Population and capital flight significantly accelerated in the 1970s as foreign economic competition contributed to the de-industrialization of the Frostbelt cities. Chicago, for example, lost 10 percent of its population and 120,000 manufacturing jobs, representing more than one-tenth of all employment, during the decade. The Steel City, hard hit by Japanese steel imports and the slump in the American automobile industry, lost nearly 20 percent of its residents and employment during the traumatic 1970s.[19]

Machines desperately searched for additional revenue to cushion the blow of the fiscal crisis on the patronage system. Property taxes were exhausted. After twenty years of steady increase, intergovernmental assistance began declining in the late 1970s. Without new revenue, the party bosses had little choice but to pare the major budget outlay—the city payroll. In Chicago, municipal employment dropped from 45,000 in 1970 to 43,000 in 1980. In Albany, the city payroll declined from 3,300 in 1970 to 3,100 in 1980. In Pittsburgh, where reform Democrats filled the leadership vacuum created by Lawrence's death and Barr's retirement, independent Mayor Peter Flaherty embarked on a vigorous austerity program designed to remedy the city's finances and prevent the rebuilding of the Democratic machine. Between 1970 and 1977, Flaherty cut city employment by one-third, from 7,200 workers to 5,000.[20]

The postwar "patronage crisis" created severe organizational maintenance difficulties for the aging Irish machines. Fewer patronage jobs meant fewer controllable machine voters. Richard Daley, Dan O'Connell, and David Lawrence could not rely on the payroll vote as Charles Francis Murphy and Frank Hague had done so successfully in the 1920s. As the supply of patronage declined, machines would be forced to bring less precious metals to the electoral auction—municipal services and collective benefits. Fewer patronage jobs hampered the organization's ability to get out the vote by reducing the number of campaign workers. The political sponsorship system's decline also created severe morale problems within the party organization. Ambitious lower-level party functionaries now faced reduced career mobility opportunities.

Patronage had represented one element of the old machine's winning electoral formula; welfare services represented another.

With the coming of the New Deal, machines lost their franchise on social services to the urban working class. Federal social insurance and welfare programs distributed benefits to the categorically eligible, not the politically deserving. Welfare-state programs weakened the old-style urban party organizations to the extent the bosses could not convert collective benefits into divisible benefits for which working-class votes could be exchanged. As welfare participation rates for poor big-city black families skyrocketed in the 1960s, the bosses found themselves potentially deprived of control over the social services that had rewarded—and disciplined—previous generations of working-class ethnic voters.

The New Deal also strengthened organized labor as a rival provider of social services to the urban working class. The Wagner Act enabled labor to unionize much of the big-city manufacturing labor force. In the conservative political climate of the late 1940s, labor turned from new membership drives to the task of protecting and enlarging existing collective bargaining agreements. By the late 1940s, unions had won the battle to include fringe benefits such as health plans and pensions in labor contracts. Nonunion companies, in turn, were forced to respond with their own fringe benefit packages, reminiscent of the welfare capitalism of the 1920s. Unions, capital, and the federal government had ended the bosses' near monopoly control over social services to the urban working class.[21]

Machines were forced back on municipal service provision. Here too they began losing their grip. As Kenneth Mladenka argues, big-city bureaucracies such as street and sanitation departments competed with the machine as major actors in local service decisions. In Chicago, city agencies by the late 1960s actively intervened in answering citizen complaints, planning neighborhood service allocations on the basis of need, and reviewing compliance. Ward politicians were reduced to a service broker role, putting constituents in touch with the right public agency. In Daley's Chicago, bureaucratic routines rather than party vote-maximization imperatives appeared to shape municipal service delivery.[22]

Even the machine's ability to set local tax rates—of considerable importance to homeowners—was reduced as ever larger portions of the city budget became noncontrollable. By the 1960s, municipal unions and federal and state officials became major actors in the local budgetary process. Public employee unions wrested wage and salary decisions—the largest element of city budgets—from local elected officials. City workers secured automatic salary increases based on cost-of-living adjustments and comparable wage increases in the private sector. Federal and state regulatory mandates on local service delivery further reduced the budgetary authority of local elected officials. As a result, the city bosses watched helplessly as city budgets and local tax rates spiraled upward in the 1960s and 1970s. The bosses were quickly losing their grip over the major levers of urban power—jobs, services, and taxes.

Indian Summer: Machine Accommodation Strategies

Resources

How did machines respond to the tandem crises? In terms of resources, machines at first were slow to revise their winning ways. Chicago's Richard Daley, for example, came to power in the 1950s invoking the old formula of high taxes and ever more patronage. After defeating reform mayor Kennelly in the hotly contested 1955 Democratic primary, Daley tried to consolidate his power among the party rank and file by the traditional method of padding the city payroll. He was stymied, however, by state taxation powers and by the city council's control of the budget. Under the terms of the Illinois constitution, the state legislature, not the mayor or the city council, had the power to set municipal real-estate tax levies. Daley's first item of business was to secure an exemption for Chicago. His second item of business was to wrest budget-making power from the "grey wolves," the aldermen who had run the city during the Kennelly years. Here too he needed state assistance.

Like earlier generations of machine builders, Daley consolidated his power with intergovernmental alliances. Daley knew Springfield, having previously served as a state representative and a senator. His state connections paid off handsomely as the legislature and governor approved his plans for placing city taxation and budget-making powers in the mayor's office.[23]

Armed with new fiscal powers, Daley undid the civil service mischief of the Kennelly years but at the price of a taxpayers' revolt. Taxation and spending in the Windy City dramatically rose in the late 1950s and early 1960s as the new boss consolidated power.

Chicago's property tax rate rose faster than any other big city in the country. The number of city employees increased by one-third—to 40,000—during the mayor's first two terms as the machine padded the payroll with fresh patronage. The property tax rate ballooned further with revelations of a burglary ring in the police department. Daley appointed reformer O. W. Wilson as police superintendent with orders to clean house. Wilson did—for a price. The police budget skyrocketed from $75 million to $200 million.[24]

Daley invoked the machine's old spending formula, and it appeared to work until 1963. Angered by a 100 percent increase in taxes since 1955, white homeowners staged a major revolt against the machine. In the 1963 general election, Republican candidate Benjamin Adamowski charged that Daley had fattened the city payroll at the expense of homeowners. Heavily taxed property owners responded, particularly Polish-Americans also incensed by the failure of the Irish to share power. Adamowski won the middle-class ethnic wards on the North Side, receiving a majority of the white vote citywide. Daley narrowly defeated the Polish challenger only because of a massive black vote in machine-controlled South Side wards.[25]

A taxpayers' revolt also threatened the O'Connell machine in upstate New York. Between 1921 and 1969 the low-tax machine had routinely won city elections with between 70 and 86 percent of the vote. In 1972, however, the machine's high-debt policies and financial sleight of hand finally unraveled. A mounting city deficit forced O'Connell to increase real-estate taxes by 84 percent. Albany's Democratic taxpayers revolted. In the 1973 city election, protesting homeowners flocked to support Republican mayoral candidate Carl Touhy. Despite a sixteen-to-one Democratic voter registration edge, Touhy came within 3,500 votes of defeating eight-term Mayor Erastus Corning II.[26]

Tax revolts taught the modern Irish bosses the risks of too rapidly expanding the relative size of the public sector. As an alternative, bosses championed downtown redevelopment projects promoting the city's growth as a whole. In Chicago, the downtown area known as the Loop was stagnating by the early 1950s. Taking power, Daley launched an ambitious revitalization program using federal urban renewal funds, eminent domain, and zoning. Growth yielded political dividends as the machine fashioned a powerful coalition of developers, bankers, and unions.[27]

The other Irish bosses also embraced the talisman of growth. Pittsburgh was a decaying city in the mid-1940s, the downtown Golden Triangle in sharp decline. Party boss David Lawrence took office as mayor in 1946, pledging himself to carry out the Steel City's facelift. Wooing wealthy industrialists and financiers, his traditional Republican rivals, Lawrence launched the Pittsburgh Renaissance project. The Renaissance rebuilt downtown, cleared the slums, and attracted corporate headquarters. Tax revenues, falling in the early 1940s, rebounded. Between 1947 and 1955 property valuations rose from $961 million to $1.12 billion.[28]

Albany's downtown facelift would be public, not private, conducted under state Republican rather than local Democratic auspices. Embarrassed by the blighted neighborhoods adjoining the state capitol in the late 1950s, GOP Governor Nelson Rockefeller proposed and built the massive ten-year $2 billion Empire State Plaza government office complex. The plaza, popularly known as the South Mall, revitalized the city's decaying South End. Completed in the mid-1970s, the plaza launched Albany's urban renaissance as private investment and $27 million in federal housing money poured into the blighted South End.[29]

Downtown revitalization required federal and state assistance, creating new political dependencies and vulnerabilities for the Irish machines. In Chicago, Daley's Loop renewal program required a substantial infusion of federal financial assistance. The federal share of local capital outlays rose from 9 percent in 1955 to 32 percent in 1977. As federal financial involvement in local growth deepened, the Daley machine became prisoner to changing federal urban policy priorities. Welcoming the expansion of federal slum clearance to include commercial redevelopment and housing (1954), the machine later found itself saddled with the consolidation of federal urban renewal and social programs (1966); the merger of planning, housing, and physical development programs (1974); and the brokering of public and private sector investment funds for purposes of commercial development (1978).[30]

Downtown redevelopment also required state assistance, which was troubling to the Irish bosses when the GOP or reform Democrats controlled the statehouse. Republican William Stratton was governor of Illinois when Daley launched his ambitious revitalization program. When Daley later turned to the Crosstown Expressway project, he found reform Democrat and arch rival Dan Walker in the governor's chair. In Pittsburgh, David Lawrence needed a state legal package to restructure the city. The package included pollution control, waste disposal, highways, mass transit, parking, and new sources of revenue. Yet in the postwar era Pennsylvania had returned to its old Republican ways. The fate of the Pittsburgh Renaissance project would be in the hands of three successive state GOP administrations. In decaying Albany, the O'Connell machine faced a potentially hostile Governor Nelson Rockefeller and a resurgent Republican-Conservative party alliance in the late 1960s and early 1970s.

Irish bosses were able to make bipartisan redevelopment deals by enlisting powerful local Republican pro-growth interests—bankers, developers, and business owners. In the Windy City, the downtown GOP business establishment enthusiastically endorsed Daley's Loop renewal program, giving the mayor increased state political leverage. Led by the Mellon family, the Steel City's business and financial community was ready to remake the city with or without the Lawrence machine. Lawrence skillfully leveraged local business support to secure state approval of his rescue package.[31]

The O'Connell organization faced a different political threat posed by downtown renewal. Because Albany's facelift was at the behest of the state GOP, the machine had little need to curry favor with local business interests. Yet the 100 acres expropriated in 1962 for the South Mall project displaced the rooming-house population crucial to the machine's success. The machine could count one-fifth of its normal citywide vote among the 9,000 refugees. The project also cut into its revenue base as tenements and businesses were removed from the tax rolls, replaced by tax-exempt state property. Faced with this twin threat, the machine initially opposed the South Mall project.[32]

Notwithstanding these costs, the machine would eventually support the massive state office project in order to gain needed political influence with the powerful Republican governor. The billion-dollar project required unprecedented financing. Rockefeller knew that a statewide bond referendum of this magnitude benefiting only one locality would likely be defeated. The Albany Democrats came up with an innovative and politically shrewd alternative. Mayor Erastus Corning proposed that Albany County, not the state, sell the bonds to build the South Mall. The county would then lease the office complex to the state for ninety-nine years at rents high enough to retire the bonds and to make up for lost tax revenues. A desperate Rockefeller agreed.[33]

The O'Connell-Corning gamble paid off handsomely in 1971 when state Republicans and local reformers tried to pry the Albany school system, its $17 million annual budget, and 1,000 employees from machine control. The school board was appointed, and the mayor packed it with machine partisans. In 1971, the city's population officially fell below 115,000, the minimum population under state law for an appointed school board. Albany would have to have an elected board. Republicans wanted a high turnout general election in November for the school board when national and state political currents could neutralize machine strength. O'Connell and Corning wanted a low turnout election in May when their full weight could be brought to bear. The machine now used its control of county bonds for the South Mall project to pressure Rockefeller. The city quietly stalled construction by canceling the sale of $70 million in project bonds. Rockefeller got the message and introduced a bill mandating a May election—good machine weather.[34]

Downtown redevelopment projects helped machines manage the postwar fiscal crisis by creating jobs and shoring up the tax base. Yet the key *organizational* resource issue was dwindling patronage. Even though the payroll vote no longer carried elections, patronage remained an essential organizational commodity. Chicago's 3,500 precinct captains, for example, depended on public jobs. Precinct captains served as vote mobilizers on election day and as service brokers the rest of the year. The machine's lower-echelon functionaries had help. In the mid-1970s, there were 12,500 patronage precinct workers, an average of four workers for each of the city's 3,000 precincts. A $200 million precinct organization—at public expense—could yield substantial electoral results.[35]

Machines handled the patronage crisis in time-tested ways. In Chicago, Richard Daley evaded civil service regulations much as James Michael Curley had done in Boston three generations earlier. Entrance examinations were given infrequently and were deliberately made difficult so that only a few applicants could qualify for permanent positions. Pleading necessity, the machine would hire numerous temporaries—for the rest of their lives. As collective bargaining agreements and affirmative action plans cut deeply into the organization's stock of public sector jobs, Daley implemented a Chicago version of Charles Francis Murphy's "businessmen's plan." Regulated businesses such as utilities, bus companies, and racetracks added party workers to their rosters.[36] In Albany, Dan O'Connell also packaged patronage from a variety of sources— the city government, the school system, county-regulated nursing homes, and state government. Even Albany County, under state civil service since 1943, was not immune from the spoils system. The county's merit system compliance record was the worst in the state.[37]

White Ethnics

Dwindling patronage and loss of monopoly control over welfare services did not weaken the postwar machine's appeal to white ethnics. Middle-class whites no longer demanded machine-supplied patronage and social services. Instead, the ethnics demanded low taxes, homeowner services, and the preservation of white neighborhoods and schools.

The antimachine tax revolts of the 1960s and early 1970s taught the bosses a valuable lesson—the need to cater to the policy preferences of white homeowners. In Chicago, the Daley machine in the mid-1960s began shifting its policies and electoral base, replacing costly patronage and welfare services delivered to poor inner-city wards with efficient low-cost homeowner services delivered to outlying middle-class wards.[38]

Daley froze the property tax rate in 1970 to placate white homeowners. The machine diversified its local revenue portfolio to include taxes on vehicles and utilities. Yet the machine's primary fiscal strategy in the post–tax revolt era was intergovernmental. Daley used his power in state and national politics to generate new revenue. In the 1960s Daley placed Otto Kerner in the governor's chair. State financial aid to the city increased as did the city's share of the state sales tax. The machine's biggest revenue coup involved federal assistance. Between 1970 and 1978 public spending in Chicago doubled—to $10 billion—although the city budget rose by only 58 percent. By 1978 federal spending in Chicago was 430 percent greater than municipal outlays from local revenue sources, up from 250 percent in 1970.[39]

Machines catered to new service as well as tax demands. While bureaucracy competed with party in influencing postwar municipal service decisions, machine politicians demonstrated an uncanny ability to intervene on behalf of voters at all stages of the service delivery process. Machines were particularly interested in maintaining control over labor-intensive and discretionary homeowner services. In Chicago, the city's building and housing codes were among the strictest in the nation. In a study of property code enforcement in the Windy City, Bryan Jones has shown that the machine thoroughly controlled the policy-making process. Ward committeemen and precinct captains stimulated citizen service demands, invoked special attention rules for particular neighborhoods, and actively intervened in the compliance process. The machine also practiced the politics of code nonenforcement, holding a powerful club over recalcitrant property owners.[40]

More generally, Daley instructed his ward bosses to act as service brokers, expediting housekeeping services such as street and sidewalk repairs, tree trimming, and garbage removal. Improved neighborhood services contributed to growing white homeowner support for the machine. As John Petrocik has shown in his study of the 1975 Chicago mayoral election, machine-provided services to white ethnics accounted for nearly one-third of Daley's overall vote plurality. For white homeowners, Chicago was "the city that works."[41]

At the same time, Daley deliberately increased the power of bureaucrats over the delivery of municipal services, particularly capital-intensive and immobile projects such as parks, schools, police, and fire stations. The mayor worked tirelessly to professionalize the upper echelons of the local public sector. His talent scouts conducted nationwide personnel searches to discover top-notch professionals needed to run the agencies responsible for delivering basic public services.[42]

There were good political reasons for bureaucratizing municipal services. Quality services bought votes, as Daley discovered in 1975. Daley also remembered his early battle with the "grey wolves." Administrators were hired by the mayor and responsible to him, not to the aldermen. Daley could both raise the level of public services, popular with voters, and weaken the power of the ward politicians. Thus service equalization and enhanced bureaucratic discretion contained a political logic, maximizing the organization's vote potential *and* the mayor's power.

To maintain his power, the mayor adroitly played the ward politicians off against the professional bureaucrats. Daley deployed his army of temporary employees in city agencies providing homeowner services. The mayor carefully ladled this service-relevant patronage to the ward leaders, rewarding them for faithful party service while enhancing their ability to serve their constituents. These boss-controlled lower-level party-bureaucratic networks represented a check on top-level bureaucrats. As Milton Rakove has observed, Daley expected his administrators "to recognize political realities in Chicago and be sensitive to the built-in relationships among city agencies, the ward organizations, and voters." [43] In Chicago, the party ruled the bureaucracy, and the mayor ruled the party.

Middle-class whites demanded that machines supply more than low taxes and homeowner services. As the northern cities filled with blacks and Hispanics, whites also demanded the preservation of white neighborhoods and continued control over such "culture-transmitting" institutions as the schools. White hegemony, not divisible benefits, increasingly served as the machine's chief attraction for the ethnic middle class. [44]

In Chicago, housing and the schools served as the twin litmus tests for white voters. The Chicago Housing Authority represented a key machine mechanism for maintaining racial residential segregation—and the white vote. The Housing Authority practiced racial discrimination in both public housing site selection and tenant assignment. In particular, the agency had to choose whether to build low-density public housing on vacant land in white neighborhoods or high-density projects on cleared slum sites. The extension of heavily black housing projects into white neighborhoods threatened the machine's traditional ethnic constituency. As the white ward bosses rose in opposition to scattered-site projects, the agency turned to building inner-city high-rise projects. Segregated public housing projects were not the only weapons the machine used to maintain white neighborhoods. Freeway routes also served as racial barriers, as did the issuance of real-estate licenses to discriminating realtors. The Albany machine practiced similar racial containment policies, confining the city's 15,000 blacks to the South End and Arbor Hill ghettos.[45]

Segregated and poorly funded public schools represented a second element in the machine's bargaining agreement with white voters. The Irish bosses had never understood the public schools except as a source of patronage. Educated in parochial schools, the bosses deliberately underfunded the public schools to make the church's educational system more attractive—and to keep the property tax rate down. In Chicago, 40 percent of the city's tax dollar went for public education compared with an average 70 percent in the surrounding suburbs. The city's meager education funds hired patronage janitors rather than teachers. Blacks and Hispanics, then, were forced to fight a two-sided battle. Minorities demanded both integrated schools and a substantial increase in public funding.[46]

Machines had to resist minority demands in order to maintain white ethnic support and staunch the exodus to the suburbs. In Chicago, school superintendent Benjamin Willis failed to integrate the city's schools or equalize resources between predominately white and black schools. Racial conflict soon spilled over into the machine's appointments to the Board of Education. In Albany, where one-half of all students were enrolled in Catholic parochial schools, the O'Connell organization refused to spend more on public schools or desegregate the school system. The machine's educational policies won the endorsement of Irish, Italian, and Polish middle-class voters—and the powerful Catholic church.[47]

The machine's defense of white racial interests solved one organizational maintenance problem while creating another. Concerning Chicago, Paul Kleppner argues that a new type of exchange relationship had developed between the machine and white voters by the 1960s. Traditional material benefits—patronage jobs and welfare services—no longer bound whites to the machine. The postwar machines had fewer benefits to offer, and middle-class whites had less need to accept. The new transactions involved power and race. Machines guaranteed the preservation of white neighborhoods, schools, and other culture-transmitting institutions for a small price—the ballot.[48]

But the machine's new policy algorithm had a major down-side risk—the minority vote. Machines could concede little to blacks on housing and schools because whites perceived these issues as zero-sum. Black gains in integrated housing or school busing equaled white losses. As minorities tipped the city's population, machines had to come to a biracial accommodation. If housing and schools were declared off-limits to blacks, machines would have to offer instead the traditional menu of patronage jobs and social services to prevent minority insurgency. With patronage dwindling and welfare preempted, machines were in a quandary.

Minorities

Before the mid-1960s shift in policies and electoral base, Irish machines had avidly courted the minority vote. In Chicago and Pittsburgh, black sub-machines were created in the late 1930s and early 1940s. In Chicago, Congressman William Dawson, the only black in the Daley machine's inner circle, ran the massive South Side ghetto. Blacks on the South Side and on the racially changing West Side supplied the margin of victory in three of Mayor Daley's six victorious campaigns between 1955 and 1976. In the 1955 general election, for example, Daley defeated Republican Robert Merriam by 127,000 votes, receiving a 125,000 vote plurality in heavily black machine-controlled wards. Despite their electoral fealty, minorities received few material rewards from the Daley organization. Rather than giving Dawson significant power or patronage, Daley rewarded him with "policy," that is, control of the numbers racket. Blacks made up 40 percent of Chicago's population in 1970, but only 20 percent of the municipal workforce, largely in menial positions.[49]

In Pittsburgh, state representative Homer Brown ran the Lawrence organization's black sub-machine. Brown did yeoman service for Lawrence. Not only did Brown dependably supply the black vote; he also served as the key leader shepherding the Pittsburgh Renaissance project through the Pennsylvania House of Representatives. A grateful Lawrence bestowed real "policy" on Brown. The Steel City's boss pushed through a fair employment practices ordinance and appointed minorities to top-level jobs in his administration.[50]

Minority demands on the big-city party organizations escalated during the turbulent 1960s. In Chicago, the black movement started growing in the early 1960s, led by Saul Alinsky's Woodlawn organization seeking better schools. In 1966 Martin Luther King, Jr., took the civil rights movement north to Chicago, demanding an end to segregated housing and discrimination in employment. As King marched through Chicago's white suburbs, racial tension increased. Riots rocked the Windy City in 1966 in the Lawndale ghetto and in 1968 in the West Side ghetto. In Albany, black neighborhood groups such as Better Homes and activist groups such as the Brothers pressured the O'Connell machine for public housing, control of federal antipoverty funds, and an end to urban renewal.[51]

Machines like the Daley organization judiciously used welfare-state programs to control the minority vote and to siphon off discontent at minimal cost to the city treasury and to tax-conscious white homeowners. Both New Deal and Great Society social programs were used for these purposes. Public housing and Aid to Families with Dependent Children (AFDC) represented the two major New Deal programs that machines used to placate blacks.

Migrating blacks confronted an acute housing shortage as the northern machines collaborated with real-estate brokers to confine blacks to crowded inner-city ghettos. By uprooting thousands of blacks, urban renewal programs contributed substantially to the inner-city housing shortage. As the northern ghettos filled in the postwar era, the big-city machines lobbied for federal housing money to build low-income public housing projects. Segregated federal housing projects not only soothed the fears of white ethnics; they also served to concentrate the black vote and make it more controllable.[52]

The postwar suburbanization of private sector jobs and industry had contributed to chronically high unemployment rates for urban blacks. Rather than grant more substantial policy and municipal employment concessions to the restive black community (which would anger the machine's white ethnic constituency), machines chose welfare as a politically cheaper response. As Frances Fox Piven and Richard A. Cloward have argued, welfare limited the scope of urban racial conflict because existing white political prerogatives were not challenged.[53]

Machines exerted little control over determining AFDC eligibility. Yet there were ways of politicizing this collective benefit program. So that it could claim credit for increasing welfare benefit levels, the Chicago machine instructed its state legislative and congressional delegations to vote for welfare liberalization measures. At the local level, Chicago's precinct captains set up welfare information bureaus in public housing projects to put prospective welfare clients in contact with the appropriate social agency. Even though the Windy City's machine politicians did not control program eligibility, they threatened welfare recipients with loss of public assistance should they vote for the machine's opponents. Under machine auspices, the welfare participation rate for black families in Chicago rose from 18 percent in 1969 to 32 percent in 1979.[54]

Machines also commandeered Great Society programs to stabilize and build political support in the black community, particularly among the emerging middle class. While the federal antipoverty programs of the 1960s such as Community Action, Job Corps, and Model Cities ostensibly were targeted at the poor, they created considerable employment for human service providers. The $2.7 billion annual federal spending for Title I of the Elementary and Secondary Education Act, for example, created 275,000 teaching and administrative positions. Nationwide, Great Society programs generated 2 million new human services jobs, primarily in local government and in nonprofit community-based organizations.[55]

The big-city bosses had strong political incentive to use federally funded human services employment to respond to growing black demands. As with welfare, federally subsidized social employment limited the scope of interracial conflict. By channeling blacks into jobs in expanding social service agencies, machine politicians minimized conflict with whites in traditional city agencies such as police and fire departments. Social welfare employment also represented one of the most tangible and effective ways the bosses could respond to the threat of urban disorder. In Chicago, 54 percent of the black job gains between 1960 and 1980 occurred in social welfare agencies. By 1980, one-third of the Windy City's blacks and nearly 60 percent of the black middle class worked in human services and government.[56]

Welfare-state programs stabilized the big-city machines by creating a large-scale social welfare economy—of middle-class service providers and lower-class recipients—in the black community. As long as social programs grew, the welfare state represented a potent partisan tool. Machine politicians carefully ensured that the party organization and not the black community controlled local antipoverty agencies. Mayor Daley successfully resisted black political demands for control of the Community Action Program by demonstrating the machine's importance in Democratic presidential politics. In 1964, Daley delivered Chicago for Lyndon Johnson by a record 675,000 votes in order to highlight the president's dependence on the machine. The lesson was not lost on federal antipoverty director Sargent Shriver, who wanted to be governor of Illinois. The president and his antipoverty chieftain sued for peace. By this show of electoral clout, reminiscent of the Kelly-Nash machine's mobilization of Chicago voters in the mid-1930s to capture control of the local WPA program, Daley received $140 million in federal antipoverty funds.[57]

In Chicago, the machine used the welfare state to dismantle and control the black vote. By the late 1960s the Daley organization had developed a new formula for success: Mobilize the white ethnic vote, particularly in wards undergoing racial transition. The large black vote of 1963 was no longer needed for victory. In fact, the black vote now loomed as a risk, particularly if black independents could capture it and challenge the machine. The machine employed a series of strategies to dilute the now superfluous minority vote. Wards on the South Side were racially gerrymandered. When black sub-lieutenant William Dawson died in 1970, the machine groomed no replacement.[58]

Above all, the machine relied on the expanding welfare state to demobilize the black vote. Minority social service providers involved themselves in intergovernmental bureaucratic politics—the grants economy—rather than in community electoral politics. The expansion of means-tested antipoverty programs such as AFDC depoliticized welfare recipients by isolating them from the work experiences encouraging political participation. Federal social programs thus represented a potent machine tool for co-opting the black middle class and depoliticizing the underclass. As the welfare state penetrated the black community, voter participation rates declined sharply. In Chicago, the black turnout rate dropped from 60 percent to 37 percent between 1964 and 1976.[59]

The welfare state even captured the residual black vote. In the Windy City, public housing projects represented the most tightly controlled precincts in the inner city. As Don Rose, one of the city's leading political strategists, observed of the welfare-state "plantation provinces," "the Organization owns a lock on a solid 20 percent of the black vote. This is the vote the Machine would deliver for a George Wallace against Martin Luther King."[60]

Not all machines needed the black vote or the welfare state. Unlike Chicago, the minority vote loomed small in Albany. As Table 14 shows, in 1980 blacks and Hispanics constituted only 18 percent of Albany's population compared with 54 percent of Chicago's. Pursuing low-tax and homeowner-service policies from the 1920s onward, the O'Connell organization did not face white ethnic insurgency until 1973—after the turmoil of the 1960s. Not needing the black vote, the machine mounted no voter registration drives in the South End and Arbor Hill ghettos.

Uncle Dan did not suffer when he failed to capture the War on Poverty. In Albany, antipoverty funds initially flowed into the Trinity Institution, a South End Episcopal Settlement House, not into the machine's coffers. Unlike the Daley organization, the O'Connell machine could not deliver the New York state vote for Democratic presidential candidates. To cripple the community-controlled antipoverty program, the machine withdrew the city's subsidy to the Trinity Institution. As a result, Albany was the last major city in the country to launch an antipoverty program. As minority unrest grew in the South End ghetto, the machine skillfully deployed Albany County's Human Resources Department. The department gave out 15,000 jobs over ten years, building a solid base among the city's poor and minorities. The department deliberately chose manpower training and jobs over cash transfers. During the 1970s, the welfare participation rate for the city's black families remained at 24 percent.[61]

For heavy users of the welfare state such as the Chicago machine, federal programs bought the organization a twenty-year lease on life by rewarding and co-opting blacks. The Daley organization had constructed a winning electoral coalition of white ethnics in the late 1960s with low taxes, homeowner services, and white hegemony. The transformed machine required minority acquiescence. Yet the systematic demobilization of the black vote contained a hitch. Up to 60 percent of the city's registered voters didn't vote in local elections—reminiscent of Tammany Hall in the 1920s.[62] Black quiescence required the services of a growing welfare state. Welfare-state contraction, however, could destabilize machines by encouraging the threatened black middle class to register and mobilize the votes of the underclass. The Chicago machine would learn of the dangers of welfare-state dependence in the early 1980s. Light users of the welfare state such as the O'Connell organization, in contrast, could more easily weather social program retrenchment.

Winter: Failures of Machine Building

The entrenched Irish machines of Chicago, Albany, and Pittsburgh adapted to the postwar market conditions of lessened resources and changing voter demands. Would-be bosses in the other once-Irish cities were not so lucky. Weakened machines reemerged in New York and Jersey City in the 1950s, only to collapse in the 1960s and early 1970s. These pluralist regimes, as Martin Shefter has termed them, never managed to get their acts together.[63] Pale imitations of the Murphy and Hague organizations, the postwar successors were weaker and more porous, forced to bargain with a powerful array of new interest groups and independent power centers.

In Boston and Philadelphia, where Irish Democratic machines had never been built, Democratic mayors tried their hand at machine building in the late 1960s and early 1970s. But the mayors succeeded only in creating personal campaign organizations, not long-lived party-based institutions. When they left office, their personal followings disintegrated.

What accounts for the postwar experience of these ersatz machines, weaker forms of the classic Irish big-city organizations? Why couldn't machine builders in these cities imitate Chicago's Daley, delivering low taxes, efficient services, and racially segregated neighborhoods and schools to white ethnic homeowners and the welfare state to minorities?

Weakened Machines

In New York City, Carmine De Sapio slowly resurrected an Italian-run "New Tammany" after World War II. During the La Guardia years, Tammany had been badly wounded by civil service reform. Not only did the Little Flower blanket city employment with a strengthened merit system; he also succeeded in eradicating the patronage system in county government, the last bastion of the Wigwam's strength. Stripped of patronage and revenue, Tammany's aging Irish chieftains were forced to sell the organization's clubhouse and sue for peace with the new ethnics. The Southern and Eastern Europeans demanded surrender. The Italian-controlled underworld threw out Christy Sullivan, the last of the Irish Tammany bosses, in 1943 after Sullivan nominated an antiracket reformer to be district attorney. Completing the Italian putsch, De Sapio took over leadership of Tammany Hall in 1949.

De Sapio's leadership did not extend to city government until 1953. In 1945, La Guardia retired and independent Democrat William O'Dwyer was elected. Though O'Dwyer initially gave Tammany some patronage, he demonstrated his independence by dispensing top appointments to the other county party leaders, all resentful of the Manhattan-based Tammany. De Sapio was further thwarted in 1950 when O'Dwyer unexpectedly resigned to become ambassador to Mexico. In the ensuing special election, De Sapio's candidate, Ferdinand Pecora, was defeated by independent Vincent Impelliteri, endorsed by underworld leader Frank Luchese.

De Sapio finally consolidated power in 1953 as the Wigwam's candidates for mayor and governor—Robert F. Wagner, Jr., and Averill Harriman—both won. De Sapio employed both patronage and policy to rebuild Tammany. Municipal employment rose by nearly one-third between 1949 and 1957, from 199,000 to 262,000, as Tammany recaptured badly needed patronage. The refurbished Tiger embraced such popular reforms as public housing, rent control, civil rights, and even permanent voter registration. With Governor Harriman beholden, De Sapio reached the zenith of his power between 1955 and 1958.[64]

Yet Italian machine-rebuilding efforts failed in New York. Despite Tammany's metamorphosis from patronage to policy, the

city's Jews remained firmly in the ranks of the reformers, organizing anti-Tammany political clubs throughout Manhattan in order
to infiltrate and capture the party bureaucracy. Loss of state and
federal patronage in the late 1950s and early 1960s seriously hampered Tammany's ability to fight the reformers. As Tammany weakened, Mayor Wagner severed his connection with De Sapio and
joined the insurgents. In the crucial 1961 mayoral election, the reformers under the leadership of a born-again Bob Wagner defeated
Tammany by capturing the non-Irish and non-Italian vote—Jews,
Yankees, Puerto Ricans, and blacks. Tammany would not be resurrected as control of the city's politics passed to reformers such as
John V. Lindsay and Ed Koch.[65]

Across the Hudson, insurgent leader John V. Kenney tried to
construct a successor organization to the Hague machine in the
1950s. Like De Sapio, Kenney pursued expansionary policies to
augment his fledgling organization's stock of resources. Between
1949 and 1957, Jersey City employment rose by one-fifth, from
6,900 to 8,300. As in Chicago, Kenney's fiscal policies backfired as
local property taxes ballooned, arousing the opposition of ethnic
homeowners. Kenney's ticket lost to a dissident Polish and Italian
faction in 1957.

Despite his return in 1961, Kenney never fully consolidated
power. After a brief fling with fiscal austerity, designed to soothe
taxpayers' nerves, the would-be boss jacked up the property tax
rate by 30 percent to enrich the party coffers—and the pockets of
his henchmen. High taxes were the price white homeowners were
willing to pay in the 1960s for the preservation of racial hegemony.
By the 1960s blacks and Hispanics represented more than one-
third of Jersey City's population. As minority unrest grew, law-
and-order Mayor Thomas J. Whelan ordered police shotgun pa-
trols in the ghetto. White homeowners were temporarily lulled.
With another record tax increase in 1970, however, Kenney's days
were numbered. As homeowners mobilized to overthrow the boss,
the federal government intervened. Kenney and eleven other Jersey
City politicians were indicted and convicted in federal court on
charges of receiving $3.5 million in kickbacks on construction
contracts. Thereafter, reformers Paul Jordan and Thomas F. X.
Smith would rule the land of Hague.[66]

What accounts for the reemergence and decline of postwar machines in New York and New Jersey? Like Daley, De Sapio and Kenney initially employed the same building blocks used by earlier generations of machine builders: intergovernmental political alliances and expanding resources. In New York, De Sapio's relationship with Governor Harriman paid off handsomely with state patronage and financial assistance. Both De Sapio and Kenney expanded the local public sector in order to create patronage for their followers and improve the delivery of municipal services to voters.

These strategies worked for a time. But a crucial difference separated New York and Jersey City from Chicago and Albany. In the latter cities, machines maintained a continuous grip on the levers of urban power, forcing interest groups both to moderate their demands and to channel them through the dominant party organization. In the former cities, machines had lost to reformers, opening up a Pandora's box of escalating group demands eluding machine recapture.

In New York, independent centers of power had grown during Tammany's twelve-year hiatus—the outer borough party organizations, special districts such as the Triborough Authority, labor unions, and, above all, a powerful reform movement. Reformers had left the Tammany-run Democratic party in the 1930s and early 1940s, channeling their energies into the American Labor party and the La Guardia administration. With La Guardia's retirement and the splintering of the ALP, many returned home. Tammany's metamorphosis in the 1950s from divisible benefits to collective goods was a tribute to the power of the reformers.[67]

As group demands exploded, would-be bosses required an extra infusion of resources. Intergovernmental alliances were particularly critical for the postwar machines. Yet vertical alliances created new political vulnerabilities as well as opportunities. In New York, De Sapio's star rose with Democratic Governor Harriman and set with Republican Nelson Rockefeller. De Sapio had used his alliance with Harriman to contain the party's reform faction, which was intent on organizing anti-Tammany clubs throughout Manhattan. In 1958 Rockefeller beat Harriman. The loss of state patronage hampered Tammany's ability to fight the reformers and heightened the importance of federal patronage as the 1960 election loomed. Wanting to be a presidential kingmaker, De Sapio committed a fatal error by maintaining his independence from the Kennedy organization until it was too late. The newly elected Irish-American president never forgot, deliberately depriving De Sapio of federal patronage. The Tiger's loss of state and federal aid emboldened local reformers. As Tammany weakened, Mayor Wagner severed his Tammany connection, realigning himself in the crucial 1961 city election with the party reformers led by ex-Governor Herbert Lehman and Eleanor Roosevelt.[68]

In Jersey City, Kenney's intergovernmental downfall was more ignominious. As the city's property tax rate soared in the 1960s to pay for machine building, Kenney turned to federal assistance. Federal grants and contracts eased pressure on local taxpayers, revitalized the decaying downtown area, rewarded the city's minorities, and enriched Kenney and his henchmen. The last purpose was impermissible. In 1970 the Nixon administration began investigating the awarding of federal construction contracts in Jersey City. A year later a federal grand jury indicted the machine's top leadership for its kickback scheme on federal projects.

True to form, new machines were more sensitive to external interventions than old machines. Yet there were higher start-up and maintenance costs for *all* machines in the Frostbelt cities in the postwar era, requiring larger dosages of external assistance. Postwar machines had to perform what James O'Connor has termed the capital accumulation and legitimation functions on an unprecedented scale.[69] Ambitious downtown revitalization projects were launched. Human service jobs and cash transfers flowed into the ghetto. With local revenue sources exhausted, the bosses tapped—and were trapped by—the intergovernmental system.

De Sapio and Kenney failed with intergovernmental alliances. Daley, Lawrence, and O'Connell succeeded. Faced with potentially hostile state and national Republican administrations in the 1950s, Daley and Lawrence fashioned local bipartisan growth coalitions to augment their intergovernmental leverage. With Democratic ascendancy in the 1960s, the two bosses took over their respective states. In Illinois, Daley put protégé Otto Kerner in the governor's chair and demonstrated his electoral indispensability to Presidents Kennedy and Johnson. In Pennsylvania, Lawrence himself moved from the mayor's office to the governor's office in 1959 and designated Irishman Joseph Barr his successor.[70]

In New York, Democratic state ascendancy came in the 1970s.

As the landlord of the Empire State Plaza project, Dan O'Connell had extracted crucial policy concessions from Governor Rockefeller. After its close escape in the 1973 city election, the Albany machine strengthened itself by actively supporting Democrat Hugh Carey for governor. Once elected, a grateful Carey diverted state patronage to the O'Connell organization. After Uncle Dan's death, successor Erastus Corning also dabbled in state politics. Corning was the first major upstate Democratic politician to support Mario Cuomo's candidacy for governor.[71]

Intergovernmental assistance allowed the strong Chicago, Pittsburgh, and Albany machines to contain their Republican and reform opponents. In strong machine cities, there was little resembling New York City's postwar machine/reform dialectic.[72] In weakened machine cities, the character of the dialectic underwent a significant transformation with the passing of citywide machines. In New York City, Tammany Hall's passing did not mean an end to political machines. No longer welcome at city hall, Democratic machines still resided at the sub-city level.

Gotham's powerful Democratic county organizations paid their last respects—and little more—to the deceased. The outer borough machines had grown in strength and organization to match their mushrooming populations. Tammany's Charles Francis Murphy had launched Ed Flynn's career as boss of the Bronx organization in 1922. Thereafter, the satellite Bronx, Brooklyn, and Queens organizations would slowly gravitate out of Tammany's orbit. Into the 1980s, the borough machines and local party organizations such as the Jefferson Democratic Club in racially embattled Canarsie would employ traditional material resources to keep their ethnic constituents in line in local races.[73]

With the demise of citywide machines, reform also underwent a transformation. In New York, Mayor Lindsay donned reformer Wagner's electoral mantle, fashioning a coalition of liberals—both WASP and Jewish—and minorities. The Wagner-Lindsay reform coalition collapsed in the early 1970s as white ethnic homeowners in the outer boroughs rebelled. Democratic Mayor Abe Beame, Lindsay's successor, proved to be no East Coast Richard Daley. Beame failed to refurbish the Democratic machine as a political home for the city's conservative-leaning white ethnic property owners.

As a result, a new type of reform—the personalized leadership of antimachine Mayor Ed Koch—became the dominant vehicle for protecting white hegemony and for expediting neighborhood services. Instead of consolidating a new citywide organization, Koch ultimately made his peace with borough power brokers in the Bronx, Brooklyn, and Queens. The price he paid became clear only after his 1981 and 1985 reelections when the scent of scandal involving these surviving county Democratic machines tainted the mayor.[74]

In New York, then, the postwar reform cycle began with a liberal cross-class Jewish-minority alliance against the machine Irish and Italians. It ended with a middle-class Jewish-Irish-Italian alliance against lower-class blacks and Hispanics presided over by a neoconservative Jew, the beau ideal of the grandchildren of the new immigrants.

Personal Organizations

In Boston, Philadelphia, and San Francisco, the postwar era would be fertile soil for the Democratic party but barren ground for machine building. The New Deal helped shape both outcomes. Where there was no preexisting machine useful to Roosevelt's reelection plans, the president could strengthen the reform wing of a revitalized local Democratic party. In Boston, FDR's patronage policies increased the influence of the anti-Curley reform forces in the faction-ridden party. In Philadelphia, the pre–New Deal Democratic ward politicians had served at the pleasure of the GOP machine. As Democratic fortunes waxed in the 1930s, Roosevelt spurned the kept ward bosses, directing federal patronage to the Democratic Warriors Club led by reformers Joseph Clark, Jr., and Richardson Dilworth.[75]

The fruit of New Deal reform would ripen slowly. In Boston, reformers suffered an apparent setback in 1946 when James Michael Curley was reelected mayor while serving time in federal prison for influence peddling. The Purple Shamrock's resurrection was short-lived as the anti-Curley forces in the city—the business community and homeowners, Yankees, Jews, and middle-class Irish and Italians—coalesced into a broad-based bipartisan reform coalition.

Representing producer interests, the reformers denounced the legacy of Curleyism—high taxes, corruption, and a depressed business climate. Failing to build a centralized political machine, the Shamrock and his allies had constructed an urban welfare state instead. In 1950, the Hub had the highest per capita expenditures in the country for welfare, health, and hospitals. Fifty-five thousand people (one out of every fourteen residents) lived in public housing, the highest proportion for any large city. The local welfare state extended to the police and fire departments. The city had the highest per capita expenditures for police and fire protection of any major city—but uniformed personnel were paid the least. Curley and his cronies had systematically padded the payroll with legions of low-paid Irish policemen and firemen. With the highest tax rate in the country, the city's property owners groaned under the weight of the local welfare state, Irish-style.[76]

Denouncing "Curleyism," the reformers captured city hall in 1951 and held on for sixteen years. Irish reform mayors John Hynes and John Collins promoted an ambitious downtown revitalization program (the "New Boston"), instituted austerity programs to lower the city's onerous tax burden, extended civil service coverage, and successfully lobbied for state assumption of welfare costs. Redevelopment was the centerpiece of the Hynes and Collins administrations. No new office building had been constructed in the downtown area between 1927 and 1958. Securing federal urban renewal funds, reformers razed blighted neighborhoods and secured construction of the Prudential and Government Center anchor projects.[77]

A challenge to Irish hegemony did not accompany the Hub's revolution in policymaking. The Irish remained the largest ethnic group, allowing Green Power and reform to coexist. The Irish dominated the city council and public payroll well into the 1960s. Yet demographic forces were at work to pick the Irish lock on local government. By 1970, the Irish share of Boston's population had dipped below one-third while the black and Hispanic share approached one-quarter. New ethnic coalitional possibilities now presented themselves—even to Irish politicians.

An enterprising Irish politico took the challenge in 1967. Kevin White fashioned an outgroup coalition of liberals, blacks, and Italians to beat Louise Day Hicks and the South Boston working-class Irish. Elected mayor, White proceeded to reward his supporters.

Between 1967 and 1979 the black proportion of the city payroll rose from 6 percent to 18 percent. Italians also entered the city workforce in record numbers. To minimize the resentment of Irish payrollers, White used federal grant funding to create job opportunities for blacks and Italians. The mayor offered other blandishments to his supporters—improved neighborhood services and "Little City Halls" to expedite service complaints to Big City Hall in Government Center.[78]

In the mid-1970s reformer White turned to machine building. White began courting the South Boston Irish, his previous foes, to create a machine. In his 1975 and 1979 reelection bids, White hired between 1,500 and 2,000 temporary city workers, many from South Boston, to staff his campaign organization. In 1977 White tried to institutionalize his power with an audacious city charter proposal. The White charter would have reinstituted the partisan ballot and increased the mayor's authority over the troubled but patronage-rich Boston school system.[79]

For all his efforts, White succeeded only in building a personal campaign organization, not a centralized party-based machine. Declining resources and state recalcitrance thwarted the mayor's plans. White's political designs on the city payroll were limited by the merit system and collective bargaining agreements. Reformers Hynes and Collins had strengthened the city's civil service system. Major municipal labor unions—the Police Patrolmen's Association, the Boston firefighters' union, and the locals of the Association of Federal, State, County, and Municipal Employees (AFSCME) and the Service Employees International Union (SEIU)—had won the right of collective bargaining the year White took office.[80]

An intertwined fiscal and racial crisis in 1975–1977 further complicated White's machine-building plans. The municipal credit market collapsed in 1975 in the wake of New York City's de facto bankruptcy. Court-mandated school desegregation cost the city an unexpected $70 million. As the city's financial woes mounted, White promised the powerful municipal unions no layoffs in exchange for no wage increases. With Morgan Guaranty Trust Company, the chief underwriter on the city's bond issues, looking over his shoulder, White was forced to dismantle his army of provisional city workers. After the 1975 election, the mayor laid off 1,200 temporary municipal employees, representing 8 percent of the city's overall workforce. In 1979, White's postelection plans included the layoff of 1,700 more temporary workers.[81]

The state also conspired against the would-be city boss. The mayor's charter proposal required state approval. Despite strenuous lobbying, White's proposal for a return to partisan patronage politics died in the state legislature. Proposition 2½, passed by Massachusetts voters in 1981, was the last nail in White's political coffin. Limiting local property taxes, the proposition cut deeply into Boston's revenue base and municipal payroll. A discouraged White announced his retirement in 1983, unable to pass his diminished campaign organization to a designated successor.

The New Deal's reform legacy also hindered Democratic machine building in Philadelphia. Strengthened with federal patronage, reformers Joe Clark, Jr., and Richardson Dilworth in the late 1930s wrested control of the local Democratic party organization from the kept ward bosses. The reformers then turned their sights on the scandal-ridden GOP Vare machine, which had suffered serious reverses in the 1930s. In 1934 Bill Vare had died with no successor in sight. The feuding Republican ward bosses temporarily united at election time as the organization lurched forward on its own momentum. In 1935 the machine narrowly averted defeat as Democrat John Kelly won at the polls but lost at the ballot counting. More trouble loomed as a New Deal coalition of Catholics, Jews, and blacks slowly took shape. Conceding defeat in national elections, the machine continued to woo the ethnics in local contests with low taxes and social services delivered by an army of precinct committeemen.[82]

The GOP machine finally succumbed in 1951. With the property tax rate frozen since 1936, basic municipal services had been deteriorating. Faced with the collapse of the city's infrastructure of streets, sewers, and public transportation, the business community called a halt. Mayor Bernard Samuel was forced to create a Committee of Fifteen to investigate the machine's fall from service— and business—grace. Philadelphia's modern-day Committee of Correspondence uncovered considerable scandal, prompting calls for a new city charter. The city's leading business, financial, and legal firms organized the Greater Philadelphia Movement to pressure for government reform. The machine reluctantly endorsed a new charter calling for home rule, the consolidation of city and county offices, a strong mayor-council system, and a sharp reduction in patronage.[83]

Philadelphia's voters approved the new charter in 1951 and called on the Democrats to implement it. Democratic mayors Joe Clark, Jr. (1952–1956), Richardson Dilworth (1956–1962), and James Tate (1962–1972) embraced much of Chicago machine-builder Daley's agenda—slum clearance and urban renewal, mass transit, and public housing. Yet the employment policies of the Chicago machine Democrats and the Philadelphia reformers diverged considerably. In the Windy City, Daley reinvigorated the patronage system to reward white ethnic partisans. In the City of Brotherly Love, reform Democrats accepted the new charter's civil service system and used it to recruit blacks. By 1970 blacks made up 43 percent of Philadelphia's municipal workforce—double their proportion in Chicago.[84]

The reformers' incorporation of blacks generated a white backlash in what became the City of Not-So-Brotherly Love. Elected mayor in 1971 with the blessing of James Tate and Democratic party chieftain Peter Camiel, former police commissioner Frank Rizzo cracked heads in the ghetto and vowed to protect white neighborhoods. Rizzo then turned to machine building to institutionalize his white ethnic political base à la Chicago's Richard Daley. Because the merit system severely limited the patronage yield of municipal employment, Rizzo invoked the intergovernmental connection. Entering into a marriage of convenience with the Nixon White House and mending his fences with liberal Democratic Governor Milton Shapp, the former police chief built a formidable campaign organization with urban renewal funding and patronage.

Like Kevin White in Boston, however, Rizzo could construct only a personal organization, not a durable party machine. His alliance with Nixon alienated Peter Camiel and the regular Democratic organization. Disbarred by the city charter from serving a third term, the law-and-order mayor was unable to designate a successor. Though William Green, the next chief executive, rose to power through the Democratic ward system, he also broke with the organization to become a Philadelphia Robert Wagner—a born-again antipatronage reformer.[85]

The postwar period, then, proved to be inhospitable for building a fourth generation of big-city machines but not for maintaining preexisting organizations. The Chicago, Pittsburgh, and Albany machines adapted to declining resources and changing voter demands by freezing the tax rate, promoting downtown revitalization, delivering homeowner services, and piggybacking the welfare state. In other cities, the postwar yield was short-lived ersatz machines. New York and Jersey City produced the closest postwar approximations to the machine ideal. Both De Sapio and Kenney took the traditional supply-side path of expanding the patronage stock and forging intergovernmental party alliances to augment and monopolize resources. As in the past, embryonic machines were most vulnerable to external shocks. The drying up of state and federal assistance hastened reform insurgency in New York City and De Sapio's early retirement. Across the Hudson, a federal indictment gave Kenney new vacation plans.

The supply-side path was available from the 1940s through the late 1960s as city payrolls grew. By the early 1970s, however, would-be bosses faced declining resources. In both Boston and Philadelphia, strong merit systems installed in the 1950s coupled with collective bargaining agreements with powerful municipal unions fashioned in the 1960s shielded the city payroll from Mayors White and Rizzo. The fiscal crisis of the 1970s further complicated the mayors' search for patronage. White, for example, was forced to slash Boston's payroll by nearly one-quarter. Both White and Rizzo turned to ersatz patronage—temporary city workers and federal project employees—to build personal campaign organizations. Yet the two mayors could not generate the resources needed to transform candidate-centered organizations into robust party-based machines.

Nor were state political alliances forthcoming to consolidate these two fledgling machines. In the postwar era, all machines were more dependent on external aid. Intergovernmental alliances were important even to entrenched organizations. During the turbulent 1960s, the Chicago and Pittsburgh machines had hitched up to workhorse Governors Otto Kerner and David Lawrence. In the 1970s and 1980s, New York Democratic Governors Hugh Carey and Mario Cuomo gave the O'Connell-Corning organization an extended lease on life with state patronage and protection.

In postwar Massachusetts, however, the statehouse remained predominately in Republican hands until 1974—the year of Watergate. Elected in 1974, Democratic Governor Michael Dukakis proved to be a defective helpmate for would-be boss Kevin White. During the Boston school busing crisis, White looked for a heavy hitter to intercede with federal judge Arthur Garrity. When Dukakis turned out to be a lightweight, White was forced to look beyond the state altogether to the establishment figure Cyrus Vance. White's machine-building plans were further frustrated in 1978 when Dukakis lost to insurgent conservative Democrat Edward J. King. King's ascension further hastened White's retirement. The mayor, who had attempted to go from John Lindsay North to Richard Daley East, called it quits.[86]

Pennsylvania politics frustrated Frank Rizzo. The state's patronage system had once been massive—50,000 jobs for the governor to dole out in the 1950s, ten times the gubernatorial patronage of New Jersey, the second leading state. Civil service reform and collective bargaining under Republicans and reform Democrats had sharply reduced the governor's patronage to 4,000 positions by the time Democrat Shapp was elected in 1971. A Philadelphia businessman, Shapp made a political career as a reformer in the 1960s, defeating the Lawrence organization's choice in the 1966 Democratic gubernatorial primary.[87]

Ideologically antagonistic to the conservative Rizzo, Shapp supported liberal opponent William Green in Philadelphia's 1971 mayoral election. Later, the reform governor and the mayor briefly aligned politically. Rizzo supported Shapp's ill-starred presidential bid while Shapp agreed to support Rizzo in ousting Peter Camiel as head of the regular Democratic organization. As Shapp's presidential campaign quickly became a fiasco, his reputation as a "Jewish Harry Truman" changed to that of a Democratic version of Harold Stassen. The strained union between the two Democratic politicians eventually helped discredit both as scandals rocked their respective administrations. In 1978, control of the statehouse passed back to the Republicans, hastening Rizzo's exit from Philadelphia politics. Weak Democratic governors had thwarted Mayors Rizzo and White as they attempted to build big-city machines by projecting a strong and continuing voice into state politics.[88]

Spring: The New Rainbow Politics

In the 1980s the new minorities would no longer work through white intermediaries in the once-Irish cities. Black mayoral candidates won in machine Chicago and reform Philadelphia and mounted a serious challenge to Irish rule in Boston. Reminiscent of the Jewish-Italian alliance of the 1930s, black challengers have tried their hand at building multiethnic coalitions uniting blacks, Hispanics, Asians, and white liberals.

What is the nature of the new big-city rainbow politics? Are today's challenging coalitions truly cross-ethnic or are they primarily black-based? The centerpiece of the new politics is the unprecedented remobilization of the black vote. What has caused this mass reentry into electoral politics? Is it the product of local forces or national developments such as welfare-state retrenchment? To what extent can black politicians continue to direct this electoral surge to buttress their claims to cross-ethnic and urban leadership? As for the treatment of their coalition partners, are today's black politicos modern-day Fiorello La Guardias or Boss Hagues? Are Hispanics and Asians being rewarded with a fair share of power, jobs, and services? Alternatively, are black politicians acting as traditional ethnic brokers, recasting themselves toward Hispanics and Asians in the parsimonious ways the Irish once accommodated Jews and Italians?

Moreover, what is the future of the new rainbow politics? Notwithstanding their reform rhetoric, are minority politicians actually seeking to build a new generation of political machines? Have the old-style machines such as Chicago's suffered irreversible decline, or can they be refurbished to serve the urban poor? To what extent is the character of the new minority politics conditioned by different big-city political traditions—machine politics in Chicago and reform in Philadelphia and Boston? To these questions we now turn.

The Indian summer of the Chicago machine ended in 1983. Black mayoral candidate Harold Washington fashioned a rainbow coalition of blacks, Hispanics, and lakeshore liberals to defeat Mayor Jane Byrne and State Senator Richard M. Daley, son of the late mayor, in the Democratic primary. In the general election, the city's white ethnics, the machine's traditional mainstays, flocked to

Republican candidate Bernard Epton, no longer a sacrificial lamb. The election was a referendum on race as a record 82 percent of eligible voters went to the polls. Eighty-eight percent of whites supported Epton while 95 percent of blacks voted for Washington. Washington barely nosed out Epton by 46,250 votes out of a record 1.3 million cast.[89]

Washington's razor-thin victory depended on a massive remobilization of the black vote. In 1979, only 35 percent of eligible blacks had voted; in 1983, an unprecedented 73 percent went to the polls. Cutbacks in federal programs contributed to the reentry of Chicago's blacks into electoral politics. In the 1960s, the welfare state had served as a crucial appendage of the Daley organization in the black community. By the late 1970s, however, social programs—and the machine—were in trouble. At the federal level, President Carter initiated cutbacks in welfare, health, and social service grants-in-aid to states and cities. At the state level, the election of Republican Governor James Thompson in 1976 signaled an era of fiscal austerity as the state cut back on social spending. By 1979 Chicago had exhausted its own revenue sources and was unable to make up for the intergovernmental shortfall.[90]

Ronald Reagan's election in 1980 led to an even more sustained attack on social programs providing employment for the black middle class and transfer payments for the poor. For fiscal year (FY) 1982, the Reagan administration reduced social outlays by $35 billion, primarily in means-tested programs for the poor. Budget reductions in subsequent years were directed at the social service programs providing minority employment—education, manpower and training, and health and social services. In FY 1983, for example, Great Society service programs were the target of more than $7 billion in cutbacks. "The 1983 budget for domestic programs," warned Henry Aaron of the Brookings Institution, "must be viewed . . . as the boldest and most controversial attempt in fifty years to roll back the place of the federal government as a guarantor of equal opportunity and provider of social services."[91]

Welfare-state retrenchment politically galvanized the black community. Threatened with job loss, minority service providers had the incentive to organize themselves and their welfare clientele to support liberal candidates. Threatened with benefit loss, welfare recipients also discovered the necessity of electoral action. The

1982 elections were the first opportunity for blacks to vote their bread-and-butter discontent with Reagan. By mid-1982, pollsters had uncovered sharp racial differences in evaluations of the Reagan domestic record. The preelection Gallup poll showed whites narrowly approving the president's job performance—47 percent to 43 percent—whereas nonwhites disapproved it by a resounding 77 percent to 12 percent margin. Blacks went to the polls in record numbers to register their disapproval of Reagan's policies. In Chicago, black Democrats flocked to the registration tables and voting booth. More than 100,000 new black voters were registered in early October. Nearly all went to the polls. For the city as a whole, 144,000 more votes were cast in 1982 than in 1978. The black electoral surge went overwhelmingly Democratic. Nationwide, the NBC News exit poll showed 93 percent of blacks voting Democratic. As Thomas Cavanagh has argued, for blacks the 1982 election was a referendum on Reagan.[92]

In Chicago, Reagan's cutbacks in social programs significantly accelerated the slowly growing black estrangement from the machine. The 1975 mayoral election had revealed the first major black disenchantment with the Daley regime. The machine's refusal to appoint blacks to top positions, coupled with charges of police brutality, not social program reductions, produced these initial stirrings of minority discontent. Daley died in late 1976 and was replaced by Alderman Michael Bilandic, a non-Catholic Croatian from Daley's Bridgeport neighborhood. Bilandic's hopes for reelection in 1978 died in a preelection blizzard, one of the worst in the city's history. The city's snow removal effort collapsed. As commuters turned from private to public transportation, Bilandic had the commuter trains bypass inner-city stations in favor of suburban locations. Blacks were outraged. With 63 percent of the black vote, Democratic maverick Jane Byrne defeated machine regular Bilandic.[93]

Despite rising discontent with the machine's policies, the black vote was not mobilized until *after* Reagan's attack on the welfare state. Before 1980, black voter participation rates remained low. As of 1979, only 520,000 out of 950,000 eligible blacks were registered. Cutbacks in federal social programs brought the black middle class back into local electoral politics. Blacks working in social service agencies, activists in community-based organizations hurt by funding reductions, and ministers orchestrated a large-scale voter registration drive in welfare agencies, unemployment offices, and the churches.

More than 200 grass-roots organizations and churches participated in the registration campaign. The welfare state was at the heart of the mobilization campaign. In mid-1982, POWER (People Organized for Welfare and Employment Rights), a coalition of sixteen community organizations, announced plans to register welfare recipients. POWER successfully fought the Chicago Board of Election Commissioners and the state public aid and labor departments in order to conduct on-site voter registration in public welfare and unemployment offices. Other minority groups joined POWER. Black United Communities, another important grass-roots umbrella organization, trained volunteers in the voter drive and enlisted the support of the Urban League and Jesse Jackson's Operation PUSH (People United to Save Humanity). Threatened with federal cutbacks in their own programs, the black churches joined the registration drive. Notwithstanding the national character of social program cutbacks, the black response was local. "All politics," as Irish-American House Speaker Tip O'Neill once observed, "is local."[94]

The black revolt against the Chicago machine forces a reconsideration of the relationship between machines and welfare-state programs. The conventional wisdom holds that the growth of social programs weakens machines by supplying voters with non-machine-controlled resources. Although the welfare state may have hindered the building of a fourth generation of machines in the postwar era, entrenched party organizations purchased a fifty-year lease on life by skillfully diverting federal social programs to the task of rewarding and co-opting minorities. However, the machine's harnessing of the welfare state was not without risk. In the postwar era, federal and state decision makers rather than local machine politicians controlled the supply of resources integrating minorities. The Reagan administration's domestic policies destabilized those big-city party organizations dependent on social programs. In Chicago, welfare-state contraction, not growth, fueled the black revolt.

The tide of black insurgency crested in other cities in 1983. In Philadelphia, Wilson Goode, the black City Managing Director, bested Frank Rizzo in the Democratic mayoral primary, going on to victory in the general election. Though the campaign was less racial in character than Chicago's, the electoral coalitions were remarkably the same. Goode received 98 percent of the high-turnout black vote while securing only 24 percent of the white vote.[95]

In Boston, former black militant Mel King mounted a voter registration campaign aimed at blacks and Latinos in his race for mayor against South Boston populist Ray Flynn. Enlisting such black leaders as Jesse Jackson and Harold Washington, the King campaign swelled the city's voter registration rolls by 25 percent in the months before the election. In the nonpartisan primary, King fashioned a rainbow coalition of blacks, Hispanics, Asians, and white liberals, forcing Flynn into a runoff election. More than 63 percent of the Hub's registered voters turned out, the highest proportion in more than two decades. Though King ultimately lost to Flynn, the Hub had witnessed the emergence of blacks and other minorities as a countervailing force to Irish rule.[96]

In crucial ways, the new big-city rainbow politics resembles the earlier mobilization of Southern and Eastern Europeans. National forces—the Al Smith candidacy, the Depression, and the New Deal—had brought the new ethnics into the electoral process in record numbers. Big-city regimes, Democratic as well as Republican, were overthrown in mobilizing elections: Tammany Hall, the Hague machine, and the GOP organizations in Chicago and Pittsburgh. Today's rainbow politics represents an electoral surge of the third-wave migrants propelled by national forces.

The character of the ethnic insurgency in the 1930s had depended on the nature of the prevailing regime. So too in the 1980s. In cities run by entrenched Irish Democratic machines, the Southern and Eastern Europeans were drawn into antimachine reform movements. In competitive-party Chicago and GOP-controlled Pittsburgh, the new ethnic revolt was harnessed to Democratic machine building. Contemporary insurgency in Chicago—white (Byrne) as well as black (Washington)—has been defined by the presence of the machine. Both Byrne and Washington adopted campaign poses as antimachine reformers. Yet the mayors have not demonstrated that they can govern Chicago effectively without accommodating the ward bosses. In Philadelphia and Boston, with postwar reform traditions punctuated only by the failed machine-building schemes of Mayors Rizzo and White, the Goode and King campaigns have been reformist.

Despite these similarities, the new rainbow politics differs in major ways from earlier cross-ethnic coalitions. Regarding resources, the prizes and the means of ethnic capture are different. Mayoral patronage, even in Chicago, is now limited. Minority capture of municipal employment depends on affirmative action plans and revised civil service examinations, not on party sponsorship. The flow of welfare-state benefits, crucial to the minority community, eludes black control. In Chicago, the coalition built by Mayor Washington may have to make its peace with Republican administrations at the federal and state levels. It may also have to come to terms with the white Democrats who control Cook County. The welfare state passes through the county offices, not city hall. Having lost control of the city council in 1986 to Washington-backed candidates who won special elections ordered by the federal courts, the white-controlled remnant of the machine headed by Aldermen "Fast Eddie" Vrdolyak and Edward Burke may retreat to the county. Neglected by Daley, the suburban Democrats are the crucial force in the future of the Cook County organization.[97]

Today's rainbow politicians are also hindered by a mounting fiscal crisis. The consolidation of ethnic power has traditionally depended on expanding resources to incorporate and reward new groups. The Irish were brought into the embryonic Democratic machines during the expansionary 1850s and 1860s. Fiscal austerity in the 1870s and 1880s encouraged working-class Irish revolts against the early machines. With the return of flush times in the early twentieth century, the machines finally incorporated the Irish working class. In the 1930s and 1940s big-city politicians—reform as well as machine—parlayed federal programs to incorporate the Southern and Eastern Europeans.

Unlike earlier ethnic politicos, newly elected black politicians lack the means to reward their followers. In an era of domestic budget retrenchment, federal programs have been slashed. Chicago lost $200 million in federal funding for 1986. Under Gramm-Rudman, the Windy City was projected to lose an additional $527 million in 1987. National retrenchment compounded the burgeoning local fiscal crisis. Handed a $150 million budget deficit upon taking office, Mayor Harold Washington reluctantly increased property taxes by $80 million.

A hostile white-controlled city council frustrated the mayor's plans to seize control of patronage and reward his restless rainbow supporters. Chicago's "Council Wars" lasted three long years. As Washington finally took control of the council in 1986, he targeted the machine's patronage reserve. The Park District, with its 3,321 full-time employees and 1,500 summer positions, was the first to go. Under the guise of agency reorganization, the mayor appointed a black city department head to oversee fifteen-year-veteran Superintendent Edmund Kelly.[98]

With few loaves and fishes, black leaders resemble the nineteenth-century Irish bosses in terms of facing insurgency from within their own ranks. Militant Irish labor leaders had challenged the leadership of conservative Irish machine politicians. In the 1980s, a black protest elite headed by ministers such as Jesse Jackson challenged black elected officials such as Harold Washington. Diminished resources also heightened tensions among black elected leaders. In Chicago, black aldermen fought Mayor Washington and the black ward committeemen for control of $80 million in federal grant funding.[99]

In order to best their ethnic rivals, black elected officials may be forced to demobilize the volatile underclass—particularly if they can't deliver jobs and services. An electoral purge of the black poor may strengthen the leadership claims of elected officials within the minority community, but it also encourages ambitious white politicians. In Philadelphia, Wilson Goode beat Republican John Egan by 152,000 votes in the 1983 general election. Since then, 147,000 voters—mostly black Democrats—have been purged from the voter registration rolls, unable to vote in the 1987 municipal elections.[100]

Diminished resources also frustrate black politicos in their efforts to cement cross-ethnic alliances. In the 1983 general election, Washington received a majority of the Hispanic vote. Yet the black-brown alliance may be unraveling as Washington's organization doles out its limited supply of patronage to blacks, its core ethnic constituency. Latino representation on the municipal payroll remains minuscule. Hispanics are only slowly being recruited as precinct captains and ward committeemen. Lacking resources, black politicians may be forced to borrow a page from the Irish brokers in their parsimonious accommodation of other ethnic groups.

The new big-city rainbow coalition is also unstable because of the different demands of its partners. Asian-Americans are prosperous and politically conservative. The Hispanic community is fractured along nationality, class, and political lines. Poor and liberal, Puerto Ricans are natural allies for blacks. Split economically and politically, Chicanos are not natural allies. Unlike the black middle class, which is heavily employed in the public sector, the Chicano middle class is largely in small business, a breeding ground for political conservatism. There is little common ground between the new black power brokers and the prosperous and deeply conservative Cuban-American community.[101]

Underneath the umbrella of rainbow rhetoric, contemporary black politicians are practicing ethnic particularism à la the Irish power brokers. The old-style Irish machines did not fashion multiethnic rainbow coalitions, rewarding each group with a fair share of the prizes drawn from a sizable pot of municipal gold. Throughout most of their history, the big-city machines were as much instruments of voter demobilization as mobilization, of ethnic exclusion as inclusion. There is little reason to believe that black politicians can succeed at cross-ethnic rainbow politics where the legendary Irish bosses failed.

Chapter Six

Machine Building, Irish-American Style

The Life-Cycle Debate

The once-mighty Irish big-city machines are nearly extinct. Tammany Hall, the Buckley organization in the Bay Area, Frank Hague's powerful Jersey City organization, the Steel City Lawrence organization—all are gone. Only Chicago and Albany remain as relics of the past. In all likelihood, though, these two vestiges will soon pass from the scene.

After dominating Chicago for decades, the Daley machine is a shambles. With its leader dead and a black mayor elected, the organization's white regulars retreated to the city council where they fought a bitter, stubborn, three-year rearguard action to retain control of the machine's power and patronage. In the end they lost. Court-ordered reapportionment and new elections wiped out the old guard's four-vote majority on the council. Mayor Harold Washington used his razor-thin council majority to seize control of the Board of Education, the huge Chicago Transit Authority, and the Chicago Park District, an independent agency with 5,000 patronage jobs and a $130-million budget.[1]

This patronage infusion may not be enough to resuscitate the machine under black leadership. The city faces an unprecedented fiscal crisis. The white regulars still control county government and the stream of welfare-state benefits sustaining former Mayor Washington's minority constituency. Even the vaunted Albany machine is in trouble, having entered an interregnum phase in 1983 following the death of Erastus Corning, Dan O'Connell's chosen successor.

Though the urban machines are largely gone, machine politics—the trading in particularistic benefits—lives. In New York, the Bronx, Queens, and Brooklyn Democratic county organizations win elections through the use of patronage, contracts, and franchises. In reaction to the big-city Democratic organizations, suburban Republicans have also tried their hand at machine building. In Long Island, the Nassau County Republican organization has wooed the Italians and Irish fleeing New York. Controlling 20,000 patronage jobs, the Nassau Republicans have built an impressive suburban machine addressing neighborhood issues and delivering homeowner services.[2]

Although these county remnants have led some to claim that the reports of the death of the political machine have been greatly exaggerated, the era of the patronage-based centralized big-city machines *is* passing. The urban machine's demise has spawned a cottage industry devoted to debating the machine's nature, functions, and dynamics. Both domestic and foreign developments have propelled the search for a summary judgment.

Domestically, as Theodore Lowi argues, "new" machines—reformed bureaucracies—have replaced the old party machines, prompting comparisons of the two urban governing arrangements.[3] In light of the general unresponsiveness of reformed structures to the interests of minorities and the working class, the dying urban machine has been given a posthumous facelift. During its heyday, boss rule was castigated by progressives as corrupt and undemocratic. In its twilight era, analysis—much of it sympathetic—replaced pejorative evaluation, and causal inquiry superseded description. Suitably refurbished, the machine is now viewed as an early, informal version of the welfare state, responding to the needs of the immigrant working class.[4]

Studies of less developed countries have also prompted a reassessment of American big-city political machines. The myth of American political exceptionalism evaporated as postwar studies of Sicily and southern Italy, India, and the emerging African and Asian states showed startling similarities to the big-city American machines. In Third World countries, party politicians behaved like the big-city bosses, trading material benefits such as patronage jobs and welfare services for political support. Seen in the broader context of political development, then, machines represented a form of clientelist politics, superseding the traditional patron-client relation between landlord and peasant in rural society. Yet party-based clientelism was considered a transitional stage between traditional and modern society, destined to dissolve in the face of organized interest groups and class-based ideological parties.[5]

The writing of the urban machine's epitaph has generated considerable controversy. Americanists have been preoccupied with what can best be termed organizational life-cycle issues—the machine's origins, longevity, and decline. Here are some of the major theoretical hotspots in this debate.

Regarding the emergence of centralized machines, two competing theories have been advanced. Group theory depicts the machine as a mass-created phenomenon. Immigrant groups such as the Irish demanded material benefits such as patronage jobs and social services. By supplying these resources, bosses built winning electoral coalitions and strong machines.

Elite theory, in contrast, argues that centralized machines are leader-created. Voters may demand material benefits, but this demand pattern does not inevitably produce a centralized machine. To consolidate power, entrepreneurial party bosses have to create governing—not merely electoral—coalitions, forging strategic alliances with the local business community to ensure adequate party finances and to mute reform opposition.

Successful machines ultimately had to fashion winning electoral coalitions as well as ruling alliances. Much of the debate over the maintenance strategies of the big-city party organizations focuses on the character of the transaction between politicians and voters. For exchange theorists, the transaction is primarily economic. Bosses seek electoral support and voters try to improve their material well-being. In this view, bosses target past and prospective supporters with material benefits. Machine longevity depends on allocating sufficient divisible benefits to build a winning electoral coalition. This long-accepted exchange model is now under challenge. Recent studies of the Chicago and New Haven machines, for example, have shown that factors other than vote maximization influence the allocation of jobs and services. Voters, in turn, may support machines in the absence of direct economic reward.[6]

The machine's demise has also triggered a coroner's inquest. The conventional wisdom traced the machine's decline to two factors—first, to a decline in both the supply and the control of resources, as a result of the inroads made by reform and the welfare state; and, second, to changes in voter demand as the machine's traditional supporters moved into the middle class. In short, machines no longer commanded the tangible benefits to purchase votes, and middle-class voters no longer wanted the machine's traditional fare of lowly patronage jobs and welfare services. This received wisdom is currently under sustained attack as studies show reform and the welfare state strengthening machines and the big-city bosses adapting their policies to middle-class tastes.

Issues of party coalition building and resource distribution have preoccupied American students of the urban machine. Comparativists, however, have examined a broader set of questions raised by machine politics: the character of the political transition from traditional to modern society, machines as forms of clientelist politics, and the relationship of the party system to state building.

On one level, the clientelist perspective on the machine emphasizes similarities between the American big-city party organizations and their urban and rural counterparts in contemporary Third World countries. Throughout the world, machine politics flourishes in the democratic interstices separating traditional and modern society, where uprooted peasants demand concrete material benefits from party leaders in exchange for their votes. First comes "democracy," that is, participatory politics; later, urban-industrial development. Machine politics persists until the lag between political development and class formation is overcome.

On another level, comparativists have distinguished between U.S. and Third World machines. In the United States, economic development was rapid, but political democracy was even more precocious. Universal suffrage triumphed remarkably early in the American federal system, generations before thoroughgoing urban-industrial transformation. In this context, the big-city machines were quintessentially nineteenth-century American phenomena—localized party structures at the periphery of a fragmented political system with minimal political and programmatic linkages to the national core. Machines both reflected and helped sustain the decentralized, parochial, and particularistic character of American politics well into the late twentieth century.

In contrast, later developing urban and rural machines in Third World countries arose in an era of centralized nation-states featuring national entitlement and development programs. In this context, Third World machines reflected and helped reinforce strong national party and programmatic structures. In the comparative party and clientelist research, there is surprisingly little dissent from this comparison of the "advanced" character of Third World machines relative to the "backward" character of the American big-city machines, the cornerstone of party development from the late nineteenth century to the mid-twentieth century.

Our analysis of four generations of machine building in eight of the once most heavily Irish-American cities, 1840 to 1985, allows us to test these theories of machine building and of American political development. The eight cities produced six strong Irish Democratic machines—Tammany Hall, the Buckley organization, the Hague machine, the O'Connell organization, the Kelly-Nash-Daley machine, and the Lawrence organization—over a one-hundred-year period. It is true that our ability to generalize from these cases to all big-city machines is limited. After all, these six cases are not a representative sample of all urban machines; Republican machines—for example, in Philadelphia, Pittsburgh, and Cincinnati—and Democratic machines in the border states—for example, Boss Crump's machine in Memphis and the Pendergast organization in Kansas City—have been excluded. Nevertheless, though not representative of all machines, the Irish big-city party organizations best approximate the pure or classic immigrant-based and welfarist machines.

Not only do we test existing theories; we also offer a new theory of machine development. This new approach departs in two critical ways from existing theories. First, it places machine development in the context of the party system, particularly in terms of intergovernmental and intraparty alliances. Urban machine building required vertical alliances to sympathetic state and national leaders, especially in the fragile gestation period, in order to monopolize public sector resources, starve factional opponents, and reward party functionaries and voters. Group and elite theories, in contrast, treat the urban political system as a hermetically sealed environment. Machine building is seen as the product of such endogenous urban factors as a large pool of needy immigrant voters.

Second, the new view emphasizes the resource side of machine politics—a Say's Law of big-city bosses and organizations. For the urban bosses, resource problems were paramount, for voter demand almost always exceeded available supply. Hence bosses spent as much time creating resources such as patronage jobs as they spent distributing them. A revised theory of machine dynamics, then, needs to specify the strategies for increasing the supply of patronage and other tangible benefits. In the long run, the scarcity of machine benefits shaped both the character and the volume of electoral demand. Rather than catering to their supporters, bosses spent much of their time deflating demand, particularly for the organization's core resources of power and patronage. In contrast, conventional wisdom assumes a cornucopia of resources and treats demand as independent of supply.

In the following pages we shall apply the findings from our case studies of the classic Irish urban machines to the theoretical debates concerning the three phases of the machine's life cycle—gestation, maintenance, and decline—before considering their relevance to issues of clientelist politics and comparative party and political development.

The Origins of Machines

Group Approaches

There is not one but several group or mass theories of the machine's birth. Let us consider three leading models. Edward Banfield and James Q. Wilson argue that machines arose as a response to the "private-regarding" ethos of working-class European immigrants. Imported from the Old World, the immigrant outlook consisted of neighborhood rather than citywide attachments. The impoverished European arrivals viewed politics as the self-interested pursuit of material gain rather than as the disinterested search for the public good. According to this model, big-city machines were fueled by this chorus of particularistic ethnic demands. Lest Banfield and Wilson be accused of offering only a demand theory of machines, they caution that sheer numbers of needy immigrants were not a sufficient condition for the development of strong machines. Machines needed resources with which to reward immigrant party workers and voters. The greater the resources, ceteris paribus, the stronger the organization and its electoral coalition.[7]

Casting his theoretical net more narrowly, Daniel Patrick Moynihan has proposed an Irish variant of the ethos account of the machine's birth. Whereas Banfield and Wilson trace the demand for machine politics to working-class Catholic groups such as the Czechs, Poles, and Italians, Moynihan highlights the peculiarly Irish role in building the big-city Democratic machines such as Tammany Hall. For Moynihan, machines were a reproduction of the social structure and value system of Irish village life. Village saloons, for example, organized local political life as they later would in American cities. The structure of the Irish Catholic church—its hierarchy and neighborhood parishes—would also serve as a template for later urban party organization. Under centuries of English oppression, the Irish assimilated the political values of their conquerors. Politics was thought of in terms of material self-interest and hierarchical patron-client relations.[8]

James Scott offers an alternative mass theory of machine building. For Scott it is not Old World values or Irish rural custom that provides the fertile soil for machines. Comparing the similarities of today's African and Asian industrializing countries to nineteenth-century America, Scott argues that machinelike parties are not a unique American big-city phenomenon. Instead, they emerge in "transitional social contexts" where traditional patterns of peasant deference to landowners and local notables have broken down and the "modern" loyalties of occupation and class have not yet taken hold.[9]

How useful are group or mass theories for understanding the origins of machines in the eight cities surveyed? At first glance, the case studies seem to provide support for a group interpretation. Centralized Irish-led machines, after all, emerged in six of the eight cities with large Irish-American populations, lending credibility to Moynihan's village transplant argument. Yet the Irish were carriers of multiple strains of politics. Pace Moynihan, there were not one but several political exits out of the Irish villages. The same rural soil produced in late nineteenth-century America a conservative organizational politics of patronage and power and in Ireland an insurgent mass politics organized around the causes of nationalism, land reform, and home rule. Only in postindependence Ireland would the supposed Irish affinity for machine politics assert itself.[10]

For the early stages of American machine development, group theories better describe the attitudes and behavior of Irish political elites—party bosses and workers—than those of the mass of working-class Celtic voters. The Irish-American community of the late nineteenth century did not uniformly support the fledgling machines. Although the Celtic politicos functioned as a conservative, self-serving elite, the working class was open to radical, mass appeals. In the 1870s and 1880s, Irish workers channeled much of their political energy into antimachine labor parties, into a class-conscious trade union movement, and into the Irish nationalist movement—hardly grist for the "private-regarding" political mill.

In fact, the urban machine itself, not Old World traits, independently shaped political values and the structure of political possibilities in the early Irish-American community. Working-class Irish revolts against boss rule evaporated in the early twentieth century as ever larger numbers of Irish were brought into the patronage system. In this manner, the big-city party organizations were not passive reactors to particularistic group demands. They were active participants in helping create what Terry Clark calls the "Irish patronage ethic."[11] Both Moynihan's rural transplant hypothesis and the Banfield and Wilson ethos theory, then, fail to consider how the Irish bosses worked tirelessly to cultivate an exclusive demand for their privatized product in the Irish-American community.

Structural limitations on the machine's supply of resources forced the Celtic bosses to frustrate mass demands among other immigrant groups. The machine's parsimonious accommodation of the non-Irish helps explain a major anomaly in ethos theory: the persistent failure of the Southern and Eastern Europeans to support the Irish machines. Given their enthusiasm for radical and reform politics, Jews were beyond the private-regarding pale. Other second-wave groups revolted against their Irish overlords. New York City's Italians voted overwhelmingly for reformer La Guardia in the 1930s and 1940s. Jersey City's Polish and Italians overthrew the Hague machine in the late 1940s. In the Windy City, Poles represented a thorn in Richard Daley's side in the late 1950s and early 1960s.

How do we explain these episodes of antimachine insurgency on the part of the machine's supposed ethnic supporters? Southern and Eastern European Catholics may well have been private-regarding.

But the entrenched Irish machines did not automatically cater to their demands. Complementing the policy of not-so-benign electoral neglect of Southern and Eastern European immigrants, the bosses offered limited benefits to the new ethnics—social services, symbolic recognition, and collective benefits—rather than a greater sharing of the scarce core resources of power and patronage. Parsimonious accommodation produced antimachine revolts by the second-wave migrants.

As with the Irish, changes in the machine's policies—not traits imported from the Old World—transformed the political outlook and behavior of newer immigrants. Private-regardingness among big-city Catholics eventually blossomed in the postwar era as machines accommodated them with a greater sharing of jobs, services, and, yes, even power, but at the price of not rewarding later-arriving blacks and Hispanics.

Why did the machines so sparsely reward newcomers, whether Southern and Eastern Europeans or blacks and Hispanics? In contrast to the Panglossian view of resource creation advanced by today's supply-side economics, there were sharp structural limits on the machine's supply of resources. A major weakness of ethos theory is that it blurs the line between voter demand and machine response, treating the latter as if it were an almost automatic reflex of group cultural and political predispositions. In actuality, there were inherent conflicts in the machine's political economy between supply and demand. Machines were structurally constrained resource-generating and resource-allocating mechanisms, which accommodated voter demand only within certain class-imposed political limits.

Elite Approaches

Group theories have been challenged from another quarter. Elite theories, such as that found in the work of Martin Shefter, see leadership alliances, not electoral coalition building, as the key factor in machine building. Drawing on Raymond Wolfinger's distinction between machine politics—as the demand for particularistic benefits—and political machines—as centralized political structures—Shefter argues that voter demand for tangible benefits did not invariably produce a citywide machine. Boston's voters were as private-regarding as New York's, but the faction-ridden Hub never produced a Tammany Hall North.[12]

According to Shefter, machine incentives can yield a variety of political structures. Individual politicians may practice "rapacious individualism," looting the city treasury to build personal followings. Alternatively, enduring factions within the dominant party may vie with one another in using tangible benefits to compete for electoral favor. Finally, a centralized machine under the direction of a single boss can monopolize the allocation of benefits.[13]

For elite theorists, successful machine builders must solve various organizational dilemmas, for example, wooing voters, ensuring party finances, controlling elected officials, and rewarding and disciplining the machine's ward bosses and precinct captains. The party-building enterprise requires governing alliances, not merely temporary electoral coalitions constructed every few years. To govern successfully, bosses must win the support of key actors in the local business community.

Shefter's account of Tammany Hall's consolidation of power in the late nineteenth century illustrates the importance of party-business alliances. Protean factionalism characterized the city's Democracy from the 1840s to the 1870s. In this premachine era of "rapacious individualism," the immigrant working-class vote assumed increasing importance. Would-be bosses built electoral followings with the patronage produced by expansionary fiscal policies. To underwrite their expansionary policies, Tammany politicians such as Fernando Wood and Boss Tweed formed alliances with contractors and speculators benefiting from municipal spending and indebtedness.

A different pattern of elite alliances and fiscal policies accompanied John Kelly's reign as Tammany's chieftain following Boss Tweed's downfall in the early 1870s. Kelly quickly aligned himself with the "Swallow-tails," the reform-minded bankers, lawyers, and businessmen demanding "tight-fisted" fiscal policies. Yet the program of municipal retrenchment demanded by conservative business interests meant little "trickle down" to the immigrant working class. With little patronage, how could Tammany consolidate its electoral base? Borrowing a page from Henry George's 1886 labor campaign, Kelly and his lieutenants devised a cheaper way to organize Tammany voters, particularly the upwardly mobile second-generation ethnics: year-round district social clubs.[14]

By the tandem tactics of capturing reform-minded businessmen with fiscal retrenchment and the immigrant working class with social clubs, Kelly supposedly weakened both business and voter support for factional opponents, particularly the reform-minded County Democracy. With the County Democracy's collapse in the late 1880s, Tammany's arrival as an unchallenged machine was complete.

In elite theory, material resources play a minimal role in machine consolidation. Tammany monopolized city patronage in the 1870s and early 1880s yet factionalism persisted within the Democratic party. Factionalism declined after 1886 even though Tammany's supply of city patronage remained the same. What did change in the late 1880s was the nature of the machine's inducements: District clubs were added to the Tiger's arsenal of enticements.

Intergovernmental Alliances

Elite theory is correct in highlighting the importance of leadership alliances for machine building. The real question is whether alliances with the business community were sufficient for machine consolidation.

Elite theory must be expanded to include other machine-building alliances. In the preceding chapters I have argued that successful aspiring bosses had to forge alliances with state and national party leaders. Vital to organizational consolidation was the monopoly of all public patronage—county, state, and national as well as city—controlled by the machine's party in the metropolis. Each patronage cache could fuel a rival party faction. To cure the mischief of faction, would-be bosses had to be oligopolists, monopolizing the raw materials needed by their competitors.

Elite theory must also be modified to include patronage as a crucial party-building ingredient. The theory views the conflict between machine and reform factions as one involving different nonmaterial incentive systems. Machine politicians used social incentives to reward voters. Reformers relied on ideological appeals. By deemphasizing the importance of patronage, the theory anachronistically projects back into the late nineteenth century developments that did not occur until the mid-twentieth century. The Democratic reform clubs of the 1950s relied heavily on ideological and programmatic appeals. Postwar machine politicians also de-emphasized old-style job patronage (relative to their early counter-parts) because the organization's electoral support increasingly rested on the provision of homeowner and welfare-state services.

Unlike the elite approach, our theory places the fight over patronage at the heart of early party factionalism. In contrast with today's reformers, the antimachine factions of the late nineteenth century relied heavily on patronage to reward both voters and campaign workers. Reform was but a thin veneer for Irving Hall and the County Democracy, Tammany's major rivals for control of the New York City Democracy in the 1870s and 1880s. All three shared the same office-for-gain ethos. In contrast, patronage was not the major axis along which Tammany fought Henry George and his followers. The labor party had to be disposed of in an ideological war to the death before the various Democratic factions could indulge themselves in the luxury of party infighting.

Let us consider the evidence for an intergovernmental, party-based, and patronage-centered interpretation of Tammany's emergence as an undisputed machine. Does control of the statehouse rather than entrée into the downtown businessmen's club, and the use of patronage rather than availability of the clubhouse, better explain Tammany's triumph over Irving Hall and the County Democracy? Yes. "Honest John" Kelly's alliance with the "Swallowtails" was short-lived as Tammany broke with Democratic reform governor Samuel Tilden in 1874 over matters of state patronage. Tilden then built an alliance with Irving Hall, funneling state resources to the reformers rather than to Tammany. The Tiger's monopoly of city patronage meant little to the rival faction sustained with state resources.

Democrat Lucius Robinson succeeded Tilden as governor, also aligning himself with the party's reform wing. With Tammany's support, Democrat Grover Cleveland succeeded Robinson. Kelly's romance with the conservative Cleveland was brief; the dalliance predictably dissolved over the distribution of state patronage to the rival city factions. Cleveland funneled state patronage to the County Democracy, reform successor to Irving Hall.

Only with Democrat David B. Hill's election in 1885 was state patronage finally channeled to Tammany. Governor Hill initially tried to placate all factions in the local Democracy. The County Democracy's collapse began with leadership scandals and an abortive fusion attempt with the Republicans. As the County Democracy began to crumble, "I Am a Democrat" Hill hastened its collapse by redirecting the County's share of state patronage to Tammany. Monopolizing both state and local patronage, the Tiger's triumph over rival factions was complete.

Tammany was not alone in seeking intergovernmental assistance to consolidate power. In the 1880s, the fledgling Irish machines of Jersey City and San Francisco forged crucial alliances with pro-machine Democratic governors. In the 1910s and 1920s, Frank Hague in Jersey City and Dan O'Connell in Albany did the same. As the Democrats became the majority party in the 1930s, federal alliances shaped the fortunes of a third generation of Irish machines in Chicago and Pittsburgh.

Republican machines also required an intergovernmental assist. In a careful study of GOP machine building in Cincinnati, James Ingram has shown the importance of state party linkages. In the 1880s the city's Republican party was split into three factions headed by George Cox, Amor Smith, and George Moerlin. "Old Boy" Cox bested his rivals for control of the party and city in 1886 by forging an alliance with Republican Governor Joseph B. Foraker. "Fire Alarm" Foraker assisted Cox in two ways. Cox was appointed state oil gauger, allowing the would-be boss to make connections with Cincinnati's business elite. Foraker also provided Cox with 2,000 state patronage jobs. Cox's army of payrollers was platooned to the various wards, there to take over the neighborhood GOP organizations. Within two years the "Old Boy" had emerged as the city's undisputed leader.[15]

The case for intergovernmental party alliances is strengthened when we consider cities where centralized machines did not emerge. Hostile state and national administrations, not the absence of alliances with the economic elite or the lack of neighborhood clubhouses, explain the failure of machine consolidation. In the late nineteenth century, Irish politicos in Boston and Chicago replicated Tammany's alliance pattern with local economic notables and its social clubs for district voters. Yet neither the Hub's Pat Maguire nor the Windy City's Mike McDonald could build a citywide machine. In early twentieth-century Boston, John F. Fitzgerald's Jefferson Club and Martin Lomasney's Hendricks Club rivaled Tammany's district clubhouses. Neither Boston politician could turn neighborhood recreational programs into citywide power. Relying on patronage rather than clubs, the Hub's James Michael Curley came closer than Fitzgerald or Lomasney to building a centralized machine.

State party politics explains the failure of machine building in early Boston and Chicago. The GOP dominated Massachusetts politics after the Civil War. Bay State Republicans established stringent taxation and indebtedness limitations for Boston, limiting the patronage take of ambitious Irish Democratic politicians. As the Irish finally took over the city, the GOP invented other forms of damage control. The patronage-rich Boston police department, for example, was placed under state authority. Even the resurgence of the state's Democratic party in the early twentieth century did not bode well for would-be Hub bosses. Yankees from western Massachusetts solidified their control over the party and thus nomination for the governorship. In order to limit the influence of Boston's feuding Irish ward bosses in state party politics, Democratic governors aligned with the western faction turned their backs on the Hub.

Hostile state administrations also prevented Irish bosses from building a Chicago machine before the 1930s. In the late nineteenth century, Mike McDonald's efforts to construct a midwestern Tammany were frustrated by "Black Jack" Logan's state GOP machine. With McDonald's death, two factions—followers of the Carter Harrisons I and II and the Hopkins-Sullivan wing—arose in the Windy City's Democratic party. Occasional Democratic governors did little to centralize Chicago Democratic politics. In the 1890s radical Governor Altgeld's policies inflamed the city's factional divisions. In the early twentieth century, reform Governor Dunne employed state patronage to build an independent Dunne wing alongside the Harrison and Hopkins-Sullivan factions. The emergence of the modern Democratic machine in Chicago would await Franklin Delano Roosevelt and the New Deal.

In a recent and important analysis of local party systems in the twentieth century, David Mayhew has also highlighted the role of state party structures in explaining the distinctive geographical patterning of the big-city machines. Local machines were concentrated in the Middle Atlantic states (New York, New Jersey, Pennsylvania), not in New England (Massachusetts) or the West (California). To explain this regional pattern, Mayhew discounts such causal variables as the size of the immigrant population. Instead, he argues that urban machines arose from the 1890s onward in states with preexisting strong traditional party organizations (TPOs). Strong TPO states featured durable, autonomous, and hierarchical party systems, which slated candidates for office and used material incentives to enforce party discipline and woo voters. Where state TPOs were weak, urban machines either did not emerge (Boston) or did not last long (San Francisco).[16]

Mayhew's theory points us in the right local machine-building direction—the state party system. Yet even within states with strong patronage-based parties, there were variations in the emergence of local machines over time and between cities. Machine politics remained strong in New York, New Jersey, and Pennsylvania from the 1860s through the late 1960s. Consistent with Mayhew's theory, these hospitable state party systems early on spawned Democratic machines in New York City, Albany, and Jersey City, and GOP machines in Philadelphia and Pittsburgh.

From the 1930s through the early 1950s, however, four of these five big-city machines were toppled. Only one strong and durable replacement was constructed—the Lawrence organization in Pittsburgh. The De Sapio and Kenny successors to Tammany Hall and the Hague organization were weak and short-lived. In Philadelphia, Mayor Frank Rizzo could not transform a personal campaign organization into a party-based machine. Despite the fertile soil of patronage-based state party systems, would-be bosses in the postwar era found the machine-building task more difficult than Mayhew's theory suggests.

Our theory of intergovernmental alliances adds an active ingredient in the state party system equation—the character of the controlling party and faction. Mayhew emphasizes the facilitating role of overall state party structures, contrasting strong patronage-based systems with all others. Yet the existence of a hierarchical and patronage-based state party system did not automatically result in local machines. To consolidate power, local party bosses needed to monopolize all public sector resources in the metropolis to strengthen their organizations and starve their opponents. Within strong patronage-based state party *structures,* intraparty (factional) *cleavages* and interparty *competition* represented important variables explaining where and when local machines emerged. For would-be urban bosses, ruling parties and factions in state and national politics mattered.

Given the crucial role of intergovernmental, intraparty alliances in machine consolidation, what explains why some aspiring bosses were successful alliance builders and others were not? Much depended on what local bosses had to offer leaders at the state and federal levels. The quid pro quo for local receipt of intergovernmental assistance involved help in furthering the careers of political higher-ups.

The forms of local assistance varied according to the needs of state and national leaders. Big-city GOP bosses were particularly eager to please Republican U.S. senators, the linchpins of state machines. As Mayhew notes, senators were "in the thick of . . . [state party structures], induced into building or tending them because of their need for state legislative majorities in order to reach and hold office in Washington (before the Seventeenth Amendment switched the power to elect Senators from legislators to popular elections). Senators were supplied, especially on the Republican side, with federal patronage (notably in post offices and custom houses) that was helpful in supporting organizations back home."[17] In return for senatorial assistance and federal patronage, local Republican bosses elected and placed at the disposal of senators the requisite state legislative majorities.

Failing to capture the White House (and federal patronage) throughout most of the period between the Civil War and the Depression, the Democrats set their sights on the statehouse. For the big-city Irish Democratic bosses, the governorship—and state patronage—was a vital adjunct to early machine building. With the coming of Roosevelt and the New Deal, the presidency and federal resources replaced governorships and state resources as necessary building blocks of strong local Democratic party organizations.

Roosevelt's treatment of the Democratic big-city bosses in the 1930s illustrates the kinds of local assistance demanded. The urban bosses captured needed federal patronage (particularly the WPA) to the extent they contributed to Roosevelt's reelection prospects. FDR had the greatest incentive to hand over federal relief to state and local party leaders in the heavily populated urban-industrial states with the greatest electoral clout and with the greatest uncertainty regarding the vote outcome. In these states, big-city bosses enhanced their prospects for federal patronage either by delivering an urban voting bloc pivotal to the state electoral outcome or by aligning themselves with the dominant wing of the state Democratic party. The Irish machines of Chicago, Pittsburgh, Jersey City, and Albany met these criteria and captured the local WPA. Failing FDR's reelection tests, Irish politicians in New York and Boston were denied federal work relief. Without federal assistance, Tammany could not mount a challenge to La Guardia, and Curley could not consolidate power in the faction-ridden Hub.

Intergovernmental intraparty alliances and patronage monopolies were most crucial in the initial stages of machine building. Consolidated machines, in contrast, merely required the existence of stable state and national political structures, regardless of the controlling party. Dominating the local party and governmental systems, established machines substantially increased the start-up costs and risks for rival parties and intraparty factions, costs that could rarely be overcome by a temporary infusion of state or federal patronage. Tammany Hall, for example, easily beat back the challenge of President Woodrow Wilson, who was anxious to have reformers capture the city's Democratic organization.

Since the New Deal, however, intergovernmental alliances have assumed increasing importance at *all stages* of the machine's life cycle. Postwar machine builders lacked the local resources of their predecessors. The twin imperatives of economic revitalization and social welfare in the older cities have required massive and continued infusions of state and federal aid. Given greater organizational fragility, modern urban bosses are at the mercy of state and federal decision makers. The postwar downfall of De Sapio in New York and Kenney in Jersey City illustrates the heightened risks of federal intervention.

Yet with the population decline of the Frostbelt and the older cities, local bosses have less to offer in return. The quadrennial presidential sweepstakes has moved to the growing Sunbelt, rendering the one-time big-city kingmakers irrelevant. In the northern urban-industrial states themselves, big-city bosses have less to contribute to state political leaders as the suburbs grow at the expense of the central cities. The failure of Kevin White in Boston and Frank Rizzo in Philadelphia to turn personal campaign organizations into machines is in part attributable to their failure to command the resources needed to cement alliances to state leaders.

Conventional elite theory fails to illuminate these crucial intraparty and intergovernmental machine-building alliances. Elite theory is further weakened by its overestimation of the attractiveness of social inducements like clubhouses to voters. It is true that machine alliances with conservative business owners limited the supply of material inducements to voters. As a consequence, the early machines offered circuses in lieu of bread to working-class immigrant voters. But district clubhouses were never as attractive as economic benefits, whether patronage jobs, welfare services, or labor legislation. The early machine's limited patronage cache explains its failure to solidify its electoral base. Only with an expanding resource base could the bosses bring working-class voters securely into the political fold. The machine's search for intergovernmental and private sector patronage can be understood as an attempt to overcome the resource constraints imposed by alliances with the conservative business community.

Maintaining the Machine

Exchange Theories

Once machines consolidated power with intergovernmental assistance, how did they maintain themselves? The conventional wisdom holds that machines fashioned elaborate exchanges with key constituencies—the business community, labor, party functionaries, and voters. Consolidating power, machines assumed control over an impressive array of valued goods and services—patronage, social services, taxation and police powers, contracts and franchises, and regulatory oversight.[18] All could be cashed in for political support, particularly for votes and campaign contributions.

There is disagreement, however, among exchange theorists regarding the terms of the transaction between voters and the machine. For pluralists such as Robert Dahl, bosses offered valuable material benefits—patronage jobs and welfare services—for votes. Each recipient of the machine's job largesse, in turn, was responsible for bringing at least five machine voters to the polls.[19] But others have stressed the nonmaterial character of the relationship between the party organization and voters. For Shefter, circuses (clubhouses) were more decisive than bread (patronage). Banfield and Wilson argue that the purchase price of votes was even cheaper. Because patronage was scarce, it was used for party workers, not voters. To solicit votes, party workers primarily traded in the currency of friendship.[20]

The vote-getting value of patronage has been challenged in a number of studies. Frank Sorauf's early pathbreaking study of state highway jobs in a rural Pennsylvania county pointed to the limits of low-level patronage as a reward for past party service, let alone prospective party work such as getting out the vote.[21] James Q. Wilson pointed out the conflicting uses of patronage—to maintain the organization or to maximize the vote—and the inevitable trade-off between rewarding all ward bosses equally or disproportionately rewarding the most effective vote producers.[22]

Recent empirical studies of urban machines have concluded that bosses allocate patronage for purposes other than maximizing the vote. In a study of the allocation of summer CETA jobs in New Haven, Michael Johnston shows that the Italian bosses practiced ethnic particularism rather than vote maximization. Most of the federally funded jobs went to Italians rather than to blacks, the party's most loyal supporters.[23] In a similar study, Thomas Guterbock examined the job and service allocation decisions of Chicago machine politicians in a typical ward in the early 1970s. Guterbock found that the machine overrewarded the fickle and independent middle class and systematically underrewarded the faithful lower class.[24] Studies such as these have supplied the evidence for a mounting attack on a vote-maximizing exchange model of machines.

Our analysis of the methods used by the Irish urban bosses to maintain power enables us to shed some light on the utility of exchange theory. At the outset, three crucial points must be made. First, there were basic differences in the terms of the machine's transaction with working-class voters compared to its transaction with their middle-class counterparts. Patronage and welfare services, not clubhouses and friendship, were the essential ingredients needed to build working-class support. Machines could dispense with public jobs in accommodating middle-class voters, but the middle class demanded its own brand of neighborhood and homeowner services. Complicating the building of cross-class alliances in the postwar era was the overlapping issue of race. Middle-class whites also demanded the preservation of white neighborhoods and schools.

Second, the big-city bosses behaved much like the congressmen studied by Richard Fenno.[25] For purposes of allocating benefits and building electoral coalitions, both sets of politicians viewed their constituency as a set of concentric circles. The bosses divided voters into supporters and opponents. Among supporters, machine politicians further distinguished between primary and secondary constituencies. For the Irish bosses the primary constituents were, first, party workers and payrollers and, second, their fellow Irishmen. Needless to say, there was substantial overlap between these two core clientele groups.[26]

Third, exchange theories implicitly assume a fixed number of claimants and a fixed amount of resources. In actuality, bosses were constantly manipulating both the supply of and the demand for machine resources to achieve minimal winning electoral coalitions. Coalition building, particularly with working-class voters, depended on a favorable *exchange ratio* between resources and political supporters. As good oligopolists in the local political marketplace, bosses actively worked to keep competitors and newcomers out. They worked as fervently to pyramid their supply of material resources, particularly patronage jobs. In the following section we present a more sophisticated exchange model of machine behavior, one that considers the *relationship* of resources to claimants and the active role of bosses in managing both.

Managing Conflicting
Constituency Demands

The behavior of the Irish big-city bosses can best be understood as the management of conflicting demands. From "Honest John" Kelly to Richard Daley, the Irish bosses deployed the machine's material resources in order to achieve three objectives: the building of winning electoral coalitions, the financing and discipline of a large-scale patronage-based party organization, and the maintenance of Irish power and prosperity.

These three goals were potentially contradictory because different claimants demanded different policy menus. For the immigrant working class, particularly the Irish, the machine represented a vast social service agency, dispensing jobs and welfare benefits. As the social service tax burden did not directly fall on their shoulders, ethnic working-class renters supported high taxes and indebtedness. Middle-class homeowners and much of the business community, however, demanded low taxes and different services. Ward bosses and precinct captains demanded expansionary resource policies. For these machine functionaries, greater patronage enhanced their power and prestige and expedited the delivery of both votes and services. But the tax burden needed to pay for the machine's patronage army was deeply resented by the middle class and the business community. Finally, continued Irish political hegemony in the face of demographic changes increased the risk of revolt by unrewarded ethnic groups.

Given these contradictory demands, how did the Irish bosses build winning electoral coalitions? Vote-getting strategies varied with the class composition of the electorate. Regarding the working class, machine politicians actively worked to create and maintain a favorable exchange ratio between voter demands and party-controlled resources. Bosses improved the terms of exchange in one of two ways: by increasing the supply of resources, or by limiting the number of voters.

Creating Resources. Bosses rarely possessed the cornucopia of benefits suggested by the rainbow theory of the machine and by exchange theorists. Machines generally faced conditions of resource scarcity as the number of claimants far exceeded available supply. Under these conditions, machines had a strong incentive to expand their resource base. Bosses possessed a hierarchy of resources with which to woo groups of voters: party and governmental offices, patronage, services, symbolic recognition, collective benefits, and, when all else failed, cash bribes. These goods can be arrayed along a continuum in terms of their value and their elasticity of supply.

Power—top party and elective offices—represented the machine's scarcest and most conflict-laden resource. Its supply was finite; its allocation, zero-sum. Nothing better illustrates the conflict between the machine's maintenance and vote-maximization goals. In the short run, the Irish monopoly of power preserved the machine. In the long run, the failure to share power with later-arriving ethnic groups eroded the organization's electoral base. The Celtic bosses developed several stratagems to forestall ethnic demands for a reallocation of power. Pliable new ethnic leaders were selected, for example, Mike Scaturchio in Jersey City and William Dawson in Chicago. As demographic changes forced the bosses' hand, the Irish retreated into the inner sanctum of major policy-making and patronage-dispensing positions, giving the new ethnic claimants lesser posts. But too rapid a sharing of power carried the risk of revolt by the machine's core Irish constituency.

Patronage represented a more elastic organizational resource than power. The size of the patronage pie could be increased, previously unrewarded groups could be given the newly created shares, and group conflict could be limited. To protect the Irish monopoly over power, the Celtic bosses encouraged the newcomers to seek patronage instead. But the redirection of group demands contained risks because the Irish also monopolized existing patronage. To protect the jobs of Irish payrollers and to minimize intergroup conflict, the bosses searched for additional job caches. Each inflationary strategy, however, had political risks as well as benefits.

Property tax hikes represented the most direct way of increasing the stock of local patronage jobs. Property taxes supplied the bulk of municipal revenue; wages and salaries represented the major budget outlay in labor-intensive local government. Yet the temptation to hike taxes to generate more patronage was tempered by the risk of homeowner-led tax revolts.

The risk of reprisal varied with the rate of homeownership. Low rates meant that absentee landlords and businesses, not local voters, would foot the machine's patronage bill. High rates meant that large numbers of voters were directly exposed to tax increases. The big-city bosses sculpted their tax policies accordingly.

The cyclical character of urban homeownership patterns—high in the late nineteenth century, low in the early twentieth century, and rising by mid-century—produced a corresponding machine taxation and patronage cycle. The low taxes and limited patronage of the first-generation machines gave way to the taxation and patronage explosion of the second-generation machines. Rising homeownership rates for white ethnics in the postwar era served as a damper on further tax hikes, a lesson learned the hard way by Chicago's Daley and Albany's O'Connell.

When machines could not tax, they went into debt. Relative to taxation, indebtedness solved an electoral problem while creating an organizational one. Machines could raise municipal debt levels without necessarily increasing the tax rate, thus reducing the risk of a taxpayers' revolt. But indebtedness created the wrong sort of patronage. Municipal bonds financed public works projects, generating temporary private sector patronage, primarily in the construction industry, rather than permanent public sector patronage, the backbone of the machine's ward and precinct organizations.

Taxation and indebtedness increased the relative size of the public sector in the local economy. But machines could also promote economic growth, siphoning off a share of the revenue added, without corresponding increases in levels of taxation and indebtedness. The tools used to promote growth were varied. Debt-financed public works projects, limited as they were as a source of permanent machine patronage, improved the urban infrastructure, encouraging business location and investment.[27] In the postwar era, federally financed downtown revitalization programs replaced locally financed public works projects as engines of growth.

Alternatively, the bosses pursued annexation to capture outward-bound businesses and residents. Annexation, while solving an organizational problem, created an electoral one. With the creation of Greater New York, for example, Tammany's patronage supply doubled. Extending the city's boundaries, however, also doubled the number of antimachine voters. The machine's outward-migrating middle-class opponents would continue to have a voice, not an exit.[28]

Given the political costs of these resource-enhancement strategies, the big-city bosses tried to piggyback other sources of patronage on the cheap. During the Progressive era, machines increasingly turned to "unofficial patronage," for example, private sector jobs with businesses franchised by or regulated by local authorities. By increasing the scope of the regulatory state, the machine's reform opponents had unwittingly created new dependencies for the bosses to exploit. Regulated firms such as private utilities and street railroads found themselves employing the machine's henchmen in exchange for favorable governmental action.

Yet there were limits to what Tammany's Murphy termed his "businessmen's plan." Businesses preferred to pay cash to the bosses rather than to hire inefficient party workers. Patronage workers in the private sector did not have the free time for party work enjoyed by their publicly employed counterparts.

Faced with these constraints, the bosses tried to capture other sources of public sector patronage. All six machines studied took over county government. Counties were a many-splendored thing. Crusading district attorneys could be silenced. The county tax assessor's and collector's offices served as vital adjuncts of machine rule. In friendly times, counties represented larger platforms than cities for projecting the bosses' voice into state politics. In unfriendly times, counties served as larger moats protecting machines from attack by state-level rivals. And, above all, counties meant more patronage.

Intergovernmental alliances could also produce state and federal patronage for the big-city bosses. Necessary for stamping out local factional opponents during the machine's embryonic phase, intergovernmental resources were also useful in the bosses' search for ways to maintain power, particularly during periods of economic crisis and local retrenchment. Yet intraparty alliances—and the resources they brought at little cost to local voters—were fragile, particularly in the postwar era as the number of suburban voters exceeded the big-city voting population. The aging machines no longer represented the balance of party or governmental power.

Cash bribes represented a less reliable material inducement than patronage to voters, particularly after the introduction of the Australian, or secret, ballot. With their jobs at stake, the machine's payrollers could be trusted to bring their friends and relatives to the polls. In contrast, the number of bribed voters depended on the machine's campaign fund, counteroffers by the bosses' opponents, and the extent of reform surveillance over the electoral process.

As Gary Cox and Morgan Kousser observe, the secret ballot changed the dynamics of electoral corruption.[29] How could the bosses tell whether bribed voters carried out their part of the bargain in the shrouded polling booth? Risk-averse bosses began bribing the machine's opponents not to vote. Some enterprising bosses like Albany's Dan O'Connell ingeniously penetrated the veil of vote secrecy. The well-oiled O'Connell machine literally refused to lubricate the Republican lever on the city's voting machines. Thus, an antimachine vote was a squeaky vote. With precinct captains listening outside, bribed electors learned to vote in silence.

The machine's core resources—job patronage and power—were given to its core constituency, the Irish. The overallocation of the machine's most valued benefits to the Irish solved group and organizational dilemmas. The Irish moved from the working class to the lower middle class. Bound by ties of ethnicity and material self-interest, Irish ward and precinct captains dutifully staffed the machine's clubhouses, dispensing services for votes. In the long run, though, the Irish resource monopoly created electoral problems as new groups demanded a reallocation of benefits.

But patronage reallocation in the interests of managing a growing electorate collided with the goals of organizational maintenance, Irish political power, and material well-being. As sources of additional patronage were exhausted, the bosses would have to take public jobs away from the Irish in order to reward the non-Irish. A zero-sum job allocation would and did provoke revolts among the machine's Irish foot soldiers.

To reconcile conflicting organizational, group, and electoral goals, the Irish bosses created new and cheap forms of patronage. The Celtic variant on the parable of the loaves and fishes involved a "patronage stretch" to include services, symbolic recognition, and collective benefits. Nearly all governmental resources and powers were converted into particularistic benefits. Nonjob forms of patronage placed fewer demands on tax-conscious city homeowners. With new resource elasticities, the Irish bosses could reward the non-Irish.

In lieu of power and jobs, the Irish bosses gave the Southern and Eastern Europeans services, for example, business licenses and in-kind welfare benefits such as food and shelter, in exchange for political support. Machines also catered to the newcomers' status and recognition needs. Tammany's "Big Tim" Sullivan, boss of the heavily Jewish Lower East Side, donned a yarmulke to solicit Jewish votes. Even the welfare state could be enlisted as a machine vote-getting device. Although the bosses exerted little control over collective benefit programs, they loudly claimed credit for passage of popular labor and social welfare legislation and actively intervened as informational and service brokers. In their quest for minority political support, the machines harnessed themselves to the New Deal and the Great Society.

But patronage elasticity did not mean fungibility. The machine's resource arsenal was pyramidal. Until the middle of the twentieth century, the great resource (and constituency) divide lay between power and patronage (for the Irish) and all other divisible benefits (for the non-Irish). As the Irish began losing the wars of ethnic succession, that divide was finally crossed—first by the Southern and Eastern Europeans, and later by blacks.

In the postwar era, the machine's core constituency shifted—and so did the forms of patronage. With the coming of civil service reform, collective bargaining, affirmative action, and the fiscal crisis, the supply of old-fashioned job patronage was depleted. No longer sufficient as a vote-getting device, job patronage was deployed to maintain the party's grass-roots service and campaign operations. As the machine's core constituency shifted from working-class Irish to white ethnic homeowners, bosses created middle-class patronage. With a sizable middle-class constituency by the 1920s, the Albany machine led the way, specializing in tax concessions and homeowner services. The Chicago machine would soon follow.

Over time, the machine's resource policies followed a cyclical pattern. Embryonic machines faced the greatest pressures to expand the public economy via old-fashioned job patronage. Consolidating machines were mobilizers, pressing newly enfranchised working-class ethnic voters into service to defeat their opponents. Political impressment was not without cost, for the new claimants lined up for the machine's employment and welfare services.

Established machines, particularly with middle-class supporters, faced fewer expansionary pressures. The new forms of middle-class patronage, particularly tax concessions to the machine's loyal voters, reduced the organization's revenue base. Expansionary pressures from the lower class could be met with other forms of new-fashioned patronage, particularly collective benefits provided from "on high" at no immediate expense to local taxpayers. As a consequence, the entrenched postwar machines had modest local public economies.[30]

Deflating Voter Demand.   The creation and distribution of resources was only part of the machine's success story. Machines also had to manage demand, particularly from the working class, in order to fashion favorable trading terms between its products and customers. Contrary to the conventional wisdom, the machine's lower-class clientele was not inert putty in the bosses' hands, susceptible to easy manipulation and low-cost bribery.

In actuality, the Irish machines were generally toppled from below, not from above. The general belief, of course, is that machines were most vigorously challenged by middle-class reform movements. It is true that reformers incessantly nipped at the bosses' heels, occasionally drawing blood and electing insurgent mayors such as New York's Seth Low and John Purroy Mitchel. But reform produced primarily short-term fluctuations in the machine's fortunes, not long-term realignments. In order to overthrow the ancien régime Celtique, reformers had to enlist ethnic and working-class helpers.

The threat of antimachine insurgency from below was real indeed. In the late nineteenth century, local labor parties, not reform movements, posed the most serious threat to the early Irish machines. In the twentieth century, insurgent leaders such as Fiorello La Guardia, John V. Kenney, and Harold Washington put together coalitions of unmobilized and unrewarded ethnic groups to topple once-powerful Irish machines.

Given the dangers to machines of failing to incorporate ethnic working-class voters, why didn't the bosses adopt a policy of total voter mobilization? Mobilization had advantages. Enlarging the size of the electoral universe allowed the bosses to preempt their opponents by reducing the pool of voters available for counter-mobilization. It also enhanced the bosses' ability to project a voice in state and national politics.

But full mobilization of all working-class ethnic groups was costly. It threatened to drain the organization's limited stock of stores and provoke a reallocation of power and patronage from Irish to non-Irish. Faced with supply-side constraints, the Irish bosses turned to the task of deflating demand from below.

Demand deflation took various forms. As oligopolists of the working-class market, the bosses drove rival producers and product lines out of town. Both repression and corruption were used to defeat the machine's labor and Socialist party rivals. The machine's henchmen intimidated labor party speakers and voters. The machine-controlled police force broke up Socialist meetings, revoked the business licenses of insurgent immigrant entrepreneurs, and enforced Sunday-closing laws to stifle Jewish dissidents. When all else failed, rivals for the labor vote were counted out at the polls, as New York's Henry George discovered in 1886. The antipathy shown by the Irish machine was more political than cultural, a jurisdictional battle for working-class allegiances rather than a conservative Catholic predilection for social stability and order.

The Irish machines also kept new ethnic customers out of the political marketplace. Once minimal winning coalitions had been constructed, the machines had little incentive to naturalize, register, and mobilize the votes of later ethnic arrivals. Mobilization of the newcomers, particularly the Southern and Eastern Europeans, would have been difficult for the bosses in any event. The new ethnics were handicapped by language and cultural barriers, contributing to their slow political mobilization. Tightened naturalization and suffrage laws created additional barriers to electoral participation.

The sharp post-1896 decline in voter participation rates in the large urban-industrial states has been the object of considerable debate. The big northern and midwestern states experienced 15 percent to 20 percent declines in voter turnout between 1896 and 1912. One leading theory of demobilization looks at the role of national economic elites in depressing political participation levels. Walter Dean Burnham has argued that the exigencies of corporate capitalism demanded that the political economy be insulated from working-class pressures during the brutal takeoff phase of industrialization.[31]

According to Burnham, the American industrial elite was particularly vulnerable because of the early extension of the franchise relative to other industrializing countries. Economic leaders brought the industrial workforce to heel by reducing interparty competition in the big urban states and by tightening the electoral rules of the game. The northern financial and industrial elite thus buffered itself from countervailing pressures from below.[32]

The Burnham corporate conspiracy thesis has been challenged by a political-institutional theory of demobilization. Philip Converse and Jerrold Rusk argue that legal-institutional changes such as personal registration laws, the secret ballot, and the direct primary were responsible for the drop in turnout (more modest than Burnham claims) in the big urban states. National economic elites displayed little interest in electoral reform and in shrinking the urban-industrial voting universe. Instead, state and local *political* leaders—urban reformers and rural party elites—led the battle for electoral rule changes in order to weaken the corrupt big-city machines. Restricted access to the ballot box, not the rise of one-party politics, represented the primary instrument causing turnout decline among the urban working class.[33]

Our case studies of the big-city Irish machines shed some light on the demobilization debate. They underscore its local and political character. Yet contrary to the Converse-Rusk argument, demobilization made strange political bedfellows—and beneficiaries. Although the big-city Irish Democratic bosses initially opposed the suffrage restriction movement, they welcomed its consequences. Entrenched machines had already fashioned minimal winning electoral coalitions. Voter restrictions weakened challengers, not supporters, of the machine by reducing the number of immigrant working-class voters available for countermobilization. Instead of strengthening the reformers' hand against the machine, electoral reform could do precisely the opposite.

Alongside these formal hurdles, the Irish Democratic bosses were busily constructing informal ones. Where Irish Democratic power was consolidated by the turn of the century, the big-city bosses actively worked to insulate local politics from challenges to *their* hegemony. Electoral calculations hinged on a manageable vote, not necessarily a large one. Party-sponsored naturalization and registration of the immigrants atrophied. Machine politicians used repression and corruption to discourage immigrant labor party opponents. The machine's electoral neglect of blacks and Hispanics in the 1970s would be a replay of its nonfeasance toward the Southern and Eastern Europeans in the early twentieth century. Only in competitive-party cities such as Chicago in the 1920s would the Irish politicos work tirelessly to help the new immigrants surmount the hurdles of naturalization, registration, and voting.[34]

A Reconsideration of Exchange Theory

Exchange theory does much to explain the behavior and success of the big-city Irish politicos. Throughout most of its history, the machine traded material benefits for electoral support. The most active trading stocks, however, varied between cities and socioeconomic classes. Where machines primarily relied on working-class constituents, patronage and welfare services were the essential bargaining chips. With the nationalization of American politics, the sources of patronage and welfare support shifted from the local to the federal government. To middle-class voters, in contrast, low taxes and local homeowner services mattered.

The machine's multiple streams of benefits and beneficiaries help explain seeming anomalies in its behavior. Studying the Daley organization in the early 1970s, Thomas Guterbock was puzzled by the "irrational" behavior of many precinct captains. The party lieutenants specialized in handling middle-class service demands, acting as brokers between homeowners and the street and sanitation departments. Local party officials devoted less attention to lower-class demands. Rather than expediting the delivery of social services to the poor, the machine's henchmen referred supplicants to the appropriate public or private social service agency. At election time, however, machine support was greater among lower-class than middle-class voters. Guterbock concluded that exchange theory does not capture the machine's behavior.[35]

Exchange theory may be equal to the task. The postwar Chicago machine had the greatest leverage over city departments such as streets and sanitation that handled homeowner demands. With high voting rates among the middle class, the machine was understandably solicitous of its needs and could do something about them. Conversely, the machine had less leverage over welfare-state programs. Here its function was largely informational, putting the needy in contact with the appropriate social agency. Yet the machine successfully claimed credit for the stream of welfare-state benefits to the poor, the organization's most loyal supporters.

Notwithstanding the general usefulness of an exchange model of machine politics, the approach needs to be broadened in two ways. First, although the conventional wisdom views machines as single-purpose institutions, relentlessly pursuing vote maximization to the exclusion of all other goals, the bosses in fact serviced multiple actors in the political marketplace—voters, party functionaries, state and federal leaders, particular ethnic groups. Each made demands on the organization's scarce resources. A revised theory needs to specify the terms and tradeoffs of these multiple transactions.

Second, exchange theory views distributional decisions as central to machine politics. Yet allocational choices were made in the broader context of resource and demand management. An adequate account of machine politics must analyze how the bosses created resources and how they managed the demands of multiple constituencies, not merely how they allocated portions of the pie to various claimants. The bosses were chefs and maître d's as well as servers.

The Machine's Decline

The machine's demise has also generated considerable controversy. Two general theories of machine decline have been advanced. *Resource* theories look at what the bosses offered to political supporters, for example, patronage jobs, welfare services, and clubhouses. In this view, diminished control over benefits hastened the end of the big-city machines. *Demand* theories look at what political supporters wanted from the machines. In this view, the assimilation of the machine's traditional ethnic supporters into the public-regarding middle class sounded the death knell of boss rule.

Resource Theories

There are several resource theories of the machine's decline. The most famous suggests that the municipal reform movement of the early twentieth century dried up the bosses' supply of enticements. In the standard progressive account, reforms such as civil service, nonpartisanship, and the direct primary brought the bosses to their knees by weakening the machines' control over both resources and voters.[36]

The reformers' victory statements were made prematurely, before all the returns were in on the machine's staying power. If reform had been successful in depleting the machine's resource supply, there should have been a subsequent decline in both the number and the strength of the big-city machines. Yet the heyday of machines was the 1920s, *after* the reform movement had crested. The postreform Tammany Hall of Charles Francis Murphy and the Hague organization in Jersey City, for example, easily outperformed their prereform predecessors as vote getters and as patronage dispensers.

At best, the urban reformers succeeded in driving the big-city bosses into temporary exile. In the eight cities studied, reform rarely produced an enduring coup d'état. Championing austerity programs unpopular with the working class, reform mayors rarely lasted more than one term. As Tammany ward chieftain George Washington Plunkitt observed, reformers "were [like] mornin' glories—looked lovely in the mornin' and withered up in a short time, while the regular machines went on flourishing forever." [37] Reform movements dethroned machines only when they produced long-lasting local electoral realignments. For this, progressives had to enlist the machine's traditional working-class ethnic supporters with a welfarist set of policy offerings.

Changes in the rules of the local game dampened the machines more than reform mayors did, particularly in the case of embryonic organizations. Already controlling government and the electorate, established bosses could circumvent such reforms as civil service and nonpartisanship. For prospective bosses, however, the task was more difficult. New machines had high start-up costs, requiring generous resource infusions to construct the requisite grassroots party organization and electoral coalition. Brand identification had to be established with voters. Ward and precinct organizations had to be created and staffed. Party henchmen had to infiltrate government so that services could be delivered on call to the machine's supporters. In the short run, would-be bosses could circumvent single reforms. In the long run, multiple reforms created barriers to machine building. Reform charters in San Francisco (circa 1898) and Philadelphia (circa 1951), for example, included strengthened civil service systems that depleted the patronage supply, making later machine building far more difficult. The gossamer threads of reform could tie down would-be Boss Gullivers.

Paradoxically, however, reform may have strengthened already established big-city machines by *increasing* the supply of particularistic benefits available for capture. The antimachine camp was divided into structural and social factions. Structural reformers such as New York Mayor Seth Low embraced changes in the formal rules of the game but not increased public expenditures. Pitted against fiscal conservatives were social reformers such as Detroit Mayor Hazen Pingree. Pingree lavishly spent public money on social and recreational programs for the working class and increased local government's regulatory oversight over public utilities and transportation companies.[38]

Social reform could be turned to the bosses' advantage. Increased spending for schools, hospitals, and parks meant more patronage once machines were reinstalled in power and civil service barriers were overcome. The regulatory state created new business dependencies on government, giving the bosses the leverage needed to demand private sector patronage and campaign contributions.

For the ethnic bosses, reform produced electoral cohesion as well as unexpected resources. Reformers tried to break up the unholy alliance between boss and immigrant. To accommodate popular demand and raise needed revenue, the machine tacitly sanctioned liquor, gambling, and prostitution. Led by Protestant ministers, the upper-middle-class Brahmin reformers attacked the trinity of machine-protected working-class pleasures. Championing literacy tests and personal registration, the reformers also attacked the immigrants at the polls. Like the Radical Republican anti-immigrant crusade of the 1860s, the progressive reform program backfired. Spurned by nativist reformers, the immigrants retreated into the bosses' embrace.

If the progressives did not bring down the big-city bosses, what did? A second resource theory argues that rival institutions, particularly the welfare state and labor unions, outbid the old-style bosses for working-class support. Presidential adviser Rexford Tugwell and novelist Edwin O'Connor have proposed the most famous version of this theory.[39] For Tugwell and O'Connor, the responsibility for the bosses' "last hurrah" was placed at the doorstep of the New Deal, which brought down the old-time urban machines by taking working-class handouts out of the bosses' hands and replacing them with Social Security and unemployment checks. With the welfare state's arrival, the bosses' monopoly over working-class benefits supposedly was broken.

Yet the New Deal's effects on the big-city machines were far more complex and contradictory than the broken-monopoly hypothesis allows. Three critical distinctions must be made. First, new machines were far more vulnerable to external shocks than were old machines. Second, the impact of the New Deal's electoral coalition needs to be distinguished from the impact of federal social legislation. Third, different pieces of the Roosevelt legislative program had different consequences for urban political organizations and the resources they controlled.

In some ways the New Deal did weaken the big-city machines. The New Deal electoral alliance overthrew or weakened established GOP machines in cities such as Pittsburgh and Philadelphia. Even the Irish Democratic machines were not immune to the new Democratic majority. Roosevelt's electoral coalition included previously nonvoting Southern and Eastern Europeans, eager to overthrow their Irish wardlords in cities like New York and Jersey City.

As with progressive reform, the New Deal's social welfare and labor legislation made it more difficult to build *new* machines. In particular, labor emerged from the 1930s a strengthened political actor in local politics. Unions began performing traditional party functions like preprimary endorsements and getting out the vote, making it more difficult for prospective bosses to build strong independent party organizations.

The New Deal also energized congressmen and senators as federal benefit dispensers, weakening postwar bosses in nonmachine cities. In faction-torn Boston, for example, welfare-state assistance and national public works projects were channeled through federal, not local, officials. Postwar machine builders in the Hub would confront a powerful and independent federal political hierarchy. In Chicago, however, the emerging local machine coalesced with the New Deal, capturing federal offices and programs in the process. The machine controlled the postwar selection of congressmen and retained control of federal benefits.[40]

Yet for the Irish Democratic machines that survived the New Deal's initial electoral onslaught and for the new generation of more ethnically heterogeneous machines built on the New Deal majority, Roosevelt's social programs represented a massive infusion of desperately needed resources. Machines contributing most to FDR's reelection prospects captured relief programs such as the WPA, more than doubling the patronage available for party distribution. The WPA meant popular neighborhood projects and services as well as patronage jobs, enhancing the machine's vote totals. As Daley demonstrated in Chicago, even the New Deal's permanent social welfare legacy of public housing and AFDC could serve as pillars of local party organization.

A third resource theory of urban party decline looks at the bosses' dwindling cache of social rather than material inducements. James Q. Wilson has argued that Tammany's clubhouses atrophied in the postwar era, presaging the Wigwam's defeat in 1961.[41] Unable to adapt to the arrival of Jews and Puerto Ricans, the aging Irish election district captains retreated to their clubhouses. For party regulars, camaraderie replaced the delivery of services and the mobilization of voters. Reformers stepped into the breach, organizing anti-Tammany clubs throughout Manhattan in order to infiltrate and capture the Democratic party.

Did the collapse of the machine's clubhouses hasten the bosses' demise? Of the Irish machines studied, there was no one-to-one relationship between the vitality of party clubhouses and electoral strength. Strong district clubs built by Tammany Hall and the Hague organization did not prevent the realigning elections of 1933 and 1949. In other cities, however, weakened machine clubhouses predated realignments. In the Bay Area, the Buckley machine's district clubs jettisoned their recreational activities by 1890, concentrating instead on voter registration and party record keeping. The San Francisco working class turned on Boss Buckley shortly thereafter.[42]

Is the clubhouse—electoral support linkage causal or casual? A decline in the bosses' material resources may have produced both the withering of local clubs and the shift of ethnic and working-class voters into the antimachine camp. In San Francisco, worsening economic conditions in the late 1880s reduced Buckley's patronage army, leading to a reduction in clubhouse manpower and responsibilities. In New York, De Sapio's loss of state patronage and prospective federal sinecures contributed to Tammany's inability to prevent reform infiltration. Declining patronage also reduced each boss's appeal to working-class voters. Collapsing clubhouses were part of a more general decline in the machine's arsenal of material inducements to voters.

Demand Theories

A second set of theories explains the machine's demise in terms of changing voter demands. Banfield and Wilson, for example, argue that machines—like the New Deal Democratic party coalition generally—self-destructed. The bosses' very successes in raising the standard of living of the immigrant working class proved their undoing. As the ethnics moved into the middle class, they dropped their private-regarding, machine-supporting ways.[43]

This so-called assimilation theory allows the immigrants—but not the bosses—to change their ways. In actuality, postwar machines did adapt to middle-class tastes. As the number of middle-class voters grew, machines switched their policy offerings from high taxes, patronage, and welfare services to low taxes and homeowner services. The policy transformation was not smooth and automatic. The O'Connell and Daley organizations, for example, needed the goad of taxpayer uprisings to shift policy gears.

Prosperity, particularly in the postwar era, may have inhibited middle-class ethnic support for a *new* generation of big-city machines. Yet a middle-class ethnic backlash is not the key to the downfall of the entrenched machines. The classic Irish Democratic organizations were destabilized from below, not from above. The unincorporated ethnic and minority working class, not the rising middle class, brought down the bosses in San Francisco, New York, Jersey City, and now in Chicago.

These machines may well have self-destructed, but in different ways than those suggested by assimilation theory. The machine's ethnically segmented electoral-mobilization and resource-allocation policies promoted interethnic conflict within the working class rather than interclass cleavages. Exclusionary policies produced antimachine mobilization on the part of unincorporated ethnic groups. Admittedly, the Lawrence organization in Pittsburgh is an outlier in this deprivation-mobilization theory of machine decline. Rather than machine exclusionary policies, a leadership vacuum in the late 1960s ushered in an era of reform in the Steel City.

Upsetting the Terms of Exchange

Explaining the demise of the classic Irish-American big-city machines is more complicated than the resource and demand theories allow. Declining resources—particularly patronage and welfare services—hurt machines with heavily working-class constituencies. Machines with middle-class constituencies and policies were less buffeted by retrenchment. But the Progressive movement, the New Deal, and the Great Society did not necessarily weaken the bosses' hold over the working class. Far from reducing either the machines' supply or monopoly of jobs and social services, each "reform" movement actually added to the bosses' stock of material inducements.

What mattered for the machine's longevity was the overall *relationship* between resources and groups of claimants. In particular, bosses strove for a favorable exchange ratio between party-supplied resources and voter demands. As the ratio rose, larger proportions of the electorate were incorporated within the machine's material reward system. The organization's electoral cushion rose. As the ratio dropped, however, larger proportions of the active electorate were deprived of the machine's resources. The ratio could drop in two ways. First, the stock of resources could drop while voter demand remained constant. Second, increases in the size of the electoral universe could outpace growth in the stock of resources. Large pools of deprived voters could be enlisted against the machines.[44]

Bosses tried to manage both the level of resources and political demand to maintain favorable exchange terms. Yet *external* political and economic forces could upset the trading terms established by the bosses in the local political marketplace, setting the stage for insurgency. Consider the role of external forces in the three major episodes of ethnic and working-class insurgency against the Celtic machines. In the 1870s and 1880s, state political leaders employed constitutional fiscal restraints to starve the Irish urban Democracy. The voter-resource ratio dropped as the patronage supply failed to keep up with the growing number of newly enrolled immigrant voters. The Buckley machine fell in San Francisco. In cities like New York, the Irish bosses were forced to use corruption and repression to best their powerful labor party opponents.

The stable second-generation Irish machines stockpiled resources and shrank the relative voting universe, reversing the exchange ratio. Yet ethnic and working-class insurgency mounted in the 1930s and 1940s in response to national economic and political forces. The Depression forced local payroll retrenchment. The New Deal coalition mobilized the unrewarded Southern and Eastern Europeans. The terms of machine exchange became unfavorable again as the number of claimants grew faster than resources. Where federal resources were not given or were subsequently withdrawn, the second-wave migrants revolted against their Irish political patrons. Tammany Hall and the Hague organization fell to the new ethnic working class.

The third-generation Irish machines required a steady infusion of federal resources to maintain favorable exchange terms with lower-class minority voters. Welfare-state benefits replaced local patronage as the primary machine inducement to the third-wave migrants. Social program retrenchment in the early 1980s, however, produced a worsening trade balance between the machine and minorities. The threatened withdrawal of previously granted benefits remobilized the black community against the aging white big-city political organizations, which failed to protect their minority clientele against federal cutbacks.

To what extent can we generalize this theory of the urban machine's life cycle? The theory is derived from a study of the evolution of the classic Irish Democratic machines in the heavily ethnic northern cities. More research is needed to determine whether the same organizational dynamics were evident in other places without Irish bosses, new immigrant constituencies, and competitive state party politics. Southern and border cities such as New Orleans, Baltimore, Memphis, and Kansas City produced Democratic machines where these conditions were missing. With smaller Irish-American populations in the southern cities, the ethnic makeup of the machine's governing circle was different. Celtic machine politicians could participate as individual players but not as ethnic prime movers. How did the lessened Irish role affect the coalition-building and resource-allocation strategies of the southern machines? In the southern cities, racial and class polarization, not ethnic conflict, constituted the dominant political cleavages long before the influx of blacks and Hispanics into the northern cities. How did this cleavage pattern affect the machine's electoral appeals and policies? Finally, the "southern relations" of the northern machines emerged in one-party states where factionalism within the Democratic party represented the dominant political cleavage. How did intraparty factionalism affect the building of the southern machines? A more general theory of the urban machine's life cycle needs to compare the northern and southern Democratic variants.[45]

A more general theory of machine building should also address the northern Republican big-city relations. Powerful GOP organizations ran cities such as Philadelphia, Pittsburgh, and Cincinnati from the Civil War to the Great Depression. Although the Republican and Democratic machines have been treated as nearly identical except for the party label, there were major differences between them.

In the urban Republican scheme of things, politically rebaptized Irish were, at best, junior coalitional partners in Yankee-controlled organizations. More reliant than their Democratic counterparts on middle-class votes, the GOP big-city juggernauts had smaller public sectors and less local patronage. As a consequence, the local Republican bosses sought and received greater infusions of state and federal patronage to compensate for the local resource shortfall. Because the fulcrum of GOP power was state and national—not local—politics, these big-city organizations were enmeshed in state and national party structures to a far greater degree than were their more autonomous Democratic counterparts. A more general theory of machine building also needs to consider the distinctive ethnic, coalitional, resource, and party alliance patterns of the GOP big-city organizations.[46]

American Machines in Comparative Perspective

While American students of machine politics have been preoccupied with organizational life-cycle issues, students of comparative politics have addressed a broader set of relations between party, state, and society. This "clientelist" perspective on the machine emphasizes the historical shift from the "old" patron-client ties linking landlord and peasant in traditional society to the "new" party-directed patronage ties connecting political leaders and voters in modernizing urban-industrial society.[47]

The clientelist approach further distinguishes between two stages of machine politics associated with the evolution of the modern state. The first stage features local, patronage-based, "orthodox" party organizations at the periphery of a weak national state characterized by limited functional responsibility and geographical fragmentation. The second stage features "neotraditional" or "mass patronage" local party structures integrated into strong national political parties and into centralized welfare and economic development programs.[48]

The Christian Democratic (DC) party in southern Italy in the postwar era has served as the model for this two-stage theory of machine development. Studying the DC machine in Catania, Mario Caciagli and Frank Belloni argue that the political demands accompanying urbanization and industrialization overwhelmed pre-existing individualistic clientelist networks. In response, the Christian Democrats solidified power by creating a new form of mass clientelism linking groups to public power. Lacking local resources, the DC bosses turned to national resources, particularly economic development programs, to build the new clientelist system.[49]

In a parallel study of the postwar Christian Democratic machine in Palermo, Judith Chubb argues that the new "mass patronage" clientelism rested on the local party's monopoly of resources rather than on an ever-increasing supply of benefits. Given economic underdevelopment and limits on both local and national resources, the Palermo bosses maintained power by astutely monopolizing resource transfers from the core to the periphery. The DC controlled the local entrepreneurial class with its state-assisted urban development and credit programs. The machine appealed to the traditional middle class and to the poor with its licensing and discretionary law enforcement powers. Finally, the DC used job patronage to control government employees.[50]

Ironically, students of southern Italian machine politics such as Caciagli, Belloni, Chubb, and Rene Lemarchand have denied the applicability of the "mass patronage" model to the American case.

They view the modern American big-city machines as "orthodox" organizations, throwbacks to the weak, localistic, and limited nineteenth-century American state. Lemarchand, for example, argues that American machines like the Daley organization use local particularistic benefits such as city jobs and services, not nationally supplied collective benefits, to construct old-fashioned individualistic (rather than modern group) clientele networks. Lemarchand concludes that "the Daley machine in Chicago has a great deal more in common with the Radical machine of Argentina in the 1920s [another orthodox party organization] than they each have with the Christian Democratic machine in contemporary Italy."[51]

Clientelist theorists misunderstand the American case. Since the late nineteenth century the once-local machines have been progressively absorbed into broader party and programmatic structures. The life cycle of the Irish Democratic machines involved a two-stage expansion of linkages—first from local to state, then from state to national. Even the "classic" early Democratic machines such as Kelly's Tammany Hall, though unable to integrate into Republican-controlled national power networks, nevertheless were "mainstream" products of a national political culture that legitimated their acquisitive ethos and distributive logic. This national "patronage culture" actually predates the Jacksonian spoils system of the 1820s, going back to the Federalist patronage machine of the 1790s. Succeeding waves of immigrants injected a "mass" potential into this initially entrepreneurial or elite system.[52]

In the twentieth century, the classical Irish urban machines have served as engines of political modernization, highly integrated into both the modern Democratic party and the national welfare state. The big-city machines and unions were the key institutional building blocks of the national Democratic party of the 1930s and 1940s.[53] By their control of local electorates and congressional representatives, the Irish machines also served as pillars of the New Deal and the Great Society. Although wedded to a "patronage logic," machines actively supported the expansion of the welfare state in order to solve local coalition-maintenance problems. National resources could be used to reward previously unincorporated ethnic groups.

Richard Daley in Chicago and the local Christian Democratic party bosses of southern Italy had much in common after all. Both American and Italian bosses in the postwar era required national welfare-state and economic development programs to maintain power. Clientelist theorists misclassify the postwar American case because they are not aware of the machine's significant post–New Deal linkages with national trends in both party development and the welfare state. Instead, they project into the twentieth century the "localized" late nineteenth-century machines for whom core-vertical linkages were limited to the state level.

America's post–New Deal "mass patronage" machines need further study, particularly in terms of their relationship to national programs. Consider, for example, the current crisis of the welfare state. Clientelist theory views the evolution of modern local machines and national social programs as mutually reinforcing. Consistent with this theory, the American big-city bosses supported and subsequently benefited from Progressive-era social welfare reforms, the New Deal, and the Great Society. The building of the American welfare state made strange political bedfellows. Samuel Beer points out how the big-city politicians actively joined forces with social service advocates in the 1960s to promote "direct federalism"—local lobbying networks in Washington and social program linkages bypassing the states.[54]

But there was a dark side to this mutual symbiosis: potential mutual destruction. While the fate of machines increasingly hinged on the benefits provided by the welfare state, the fate of the welfare state hinged on the votes produced by the decaying big-city party organizations. Yet local politicians were lulled into political inertia by the seemingly automatic nature of social program gains achieved under both Republican (Nixon, Ford) and Democratic (Kennedy, Johnson, Carter) administrations. National bureaucratic incrementalism exacted a local political price. In Chicago, for example, voter turnout rates dropped in the late 1960s and early 1970s as the machine dispensed with mobilizing its welfare-state clientele. Yet this unraveling of the electoral base of the party system, as Claus Offe points out, accentuated the legitimation crisis of the Keynesian welfare state. Machines—and the party system generally—were no longer able to fulfill their mass mobilization function in support of government social programs.[55]

The contradictory relationship between the urban Democratic party and the welfare state deserves far more attention than it has received. In the 1980s it became fashionable to view postwar urban politics through the lens of "pro-growth" coalitions and federal economic development programs rather than through the prism of national social programs. But "pro-welfare" coalitions were as central to the making—and unmaking—of the postwar urban Democratic party as were the "pro-growth" coalitions so provocatively analyzed by John Mollenkopf. Mollenkopf argues that federal urban development programs since the 1930s have been the "principal means" through which the modern Democratic party was created.[56]

The single prism of national revitalization programs such as urban renewal is too narrow to do justice to postwar urban Democratic politics. The welfare state also had a significant political impact on the Democratic-controlled big cities, particularly on those cities dominated by machines (Chicago, Pittsburgh). Mollenkopf, however, studied reform cities (San Francisco, Boston) dominated by pro-growth coalitions and policies. Yet welfare politics affected even these reform cities, for although growth policies preoccupied local decision makers in Boston and San Francisco in the 1950s and 1970s, welfare policies dominated their decision making in the 1930s and 1960s.

By studying reform cities rather than machine cities, Mollenkopf overestimates the antiparty logic of national urban policy since the New Deal. He argues that the New Deal revolutionized the urban political landscape by substituting a program-based, nationally directed bureaucratic strategy for amassing power for a patronage-based, locally rooted party strategy. In this fashion, Roosevelt supposedly built a new reform coalition in the cities.[57]

But the New Deal was most creative in redirecting urban political reality by its *fusion* of party and bureaucracy, of patronage and policy. Far from being antiparty instruments to modernize local government, federal relief programs like the WPA were carefully calibrated to co-opt existing machines and even to help build new ones. Similarly, in machine cities like Chicago, Great Society programs were a complement, not a substitute, for local party organization.[58]

As for future urban coalition building, the welfare state—and local regimes grafted onto it—may contain a dark antigrowth side. Accepting pro-growth politics as an automatic given, Mollenkopf calls for building a new coalition of minority neighborhood organizations and young white professionals.[59] Harold Washington's initial victory by a coalition of South Side and lakefront voters and the recent downtown Chicago building boom seem to bear out this thesis.

Washington tried to ride two political horses—growth *and* welfare services—and was trapped by their contradictory pull. In power, the mayor jockeyed himself into a partnership with bankers and developers to construct a *governing* coalition. But the horse on which he first rode to power was a minority-welfare state clientele jeopardized by Reagan's cutbacks in social programs. This *voting* constituency represented the foundation of Washington's support and has benefited little from his growth policies. In an era of declining welfare, the late mayor also experienced difficulty maintaining existing social service levels to his core constituency.

The future does not augur well for big-city minority mayors such as Harold Washington. Economic trends in aging heartland cities like Chicago (rather than coastal oases like Boston and San Francisco) point toward continuing deindustrialization and accelerating racial and class polarization, not toward the building of multiethnic, cross-class growth coalitions.

Perhaps students of southern Italian politics can provide a lesson about the possible mutually reinforcing character of local economic backwardness and entrenched machines. In her study of the Palermo Christian Democratic party, Judith Chubb argues that economic underdevelopment enhanced the machine's power. Monopolizing national and local resources, the party became "the obligatory intermediary to all transactions involving individuals and public power." Economic growth, however, threatened the DC machine by "creating new sources of wealth and privilege and potential opposition groups."[60]

The post–New Deal American machines developed at the same time as their Italian counterparts and, more significantly, in regions characterized by increasing industrial backwardness. Under new ethnic ownership, the decaying big-city machines of the American rustbowl may turn out to be parasitic of the metropolitan industrial decay they promise to ameliorate, but just as regularly exacerbate, through redevelopment programs. The last of the Democratic machines are also parasitic of the welfare-dependent underclass. The talisman of unbridled growth may not be grabbed as eagerly by big-city minority politicians as some analysts would have us believe, particularly if it entails welfare-state cutbacks.

The political and economic situation of today's urban minorities raises questions about the historical use of local party and state structures to advance the interests of working-class ethnic groups. Paul Peterson has downplayed the political machine's "redistributional" role, arguing instead that the local bosses umpired modest ethnic group "allocational" contests over patronage. For Peterson, redistributional policies are best left to the federal government, not to city hall. Viewed historically, how accurate is the Petersonian model of limited local redistributional politics?[61]

More generally, how did the big-city machines contribute to the oft-noted pattern of American political exceptionalism—the failure to produce European-style social democratic political parties and universal social welfare programs? Ira Katznelson argues that the institutional separation of party machines and unions fragmented American working-class politics by encouraging different ways of thinking and behaving in the community and workplace. Machines encouraged ethnic divisions in the community; unions, class divisions in the workplace.[62] Is institutional incongruity the key to explaining America's muted working-class politics, as Katznelson would have it? Or did the big-city machines and unions work in tandem to fracture the working class along ethnic-racial lines, pitting older arrivals against newcomers? These questions about the machine's ability to *represent* ethnic group and working-class interests are the subject of the next chapter.

Chapter Seven

Rainbow's End:
Machines, Immigrants,
and the Working Class

Cui Bono? The Beneficiary Debate

The performance of the classic immigrant-based big-city machines has sparked a second controversy, which is concerned with the consequences of boss rule. During the machine's heyday, reformers had attacked the urban bosses for weakening democracy and promoting plutocracy. Traditional liberals such as James Bryce and M. Ostrogorski deplored the capture of the postbellum party system by professional officeseekers eager for patronage, power, and profit. For Bryce, America's corrupt spoilsmen were a far cry from the liberal democratic ideal of enlightened party statesmen involved in principled confrontation over the burning issues of the day. Bryce singled out the Irish-American big-city bosses for particular criticism. In their quest for power and spoils, the demagogic Celtic bosses supposedly manipulated the masses of ignorant foreign-born voters, thereby upsetting the counterbalancing role of public opinion over narrow, venal elites.[1]

Social welfare liberals such as Frederick Howe and Lincoln Steffens added a new dimension to Bryce's critique by attacking the unholy alliance between the big-city bosses and the utility and transportation magnates. For Howe, machine politics promoted plutocracy and the exploitation of the poor by the wealthy. Granted lucrative public franchises, monopolists charged the working class all that the traffic would bear. The machine's tax concessions to the wealthy limited the provision of public amenities and welfare services to the needy.[2] For progressive reformers, machine politics had produced the ultimate horror—"the rule of mob and money."[3]

In the machine's twilight era, however, a much different evaluation of its performance has been advanced. In the new pluralist or "rainbow" view, the machine, though imperfectly democratic, incorporated the immigrant working class. Facing competition in the electoral marketplace, big-city bosses found it in their interests to serve as ethnic middlemen, quickly naturalizing and registering successive waves of immigrants. In this fashion, machines ostensibly assimilated the newcomers, fashioning multiethnic "rainbow" coalitions.

For pluralists such as Robert Dahl, the resource-laden machines served as redistributional devices. The votes of lower-class immigrants could be traded for public jobs and other material benefits. The Irish were the machine's beneficiaries par excellence. Capturing the levers of urban power, the Irish could build a middle class on a base of patronage jobs. In the pluralist scheme of things, ethnic political assimilation and economic reward ameliorated working-class grievances. Ethnic-machine politics in this manner is said to have muted more radical forms of working-class political action.

Notwithstanding the big-city machine's decline, this rainbow theory has figured prominently in contemporary minority power debates, promising a pot of gold for today's ethnic groups. In the 1960s and 1970s, blacks mobilized to capture the big cities. The legend of the Irish machines served as an important yardstick in the black power debates, showing how group voting strength could be turned into local political power. Group power, in turn, promised to yield sizable economic rewards such as public jobs and contracts. In the 1980s, big-city minority politicians claim to have expanded their electoral constituency. One part Jesse Jackson and one part Boss Tweed, the new coalitional formula calls for multiethnic "rainbow" politics.[4]

But as the new minorities embraced the pluralist model of group power and coalition building, the model underwent academic revision. A variant interpretation emphasized the machine's symbolic, not material, accommodation of the immigrants. For revisionists such as Raymond Wolfinger, middle-class leadership, not working-class votes, represented the crucial building block of ethnic group power. Ethnic capture of city hall, in turn, promised very little group economic yield. In a recent and influential study, Paul Peterson has pointed out the sharp constraints on local redistributional politics.

At issue in the pluralist-revisionist debate was the machine's capacity to represent ethnic group and working-class interests. In this chapter we reconsider the pluralist and revisionist models, using the data from our analysis of the classic Irish-American big-city machines. Did the old-style urban party organizations politically assimilate the successive waves of immigrants, as the pluralists would have it? Were machines redistributional devices serving as a route of social mobility for groups such as the Irish? How did machines contribute to American political exceptionalism—the failure to produce strong labor parties with social welfare programs?

This debate over the machine's performance in redressing group inequalities is of compelling relevance for today's urban minorities. As blacks take over the citadels of once-Irish big-city power, the question again arises whether group political power can be translated into economic advancement. Though the terrain of urban politics has changed since the heyday of the Irish bosses, with reformed bureaucracies replacing party machines as the chief instruments of governance, the question of the machine's historical role in promoting ethnic assimilation and economic redistribution is still current.

To the extent that the controversy over the future of black, Hispanic, and Asian-American politics in the big cities is dominated by the long shadow of the legendary Irish machine, we need to understand the difference between historical fact and historical fiction. Hence, this chapter concludes by assessing the relevance of machine politics for today's urban minorities and by examining the political mechanisms for incorporating more recent ethnic arrivals to the cities.

Machines and Ethnic Assimilation

The Pluralist Approach

In the postwar era, social scientists eulogized the dying and much-maligned machine. In the 1940s and 1950s, a new generation of empirically trained sociologists such as William Foote Whyte, Robert K. Merton, and Daniel Bell used the machine as a test case to critique the middle-class Protestant value orientation that had dominated social analysis. Buttressing their claims for a value-neutral, functional approach to social science, the Young Turks argued that the censorious view of machine politics ignored the positive functions performed by lower-class ethnic institutions offering unconventional mobility routes. Finding their career opportunities blocked in the Protestant-controlled business world, the Irish had turned to the machine; the Italians, to the mob. Because it served the material needs of the immigrant working class, machine politics persisted, despite middle-class Protestant opposition.[5]

By the 1960s, political scientists such as Dahl, Fred Greenstein, Elmer Cornwell, and Edgar Litt had joined the chorus of machine defenders, arguing that the big-city party bosses had been both ethnic integrators and system stabilizers-transformers.[6] In the hands of the pluralists, the machine became a local precursor to the New Deal ethnic coalition and the welfare state; the boss, a new paradigm of democratic leadership and mass politics.

The pluralist locus classicus was *Who Governs?*, Robert Dahl's 1961 survey of New Haven's political development over two centuries. Dahl's treatment of the Irish party bosses represented part of a larger analysis of successful regime transformation. In nineteenth-century New Haven, an oligarchic system of cumulative inequalities and overlapping privileges (the same hands holding wealth, social standing, and power) gradually and peacefully gave way to a pluralist system of dispersed inequalities and advantages (in which different people controlled different resources).[7]

By the mid-nineteenth century, a new breed of Yankee businessmen-politicians had displaced the "Old Standing Order" of leading Federalist and Congregationalist families. From humble origins, the new self-made entrepreneurs fought to end property restrictions on voting in order to mobilize a new electoral majority of native-born artisans and laborers. But this insurgent elite's primary weapon of victory—the vote—would soon be turned against them. Successfully challenging Yankee leadership at century's end, Irish Democratic politicians naturalized, registered, and claimed the votes of their countrymen in order to forge a new electoral majority.[8]

The Irish bosses then turned to the task of group economic uplift. According to Dahl, politics and city jobs served as "major springboards" for the Irish into the middle class. Controlling the levers of urban power, the Irish traded votes for patronage, accelerating their movement out of the laboring classes. The early machine's patronage cache awaiting capture appeared sizable indeed. In the pre–New Deal era, the big-city machines controlled thousands of public sector and private sector patronage jobs. Tammany Hall, for example, had more than 40,000 patronage jobs at its disposal in the late 1880s. Furthermore, the public sector offered greater social mobility opportunities than did the private sector. In San Francisco at the turn of the century, nearly one-quarter of all public employees were in professional and managerial positions compared with only 6 percent of the privately employed workforce.[9]

Using machine patronage, the Irish supposedly built a middle class with surprising rapidity considering their meager job skills and the discrimination they encountered. In the big cities, the proportion of first- and second-generation Irish in white-collar jobs rose from 12 percent to 27 percent between 1870 and 1900. Among the non-Irish, the white-collar increase was smaller, from 27 percent to 34 percent. As Andrew Greeley has shown, Irish-Americans are now the most affluent of the country's non-Jewish ethnic groups, having translated their apparently early white-collar job gains into a solid middle and upper middle class anchored in business and the professions in the post–World War II era.[10]

Dahl's account of the rise of the Irish "ex-plebes" and the accompanying systemic shift from cumulative to dispersed inequalities is central to a larger pluralist theory of American politics. Placing himself in an Aristotelian-Machiavellian tradition, Dahl highlighted the creative role of political elites such as the Irish party bosses in promoting both change and stability in the modern city-state. In the hands of gifted leaders, the mechanisms of political equality—popular sovereignty, universal suffrage, competitive parties, and the patronage system—could be used to reduce social and economic inequalities.

Our case studies support the pluralist argument regarding the machine's *political* assimilation of the Irish. The English-speaking famine Irish arrived as the competitive second party system was entering its modern or mobilization phase. As the Irish allegiance to the Democratic party solidified, the embryonic machines actively worked to naturalize and enroll Irish voters. Group mobilization allowed the Irish to infiltrate and take over the helm of the big-city Democratic machines.

Yet the machine's *economic* assimilation of the Irish—and its redistributional potential generally—was smaller than pluralists allow. For one thing, early Irish economic progress was slower and more uneven than the growth in white-collar jobholders indicates. As Stephan Thernstrom has carefully shown for Boston, many middle-class gains by first- and second-generation Irish were marginal at best, signaling entry into poorly paid clerical and sales work rather than into business and the professions.[11]

Thernstrom also cautions that it is misleading to compare Irish economic progress with the sluggish performance of the new immigrants. The new immigration was made up of successive waves of impoverished Southern and Eastern Europeans. More instructive is his comparison of the progress of the politically powerful Irish in Boston's labor market relative to that of other early-arriving but politically weaker immigrant groups. First- and second-generation Germans, Scandinavians, and English all climbed the economic ladder more quickly than did their Irish counterparts.

Our case studies of the classic Irish machines suggest that the pluralist model overestimates the magnitude of machine resources and the Irish ability to use them for sizable group economic gain. The Democratic machines of the late nineteenth century offered impressive channels of advancement for *individual* Irish politicians and contractors. But the early machines could do only so much for Irish *group* mobility.

Political and class constraints hampered the early bosses in their search for greater resources. Middle-class Yankee Republicans had not yet migrated to the suburbs. They vigorously contested local elections, demanding fiscal retrenchment. The early Irish bosses like John Kelly also had to contend with opponents in their own ranks: Democratic businessmen-reformers advocating "tight-fisted" economic policies. This bipartisan conservative coalition forced the nascent Celtic machines to pursue cautious fiscal policies, limiting their patronage take.

Republicans dominated state politics during much of this era, reinforcing the fiscal conservatism of the early Irish machines. Republican governors and legislators imposed constitutional restrictions, severely limiting the bosses' ability to raise taxes, increase municipal debts, and reward their working-class ethnic followers. Consequently, as Chapter 2 has argued, only a small minority of the Irish working class in the late nineteenth century could crowd into the machine's patronage enclave.

The twentieth-century machines did a better job of economically aiding the Irish. Political and legal constraints on the bosses' ability to raise and spend money—and thus to create patronage jobs—began to ease as the machine's middle-class Republican and reform opponents moved to the suburbs, as home rule lifted state fiscal restraints, and as the millions of Southern and Eastern Europeans filling the cities demanded new services. Machines directly and indirectly controlled more than 20 percent of post-1900 urban job growth, double their pre-1900 share. In the Irish-run machine cities of New York, Jersey City, and Albany, the Irish were rewarded with more than 60 percent of this newly created patronage. As a result, on the eve of the Depression, at least one-third of the Irish-stock workforce toiled in machine-sponsored jobs.

The second-generation machine's patronage policies appear to support the pluralist argument that politics served as an important conduit of Irish economic advancement. Compared with Yankees, Germans, and Jews, though, the Irish were slow to build a middle class in business and the professions. Today's Irish affluence was latecoming, postdating the heyday of the machine. As even Greeley admits, the Irish middle class was only emerging on the eve of the Depression; its arrival would not occur until after World War II.[12]

In light of Irish political success, why was Irish middle-class status so slow in coming? Was there an *inverse* relation between political success and economic advancement? The Irish crowded into the largely blue-collar urban public sector in the late nineteenth and early twentieth centuries. Yet as low-paid policemen, firemen, and city clerks, the Irish were solidly lower-middle- rather than middle-class. The relative security of blue-collar jobs in public works, police, and fire departments may have hindered the building of an Irish middle class by encouraging long tenure in poorly paid bureaucratic positions. The pluralist machine's apparent cornucopia of resources could turn into a blue-collar cul-de-sac.[13]

It can be argued that by channeling so much of their economic energy into the public sector, the Irish forsook opportunities in the private sector save for industries such as construction that depended on political connections. As Moynihan has accurately observed, the economic rewards of America have gone to entrepreneurs, not to functionaries. Moreover, the Irish public sector job gains were fragile. The Depression forced the cities to cut their payrolls. The 1930s also witnessed the long-awaited revolt of the Southern and Eastern Europeans against their Irish overlords. Thousands of Irish-American payrollers lost their jobs as a result of retrenchment and machine overthrow. Only with lessened job dependence on the machine in the prosperous post–World War II era were the third- and fourth-generation Irish able to move rapidly into business and the professions.

The puzzling question is why the Irish embraced the machine's blue-collar patronage system with such enthusiasm. Dahl has advanced a "blocked mobility" explanation. In his account, the Irish quickly assimilated the American value of upward mobility. However, limited job skills and anti-Catholicism blocked Irish advancement in the private sector. Thus, the Irish, in Dahl's words, "eagerly grabbed the 'dangling rope' [of politics] up the formidable economic slope." [14]

If the Irish so easily assimilated the American success ethic, why did they allow the dangling rope of politics to become a noose? There are both cultural and resource explanations for the Irish overreliance on the patronage system. Moynihan has taken issue with Dahl, arguing that the Irish displayed a "distaste for commerce," valuing security over entrepreneurial success. Seeking safe bureaucratic havens, the Irish settled for marginal advancement through politics. [15]

Borrowing a page from Max Weber, Edward Levine similarly argues that the Irish working class consciously rejected the middle-class Protestant value of economic achievement. Alienated from Protestant values and institutions, the Irish constructed the Democratic party and the Catholic church as mutually reinforcing institutions rooted in working-class Irish Catholic values. For the Irish, power and security, not money or status, represented the highest values. In this scheme of things, social and geographical mobility meant apostasy. Reinforcing their separateness from the Protestant mainstream, politics enveloped the Irish, becoming *the* approved secular career. As the machines have declined, however, the Irish have gradually replaced the values of power and security with those of money and status.[16]

A resource explanation for limited Irish patronage mobility looks to the machine's maintenance needs. To win the jurisdictional battles for working-class support, machines quickly realized the potency of economic appeals. Yet scarce economic benefits had to be spread as widely as possible to realize their full vote-getting value. Thus the Irish bosses stretched patronage, creating large numbers of poorly paid blue-collar positions to maximize the number of working-class voters rewarded. The machine's job growth strategy created ever more blue-collar public employment for the Irish at a time when the cities were moving from a manufacturing to a service economy and when the greatest increases in private sector employment occurred in white-collar ranks.

The party's maintenance needs conflicted with the long-run goal of Irish prosperity. But patronage had short-run economic advantages. The machine's job system allowed unskilled and semiskilled Irish workers to move to the next rung above the working class. In fact, the ready availability of blue-collar patronage helped to *shape* Irish economic horizons, encouraging the values of security, seniority, and slow bureaucratic advancement.

The pluralist view of the machine as an integrator of the immigrants has been applied to the Southern and Eastern Europeans. Elmer Cornwell, for example, argues that the Irish bosses in the northern cities were forced to politically assimilate the second-wave immigrants in order to continue to win elections.[17] Competitive electoral pressures encouraged the Irish bosses to naturalize and register the newer arrivals. Our survey of the classic Irish machines found that the machine's invisible hand did not automatically embrace the newcomers. Mature machines were one-party regimes lacking the political incentive to mobilize the second-wave immigrants. The Irish Democratic bosses had already constructed winning electoral coalitions among early-arriving ethnic groups. The newcomers' political assimilation would only encourage demands for a redistribution of power and patronage.

In entrenched machine cities like New York and Jersey City, naturalization and voter registration rates for the Southern and Eastern Europeans remained quite low until the late 1920s. Electoral participation rates for the second-wave immigrants increased thereafter in response to national candidates and issues rather than to sponsorship by local party bosses.

In competitive party cities, however, the Irish party chieftains worked energetically to mobilize the Southern and Eastern Europeans. The fledgling Democratic machines of Chicago and Pittsburgh most successfully mobilized the newcomers. As the minority party in these cities in the 1920s, the Democrats were forced into actively courting the new ethnics. Chicago's Democratic precinct captains naturalized and registered the new immigrants far more quickly than did their counterparts in one-party New York, Jersey City, and Boston.

Entrenched machines did little to further economic assimilation among the Southern and Eastern Europeans before the latter mobilized in the 1930s. With so much of Irish well-being and group identity dependent on continued control of the machines, Irish politicos were understandably loath to share power and patronage. To preserve their hegemony, the Irish accommodated the slowly mobilizing newcomers in parsimonious fashion, dispensing social services, symbolic recognition, and collective benefits rather than the organization's core resources of power and patronage.

At critical moments the Irish were forced by electoral pressures to enter tactical alliances with some groups for a greater share of the machine's jealously guarded core resources. As Jews flexed their political muscle in New York in the 1920s, the Irish offered them minor offices and a greater share of municipal employment, particularly in the rapidly expanding school system. The Celtic bosses worked as actively to reduce Italian influence by gerrymandering Italian neighborhoods.

Postwar machines such as the Daley organization accommodated the Southern and Eastern Europeans in different and less costly ways than those in which the prewar machines had rewarded the Irish. Wartime and postwar prosperity benefited the second-wave immigrants and their children, propelling large numbers into the property-owning middle class. As homeowners, white ethnics objected to high property taxes to pay for patronage jobs they did not need. The Southern and Eastern Europeans demand a different set of machine policies: low property taxes, the preservation of property values and white neighborhoods, and homeowner rather than welfare services. The postwar Irish-led machines accommodated these taxation and service demands—as long as the Irish maintained control over key party positions and those city offices with major policy-making and patronage-dispensing responsibilities.

Machines did little to assimilate blacks and Hispanics. In the pre-1960 period, black sub-machines to the white machines had emerged in cities such as Chicago and Pittsburgh. Congressman William Dawson, the only black in the Daley machine's inner circle, ran the black sub-machine in the South Side ghetto. To counter the threat of Polish insurgency, Dawson and his lieutenants mobilized the minority vote for Mayor Daley. As the threat of white revolt diminished in the 1960s, the threat of black revolt grew. Using welfare-state benefits, the machine systematically demobilized the black vote.

Contrary to pluralist theory, the big-city machine's political and economic incorporation of ethnic groups was limited. The Irish represent the theory's par excellence case. The nascent Democratic machines actively assisted the Irish in acquiring citizenship, in voting, and in securing patronage jobs. Yet pluralist theory exaggerates the ability of the Irish to turn political into economic success. The economic disadvantages suffered by the Irish could not readily be overcome by politics; they may even have been aggravated. Celtic economic success came *after* the machine's heyday. Failing to consider the class and political constraints on the machine's creation and distribution of resources, pluralists overestimate the old-style party organization's redistributional capacity.

The pluralist case is further weakened when we consider the machine's limited assimilation of other ethnic groups. The entrenched Democratic machines did little to mobilize and reward the new arrivals from Southern and Eastern Europe, the South, the Caribbean, and Latin America. Deprived of machine sponsorship, the newcomers would have to rely on internal group resources to contest urban power.

The Revisionist Approach

Raymond Wolfinger recognizes that machines did little to aid ethnic assimilation. Rather than relying on majority party sponsorship, ethnic groups had to develop their own resources to amass power. Where votes represent the crucial group resource for pluralists, Wolfinger points to the importance of middle-class leadership.[18]

The revisionist critique posits an economic determinism wherein ethnic political power follows from the development of "bourgeois" economic power within the newcomer community. Ethnic power is an elite-driven process. Middle-class leaders possess the organizational and communication skills needed to press the group's demands. Because a middle class takes time to build, there is a generational time lag before group influence is achieved.[19]

The model also posits a political determinism in which middle-class ethnic demands must be "linked" to the political system for group influence to occur. Minority parties have greater incentive than majority parties to mobilize and reward the new ethnic group. Minority party bosses forge a group-party linkage by nominating middle-class ethnic leaders to major offices, particularly the mayorality. Only with this ethnic-party elite alliance does group political mobilization occur. The nomination of ethnic leaders seals the party-group "tie," encouraging the group to register and vote en masse.[20]

But ethnic power, even when finally achieved, had limited redistributional potential. Following Oscar Handlin, Wolfinger argues that ethnic group demands were not expansive but conservative, traceable to the immigrants' Catholic peasant origins.[21] Machines, in turn, controlled limited material benefits. As a consequence, machines gave immigrants few tangible benefits. "Politics," Wolfinger concludes, "has not been a pathway enabling ethnics to attain equality in social and economic life."[22] Instead, the party system specialized in symbolic inducements. Catering to the status needs of the emerging ethnic middle class rather than to the material needs of the working class, local bosses successively "recognized" aspiring groups with elite nominations to public office.

Wolfinger's theory accurately describes the case it is based on— New Haven's Republican-leaning Italians. In the early twentieth century, the Irish controlled the city's majority Democratic party and did little to assimilate the Italians. Led by the farsighted Ullman brothers, the Republican party actively courted the Italian vote. As the Italians moved from the working class into the middle class, the Republicans nominated William Celentano for mayor in

1939, the first Italian selected for a major public office. Celentano won in 1945 as thousands of newly registered Italian Republicans went to the polls, sealing the local ethnic-party alliance.

But New Haven's Italian Republicans were an atypical case. In other Democratic cities, the GOP was slow to pick up the ethnic slack. Republicans in New York and Boston soured into nativism and conservatism in the 1920s, turning their backs on the new immigrants. Tammany Hall got the Jewish and Italian vote by default. The Irish Democratic bosses complicated minority party challenges by grooming their own kept ethnic leaders. Ever on the lookout for potential opposition, the Hague machine gave the city's sanitation contract to Italian loyalist Mike Scaturcchio. In cities like Chicago and Pittsburgh, the national Democratic realignment of the 1930s overshadowed local party-group alliances as a prime energizer of new ethnic leaders and voters. Italian Fiorello La Guardia and Czech Anton Cermak, for example, rode the New Deal's ethnic turnout surge into the mayor's office in the nation's two largest cities.

In northern cities, the Italians lacked group voting power, as important for building group influence as a large middle-class and party sponsorship. High rates of return migration to Italy, limited familiarity with English, and literacy test barriers for naturalization and voting drastically limited the number of Italian-American voters, creating disincentives for *any* party to mobilize the newcomers. Growing Italian voting strength, however, changed the party calculus. In New Haven, rising Italian voter participation rates in the 1930s encouraged the GOP to first nominate Celentano for mayor in 1939.

The first-wave immigrants from Western Europe clearly represent confounding cases for Wolfinger's middle-class hypothesis. The Germans, English, and Scandinavians, who were the first to develop middle classes, had their politicization impeded precisely for this reason. For the Irish, in contrast, the possession of political power long predated the development of a middle class. As saloonkeepers, volunteer firemen, and foremen on public works projects, early Irish leadership emerged from the working class and lower-middle class. Green Power did not await elite nominations and recognition from on high. Instead, the Irish built power from the grass roots, infiltrating the bottom of the political hierarchy as precinct and ward captains and as nominees for minor public offices. Working-class Irish built a politics of group electoral mobilization, party activism, and patronage.

Machines and Working-Class Politics
The Pluralist Account

Both pluralists and revisionists agree that machines retarded the development of labor parties. However, they disagree about the mechanisms used to produce this outcome. For Dahl, machines rapidly mobilized and paid off ethnic groups with divisible benefits. It was precisely the machine's large-scale distribution of jobs and services to the immigrant working class that was responsible in the pre–New Deal era for defusing the potential of militant labor parties and for delaying demands for collective welfare benefits. The Irish party bosses simply outbid their rivals for working-class political support, beating back the challenge of local labor parties in the late nineteenth century and the Socialist party after the turn of the century.[23]

Our case studies suggest that the pluralist model accurately describes the patronage system's conservatizing effects on assimilated ethnic groups. Patronage helped quell Irish working-class radicalism. The late nineteenth-century machines had little patronage at their disposal to reduce working-class support for local labor parties. The patronage-rich machines of the early twentieth century, in contrast, put the Irish on the city payroll in droves, dimming their enthusiasm for labor politics.

Yet the machine's triumph over militant opponents was a product of more than ethnic assimilation and patronage. Other means of fending off challenges were employed. First, the Irish machines pursued a divide-and-conquer electoral strategy that set ethnic groups at one another's throats. Having discovered a winning electoral formula, mature machines fractured the working class into incorporated and unincorporated ethnic groups. In the pre–New Deal period, the Democratic machines mobilized and rewarded the Irish but not the Jews, Italians, and Slavs. In the post–New Deal period, machines systematically mobilized and rewarded white ethnics but not blacks and Hispanics. Selective incorporation by the machine heightened ethnic conflict, thereby inhibiting unified working-class political action.

In this fashion, the big-city bosses actively participated in reducing the size of the working-class voting universe, thereby increasing any challenger's mobilization costs. Rival parties would have to naturalize, register, and secure the votes of the working-class nonparticipants. In the post-1896 period, entrenched machines abetted capital in insulating the political system from pressures from below that might challenge their respective political and economic hegemonies.

Second, machines split off the ethnic masses from their potential leaders through the process of co-opting the emerging lower-middle class. Michael Rogin has accurately observed that ethnic party and union leaders were more conservative than the ethnic masses.[24] The fragile nineteenth-century machine's maintenance needs forced the early Celtic bosses to placate business by imposing retrenchment on the working class. But as the robust twentieth-century machines inducted ever-more Irish into the patronage system, elite prudence became mass conservatism. The bosses also used tangible benefits to co-opt aspiring non-Irish leaders, splitting emerging ethnic elites off from the masses.

Third, machines used both divisible *and* collective benefits to establish hegemony over the working class. The pluralist model views the two types of benefits as competing with each other; in fact, they were politically complementary. The Irish party bosses allotted their cache of divisible benefits—patronage—to their core constituency—the Irish. The limited divisible leftovers were given to the strongest ethnic challengers at the coalition's periphery. Yet the patronage-based big-city party organizations also supported welfare-state programs. The Irish party bosses lined up behind Progressive-era workman's compensation and factory safety legislation and supported New Deal labor and social welfare programs. Machines supported collective benefit initiatives in part to dampen new immigrant enthusiasm for progressivism, socialism, and anti-machine reform.

Fourth, the pluralist model ignores the machine's darker, repressive side. The bosses used nightsticks as well as patronage carrots to maintain power. Irish-controlled police departments were frequently used to break up labor party and socialist rallies and to discourage insurgents from going to the polls. Where repression failed, corruption succeeded. The machine's labor challengers were all too often counted out at the polls in close elections.

Ira Katznelson has developed an important neopluralist account of the machine's role in fracturing working-class politics. What is distinctive about the American workforce is its conservatism in the community and its militancy in the workplace. In the community, the rapid extension of the vote to white males in the 1820s and 1830s allowed the early machines to incorporate the immigrant working class. In the workplace, the union movement also developed in the permissive political climate of the antebellum period. Then during the postbellum period, ethnic ghettos reinforced the communal logic of machine politics while organized labor continued to woo successive waves of immigrant workers.[25]

Unlike their European counterparts, who struggled simultaneously to acquire the vote *and* to unionize, institutional dynamics, according to Katznelson, encouraged the American working class to develop different ways of thinking and acting in the community and workplace. Neighborhood-based machines encouraged ethnic and racial identification, demands, and organization. Workplace-based unions, however, encouraged a militant class consciousness. This institutional split created a fissure in working-class political attitudes and behavior, hindering the development of a party-class alignment on the European social democratic pattern.[26]

The problem with this "institutional separation" hypothesis is that neither big-city machines nor unions ever fully incorporated the immigrant working class. Both were ethnically exclusive institutions, fracturing the working class into assimilated and nonassimilated groups. As demonstrated in the case studies, machine-umpired ethnic wars of succession in the community pitted older working-class ethnic arrivals against newcomers. Katznelson's community-workplace dichotomy merely aggravated more fundamental ethnic-class discords orchestrated by political elites.

Organized labor also fought its own internal wars of ethnic succession. Wendy Mink has shown a similar pattern of newcomer exclusion practiced by unions in the late nineteenth and early twentieth centuries. "Trade union nativism" characterized the labor politics of the period. To protect existing union prerogatives and to guarantee jobs for Irish, Yankee, and German union members, the conservative craft union leadership excluded Southern and Eastern Europeans. With the Irish-led old immigrants dominating the big-city craft unions, Jews turned to organizing the needle trades. Later, the Southern and Eastern Europeans would be active participants in organizing the insurgent industrial unions (the CIO) that would challenge the craft unions of the AFL for leadership of the labor movement.[27]

The Katznelson hypothesis is further weakened when we consider the tacit alliance constructed between the Irish machines and the Irish-controlled trade unions. In the Democratic-controlled cities, machine-union ties were forged in the late nineteenth century, creating additional obstacles to party-class alignments. The partnership had a strong caste overlay. The Irish controlled the northern Democratic machines and headed more than half of the big-city American Federation of Labor locals.[28]

But the alliance was as much a product of mutual self-interest as it was an expression of ethnic primordialism. Bosses could do much for local unions. Sympathetic judges and police hampered the ability of capital to break strikes and boycotts. The construction industry, backbone of the early big-city labor movement, valued public works projects. Union officials appointed to public works boards ensured that these projects bore the union label. Unions could do much for the bosses. Tacit alliances co-opted organized labor and its vote, thereby weakening labor party challenges. In turn, machine protection strengthened labor's hand relative to capital, encouraging the very militancy in the workplace that the separation hypothesis takes as a given.

Structural tensions within the working class, then, were as much horizontal as vertical. Katznelson subscribes to a vertical conflict between party-based ethnic divisions in the community and union-based class divisions in the workplace. But there were cross-cutting cleavages. The early machines and craft unions worked in tandem to fracture the working class, pitting an ethnic "aristocracy of labor and politics" against later arrivals. Institutional and ethnic hegemony represented twin motive forces producing these horizontal political fissures.

The Revisionist Account

Pluralism's critics have developed a variant interpretation for the failure of working-class radicalism. Two arguments stand out in the revisionist model. First, the critics downplay the magnitude of the challenge by placing great store in the conservatism of the European peasant immigrants. For revisionists, the cautious immigrants eschewed radical politics. The uprooted also appeared unmoved by populist and progressive insurgency.

Second, the party system performed a different buffering role for the masses than bread-and-butter pluralism allows. For Wolfinger, the party system "horizontally divided" ethnic groups by accommodating in limited fashion the tangible demands of their emerging middle-class leadership strata while denying the masses anything but the intangibles of symbolic recognition. Placing ethnic leaders in high offices was the sine qua non of recognition politics. Recognition, in turn, muted class politics. Symbolic gratification diverted attention from material needs and demands. Group recognition also heightened the salience of ethnic consciousness, thus inhibiting the development of cross-ethnic class consciousness.[29]

There are problems with the revisionist argument. For one thing, it exaggerates the immigrants' conservatism. In the cities, the Irish and German working class supported local labor parties in the 1870s and 1880s. In the twentieth century, the new immigrants endorsed progressive candidates such as Theodore Roosevelt, Woodrow Wilson, and Hiram Johnson. New York City's Jews and Milwaukee's Germans were ardent supports of the Socialist party. In the countryside, Scandinavian farmers supported populism and progressivism.

For another thing, the theory underplays the machine's very real carrots and sticks. Machines specialized in supplying tangible benefits to their core ethnic supporters, reserving "recognition" for weak groups excluded from a meaningful share of power and patronage. If the manipulation of symbols was the essence of machine politics, why did the bosses work so tirelessly to increase their stock of material benefits? Machines also used repression and corruption to prevent leftist parties from winning elections. Far from eschewing radical politics, the immigrants were frequently denied the opportunity of choosing.

Finally, the theory overestimates the potency of symbolic appeals to ethnic groups. Riding the crest of group mobilization, aspiring ethnic elites found they had to satisfy group material needs
as well as status yearnings. The carriers of symbolic politics were
normally the status-conscious *nouveau* middle classes, not the
huddled ethnic masses. Working-class immigrants demanded sub-
stantive, not merely formal, representation. La Guardia, for example, embarked on an ambitious program of civil service reform
and human service spending to create the jobs and services needed
to reward his ethnic supporters and to create a durable electoral
coalition.

Machine Redistribution
Historically Reconsidered

In the 1980s, public choice economists joined the revisionist camp.
Taking his cue from economic theory, Paul Peterson has made a
powerful case against local redistributional politics machine-style.
Peterson's approach can best be considered neorevisionist as he
borrows from the revisionists the "output" argument that local institutions like the machine can do little to redistribute wealth from
the rich to the poor, while taking from the pluralists the "input"
argument of extensive ethnic group bargaining over allocational
issues such as public employment.[30]

For Peterson, economics shapes policy, and policy shapes patterns of urban political decision making and participation. The
Petersonian model divides urban policymaking into three parts:
developmental, redistributional, and allocational.[31] Developmental policies promoting economic growth are the city's raison d'être.
With permeable economies and mobile capital, cities find themselves in a competitive sweepstakes with other locales. To promote
prosperity, local politicians offer investors favorable taxation and
expenditure policies. Because capital can flee in reaction to unfavorable taxation-benefit ratios, local leaders avoid redistributional transfers from the rich to the poor. Public employment and
service policies are allocational policies—the essence of machine
politics. Unlike developmental and redistributional policies, their
economic impact on the city's market position is limited and
uncertain.[32]

Different patterns of political decision making and participation characterize the three policy arenas. Developmental policies feature covert business-political elite alliances. Decision making is done in private, and conflict is kept to a minimum. Redistributional policies represent a species of local nondecision making. Local elites keep them off the urban political agenda, kicking them upstairs to the state and national levels. With greater control of the economy, national decision makers can tax capital to pay for welfare-state programs for the needy. An intermediate category in the policy tug of war between the imperatives of growth and redistribution, allocational policies are the stuff of local public decision making. In the pluralist arena, community groups bargain with local decision makers over their relative shares of public jobs and services.[33]

In this neorevisionist model, the machine serves as the allocational device par excellence. Even for party bosses, economic priorities take precedence over political imperatives. The city's economic well-being has higher standing than the machine's maintenance needs. Accordingly, the machine heeds the business community more than the working class. The taxation and expenditure policies needed to promote development sharply constrain the machine's redistributional capacity. As a result, the machine uses ethnic-racial appeals as a strategy to convert redistributive demands into allocational contests over job and service distribution—group contests that can be won or lost without fundamental alteration in the urban capitalist political economy.[34]

Even the machine-reformer conflict is sanitized from the taint of redistributional class politics in this model. For reformers, the primary antimachine issues were corruption and patronage, not the bosses' predatory taxation of property owners. The merit system served as the reformers' consensual holy grail. In the Petersonian scheme of things, the reform-machine conflict over public employment practices was another group allocational issue. But contrary to Peterson the charge of machine corruption had indelible class components. The issue deeply split the business community, as entrepreneurs benefited from the bosses' easing of the legal obstacles to capital formation. Turning a blind eye to "white-collar crime" benefiting members of the business community, reformers instead excoriated the evils of the blue-collar ethnic patronage system.[35]

How accurate is the Petersonian model of the machine, its primarily allocational character, and the limited possibilities for local redistributional policies? The model is rooted in the post–New Deal present, yet claims to speak for the pre–New Deal past. Since the 1930s, developments have taken place that confirm essential elements of the approach. New Deal and Great Society welfare-state programs have highlighted the national government's redistributional role. The creation of national and international markets coupled with new technologies have given capital undreamed-of mobility opportunities. With the American economy stalled in the 1970s, growth became the centerpiece of the domestic political agenda. With highly permeable local economies, a new generation of municipal development specialists competed with one another to entice investors to their city with evermore favorable taxation and policy packages.[36]

But what of the past? Peterson freezes his subject matter in time, treats the transient present as permanent, and fails to appreciate the virtues of a dynamic view of the contingent relationship between present and past. Consider his intergovernmental theory of redistributional policy. For Peterson, nationals redistribute; locals do not. But in the pre–New Deal period, it was precisely the locals who did and the state and nationals who did not. The big-city Irish Democratic machines constantly faced redistributional pressures from below. State and national governments, particularly when controlled by the GOP or reform Democrats, were the biggest *obstacles* to local redistribution.

In the early twentieth century, the Irish machines did serve as limited redistributional devices, taxing business and the middle class in order to put lower-middle class Irish on the city payroll. The patronage practices of the Hague machine—and the taxes needed to support his Irish version of the welfare state—were, as his reform opponent argued, a redistributional issue.

Claiming to offer an intergovernmental perspective on urban politics, Peterson instead reifies the different governmental levels, treating them more like alien essences than as dynamic components of an ever-changing core-periphery system. His picture of how redistributional issues have been kept out of local politics distorts the historical record and accepts as a "given" emerging differences between local and national arenas that, instead, have to be explained.

A more historically oriented model would recognize how nine-teenth-century big-city politics significantly diverged from the Petersonian model. As Amy Bridges points out, during the heyday of the second party system, national policy debates and federal patronage sources were the very stuff of New York City politics.[37] With the breakup of the second party system and continuing after the Civil War, local politics developed its own autonomous par-tisan structure and policy agenda. Yet, contrary to Peterson, these changes, at least for a generation or two, made city governments more—not less—responsive than the federal government to re-distributive pressures and initiatives.

Changes initiated during the Progressive era and accelerated during the New Deal period—the welfare state—gradually insu-lated city governments from redistributional pressures and moved urban political issues such as public employment within the "al-locational" parameters that the Peterson model takes as an un-changing datum. If local politics "stayed the same"—and the lid was kept on local insurgent forces—the reason was that local po-litical elites and newly mobilized lower-class claimants in the 1930s and 1960s generated political forces that made the federal govern-ment expand its role.

A more historically oriented model would also appreciate how big-city economies were more susceptible than at present to local redistributional politics. In the late nineteenth and early twentieth centuries, much of the urban economy was local. Business owners were captives of local markets and customers, unable to move freely as tax burdens shifted. It was precisely their geographical immobility that propelled them into active political involvement, making them guardians of the city treasury.

Capital tied to national markets was less interested in local poli-tics. But even national businesses could be incorporated into local redistributional schemes. Some national businesses were geographi-cally immobile and thus subject to local tax extortion. Needing terminal space in Jersey City in order to transfer freight to New York City, the country's major railroads were forced to pass along the high cost of Boss Hague's welfare state to their customers. In the postwar era, however, the growth of markets and technologies has given capital the upper hand vis-à-vis local political elites that it previously lacked.[38]

The real problem with the Peterson model is that it substitutes a

reified citywide economic logic for political and institutional imperatives. Class interpretations of urban politics sometimes com-
mit the sin of reductionism—reducing structures and policies to
the mere reflex of the groups that articulate them. Peterson, however, surrenders to the opposite, hedgehog-like vice of economically reifying "the interests of the city, taken as a whole," independent of underlying political institutions and forces.[39]

Political machines are a cardinal case in point. The big-city
bosses responded to contradictory economic pressures in terms of
a political logic of building the governing alliances and electoral
coalitions needed to maintain the organization in power. The weak
nineteenth-century Irish bosses had bowed to business pressures,
risking insurgency from below. The strong early twentieth-century
bosses played to the "old" ethnic working class, imposing the cost
of redistribution on property owners. Capital's position in the
urban political economy had become increasingly precarious.
Working-class renters could vote; absentee suburban property
owners could not. Bosses increased the tax rate—supposedly in-
jurious to the economic health of the city as whole—to maintain
the political health of the party organization and its working-class
electoral base. Bosses subsequently cut back on tax hikes when
faced with political reprisal—taxpayer revolts—rather than investment strikes.

Having treated the highly circumscribed boundaries of contemporary city politics as a given, Peterson finally reverses himself,
concluding that, after all, our federal system is an "aberration"
and that "city limits" can be transcended by such tinkering as putting the full faith and credit of the federal government behind all
state and local governmental indebtedness. However, he never ventures a searching historical explanation of why our aberrant federal system developed in the way it did.

From the Founding Fathers on, federalism has been, among
other things, a strategy to kick class-based issues upstairs and thus
keep them out of arenas—like local politics—that are "too close
to home" to allow safe resolution. Creating a powerful national
government that, ultimately, might become an instrument of redistribution as well as of growth was the risk taken by Hamiltonians
intent on restricting the operation of redistributional forces such as
the ethnically based machines in the state and local arenas.[40]

Today's Big-City Rainbow Politics: Machines Revividus?

In the past twenty years the baton of urban power has slowly been passed to the third- and fourth-generation ethnic arrivals—blacks, Hispanics, and Asians. Black mayors have been elected in Los Angeles, Chicago, Philadelphia, Detroit, Atlanta, Washington, Cleveland, Gary, Newark, and New Orleans. Blacks have also been elected in large numbers to city councils and school boards. The new black power is bureaucratic as well as electoral. In the big cities, black administrators have been appointed to such top policy-making positions as city manager, police chief, and school superintendent.[41]

In the Sunbelt, Hispanics and Asians are beginning to transform urban political life. San Antonio's voters in 1981 elected Henry Cisneros as the first Mexican-American mayor of a major U.S. city. Miami has a Cuban-American mayor and a Hispanic majority on the city council. Reversing a century-old legacy of racism and discrimination against Asians, California's cities are witnessing the first stirrings of Asian-American power. Los Angeles's voters elected Michael Woo to the city council, and San Francisco Mayor Dianne Feinstein appointed Thomas Hsieh to the city's Board of Supervisors.[42]

As the new minorities mobilize, particularly the black and Mexican-American communities with large lower-class populations, they have searched for strategies of group uplift. The viability of the machine model was problematic for the new groups. Before the 1960s, minorities were deliberately kept out of the established system of "city trenches." Except for a few independent politicians such as New York's Adam Clayton Powell, the legacy of the machine era for blacks was "plantation politics" Chicago-style. When the minority assault finally came, the old-style party organizations were in the last stages of decline.[43]

In the postmachine era, the prizes of urban politics seemed hollow indeed. The northern cities where blacks had migrated in massive numbers had experienced economic decline, their treasuries nearing bankruptcy. The rapidly growing Sunbelt cities had small, lean public sectors (the legacy of conservative reformers), limiting government job opportunities. To make matters worse, white civil

service commissioners and municipal union stewards zealously
guarded the prerogatives of the heavily white public sector workforce, making it difficult for minorities to translate political gains
into economic advancement.[44]

Even the means of ethnic capture were more difficult. The new
minorities were the victims of reform. In the process of wresting
power from the Irish, the Southern and Eastern Europeans had
created additional barriers for later-arriving groups. The second-
wave ethnics joined Yankee reformers in bringing to the eastern
cities the reforms first implemented by progressives in the West
and South: at-large city council elections, nonpartisanship, educational requirements for public employment, and expanded civil
service coverage. At-large electoral systems, in particular, made it
harder for blacks to gain representation on city councils. Designed
to prevent the machine's reemergence, reforms also made it more
difficult for working-class blacks and Hispanics to gain group influence and benefits.[45]

In this bleak age of reform, a possible return to machine politics
didn't seem so bad after all. Black politicians in particular called
for the machine's resurrection in part or in toto. During the 1960s,
black moderates committed to "working within the system" had
embraced the Irish model of group electoral politics to counter
radical separatist demands. The radical rhetoric of militant nationalism and community control ultimately proved an empty threat,
revealing an incrementalist and patronage core that could be accommodated as the emerging black bourgeoisie took over such
community institutions as schools and health clinics. By the 1970s,
blacks of diverse ideological inclinations had moved "from protest
to politics," emulating the strategy of ethnic group mobilization—
registration, turnout, and bloc voting en masse—first perfected by
the Irish.[46]

To appeal to both militants and moderates in the minority community, contemporary black politicians disingenuously coupled
radical-reformist rhetoric with venerable machine-building techniques designed to enhance group influence and payoffs. Claiming
that at-large electoral systems discriminated against racial minorities, followers of rainbow "reformer" Jesse Jackson in cities such
as Pittsburgh and Cincinnati have pursued the machine gambit of
reviving the ward system. Chicago's "antimachine" Mayor Harold

Washington ransacked city hall and special district governments for additional patronage to pay off his supporters and consolidate power. Reformer Washington also vigorously opposed a move to make the city's elections nonpartisan.[47]

Are black politicians correct in looking to the machine past? What lessons could the departed Irish bosses offer today's minorities about group influence, electoral coalition building, and economic advancement through local politics? Moynihan has argued that the twentieth-century black experience needs to be understood in terms of a critical comparison with the nineteenth-century Irish experience.[48]

Both groups have tried their hand at public sector politics, seeking governmental channels of group mobility. The Irish political experience cannot fully be emulated by blacks because the big-city machines—centralized party structures—are unlikely to be revived in anything like their historical form. Yet machine politics—the trading in divisible benefits—has staying power in local politics. The Irish bosses were the undisputed masters of this game. Can their example educate today's minority power brokers about both the possibilities and the limits of ethnic politics?

On the positive side, the Irish experience demonstrates some potential for group economic uplift through the local political process. The votes of the Irish working class could be translated into group power and a major share of city jobs and services. The twentieth-century Celtic municipal engines served as modest redistributional devices, reallocating economic burdens and benefits within the middle of the class structure. To the extent that the Irish bosses were Robin Hoods, they were selective about their victims and beneficiaries. Rather than taking from the very rich and giving to the very poor, the Irish politicos took from the Yankee middle class and gave to the lower-middle-class payroll Irish.

On the negative side, the Irish machines were as much instruments of social control as of economic reward. The nineteenth-century Irish bosses imposed retrenchment on their followers as the price of keeping power. Black mayors are under the same fiscal constraints today. Retrenchment produced ideological-class schisms among the Irish in the 1880s and is doing the same for blacks in the 1980s. The conflict between Tammany's conservative "long-hair" Irish faction and the militant working-class "shorthairs" finds contemporary expression in the tensions between moderate black mayors and militant followers of the Jacksonian rainbow.

The early Irish bosses parsimoniously accommodated later arrivals on the rainbow bandwagon. With limited resources and pressing group demands, black politicians may have to do the same with Hispanics and Asians. The down-side risk of today's slow-growth politics is that the new rainbow coalition may produce a small pot of gold for the black political elite, while browns, yellows, and even the black underclass are left chasing the mirage.

Concluding the Irish-black comparison on an even more pessimistic note, what will urban politics look like at century's end if present trends in conservative national politics and uneven regional economic development continue? Will big-city minority politicians in declining Frostbelt cities be called on to implement an updated "System of '96"—for 1996? Will black leaders soothe the "mixed multitudes" with populist rhetoric while cutting deals with conservative national politicians? And will federally funded "urban enterprise zones" prove to be the newest species of "plantation politics" designed to discipline the have-nots? Big-city minority politicians might have to take a lesson from the Christian Democratic party bosses of stagnant Palermo after all.

Blacks are now emulating the Irish by using political strategies of group uplift. The means employed, however, are different. The Irish used the big-city party organizations; blacks use local and national bureaucracies. The locus of urban power has shifted from political machines to independent and semiautonomous bureaucracies, organized along functional lines. Furthermore, urban politics has been nationalized. In the post–New Deal era, the political access and economic distribution functions once monopolized by local machines now are nationally performed by the Democratic party and federal welfare-state bureaucracies.[49]

Peter Eisinger finds black mayors pursuing a dual strategy of group advancement in this new arena of urban politics. The first prong consists of the politics of public sector bureaucracies. Black leaders in cities such as Detroit and Atlanta have used their appointment powers to name minorities to head city personnel departments and other major agencies. Minority administrators, in turn, have launched aggressive affirmative action programs, producing a dramatic increase in the minority share of public employment. Black mayors are also using affirmative action to award city contracts to minority businesses. Newark's former Mayor Kenneth Gibson, for example, set aside 25 percent of all federal public works project monies for minority contractors.[50]

The second prong consists of a strategy of "trickle down" from private sector economic growth. Black mayors in Los Angeles, Chicago, Detroit, Washington, Atlanta, and Newark have formed alliances with the white business community to promote downtown redevelopment, hoping to create private sector job opportunities for minorities.

The Irish experience suggests the limits of this dual strategy. On the public sector side, the approach has a major down-side risk—retrenchment. The Irish were the principal beneficiaries of city payroll growth from 1900 to 1929; after 1929, however, they were also the victims of retrenchment. Blacks clearly benefited from the halcyon municipal employment growth of the 1960s and early 1970s. The late 1970s, however, brought municipal austerity, threatening to reverse black city payroll gains. As the last hired, minorities were frequently the first victims of budgetary cutbacks. Detroit's black Mayor Coleman Young, for example, was forced by budget-balancing pressures to fire hundreds of minority police, undoing in a single afternoon ten years of hard-fought affirmative action in police hiring.

Black politicians and civil servants may also face a political challenge to their power and prerogatives. In the 1930s and 1940s, the Irish machine's jerry-built rainbow coalition unraveled as the new immigrants countermobilized, jeopardizing the jobs of thousands of Irish payrollers. In the 1990s, Asian-Americans and Hispanics could challenge blacks for control of the big cities, particularly if black politicians are unable or unwilling to share power and patronage. With a large and prosperous middle class, Asian-Americans in particular might assume the broker role, financing and leading an Asian-Hispanic coalition that could threaten today's black municipal workers.

The Irish experience also suggests caution regarding the extent of "trickle down" to the black masses from publicly subsidized private sector growth. Public investment in urban infrastructure was the early equivalent of today's publicly assisted downtown redevelopment projects. Public works contracts benefited individual Irish contractors while providing temporary low-wage employment for the masses of unskilled and semiskilled Irish workers.

Today, black mayors offer public seed money, tax and zoning abatements, and lease-back arrangements to downtown developers. Ambitious redevelopment projects like Detroit's Renaissance Center and Atlanta's Peachtree Plaza are sold to minorities and the poor on the premise that economic benefits—primarily in the form of job opportunities—will filter down to them. But new convention centers, hotels, and shopping centers are not a viable vehicle of group uplift. Too few jobs are created to make an appreciable dent in inner-city poverty. The limited pool of high-paying professional and managerial positions disproportionately goes to upper-middle-class white suburbanites. Minority "trickle down" has primarily taken the form of a limited number of low-wage service jobs.[51]

There is a vital third element to today's black advancement strategy—federal social programs. Both Irish and black politicians have used the expanding welfare state to consolidate power. The nascent Irish Democratic machines of the 1930s fused with New Deal programs. A generation later, the Great Society served as a catalyst for black power. Studying minority politics in ten northern California cities, Rufus Browning, Dale Marshall, and David Tabb argue that the Great Society programs "provided the functional equivalent of earlier forms of patronage." In the Bay Area cities, federal social initiatives encouraged minority political mobilization, promoted their incorporation into local governing coalitions, and secured greater local governmental responsiveness to minority job and service demands.[52]

The expanding welfare state was more than a vehicle for black assimilation into local politics. It was a primary route of group *economic* advancement. Where the Irish had used machine patronage, blacks now relied on federally funded social programs. In the 1960s and early 1970s, the new black middle class found jobs in the expanding federally funded human services sector—health, education, and welfare. By the late 1970s, nearly half of all black professionals and managers worked in the social welfare sector, compared with less than one-quarter of comparably situated whites.[53]

The welfare state meant more than jobs for the black middle class; it also represented cash and in-kind welfare payments for the underclass. From the mid-1960s onward, the black poor increasingly relied on transfer payments. Two-thirds of poor black families received welfare in the late 1970s, up from one-third in the late 1960s. Economically, blacks were more integrated into the public sector in the late 1970s than the Irish had been during the machine's heyday—but under *federal* and *bureaucratic* auspices.[54]

But black politicians lack integrating mechanisms like the machine that can fuse together the disparate elements of today's urban politics—national versus local, bureaucratic versus electoral. As a result, big-city and minority politics reflect their unreconciled imperatives. The continued flow of welfare-state jobs, transfer payments, and social services, which sustain the black middle class and underclass, depend on group influence and alliance building at the national and state levels where social policy is made and funded. Blacks, however, are not as well organized to press their claims outside the local political arena.

In the absence of local machines capable of mobilizing voters, bureaucratic politics has acted as a depressant on electoral participation. The relationship between the bureaucratic service provider and the recipient differs from the relationship between the party cadre and the voter. Precinct workers are encouraged to mobilize loyal voters on election day. Human service workers, however, have little incentive to politically mobilize their clientele—as long as social programs and budgets grow. In the 1970s, minority service providers increasingly involved themselves in bureaucratic politics within the intergovernmental grant system rather than in mobilizing their clientele in local electoral politics. The expansion of means-tested programs such as AFDC depoliticized welfare recipients by isolating them from the work experiences encouraging political participation.[55]

Whatever the Great Society's initial mobilization effect, it soon acted as a brake on black voter turnout. During the period of welfare-state expansion, from 1964 to 1976, the mass electoral base of black politics in the northern cities eroded. The voting rate for young urban blacks plummeted, from 56 percent to 29 percent, while the rate for unemployed blacks dropped nearly as sharply, from 62 percent to 37 percent. Low turnout hurt big-city black politicians seeking to challenge white-controlled machine and reform regimes.[56]

Welfare-state contraction in the 1980s, however, reversed the bureaucratic expansion-electoral decline cycle. Threatened with job and benefit loss by the Reagan cutbacks, minority social service providers and recipients quickly rediscovered the value of electoral politics. Though primarily generated by national forces, the remobilization drive could be used in local politics. In machine Chicago and reform Philadelphia, black mayoral candidates rode the electoral surge to victory.

It is ironic that the policies of a president who points to his Irish ancestry during campaigns helped to produce the last hurrah for the Irish Democratic machines. Black mayors have ridden the turbulent waves of Reaganite austerity into office. Yet the practitioners of the new ethnic politics are trying to consolidate power with limited local resources and diminished welfare-state largesse. Lacking the tangible benefits demanded by their supporters, the new minority power brokers may discover what was learned the hard way by the now-departed Irish bosses: the real lessons at rainbow's end.

Notes

*All works that appear in abbreviated form in the
notes are cited in full in the bibliography.*

Chapter One

1. Daniel Patrick Moynihan, "The Irish," in Nathan Glazer and Daniel Patrick Moynihan, *Beyond the Melting Pot,* pp. 217–287.

2. James Bryce, *The American Commonwealth,* pp. 101–135; Harold Zink, *City Bosses in the United States.*

3. John Paul Bobcock, "The Irish Conquest of Our Cities," pp. 186–195.

4. Edward M. Levine, *The Irish and Irish Politicians,* pp. 138, 142–143.

5. Lincoln Steffens, *The Shame of the Cities,* pp. 136–138.

6. Ibid., pp. 5, 16–18.

7. Frederick C. Howe, *The City: The Hope of Democracy,* pp. 61–91.

8. M. Ostrogorski, *Democracy and the American Party System,* pp. 225–281.

9. See Robert K. Merton, *Social Theory and Social Structure,* pp. 125–136; Robert A. Dahl, *Who Governs? Democracy and Power in an American City,* pp. 32–62. The rainbow theory of the machine also figures prominently in Elmer E. Cornwell, "Bosses, Machines, and Ethnic Groups," pp. 27–39; and in the Kerner Commission's findings in U.S. National Advisory Commission on Civil Disorders, *Report,* pp. 143–145.

10. Steven P. Erie, "Politics, the Public Sector, and Irish Social Mobility: San Francisco, 1870–1900," pp. 274–289.

11. Dahl, *Who Governs?* pp. 40–42; Steven P. Erie, "Two Faces of Ethnic Power: Comparing the Irish and Black Experiences," pp. 263, 272.

12. For evidence of Irish big-city public employment gains, see Carl Wittke, *The Irish in America,* pp. 108–110; Terry Nichols Clark, "The Irish Ethic and the Spirit of Patronage," pp. 327–343. The figures for 1870 and 1900 are reported in U.S. Census Office, *Ninth Census, 1870,* vol. 1, Tables 29, 32; and U.S. Bureau of the Census, *Special Reports: Occupations at the Twelfth Census,* Tables 41, 43.

13. Charles V. Hamilton, "Blacks and the Crisis of Political Participation," pp. 191–193. A sizable body of black power literature uses the

legend of Irish power in this fashion. For representative discussions, see Harold Cruse, *The Crisis of the Negro Intellectual: From Its Origins to the Present,* pp. 315–316; Chuck Stone, *Black Political Power in America,* pp. 110–118; James P. Comer, "The Social Power of the Negro," in Floyd B. Barbour, ed., *The Black Power Revolt,* pp. 72–84; and Robert M. Fogelson, *Violence as Protest,* pp. 128–137.

14. Levine, *Irish and Irish Politicians,* p. 185.

15. Andrew Greeley, *That Most Distressful Nation: The Taming of the American Irish,* pp. 122–128; Andrew Greeley, *Ethnicity, Denomination, and Inequality,* pp. 54–55.

16. Edward C. Banfield and James Q. Wilson, *City Politics,* pp. 33–46, 115–127; James Q. Wilson and Edward C. Banfield, "Public-Regardingness as a Value Premise in Voting Behavior," pp. 876–887; Glazer and Moynihan, *Beyond the Melting Pot,* pp. 223–229.

17. Martin Shefter, "The Emergence of the Political Machine: An Alternative View," in Willis Hawley et al., eds., *Theoretical Perspectives on Urban Politics,* pp. 14–44.

18. William L. Riordan, comp., *Plunkitt of Tammany Hall,* p. 17.

19. Rexford Tugwell, *The Brains Trust,* pp. 366–371; Edwin O'Connor, *The Last Hurrah,* pp. 329–330.

20. Regarding labor in Detroit politics, see J. David Greenstone, *Labor in American Politics,* pp. 110–140.

21. For New Haven, see Dahl, *Who Governs?* pp. 32–62; Raymond E. Wolfinger, *The Politics of Progress,* pp. 30–129; and Jerome K. Myers, "Assimilation in the Political Community," pp. 175–182. For Providence, see Elmer E. Cornwell, "Party Absorption of Ethnic Groups: The Case of Providence, Rhode Island," pp. 205–210; Elmer E. Cornwell, "Some Occupational Patterns in Party Committee Membership," pp. 87–98; and Leo E. Carroll, "Irish and Italians in Providence, Rhode Island, 1880–1960," pp. 67–74.

22. Dennis Clark, *The Irish in Philadelphia: Ten Generations of Urban Experience,* p. 172.

23. Bryce, *American Commonwealth,* p. 115.

Chapter Two

1. Oliver MacDonagh, "The Irish Famine Emigration to the United States," pp. 430–433.

2. For representative definitions of the machine, see Edward C. Banfield and James Q. Wilson, *City Politics,* pp. 115–117; James C. Scott, "Corruption, Machine Politics, and Political Change," pp. 1143–1145;

Raymond E. Wolfinger, "Why Political Machines Have Not Withered Away and Other Revisionist Thoughts," pp. 374–375. For a definition stressing nonmaterial as well as material rewards, see Fred I. Greenstein, "The Changing Pattern of Urban Party Politics," pp. 2–3.

3. For an excellent analysis of the building of Tammany Hall in the antebellum era, see Amy Bridges, *A City in the Republic*.

4. Based on a surname analysis. For lists of Democratic party leaders, see *San Francisco Evening Bulletin*, September 15, 1886; Chicago Daily News, *Almanac, 1891*, p. 299; New York World, *World Almanac, 1893*, p. 331.

5. Daniel Patrick Moynihan, "The Irish," in Nathan Glazer and Daniel Patrick Moynihan, *Beyond the Melting Pot*, pp. 223–226.

6. For an analysis of the differences between Irish and Irish-American politics, see Thomas N. Brown, "The Political Irish: Politicians and Rebels," in David Noel Doyle and Owen Dudley Edwards, eds., *America and Ireland, 1776–1976*, pp. 133–150.

7. Martin Shefter, "The Emergence of the Political Machine: An Alternative View," in Willis Hawley et al., eds., *Theoretical Perspectives on Urban Politics*, pp. 14–44. Also see David R. Cameron, "Toward a Theory of Political Mobilization," pp. 140–142.

8. Robert E. Kennedy, Jr., *The Irish: Emigration, Marriage, and Fertility*, pp. 20–21.

9. Emmet Larkin, "Church, State, and Nation in Modern Ireland," pp. 1248–1251.

10. Donald H. Akenson, *The Irish Educational Experiment*, pp. 49–56, 202–213, 376–391.

11. On German-American politics, see Frederick C. Luebke, *Immigrants and Politics: The Germans of Nebraska, 1880–1900*, pp. 179–185; Carl Wittke, *Refugees of Revolution*, pp. 203–218.

12. Robert Kelley, *The Cultural Patterns in American Politics*, pp. 154–155, 172, 187. Tammany Hall is normally credited with using this patronage strategy to win Irish votes. However, it was first used against Tammany. In the 1820s, gubernatorial candidate DeWitt Clinton successfully outbid Tammany for Irish votes with promises of construction jobs on the Erie Canal.

13. Ibid., pp. 172–173.

14. Steven P. Erie, "The Development of Class and Ethnic Politics in San Francisco, 1870–1910: A Critique of the Pluralist Interpretation," Tables 5.11, 5.12, pp. 293–296.

15. Frederick A. Bushee, *Ethnic Factors in the Population of Boston*, Table 31, p. 124; Chicago Daily News, *Almanac, 1894*, p. 318 (nationality of registered foreign-born voters); U.S. Census Office, *Eleventh Cen-*

sus of the United States, 1890, vol. 1, pt. 1: Table 34, p. 670, Table 78, p. 752; vol. 1, pt. 2: Table 72, p. 282, Table 74, p. 288.

16. James C. Mohr, *The Radical Republicans and Reform in New York During Reconstruction,* pp. 208–209, 219–223, 235–238.

17. Jerome Mushkat, *The Reconstruction of the New York Democracy, 1861–1874,* pp. 145–146, 163–164.

18. Gustavus Myers, *History of Tammany Hall,* pp. 183, 187, 211.

19. Mohr, *Radical Republicans,* pp. 23–24, 84, 106–111; Mushkat, *Reconstruction,* pp. 64–65, 93.

20. Douglas V. Shaw, *The Making of an Immigrant City: Ethnic and Cultural Conflict in Jersey City, New Jersey, 1850–1877,* pp. 113, 217.

21. Jerome Mushkat, *Tammany: The Evolution of a Political Machine, 1789–1865,* pp. 82–83, 96–99, 110–111, 116, 128–135, 143–144; Herbert Bass, "The Politics of Ballot Reform in New York State, 1888–1890," pp. 253–272.

22. Herbert Bass, *"I Am a Democrat": The Political Career of David Bennett Hill,* pp. 82–83, 96–99, 110–111, 128–135, 143–144.

23. John Kincaid, "Political Success and Policy Failure: The Persistence of Machine Politics in Jersey City," p. 433.

24. R. Hal Williams, *The Democratic Party and California Politics, 1880–1896,* pp. 24–26, 102–105.

25. Geoffrey Blodgett, *The Gentle Reformers: Massachusetts Democrats in the Cleveland Era,* pp. 60, 64–69, 141, 143, 149–153. For accounts of the political mobilization of the Irish in Boston and of the nativist reaction, see Peter K. Eisinger, *The Politics of Displacement: Racial and Ethnic Transition in Three American Cities,* pp. 29–54; and Oscar Handlin, *Boston's Immigrants: A Study in Acculturation,* pp. 191–206.

26. John F. Stack, Jr., *International Conflict in an American City,* pp. 32–33; Richard H. Abbott, "Massachusetts: Maintaining Hegemony," in James C. Mohr, ed., *Radical Republicans in the North: State Politics During Reconstruction,* pp. 5–8, 18.

27. Richard Harmond, "The 'Beast' in Boston: Benjamin F. Butler as Governor of Massachusetts," pp. 267–268; Blodgett, *Gentle Reformers,* pp. 15, 18.

28. Harold U. Faulkner, *Politics, Reform, and Expansion, 1890–1900,* pp. 94–110; Blodgett, *Gentle Reformers,* pp. 84–93, 154 (O'Neill quote).

29. Murray B. Levin, *The Compleat Politician: Political Strategy in Massachusetts,* p. 17; Joseph F. Dineen, *The Purple Shamrock: The Honorable James Michael Curley of Boston,* pp. 17, 25, 29; Blodgett, *Gentle Reformers,* pp. 26–28, 30, 109–113, 166–170.

30. Richard M. Abrams, *Conservatism in a Progressive Era: Massachusetts Politics, 1900–1912*, pp. 44–45, 119, 168.

31. For a discussion of how state politics shaped the evolution of big-city machines, see Kincaid, "Political Success," pp. 24–26, 60, 95, 217–225.

32. Dennis Clark, *The Irish in Philadelphia: Ten Generations of Urban Experience*, pp. 120–121, 136–141, 172. For an analysis of the state Republican machine, see James A. Kehl, *Boss Rule in the Gilded Age: Matt Quay of Pennsylvania*.

33. Lincoln Steffens, *The Shame of the Cities*, pp. 138, 142–143.

34. Matthew Josephson, *The Politicos, 1865–1896*, pp. 87–99.

35. Paul Michael Green, "The Chicago Democratic Party, 1840–1920: From Factionalism to Political Organization," pp. 16, 33–34, 89–92; Lloyd Wendt and Herman Kogan, *Bosses in Lusty Chicago: The Story of Bathhouse John and Hinky Dink*, pp. 200–207, 239–241.

36. Ray Ginger, *Altgeld's America: The Lincoln Ideal Versus Changing Realities*, pp. 71–72, 168–169; Carter H. Harrison, Jr., *Stormy Years*, pp. 39–41.

37. For evidence of Irish-American preferences for higher urban public expenditures as compared with other ethnic groups, see Terry Nichols Clark, "The Irish Ethic and the Spirit of Patronage," pp. 327–343; James J. Vanecko and Jennie Kronenfeld, "Preferences for Public Expenditures and Ethno-Racial Group Membership: A Test of the Theory of Political Ethos," pp. 311–366; and John W. Foley, "Community Structure and Public Policy Outputs in 300 Eastern American Communities: Toward a Sociology of the Public Sector," pp. 222–234. For an analysis of turn-of-the-century expenditures in medium-sized cities, see J. Rogers Hollingsworth and Ellen Jane Hollingsworth, "Expenditures in American Cities," in William O. Aydelotte et al., eds., *The Dimensions of Quantitative Research in History*, pp. 347–389.

38. Martin Shefter, "New York City's Fiscal Crisis: The Politics of Inflation and Retrenchment," pp. 101–105.

39. M. R. Werner, *Tammany Hall*, p. 276; Myers, *History of Tammany Hall*, pp. 254–256.

40. William A. Bullough, *The Blind Boss and His City: Christopher Augustine Buckley and Nineteenth-Century San Francisco*, pp. 92, 136. For contemporary accounts of Buckley's rule, see Jeremiah Lynch, *Buckleyism: The Government of a State*; and *San Francisco Morning Call*, November 10, 1892.

41. Arthur Genen, "John Kelly: New York's First Irish Boss," pp. 126–128; Martin Shefter, "The Electoral Foundations of the Political Ma-

chine: New York City, 1884–1897," in Joel H. Silbey, et al., eds., *The History of American Electoral Behavior*, p. 290.

42. Bullough, *Blind Boss*, pp. 97, 160–163, 232–233.

43. Moynihan, "The Irish," pp. 229, 259–260. A similar argument is made by Raymond E. Wolfinger in "The Development and Persistence of Ethnic Voting," pp. 896–908.

44. James Bryce, *The American Commonwealth*, p. 434.

45. For an early and sympathetic account of the Workingmen's party of California by journalist Henry George, later nominated for mayor of New York City on a labor party ticket, see his article "The Kearney Agitation in California," pp. 433–453. On labor politics generally in San Francisco, see Alexander Saxton, *The Indispensable Enemy: Labor and the Anti-Chinese Movement in California*, pp. 113–156; and Erie, "Development of Class and Ethnic Politics in San Francisco," pp. 128–145. Regarding labor politics in Chicago, see Howard H. Quint, *The Forging of American Socialism*, p. 14.

46. David Montgomery, "The Irish and the American Labor Movement," in David Noel Doyle and Owen Dudley Edwards, eds., *America and Ireland, 1776–1976*, pp. 207, 211, 213; Daniel Bell, *Marxian Socialism in the United States*, pp. 24–25.

47. Eric Foner, "Radicalism in the Gilded Age: The Land League and Irish-America," pp. 8–15, 24–25, 28; Montgomery, "Irish and the American Labor Movement," p. 216. On the Irish nationalist movement in Chicago, see Michael F. Funchion, *Chicago's Irish Nationalists, 1881–1890*.

48. Florence E. Gibson, *The Attitudes of the New York Irish Toward State and National Affairs, 1848–1892*, p. 245 (Rossa quote).

49. Martin Shefter, "The Emergence of the Political Machine," in Willis Hawley et al., eds., *Theoretical Perspectives on Urban Politics*, pp. 29–32.

50. Alfred Connable and Edward Silberfarb, *Tigers of Tammany: Nine Men Who Ran New York*, p. 155; Myers, *History of Tammany Hall*, p. 217; Werner, *Tammany Hall*, pp. 135–136. For evidence of the success of San Francisco's Democratic politicians in naturalizing and registering the Irish in the late 1860s, see R. A. Burchell, *The San Francisco Irish, 1848–1880*, p. 18.

51. Werner, *Tammany Hall*, p. 170. By 1868 Boss Tweed controlled state as well as local government. Tweed broadened his appeal to immigrant and working-class voters by state subsidies to Catholic schools and to religious charities. See John W. Pratt, "Boss Tweed's Public Welfare Program," pp. 396–411.

52. C. K. Yearley, *The Money Machines: The Breakdown and Reform of Governmental and Party Finance in the North, 1860–1920*, pp. 3–74.

53. Yearley observes that demands for liberalized debt policies came from the top as well as the bottom of the class structure. "Men of substance, realtors, bankers, construction men, contractors, manufacturers, and suppliers of the varied equipage essential to urban growth . . . succumbed to tempting speculations which public indebtedness could and did abet; the roads, sewers, utilities, schools, and other public improvements useful to increasing the value of existing realty and attracting even larger populations to particular areas could thereby come more swiftly" (ibid., p. 264).

54. Horace Secrist, *An Economic Analysis of the Constitutional Restrictions upon Public Indebtedness in the United States*, vol. 8, no. 1, pp. 56–63. States also imposed constitutional limitations on city taxation powers. See Richard T. Ely, *Taxation in American States and Cities*, pp. 396–397.

55. Jon C. Teaford, *City and Suburb: The Political Fragmentation of Metropolitan America, 1850–1970*, pp. 39, 62, 77.

56. Werner, *Tammany Hall*, p. 451.

57. Yearley, *Money Machines*, pp. 97–118; Werner, *Tammany Hall*, pp. 348, 356–357.

58. Werner, *Tammany Hall*, p. 449.

59. U.S. Census Office, *Ninth Census, 1870*, vol. 1, Table 32; U.S. Bureau of the Census, *Special Reports: Occupations at the Twelfth Census*, Tables 41, 43. For the occupational ranking scheme, see Stephan Thernstrom, *The Other Bostonians: Poverty and Progress in the American Metropolis, 1880–1970*, Appendix B: "On the Socioeconomic Ranking of Occupations," pp. 289–302.

60. For an excellent summary of the scope of the machine's resources, see Charles Merriam, *The American Party System*, pp. 160–163. See also E. L. Godkin, "Criminal Politics," pp. 706–723.

61. Steven P. Erie, "Politics, the Public Sector, and Irish Social Mobility: San Francisco, 1870–1900," Table 2, p. 281.

62. Ibid., Table 4, p. 283.

63. Ibid. For a case study of an Irish machine's proletarianization of the public sector, see Frank S. Robinson, *Machine Politics: A Study of Albany's O'Connells*, pp. 166–168, 182.

64. Erie, "Politics, the Public Sector," Table 4, p. 283, and n. 37, pp. 287–288.

65. Montgomery, "Irish and the American Labor Movement," pp. 205–217.

66. Robert C. Brooks, *Political Parties and Electoral Problems*, p. 214. The machine's private sector patronage is also discussed in William Bennett Munro, *The Government of American Cities*, pp. 172–174.

67. U.S. Bureau of the Census, *Special Reports: Occupations at the Twelfth Census*, Table 43, pp. 720–725.

68. San Francisco Board of Supervisors, *San Francisco Municipal Reports, 1880–1881*, pp. 491–556.

69. Thernstrom, *Other Bostonians*, pp. 132–133, 142; Moynihan, "The Irish," pp. 229, 259–260. For a similar argument about sluggish Irish economic progress and the limited opportunities available in the public sector, see Dennis P. Ryan, *Beyond the Ballot Box: A Social History of the Boston Irish, 1845–1917*, pp. 148–153.

70. U.S. Census Office, *Ninth Census, 1870*, vol. 1, Table 32; U.S. Bureau of the Census, *Special Reports: Occupations at the Twelfth Census*, Tables 41, 43.

71. Erie, "Politics, the Public Sector," Table 5, p. 285.

72. San Francisco Recorder, *General List of Citizens of the United States Registered in the Great Register, 1867*, p. 2; San Francisco Board of Supervisors, *San Francisco Municipal Reports, 1900–1901*, pp. 373–374. For 1900, second-generation Irish and German voters have been included. See Erie, "Development of Class and Ethnic Politics in San Francisco," Table 4, p. 283.

73. Foner, "Radicalism in the Gilded Age," p. 29; Genen, "John Kelly," pp. 261–323.

74. Bullough, *Blind Boss*, p. 177.

75. Shefter, "Electoral Foundations," pp. 263–298.

Chapter Three

1. For studies of the impact of the 1893 depression on the fortunes of the Democratic party, particularly in the northern cities, see Samuel T. McSeveney, *The Politics of Depression: Political Behavior in the Northeast, 1893–1896*, pp. 43, 87–133, 163–221; and Carl N. Degler, "American Political Parties and the Rise of the City: An Interpretation," in Alexander B. Callow, Jr., ed., *American Urban History*, pp. 469–470.

2. Andrew Greeley, *That Most Distressful Nation: The Taming of the American Irish*, pp. 122–128; Andrew Greeley, *Ethnicity, Denomination, and Inequality*, pp. 54–55.

3. John Kincaid, "Political Success and Policy Failure: The Persistence of Machine Politics in Jersey City," pp. 233–234, 287–289.

4. Dayton David McKean, *The Boss: The Hague Machine in Action*, pp. 37–44.

5. Frank S. Robinson, *Machine Politics: A Study of Albany's O'Connells,* pp. 14, 49–54.

6. M. R. Werner, *Tammany Hall,* pp. 516–517.

7. Gustavus Myers, *History of Tammany Hall,* pp. 353–363.

8. Walton E. Bean, *Boss Reuf's San Francisco: The Story of the Union Labor Party, Big Business, and the Graft Prosecution;* Steven P. Erie, "The Development of Class and Ethnic Politics in San Francisco, 1870–1910: A Critique of the Pluralist Interpretation," pp. 196–216, 227, and Table 5.13, p. 300.

9. George Mowry, *The California Progressives;* Spencer Olin, *California's Prodigal Sons: Hiram Johnson and the Progressive Movement, 1911–1917;* Alexander Saxton, "San Francisco Labor and the Populist and Progressive Insurgencies," pp. 421–438; Michael Rogin, "Progressivism and the California Electorate," pp. 297–314; John L. Shover, "The Progressives and the Working-Class Vote in California," pp. 584–601.

10. Richard M. Abrams, *Conservatism in a Progressive Era: Massachusetts Politics, 1900–1912,* pp. 45–48, 105–107, 147–187, 287; Geoffrey Blodgett, *The Gentle Reformers: Massachusetts Democrats in the Cleveland Era,* pp. 256, 271. Even if Governor Walsh had wanted to centralize Boston's Democratic politics, as Governor "Billy" Russell had briefly attempted to do in 1890, his efforts might have been frustrated by federal patronage policies. The Wilson administration appointed New Yorker Dudley Field Malone as the state's chief patronage dispenser with express orders to wage warfare against Boston's Irish machine politicians. Malone used federal appointments to create more havoc in the Hub's already chaotic politics—all in the name of reform. Regarding Fitzgerald's patronage practices, see the Boston Finance Commission, *Reports and Communications,* vol. 2, pp. 194–227.

11. Alex Gottfried, *Boss Cermak of Chicago: A Study of Political Leadership,* pp. 70, 80–82.

12. Robert D. Marcus, *Grand Old Party: Political Structure in the Gilded Age,* p. 223.

13. Joel A. Tarr, *A Study in Boss Politics: William Lorimer of Chicago,* p. 196.

14. For the cost-of-living measures used to adjust city spending and indebtedness for the period 1880 to 1932, see U.S. Bureau of the Census, *Historical Statistics of the United States: Colonial Times to 1957,* series E 157–160, p. 127.

15. U.S. Census Office, *Special Reports: Wealth, Debt, and Taxation,* Table 86, pp. 452–612; U.S. Bureau of the Census, *Financial Statistics of Cities Having a Population over 100,000, 1932,* Table 18, pp. 176–179.

16. For an excellent study of the urban transportation revolution and

suburban growth in late nineteenth-century Boston, see Sam Bass Warner, Jr., *Streetcar Suburbs: The Process of Growth in Boston, 1870–1900*.

17. Jon C. Teaford, *City and Suburb: The Political Fragmentation of Metropolitan America, 1850–1970*, pp. 77, 90–94.

18. U.S. Bureau of the Census, *Census of Population, 1920*, vol. 2, Table 7, p. 1288.

19. Richard L. McCormick, *From Realignment to Reform: Political Change in New York State, 1893–1910*, pp. 120–134.

20. Ibid., pp. 168–171; U.S. Bureau of the Census, *State and Local Government Special Studies: Historical Review of State and Local Government Finances*, G-SS-no. 25, Table 1, p. 13. In some states, particularly where Republicans controlled the statehouse and Democrats city hall, the reform package included limits on city borrowing authority. For example, Massachusetts in 1921 placed a 2.5 percent debt ceiling (as a percentage of the total assessed value of taxable property) on the cities. Local borrowing in the Bay State also had to be approved by two-thirds of the voters. New Jersey in 1916 placed a 7 percent debt limit on the cities, while New York enacted a 10 percent debt ceiling. See Lance W. Lancaster, "State Limitations on Local Indebtedness," in International City Managers' Association, *Municipal Year Book, 1936*, pp. 313–327, esp. Table 8, pp. 319–323.

21. Steven P. Erie, "Progressivism and San Francisco Labor, 1899–1917," pp. 33–34.

22. Kincaid, "Political Success," pp. 414–415, 429.

23. McKean, *The Boss*, p. 44. Hague's tax policies were also shaped by New Jersey's 7 percent ceiling on municipal debts. In order to borrow, Hague increased the city's assessment base by taxing property at 100 percent of true value. See ibid., pp. 253, 259–260.

24. Ibid., pp. 249–259.

25. Robinson, *Machine Politics*, pp. 137–139.

26. For analyses of the growth of urban public employment, 1900–1930, see Steven P. Erie, "Politics, the Public Sector, and Irish Social Mobility: San Francisco, 1870–1900," Table 2, p. 281; Willford I. King, *The National Income and Its Purchasing Power*, pp. 360–363; William E. Mosher and Sophie Polah, "Public Employment in the United States," pp. 51–72; and Simon Kuznets, *National Income and Its Composition, 1919–1938*, vol. 2, Table G–7, p. 814.

27. For a survey of municipal civil service systems, see the International City Managers' Association, *Municipal Year Book, 1941*, Table 4–A, pp. 130–132. Regarding Tammany's personnel practices, see Charles Garrett, *The La Guardia Years: Machine and Reform Politics in New York City*, pp. 133–134.

28. U.S. Bureau of the Census, *Fifteenth Census of the United States,*
1930, vol. 2, Table 11, vol. 4, Table 12. For an analysis of the importance
of counties for machine consolidation, see Kincaid, "Political Success,"
pp. 264–266.

29. Steven P. Erie, "Two Faces of Ethnic Power: Comparing the Irish
and Black Experiences," p. 263.

30. Werner, *Tammany Hall,* p. 557. The other Irish bosses also relied
heavily on private sector patronage. Hague, for example, milked the wa-
terfront and large packing companies such as Swift and Armour. See
Richard J. Connors, *A Cycle of Power: The Career of Jersey City Mayor*
Frank Hague, p. 88.

31. Unlike the 1900 census, the 1930 census does not report the number of Irish-stock public employees for the cities. I used the following procedure to estimate the number of Irish public servants for 1930. Regarding Albany, Terry Clark has done a surname analysis of the city payroll
from 1870 to 1970. For 1930, approximately 41 percent of the city's
elected officials, policemen, firemen, and other employees were of Irish
descent. See Clark, "The Irish Ethic and the Spirit of Patronage," Fig. 3,
p. 342. For New York and Jersey City, I have used a conservative estimating procedure. The New York World's *World Almanac* for 1931 provides
rosters of top officials for New York (N = 428) and Jersey City–Hudson
County (N = 56). Fifty-two percent of New York City's officials and
58 percent of the leadership of Jersey City–Hudson County had Irish sur-
names. These proportions were used to estimate the Irish share of overall
city and county employment. I believe this is a reasonable estimating procedure for the following reasons. First, as Theodore J. Lowi has shown
for New York City, ethnic ticket-balancing considerations were most pro-
nounced for top elective and appointive positions. See Theodore J. Lowi,
At the Pleasure of the Mayor: Patronage and Power in New York City,
1898–1958, pp. 29–46, esp. Fig. 2.1, p. 36. Top leadership, then, should
have included *fewer* Irish than the rank and file. If anything, the ethnicity
of public employees should more closely reflect that of the chief patronage dispensers, the party central committee members and the ward bosses.
In 1932, nearly 70 percent of Tammany's district leaders in Manhattan
were Irish. Second, the New York City and Jersey City estimates are consistent with a sample survey of 1,600 family heads in New Haven conducted in 1931–1933. In Irish-run New Haven, 49 percent of all public
workers in the survey were Irish. See John W. McConnell, *The Evolution*
of Social Classes, pp. 82–84, 214. As a final check, I did a surname
analysis of the 1927 and 1933 rosters of top New York City and Jersey
City officials. The Irish share of top positions remained remarkably constant. One final estimation problem remained. The surname analysis cap-

tured all Irish regardless of generation while the 1930 census only included first- and second-generation Irish. Based on secondary literature estimates and on the generational dropoff resulting from mixed marriages, I have estimated the size of the third-generation Irish workforce at roughly one-half that of the second generation.

32. Thomas M. Henderson, *Tammany Hall and the New Immigrants: The Progressive Years*, pp. 83–87, 166; U.S. Bureau of the Census, *Special Reports: Occupations at the Twelfth Census*, Tables 41, 43; U.S. Bureau of the Census, *Fifteenth Census of the United States, 1930*, vol. 2, Table 11, and vol. 4, Table 12.

33. Ronald H. Bayor, *Neighbors in Conflict: The Irish, Germans, Jews, and Italians of New York City, 1929–1941*, p. 26; New York World, *World Almanac* for 1931, pp. 545–549.

34. U.S. Bureau of the Census, *Special Reports: Occupations at the Twelfth Census*, Tables 41, 43; U.S. Bureau of the Census, *Fifteenth Census of the United States, 1930*, vol. 2, Table 11, vol. 4, Table 12; and Alba M. Edwards, *A Socio-Economic Grouping of the Gainful Workers of the United States*, Appendix, p. 275.

35. Alfred Connable and Edward Silberfarb, *Tigers of Tammany: Nine Men Who Ran New York*, p. 243; Kenneth Finegold, "Progressivism, Electoral Change, and Public Policy in New York City, 1900–1917," Occasional Paper no. 83–1, pp. 18–28; Myers, *History of Tammany Hall*, p. 309; Henderson, *Tammany Hall*, pp. 91, 124. The slowly growing Irish middle class began experimenting with antimachine reform politics as labor insurgency died. In New York, the anti-Tammany fusion ticket of 1913 was heavily Irish—John Purroy Mitchel for mayor and Prendergast and McAneny for citywide office—and drew substantial Irish middle-class support.

36. Connors, *Cycle of Power*, p. 94; Kincaid, "Political Success," pp. 429–431.

37. John Palmer Gavit, *Americans by Choice*, pp. 77–142, 232–233.

38. Ibid., p. 241; U.S. Bureau of the Census, *Historical Statistics of the United States, Colonial Times to the Present*, series C 168–180, p. 115.

39. For the enterprising reader, state voter qualifications are reported annually in the New York World Telegram's *World Almanac*. For an analysis of the Michigan movement to abolish alien suffrage, see Melvin G. Holli, *Reform in Detroit: Hazen S. Pingree and Urban Politics*, p. 151.

40. William M. Johnson, "On the Outside Looking In: Irish, Italian, and Black Ethnic Politics in an American City," p. 185.

41. McCormick, *From Realignment to Reform*, p. 54.

42. Harold F. Gosnell, *Machine Politics: Chicago Model*, Table 8,

p. 71. For evidence of how Chicago's competitive parties also registered and voted the new immigrants, see Charles E. Merriam and Harold F. Gosnell, *Non-Voting: Causes and Methods of Control,* pp. 202, 228–230.

43. U.S. Bureau of the Census, *Census of Population, 1920,* vol. 2, Table 16. Chicago's higher naturalization rates relative to New York were not a function of an older, settled population. Chicago's immigrants were newer arrivals. Forty-three percent of the Windy City's Russian-born, for example, had arrived after 1910 compared with 38 percent of New York's. See U.S. Bureau of the Census, *Fifteenth Census of the United States, 1930,* vol. 2, Tables 18, 19.

44. Werner, *Tammany Hall,* p. 436; Frederick A. Bushee, *Ethnic Factors in the Population of Boston,* Table 31, p. 124 (nationalities of 1896 registered voters). Naturalization rates for the Hub's ethnic groups are estimated from the censuses of 1890, 1900, and 1910.

45. U.S. Census Office, *Eleventh Census of the United States, 1890,* vol. 1, pt. 1, Table 78, vol. 1, pt. 2, Tables 72, 74; U.S. Bureau of the Census, *Census of Population, 1920,* vol. 2, Tables 16, 34; New York World, *World Almanac,* and New York municipal reports, variously dated.

46. Sources for New York City voting returns, 1870 to 1890, are New York Tribune, *Tribune Almanac and Political Register;* and New York State Legislature, *Red Book, State of New York.* For voting-age males and municipal employment, see U.S. Census Office, *Ninth Census, 1870,* vol. 1, pt. 1, Table 78, and vol. 1, pt. 2, Table 118.

47. For contemporary estimates of the size of the payroll vote in the big cities, see William Bennett Munro, *The Government of American Cities,* pp. 265–293, 401–440; and Robert C. Brooks, *Political Parties and Electoral Problems,* pp. 190–251, 541–574. For an early account of vote buying in New York, see John Gilmer Speed, "The Purchase of Votes in New York City," pp. 386–387, reprinted in Arnold J. Heidenheimer, ed., *Political Corruption: Readings in Comparative Analysis,* pp. 422–426.

48. Irving Howe, *World of Our Fathers,* pp. 80–84, 101–115, 287–324; Thomas Kessner, *The Golden Door: Italian and Jewish Immigrant Mobility in New York City, 1880–1915,* pp. 28–31.

49. New York World Telegram, *World Almanac* for 1932, p. 920; Norman Martin Adler, "Ethnics in Politics: Access to Office in New York City," esp. pp. 20–23, 48, 88–100, 197–227; Connable and Silberfarb, *Tigers of Tammany,* pp. 307–311; Lowi, *At the Pleasure of the Mayor.*

50. Herbert J. Gans, *The Urban Villagers: Group and Class in the Life of Italian-Americans,* pp. 174–175; William M. DeMarco, *Ethnics and Enclaves: Boston's Italian North End,* pp. 22–23.

51. John M. Allswang, *A House for All Peoples: Ethnic Politics in*

Chicago, 1890–1936, pp. 35–36, 104, 161; Paul Michael Green, "The Chicago Democratic Party, 1840–1920: From Factionalism to Political Organization," pp. 156–158, 333.

52. Henderson, *Tammany Hall,* pp. 4–5, 137; Howe, *World of Our Fathers,* pp. 360–383.

53. Joseph F. Dineen, *The Purple Shamrock: The Honorable James Michael Curley of Boston,* pp. 85, 172; Charles Angoff, *The Tone of the Twenties and Other Essays,* pp. 150–155.

54. Robert A. Woods, ed., *Americans in Process,* p. 64.

55. Lawrence H. Fuchs, *The Political Behavior of American Jews,* pp. 56, 63, 123, 135–139; Howe, *World of Our Fathers,* pp. 310–321.

56. Nancy Joan Weiss, *Charles Francis Murphy, 1858–1924: Respectability and Responsibility in Tammany Politics,* pp. 81–85; J. Joseph Huthmacher, "Urban Liberalism and the Age of Reform," pp. 234–238; Mark S. Foster, "Frank Hague of Jersey City: The Boss as Reformer," pp. 106–116. For an account of Lomasney's sponsorship of progressive legislation in Massachusetts, see John D. Buenker, "The Mahatma and Progressive Reform: Martin Lomasney as Lawmaker, 1911–1917," pp. 404–405.

57. J. Joseph Huthmacher, *Massachusetts People and Politics, 1919–1933,* pp. 93, 119–120; Henderson, *Tammany Hall,* pp. 249–251, 264–270.

58. Fuchs, *Political Behavior,* p. 127; Henderson, *Tammany Hall,* pp. 212–231.

59. Bayor, *Neighbors in Conflict,* pp. 26–31; Adler, "Ethnics in Politics"; Henderson, *Tammany Hall,* pp. 4–5, 137. For an account of how Chicago's Irish politicians also gerrymandered Italian neighborhoods, see Humbert S. Nelli, "John Powers and the Italians: Politics in a Chicago Ward, 1896–1921," pp. 67–84.

60. Gottfried, *Boss Cermak,* pp. 169–199; Allswang, *House for All Peoples,* pp. 105–106, 152–156.

Chapter Four

1. See Edwin O'Connor, *The Last Hurrah,* pp. 329–330; and Rexford G. Tugwell, *The Brains Trust,* pp. 366–371.

2. Lyle W. Dorsett, *Franklin D. Roosevelt and the City Bosses,* pp. 1–8, 113–116.

3. Robert A. Caro, *The Power Broker: Robert Moses and the Fall of New York,* pp. 326–327.

4. James T. Patterson, *The New Deal and the States: Federalism in Transition,* pp. 26–31; International City Managers' Association, *Munic-*

ipal Year Book, 1934, Table 11, pp. 206–211; U.S. Works Progress Administration, *Family Unemployment,* Table 20, pp. 125–126; International City Managers' Association, *Municipal Year Book, 1937,* Table 9, pp. 356–357.

5. Quoted in William Whyte, *Financing New York City,* pamphlet series no. 2, p. 5.

6. Barbara Blumberg, *The New Deal and the Unemployed: The View from New York City,* p. 27; Richard J. Connors, *A Cycle of Power: The Career of Jersey City Mayor Frank Hague,* p. 159.

7. International City Managers' Association, *Municipal Year Book, 1934,* Table 12, pp. 212–217; Martin Shefter, "Economic Crises, Social Coalitions, and Political Institutions: New York City's Little New Deal," p. 23.

8. Donald S. Watson, "Financing Relief and Recovery: [The] Reconstruction Finance Corporation," in International City Managers' Association, *Municipal Year Book, 1937,* pp. 375–381, esp. Table 2, pp. 380–381.

9. William O. Suiter, "State Limits on Local Property Taxes," in International City Managers' Association, *Municipal Year Book, 1936,* pp. 328–339, esp. Table 10, pp. 334–337; Robert P. Ingalls, *Herbert H. Lehman and New York's Little New Deal,* p. 51.

10. Shefter, "Economic Crises," pp. 32–33; Connors, *Cycle of Power,* p. 159; International City Managers' Association, *Municipal Year Book, 1935,* Table 5, pp. 204–208.

11. Charles Garrett, *The La Guardia Years: Machine and Reform Politics in New York City,* p. 104; Caro, *Power Broker,* p. 327; Harold F. Gosnell, *Machine Politics: Chicago Model,* p. 17.

12. Arthur Mann, *La Guardia Comes to Power, 1933,* pp. 138–149.

13. John Kincaid, "Political Success and Policy Failure: The Persistence of Machine Politics in Jersey City," pp. 472–473; Connors, *Cycle of Power,* pp. 141–183.

14. Alex Gottfried, *Boss Cermak of Chicago: A Study of Political Leadership,* pp. 262–263, 304–305.

15. Bruce M. Stave, *The New Deal and the Last Hurrah: Pittsburgh Machine Politics,* pp. 27–29, 86–88, 94.

16. Charles H. Trout, *Boston, the Great Depression, and the New Deal,* pp. 30–40, 50–59, 99, 286.

17. Stave, *New Deal,* pp. 165–169.

18. David Burner, *The Politics of Provincialism: The Democratic Party in Transition, 1918–1932,* pp. 215–243; John M. Allswang, *A House for All Peoples: Ethnic Politics in Chicago, 1890–1936,* p. 42. For more general studies of the role of the new ethnics in the 1928–1936 re-

alignment, see Samuel Lubell, *The Future of American Politics*, pp. 43–55; Jerome M. Clubb and Howard W. Allen, "The Cities and the Election of 1928: Partisan Realignment?" pp. 1205–1220; and Kristi Andersen, *The Creation of a Democratic Majority, 1928–1936*, pp. 19–52. For evidence of a parallel 1928 mobilization of rural Protestant women for Hoover, see Allan J. Lichtman, *Prejudice and the Old Politics: The Presidential Election of 1928*.

19. Mann, *La Guardia Comes to Power*, pp. 26, 113; Garrett, *La Guardia Years*, p. 110.

20. Ronald H. Bayor, *Neighbors in Conflict: The Irish, Germans, Jews, and Italians of New York City, 1929–1941*, p. 127; Mann, *La Guardia Comes to Power*, pp. 124, 138–146.

21. Bayor, *Neighbors in Conflict*, p. 135; Garrett, *La Guardia Years*, p. 134.

22. Garrett, *La Guardia Years*, pp. 147, 366 (n. 6).

23. Bayor, *Neighbors in Conflict*, p. 26.

24. Warren Moscow, *The Last of the Big-Time Bosses: The Life and Times of Carmine De Sapio and the Rise and Fall of Tammany Hall*, pp. 54–59; Daniel Bell, "Crime as an American Way of Life," pp. 131–154.

25. Connors, *Cycle of Power*, pp. 142–183; Kincaid, "Political Success," pp. 502–511.

26. Andersen, *Creation of a Democratic Majority*, pp. 34–37.

27. Frank S. Robinson, *Machine Politics: A Study of Albany's O'Connells*, pp. 138–139.

28. Dayton David McKean, *The Boss: The Hague Machine in Action*, p. 127.

29. Imposing state oversight over Albany's registration and election procedures, Republican Governor Thomas E. Dewey was able slowly to reduce the O'Connell machine's padded registration and vote totals. Between 1940 and 1960 the city's 85,000 registered voters were trimmed to 58,000, despite only a slight drop in population. Robinson, *Machine Politics*, pp. 163–164.

30. Milton L. Rakove, *Don't Make No Waves, Don't Back No Losers: An Insider's Analysis of the Daley Machine*, pp. 1–5; Gottfried, *Boss Cermak*, p. 326; Gosnell, *Machine Politics*, pp. 13, 109, 173; Andersen, *Creation of a Democratic Majority*, pp. 31, 83–120; Allswang, *House for All Peoples*, pp. 40–47.

31. Gosnell, *Machine Politics*, pp. 52–53, 71.

32. Stave, *New Deal*, pp. 6, 180, Table 23.

33. Stave reports robust ward-level correlations between the foreign stock population and the 1928 Smith vote ($r = .87$) and the 1932 Roosevelt vote ($r = .67$). Ibid., p. 203.

34. Stave notes the anemic correlation between the 1932 Roosevelt vote and the 1933 McNair vote (r = .16) compared with the strong linkage between the 1936 vote for FDR and the 1937 vote for Scully (r = .88). Ibid., pp. 209, 222.

35. Trout, *Boston*, pp. 11, 258–267; John F. Stack, Jr., *International Conflict in an American City*, pp. 32–39.

36. Trout, *Boston*, p. 116.

37. Arthur W. MacMahon et al., *The Administration of Federal Work Relief*, pp. 3–18.

38. U.S. Works Progress Administration, *Summary of Relief and Federal Work Program Statistics, 1933–1940*, Table 1, pp. 46–49.

39. Donald S. Howard, *The WPA and Federal Relief Policy*, Table 20, p. 399; U.S. Social Security Board, "Relief in Urban Areas," in International City Managers' Association, *Municipal Year Book, 1939*, pp. 460–465, esp. p. 461.

40. Stave, *New Deal*, pp. 147–169; MacMahon, *Administration*, pp. 285–286; Gosnell, *Machine Politics*, p. 75.

41. Blumberg, *New Deal*, p. 282. Urban Democratic machines could build formidable public sector coalitions by mobilizing municipal employees, WPA workers, and direct relief recipients. In New York, Jersey City, Chicago, and Pittsburgh these three groups constituted one-quarter to one-third of all voters.

42. Caro, *Power Broker*, p. 325.

43. Blumberg, *New Deal*, p. 126; Trout, *Boston*, pp. 170–171, 301, and Table 8.2, p. 193; MacMahon, *Administration*, p. 303.

44. Blumberg, *New Deal*, p. 126.

45. Searle F. Charles, *Minister of Relief: Harry Hopkins and the Depression*, p. 175. Before the 1936 election the WPA issued regulations making partisan interference with WPA officials and workers illegal. Solicitation of campaign funds, voter canvassing, and votes from WPA personnel were prohibited. WPA enforcement of partisan prohibitions was spotty at best. Ibid., pp. 180–181.

46. Ibid., pp. 54, 74–78, 142–143; McKean, *The Boss*, p. 99.

47. Dorsett, *Roosevelt*, p. 103; Kincaid, "Political Success," p. 471; McKean, *The Boss*, p. 104.

48. Ingalls, *Lehman*, p. 12; Mann, *La Guardia Comes to Power*, p. 123.

49. Blumberg, *New Deal*, pp. 49–50, 70–71, 99–101, 266–267, 296–297.

50. Gosnell, *Machine Politics*, pp. 11, 19, 24, 75–78, 89.

51. Dorsett, *Roosevelt*, p. 91; Gosnell, *Machine Politics*, pp. 71, 78–80, 90.

52. Stave, *New Deal*, pp. 27–35, 64–88, 108–113, 139–144, 155,

162–181. For an account of Lawrence's political career, see Paul B. Beer, *Pennsylvania Politics Today and Yesterday: The Tolerable Accommodation,* pp. 239–266.

53. Harold Gorvine, "The New Deal in Massachusetts," in John Braeman et al., eds., *The New Deal: The State and Local Levels,* pp. 4–5; Dorsett, *Roosevelt,* pp. 15–16, 21–28.

54. Gorvine, "New Deal," pp. 24–25; Trout, *Boston,* pp. 164–168. Control of pre-WPA federal relief programs also eluded Curley's grasp. Both the PWA and Federal Emergency Relief Administration (FERA) grant-in-aid program required project approval by the state relief board. The Bay State's Emergency Relief Administration and the state Emergency Finance Board were both controlled by the Walsh-Ely western wing of the state Democratic party. As leader of the rival Boston wing, Curley found his proposed PWA and FERA projects blocked or delayed by state boards controlled by the Walsh-Ely faction. Curley briefly controlled some WPA patronage in 1936. During the superheated 1936 U.S. senatorial campaign, state relief boss Edwards relented and gave candidate Curley appointment power over a few lower-level WPA administrative positions. Curley exaggerated his relief influence, claiming to control 2,200 WPA project supervisors during his unsuccessful campaign for a U.S. Senate seat.

55. Trout, *Boston,* pp. 170–171, 278–279.

56. For an insightful analysis of how presidential elections after 1928 were influenced by the big-city vote in the urban-industrial states, see Samuel J. Eldersveld, "The Influence of Metropolitan Party Pluralities in Presidential Elections Since 1920: A Study of Twelve Cities," pp. 1189–1209.

57. Gavin Wright, "The Political Economy of New Deal Spending: An Econometric Analysis," pp. 30–38.

58. For a discussion of how state WPA job quotas were determined, see MacMahon, *Administration,* p. 101.

59. For an account of the "prospective" character of FDR's state patronage policies, see James T. Patterson, *The New Deal and the States: Federalism in Transition,* pp. 168–193.

60. Eldersveld, "Influence of Metropolitan Party Pluralities," pp. 1198–1202.

61. Regarding Lawrence's alliance with state Boss Guffey, see Richard C. Keller, "Pennsylvania's Little New Deal," in John Braeman et al., eds., *The New Deal: The State and Local Levels,* pp. 45–76; and Thomas H. Coode and John F. Bauman, "Democratic Politics and Pennsylvania, 1932–1938," in Thomas H. Coode and John F. Bauman, eds., *People, Poverty, and Politics: Pennsylvanians During the Great Depression,* pp. 224–250.

62. J. Joseph Huthmacher, *Massachusetts People and Politics, 1919–1933*, pp. 236, 250–263; Gorvine, "New Deal," pp. 4–13.

63. Patterson, *New Deal*, p. 171.

Chapter Five

1. For an analysis of the distinction between machine politics and political machines, see Raymond E. Wolfinger, "Why Political Machines Have Not Withered Away and Other Revisionist Thoughts," pp. 374–375.

2. John H. Mollenkopf, *The Contested City*, pp. 28–36.

3. U.S. Bureau of the Census, *Statistical Abstract of the United States, 1950*, Table 908, pp. 759–760; U.S. Bureau of the Census, *Census of Housing, 1980*, vol. 1, ch. A, Table 18.

4. Frances Fox Piven and Richard A. Cloward, *Regulating the Poor: The Functions of Public Welfare*, pp. 200–205.

5. John F. Kain, "Housing Segregation, Negro Employment, and Metropolitan Decentralization," pp. 175–197; John F. Kain, "The Distribution of Jobs and Industry," in James Q. Wilson, ed., *The Metropolitan Enigma*, pp. 23–30.

6. Bennett Harrison, *Urban Economic Development*, pp. 27–31; Bennett Harrison and Paul Osterman, "Public Employment and Urban Poverty: Some New Facts and a Policy Analysis," pp. 305–313, 363–366; Steven P. Erie, "Public Policy and Black Economic Polarization," pp. 308–309.

7. Mike Royko, *Boss: Richard J. Daley of Chicago*, pp. 136–137, 141; Arnold R. Hirsch, *Making the Second Ghetto: Race and Housing in Chicago, 1940–1960*.

8. Milton L. Rakove, *Don't Make No Waves, Don't Back No Losers: An Insider's Analysis of the Daley Machine*, pp. 34–37; Frank S. Robinson, *Machine Politics: A Study of Albany's O'Connells*, pp. 139–148.

9. Warren Moscow, *The Last of the Big-Time Bosses: The Life and Times of Carmine De Sapio and the Rise and Fall of Tammany Hall*, pp. 62–97.

10. Len O'Connor, *Clout: Mayor Daley and His City*, p. 85.

11. Robinson, *Machine Politics*, p. 169.

12. William J. Grimshaw, "The Daley Legacy: A Declining Politics of Party, Race, and Public Unions," in Samuel K. Gove and Louis H. Masotti, eds., *After Daley: Chicago Politics in Transition*, p. 64; John Waner, quoted in Milton L. Rakove, ed., *We Don't Want Nobody Nobody Sent: An Oral History of the Daley Years*, pp. 284–285.

13. Grimshaw, "Daley Legacy," pp. 69–71, 80.

14. R. L. McManus, Jr., "The Mayor's Stormy Pond," p. A–5.

15. Michael B. Preston, "Black Politics in the Post–Daley Era," in Gove and Masotti, eds., *After Daley*, pp. 101–107; Royko, *Boss*, pp. 67–68.

16. Grimshaw, "Daley Legacy," p. 77.

17. *Shakman* v. *the Democratic Organization of Cook County et al.*, no. 69 C 2145 (U.S. District Court for the Northern District of Illinois, Eastern Division), Memoranda and Stipulations. I am grateful to John Petrocik for sharing these materials with me.

18. Mollenkopf, *Contested City*, pp. 20–28.

19. U.S. Bureau of the Census, *1970 Census of Population*, vol. 1, Table 87; U.S. Bureau of the Census, *1980 Census of Population*, vol. 1, ch. C, Table 122.

20. U.S. Bureau of the Census, *Local Government Employment in Selected Metropolitan Areas and Large Counties, 1970*, Table 4; U.S. Bureau of the Census, *Local Government Employment in Selected Metropolitan Areas and Large Counties, 1981*, Table 4; Wendell Rawls, Jr., "Pittsburgh Nears End of Era as Flaherty Prepares to Move."

21. Michael K. Brown, "The Segmented Welfare State: The Political Origins and Consequences of U.S. Social Policy, 1938–1980," pp. 5–6.

22. Kenneth R. Mladenka, "The Urban Bureaucracy and the Chicago Political Machine: Who Gets What and the Limits to Political Control," pp. 991–998; Kenneth R. Mladenka, "Citizen Demands and Urban Services: The Distribution of Bureaucratic Response in Chicago and Houston," pp. 693–714.

23. O'Connor, *Clout*, pp. 172–173; Royko, *Boss*, p. 98; Samuel K. Gove, "State Impact: The Daley Legacy," in Gove and Masotti, eds., *After Daley*, p. 205.

24. O'Connor, *Clout*, pp. 149, 170–176.

25. Royko, *Boss*, pp. 129–132.

26. Alan C. Miller, "Corning: From the Shadow to 'Absolute King,'" p. A–19; Robinson, *Machine Politics*, pp. 139–140.

27. Ralph Whitehead, Jr., "The Organization Man," p. 352; O'Connor, *Clout*, p. 134.

28. Frank Hawkins, "Lawrence of Pittsburgh: Boss of the Mellon Patch," pp. 57–61.

29. Joann Crupi, "Corning: Last of the Traditional Political Bosses," pp. 12–13.

30. Donald H. Haider, "Capital Budgeting and Planning in the Post–Daley Era," in Gove and Masotti, eds., *After Daley*, pp. 161–165.

31. For a general analysis of postwar big-city pro-growth coalitions,

see Mollenkopf, *Contested City*. Regarding pro-growth politics in Chicago, see Royko, *Boss,* pp. 100–103; O'Connor, *Clout,* pp. 132–134, 149. Regarding Pittsburgh's growth politics, see Hawkins, "Lawrence of Pittsburgh," pp. 57, 60–61.

32. William Kennedy, *O Albany!* pp. 307–308, 316.

33. R. L. McManus, Jr., "Corning Dead: Last of the Traditional Political Machine Bosses," p. A–5.

34. Kennedy, *O Albany!* p. 316. In an interview a year before his death, Albany Mayor Erastus Corning revealed his method for handling Rockefeller: "When you're dealing with someone on a higher authority, you've got to deal from a position of strength. In other words, you've got to have something you can do to help, if you want them to help you. That's the art—to find something you can do, and then know what you'd like to trade for it." Quoted in McManus, "Mayor's Stormy Pond," p. A–5.

35. *Shakman* v. *the Democratic Organization of Cook County et al.,* no. 69 C 2145 (U.S. District Court for the Northern District of Illinois, Eastern Division), "Memorandum in Support of Plaintiffs' Motion for Partial Summary Judgment," pp. 23–41.

36. Royko, *Boss,* pp. 67–69, 78; O'Connor, *Clout,* pp. 128–129.

37. Robinson, *Machine Politics,* p. 169.

38. Roger E. Kasperson, "Toward a Geography of Urban Politics: Chicago, a Case Study," pp. 95–107; Whitehead, "Organization Man," pp. 355–356.

39. Len O'Connor, *Requiem: The Decline and Demise of Mayor Daley and His Era,* p. 134; "The City That Survives," *The Economist,* March 29, 1980.

40. Bryan Jones, "Party and Bureaucracy: The Influence of Intermediary Groups on Urban Public Service Delivery," pp. 688–689; Royko, *Boss,* p. 136. For evidence of political influence over municipal service delivery in Boston, see David L. Cingranelli, "Race, Politics, and Elites: Testing Alternative Models of Municipal Service Distribution," pp. 664–692; and Frederic N. Bolotin and David L. Cingranelli, "Equity and Urban Policy: The Underclass Hypothesis Revisited," pp. 209–219.

41. John Petrocik, "Voting in a Machine City: Chicago, 1975," p. 334. For evidence that citywide services represented a collective rather than an individual good in Chicago, see Ester R. Fuchs and Robert Y. Shapiro, "Government Performance as a Basis for Machine Support," pp. 537–550.

42. Milton L. Rakove, "Jane Byrne and the New Chicago Politics," in Gove and Masotti, eds., *After Daley,* p. 221.

43. Ibid.

44. For evidence of middle-class white demands for cultural dominance, see Anthony Downs, *Opening Up the Suburbs.*

45. Paul Kleppner, *Chicago Divided: The Making of a Black Mayor,* pp. 43–50; Royko, *Boss,* pp. 136–141; Kennedy, *O Albany!* p. 264.

46. John Hoellen, quoted in Rakove, *We Don't Want Nobody Nobody Sent,* pp. 300–301.

47. Grimshaw, "Daley Legacy," p. 69; Robinson, *Machine Politics,* pp. 179–182.

48. Kleppner, *Chicago Divided,* pp. 83–84; Kathleen A. Kemp and Robert L. Lineberry, "The Last of the Great Urban Machines and the Last of the Great Urban Mayors? Chicago Politics, 1955–1977," in Gove and Masotti, eds., *After Daley,* pp. 2–12, 18–20.

49. Martin Kilson, "Political Change in the Negro Ghetto, 1900–1940s," in Nathan I. Huggins et al., eds., *Key Issues in the Afro-American Experience,* pp. 182–189; O'Connor, *Clout,* pp. 120–121; Rakove, *Don't Make No Waves,* pp. 16, 110–111.

50. Constance A. Cunningham, "Homer S. Brown: First Black Political Leader in Pittsburgh," pp. 304–317; Hawkins, "Lawrence of Pittsburg," p. 61.

51. Royko, *Boss,* pp. 141–142; O'Connor, *Clout,* pp. 192–193; Kennedy, *O Albany!* pp. 166–167, 173, 260–264.

52. Hirsch, *Making the Second Ghetto;* Royko, *Boss,* pp. 136–144.

53. Piven and Cloward, *Regulating the Poor,* pp. 242–243.

54. Edward C. Banfield, *Political Influence: A New Theory of Urban Politics,* p. 74; Royko, *Boss,* p. 138; U.S. Bureau of the Census, *1970 Census of Population,* vol. 1, Table 94; U.S. Bureau of the Census, *1980 Census of Population,* vol. 1, ch. C, Table 137.

55. Michael K. Brown and Steven P. Erie, "Blacks and the Legacy of the Great Society: The Economic and Political Impact of Federal Social Policy," pp. 302–304; U.S. Bureau of Labor Statistics, *Manpower Impact of Federal Government Programs: Selected Grants-in-Aid to State and Local Governments,* Report 424, pp. 18–21.

56. U.S. Bureau of the Census, *Census of Population: 1960,* vol. 1, Table 129; U.S. Bureau of the Census, *1980 Census of Population,* vol. 1, ch. C, Tables 129, 135.

57. David L. Protess, "Banfield's Chicago Revisited: The Conditions for and Social Policy Implications of the Transformation of a Political Machine," pp. 184–202; O'Connor, *Clout,* p. 107.

58. Grimshaw, "Daley Legacy," p. 72; Rakove, *Don't Make No Waves,* pp. 110–111, 259.

59. Steven P. Erie, "Rainbow's End: From the Old to the New Urban

Ethnic Politics," in Joan W. Moore and Lionel Maldonado, eds., *Urban Ethnicity in the United States,* pp. 268–269; Charles V. Hamilton, "Public Policy and Some Political Consequences," in Marguerite R. Barnett and James A. Hefner, eds., *Public Policy for the Black Community,* pp. 239–255.

60. Quoted in Kleppner, *Chicago Divided,* p. 78.

61. Alan C. Miller, "His Honor, the Boss," p. 14; Kennedy, *O Albany!* pp. 173, 277–278, 328.

62. Kleppner, *Chicago Divided,* p. 83.

63. Martin Shefter, *Political Crisis/Fiscal Crisis: The Collapse and Revival of New York City.*

64. Wallace S. Sayre and Herbert Kaufman, *Governing New York City: Politics in the Metropolis,* Table 9, p. 48; Moscow, *Last of the Big-Time Bosses,* pp. 62–97, 105, 114–115, 127.

65. James Q. Wilson, *The Amateur Democrat: Club Politics in Three Cities,* pp. 32–64; Alfred Connable and Edward Silberfarb, *Tigers of Tammany: Nine Men Who Ran New York,* pp. 297–299.

66. Thomas F. X. Smith, *The Powerticians,* pp. 213, 226–227, 250–272.

67. Warren Moscow, *Politics in the Empire State,* pp. 97–109, 135; Shefter, *Political Crisis,* pp. 29–37.

68. Moscow, *Last of the Big-Time Bosses,* pp. 124–127, 159–183.

69. James O'Connor, *The Fiscal Crisis of the State.*

70. Royko, *Boss,* p. 58; O'Connor, *Clout,* pp. 180–181, 187; Hawkins, "Lawrence of Pittsburgh," p. 57.

71. Crupi, "Corning," pp. 12–13; Kennedy, *O Albany!* p. 316.

72. For an analysis of the machine-reform dialectic in New York politics, see Shefter, *Political Crisis,* pp. 13–104.

73. Jonathan Rieder, *Canarsie: The Jews and Italians of Brooklyn Against Liberalism,* pp. 51–54, 76–77, 123–129, 163–164, 216–263; Sayre and Kaufman, *Governing New York City,* p. 18.

74. For analyses of post–Tammany New York politics and mayoral coalition building, see Charles R. Morris, *The Cost of Good Intentions: New York City and the Liberal Experiment, 1960–1975;* Edward Koch, *Mayor;* Roger Starr, "John V. Lindsay: A Political Portrait," pp. 25–46; and Nat Hentoff, "Profile: The Mayor [Lindsay]."

75. John L. Shover, "The Emergence of a Two-Party System in Republican Philadelphia, 1924–1936," p. 1001.

76. Edward C. Banfield and Martha Derthick, *A Report on the Politics of Boston,* pp. VI-1–VI-13.

77. Ibid., pp. II-20–II-25, II-36, VI-14.

78. Martha Wagner Weinberg, "Boston's Kevin White: A Mayor Who

Survives," pp. 87–106; Alan Lupo, *Liberty's Chosen Home: The Politics of Violence in Boston,* p. 188.

79. Philip B. Heymann and Martha Wagner Weinberg, "The Paradox of Power: Mayoral Leadership on Charter Reform in Boston," in Walter Dean Burnham and Martha Wagner Weinberg, eds., *American Politics and Public Policy,* pp. 280–303; "Boston: White ex machina," p. 28.

80. Chris Black, "City, Unions Not the Best of Friends."

81. Peter Cowan, "1,600 Facing Hub Layoffs"; Black, "City"; Weinberg, "Boston's Kevin White," pp. 87–106.

82. Roger Butterfield, "Revolt in Philadelphia," November 15, 1952, pp. 40–41, 65–67, 70.

83. Ibid., November 1, 1952, pp. 19–21, 106–107; November 22, 1952, pp. 13, 36–39.

84. Melvin G. Holli and Peter d'A Jones, eds., *Biographical Dictionary of American Mayors, 1820–1980: Big City Mayors,* pp. 67–68 (Clark), 103–104 (Dilworth), 355–356 (Tate).

85. "Rizzo's Town"; "Philadelphia: Man or Machine?" For accounts of Rizzo's political career, see Fred Hamilton, *Rizzo;* and Joseph R. Daughen and Peter Binzen, *The Cop Who Would Be King.*

86. J. Anthony Lucas, *Common Ground: A Turbulent Decade in the Lives of Three American Families,* pp. 610–623; George V. Higgins, *Style Versus Substance: Boston, Kevin White, and the Politics of Illusion,* pp. 125–128, 179–187.

87. Reed M. Smith, *State Government in Transition: Reforms of the Leader Administration, 1955–1959,* pp. 80–85; Paul B. Beer, *Pennsylvania Politics Today and Yesterday: The Tolerable Accommodation,* pp. 210–215, 268, 348–349, 372–374.

88. Hamilton, *Rizzo,* pp. 162–163; Beer, *Pennsylvania Politics,* pp. 363–387.

89. Kleppner, *Chicago Divided,* pp. 149, 217–218.

90. "The City That Survives."

91. Henry Aaron, "Nondefense Programs," in Joseph A. Pechman, ed., *Setting National Priorities: The 1983 Budget,* pp. 149–150; Michael K. Brown, "Gutting the Great Society: Black Economic Progress and the Budget Cuts," pp. 11–24.

92. Thomas E. Cavanagh, *The Reagan Referendum: The Black Vote in the 1982 Elections,* pp. 3–6, 8.

93. O'Connor, *Requiem,* pp. 50, 121; Michael B. Preston, "Black Politics and Public Policy in Chicago: Self-Interest Versus Constituent Representation," in Michael B. Preston et al., eds., *The New Black Politics: The Search for Political Power,* pp. 168–174.

94. Manning Marable, "How Washington Won: The Political Econ-

omy of Race in Chicago," pp. 57–60; Ralph Whitehead, Jr., "The Chicago Story: Two Dailies, a Campaign—and an Earthquake," p. 30; Edward Thompson III, "Race and the Chicago Election," p. 4; Kleppner, *Chicago Divided*, p. 135 (O'Neill quote), pp. 146–147.

95. Kleppner, *Chicago Divided*, p. 250.

96. Fox Butterfield, "Signs of Change Appearing in Boston Electorate"; Higgins, *Style Versus Substance*, p. 179.

97. Rakove, *Don't Make No Waves*, pp. 3–14; Lawrence N. Hansen, "Suburban Politics and the Decline of the One-City Party," in Gove and Masotti, eds., *After Daley*, pp. 175–202.

98. Chinta Strausberg, "Mayor Asks Illinois' Cities to Battle Feds"; Chinta Strausberg, "Mayor Seizes Control of Park Board."

99. Adolph L. Reed, Jr., *The Jesse Jackson Phenomenon*, pp. 1–11; Chinta Strausberg, "Wallace Won't Quit"; Chinta Strausberg, "Hutch, Humes Answer Critics"; Chinta Strausberg, "Humes, Stroger Trade Blows."

100. *Philadelphia Tribune*, June 24, 1986. For evidence of white acquiescence to black rule in Detroit and Atlanta, see Peter K. Eisinger, *The Politics of Displacement: Racial and Ethnic Transition in Three American Cities*.

101. Joanne Jacobs, "Asian-American Political Muscle"; Bruce E. Cain and D. Roderick Kiewiet, *Minorities in California*; Kevin Phillips, "New Americans for the Next America"; Joanne Belenchia, "Latinos and Chicago Politics," in Gove and Masotti, eds., *After Daley*, pp. 118–145. For evidence of liberal cross-ethnic coalitions in California cities, see Rufus P. Browning et al., eds., *Protest Is Not Enough*.

Chapter Six

1. Larry Green, "Chicago's Mayor Finally Grasps Power and Spoils," pp. 1, 18.

2. Jeff Greenfield, "Payoffs Still Define Politics in Some Cities"; Tom Watson, "All Powerful Machine of Yore Endures in New York's Nassau," pp. 1623–1625.

3. Theodore J. Lowi, "Machine Politics—Old and New," pp. 83–92.

4. For a comparison of the two perspectives on the machine, see J. David Greenstone and Paul E. Peterson, "Reformers, Machines, and the War on Poverty," in James Q. Wilson, ed., *City Politics and Public Policy*, pp. 268–272. The revisionist theory of the machine is presented in Fred I. Greenstein, "The Changing Pattern of Urban Party Politics," pp. 1–13; Elmer E. Cornwell, "Bosses, Machines, and Ethnic Groups," pp. 27–39; and Robert K. Merton, *Social Theory and Social Structure*, pp. 125–136.

5. Alex Weingrod, "Patrons, Patronage, and Political Parties," pp. 377–400; James C. Scott, "Corruption, Machine Politics, and Political Change," pp. 1142–1158.

6. Thomas M. Guterbock, *Machine Politics in Transition: Party and Community in Chicago;* Michael Johnston, "Patrons and Clients, Jobs and Machines: A Case Study of the Uses of Patronage," pp. 385–398.

7. Edward C. Banfield and James Q. Wilson, *City Politics,* pp. 33–46; James Q. Wilson and Edward C. Banfield, "Public-Regardingness as a Value Premise in Voting Behavior," pp. 876–887. Regarding the debate over ethos theory, see Raymond E. Wolfinger and John Osgood Field, "Political Ethos and the Structure of City Government," pp. 306–326; Robert L. Lineberry and Edmund P. Fowler, "Reformism and Public Policies in American Cities," pp. 701–716; Timothy E. Hennessy, "Problems in Concept Formation: The Ethos 'Theory' and the Comparative Study of Urban Politics," pp. 537–564; and Edward C. Banfield and James Q. Wilson, "Political Ethos Revisited," pp. 1048–1062.

8. Daniel Patrick Moynihan, "The Irish," in Nathan Glazer and Daniel Patrick Moynihan, *Beyond the Melting Pot,* pp. 217–287. The role of the Catholic church as an organizational model for the machine is discussed in Edward M. Levine, *The Irish and Irish Politicians,* pp. 123–134.

9. Scott, "Corruption," pp. 1145–1148, 1155. For an application of the uprooted hypothesis to Irish-American politics, see Oscar Handlin, *The Uprooted,* pp. 201–226. Amy Bridges offers a similar account. In the United States, the franchise expanded at the beginning of industrialization, bringing the social conflicts created by economic transformation into the arena of party politics. In the cities the result was machine politics. According to Bridges, if England had had manhood suffrage in the early nineteenth century the outcome would have been machine politics in cities such as Manchester, Liverpool, and London (Amy Bridges, *A City in the Republic*). For the comparative argument, see Amy Bridges, "Rethinking the Origins of Machine Politics," in John Mollenkopf et al., eds., *Power, Structure, and Place.*

10. As Thomas N. Brown has observed, "The rebel resides in Ireland; the politician in America." For the differences between Irish politics in late nineteenth-century Ireland and America, see Thomas Brown, "The Political Irish: Politicians and Rebels," in David Noel Doyle and Owen Dudley Edwards, eds., *America and Ireland, 1776–1976,* pp. 133–150. Ireland's rebels turned politicians in the twentieth century. For case studies of local machine building in modern Ireland, see Paul Martin Sacks, *The Donegal Mafia: An Irish Political Machine;* and Max Bart, "The Political Machine and Its Importance in the Irish Republic," pp. 6–20.

America's Irish politicians turned rebels in the twentieth century. For evidence of Irish-American liberalism and public-regardingness, see Lawrence J. McCaffrey, *The Irish Diaspora in America*, pp. 146–147.

11. Terry Nichols Clark, "The Irish Ethic and the Spirit of Patronage," pp. 327–343.

12. Martin Shefter, "The Emergence of the Political Machine: An Alternative View," in Willis Hawley et al., eds., *Theoretical Perspectives on Urban Politics*, pp. 14–44.

13. Shefter, "Emergence of the Political Machine," pp. 21–27.

14. Martin Shefter, "The Electoral Foundations of the Political Machine: New York City, 1884–1897," in Joel H. Silbey et al., eds., *The History of American Electoral Behavior*, pp. 263–298.

15. James Warren Ingram III, "The 'Old Boy' Triggers the 'Fire Alarm': Boss Cox, Governor Foraker, and Machine Building in Cincinnati, 1885–1915," esp. pp. 45–48.

16. David R. Mayhew, *Placing Parties in American Politics*, pp. 20–21, 212–236.

17. Ibid., p. 212.

18. Regarding exchange theory, see George C. Homans, "Social Behavior as Exchange," pp. 597–606; Richard M. Emerson, "Power-Dependence Relations," pp. 31–40; Peter Blau, *Exchange and Power in Social Life*; R. L. Curry and L. L. Wade, *A Theory of Political Exchange*; Sidney Waldman, *Foundations of Political Analysis*; and the selections in *Sociological Inquiry* 42, nos. 3 and 4 (September and December 1972). For an estimate of the diverse kinds of resources machines could exchange for political support in a city of 100,000, see Charles Merriam, *The American Party System*, pp. 160–163.

19. Robert A. Dahl, *Who Governs? Democracy and Power in an American City*, pp. 32–51. The estimate of the vote yield of patronage is supplied by D. W. Brogan, *Politics in America*, pp. 114–115.

20. Banfield and Wilson, *City Politics*, pp. 117–118; Peter B. Clark and James Q. Wilson, "Incentive Systems: A Theory of Organizations," pp. 129–166.

21. Frank Sorauf, "State Patronage in a Rural County," pp. 1046–1056. See also Frank Sorauf, "The Silent Revolution in Patronage," pp. 28–34; and W. Robert Gump, "The Functions of Patronage in American Party Politics: An Empirical Reappraisal," pp. 87–107.

22. James Q. Wilson, "The Economy of Patronage," pp. 369–380.

23. Johnston, "Patrons and Clients," pp. 385–398.

24. Guterbock, *Machine Politics*, pp. 146–169. In another mid-1970s study of the Chicago machine, Ester R. Fuchs and Robert Y.

Shapiro argue that the Daley organization built voter support by effi-
ciently delivering citywide services, not merely by providing individual
benefits. See Fuchs and Shapiro, "Government Performance as a Basis for
Machine Support," pp. 537–550.

25. Richard F. Fenno, Jr., *Home Style: House Members in Their Districts,* pp. 1–30.

26. For an application of Fenno's model of electoral coalition building to the big-city machines under conditions of risk aversion, see Gary
W. Cox and Matt McCubbins, "Electoral Politics as a Redistributive
Game," pp. 370–389. Cox and McCubbins argue that risk-averse
bosses overreward primary constituencies and underreward secondary
constituencies.

27. Regarding machine growth policies, see Roger W. Lotchin, "Power
and Policy: American City Politics Between the Two World Wars," in
Scott Greer, ed., *Ethnics, Machines, and the American Urban Future,*
pp. 30–37.

28. The terms *voice* and *exit* are Albert O. Hirschman's; see his *Exit,
Voice, and Loyalty.*

29. Gary W. Cox and Morgan Kousser, "Turnout and Rural Corruption: New York as a Test Case," pp. 646–663.

30. Regarding machine fiscal policies, see Mayhew, *Placing Parties,*
pp. 262–307.

31. Walter Dean Burnham, "The Changing Shape of the American
Political Universe," pp. 7–28.

32. Walter Dean Burnham, *Critical Elections and the Mainsprings of
American Politics,* pp. 71–90; Walter Dean Burnham, "Theory and
Voting Research," pp. 1002–1023.

33. Philip E. Converse, "Comment on Burnham's 'Theory and Voting
Research,'" pp. 1024–1027; Jerrold G. Rusk, "Comment: The American Electoral Universe: Speculation and Evidence," pp. 1028–1049. Surprisingly, Converse and Rusk fail to note the role played by the 1906
Naturalization Act in dampening turnout rates (see Chapter 3).

34. For evidence of party-sponsored registration and voting of the immigrants in Chicago's 1923 mayoral election, see Charles E. Merriam
and Harold F. Gosnell, *Non-Voting: Causes and Methods of Control,*
pp. 202, 228–230. Not all entrenched machines were demobilizers.
Bosses in noncompetitive cities but in competitive-party and critical
states often pursued mobilization strategies. Walter Dean Burnham notes
that the GOP "steamrollers" of Philadelphia and Pittsburgh rolled up
massive vote pluralities in order to project their influence into state and
national politics. See Burnham, *Critical Elections,* pp. 51–53.

35. Guterbock, *Machine Politics*, pp. 146–169.

36. For accounts of the early successes of the reformers, see Harold A. Stone et al., *City Manager Government in the United States: A Review After Twenty-Five Years*; Frank M. Stewart, *A Half Century of Municipal Reform*; Richard S. Childs, *Civic Victories: The Story of an Unfinished Revolution*; Richard Hofstadter, *The Age of Reform*; Lorin Peterson, *The Day of the Mugwump*; and George Mowry, *The California Progressives*. A model study of national civil service reform and its limits is Stephen Skowronek's *Building a New American State*, pp. 47–84, 177–211. For an overview of theories of machine decline, see Harvey Boulay and Alan DiGaetano, "Why Did Political Machines Disappear?" pp. 25–50.

37. William L. Riordan, comp., *Plunkitt of Tammany Hall*, pp. 17–20.

38. Melvin G. Holli, *Reform in Detroit: Hazen S. Pingree and Urban Politics*, pp. 393–403; C. K. Yearley, *The Money Machines: The Breakdown and Reform of Governmental and Party Finance in the North, 1860–1920*, pp. 253–269.

39. Rexford Tugwell, *The Brains Trust*, pp. 366–371; Edwin O'Connor, *The Last Hurrah*, pp. 329–330.

40. Leo M. Snowiss, "Congressional Recruitment and Representation," esp. pp. 629–631.

41. James Q. Wilson, *The Amateur Democrat*, pp. 32–64, 301–316.

42. William A. Bullough, *The Blind Boss and His City: Christopher Augustine Buckley and Nineteenth-Century San Francisco*, pp. 232–233.

43. Banfield and Wilson, *City Politics*, pp. 121–125. For a provocative analysis of the self-destructive tendencies of the post–New Deal Democratic party, see Thomas Byrne Edsall, *The New Politics of Inequality*, pp. 23–66.

44. James C. Scott and Benedict J. Kerkvliet, "How Traditional Rural Patrons Lose Legitimacy," in Steffen W. Schmidt et al., eds., *Friends, Followers, and Factions: A Reader in Political Clientelism*, pp. 439–458; Boulay and DiGaetano, "Why Did Political Machines Disappear?" pp. 36–38.

45. Here is a sampling of the research on the southern relations: Regarding New Orleans machine politics, see John R. Kemp, ed., *Martin Behrman of New Orleans: Memoirs of a City Boss*; Joy J. Jackson, *New Orleans in the Gilded Age: Politics and Urban Progress, 1880–1896*; George M. Reynolds, *Machine Politics in New Orleans, 1897–1926*; and Edward F. Haas, *DeLesseps S. Morrison and the Image of Reform: New Orleans Politics, 1946–1961*. On boss rule in Baltimore, see Edwin

Rothman, "Factional Machine-Politics: William Curran and the Baltimore City Democratic Party Organization, 1929–1946"; James B. Crooks, *Politics and Progress: The Rise of Urban Progressivism in Baltimore, 1895 to 1911;* and Henry Bain, "Five Kinds of Politics: A Historical and Comparative Study of the Making of Legislators in Five Maryland Constituencies," pp. 816–919. Regarding the Crump machine in Memphis, see William D. Miller, *Mr. Crump of Memphis;* D. Tucker, *Lieutenant Lee of Beale Street;* Alfred Steinberg, *The Bosses,* pp. 72–133; David M. Tucker, *Memphis Since Crump: Bossism, Blacks, and Civic Reformers, 1948–1968;* and Kenneth D. Wald, "The Electoral Base of Political Machines: A Deviant Case Analysis," pp. 3–29. On the Pendergast organization in Kansas City, see William Reddig, *Tom's Town: Kansas City and the Pendergast Legend;* A. Theodore Brown, *The Politics of Reform: Kansas City's Municipal Government, 1925–1950;* Lyle W. Dorsett, *The Pendergast Machine;* and Steinberg, *The Bosses,* pp. 307–366.

46. Regarding the northern GOP relations, consult the following sources: On Philadelphia machine politics, see Lincoln Steffens, *The Shame of the Cities,* pp. 134–161; Harold Zink, *City Bosses in the United States,* pp. 194–229; David Harold Kurtzman, *Methods of Controlling Votes in Philadelphia;* J. T. Salter, *Boss Rule: Portraits in City Politics;* Dennis Clark, *The Irish in Philadelphia: Ten Generations of Urban Experience,* pp. 117–179; John L. Shover, "The Emergence of a Two-Party System in Republican Philadelphia, 1924–1936," pp. 985–1002; and James Reichley, *The Art of Government: Reform and Organization Politics in Philadelphia.* On Pittsburgh GOP machine politics, see Steffens, *Shame of the Cities,* pp. 101–133; Zink, *City Bosses,* pp. 230–256; and Bruce M. Stave, *The New Deal and the Last Hurrah: Pittsburgh Machine Politics,* pp. 24–52. Regarding the Cox machine in Cincinnati, see Zink, *City Bosses,* pp. 257–274; and Zane L. Miller, *Boss Cox's Cincinnati: Urban Politics in the Progressive Era.*

47. For an introduction to the clientelist approach to machine politics, see Scott, "Corruption"; Weingrod, "Patrons"; James C. Scott, "Political Clientelism: A Bibliographic Essay," in Steffen W. Schmidt et al., eds., *Friends,* pp. 483–505; and René Lemarchand, "Comparative Political Clientelism: Structure, Process, and Optic," in S. N. Eisenstadt and René Lemarchand, eds., *Political Clientelism, Patronage, and Development,* pp. 7–31.

48. Weingrod, "Patrons," pp. 377–395; Lemarchand, "Comparative Political Clientelism," pp. 21–24.

49. Mario Caciagli and Frank Belloni, "The 'New' Clientelism in

Southern Italy: The Christian Democratic Party in Catania," in Eisenstadt and Lemarchand, eds., *Political Clientelism*, pp. 35–55.

50. Judith Chubb, "The Social Bases of an Urban Political Machine: The Case of Palermo," pp. 107–125; Judith Chubb, *Patronage, Power, and Poverty in Southern Italy*.

51. Lemarchand, "Comparative Political Clientelism," p. 22. On the supposed "backward" character of the American machines, see Caciagli and Belloni, "'New' Clientelism," p. 43; Judith Chubb, "The Social Bases of an Urban Political Machine: The Christian Democratic Party in Palermo," in Eisenstadt and Lemarchand, eds., *Political Clientelism*, pp. 84–85.

52. Matthew A. Crenson, *The Federal Machine: Beginnings of Bureaucracy in Jacksonian America*, pp. 11–17, 31–57, 72–101; Carl E. Prince, *The Federalists and the Origins of the U.S. Civil Service*, pp. ix–xiii, 1–20; Richard L. McCormick, "The Party Period and Public Policy: An Exploratory Hypothesis," pp. 279–298.

53. Mayhew, *Placing Parties*, p. 324.

54. Samuel Beer, "Political Overload and Federalism," pp. 5–17; Samuel Beer, "The Adoption of General Revenue Sharing: A Case Study in Public Sector Politics," pp. 127–195. For the pre–Great Society roots of direct federalism, see Philip Funigiello, *The Challenge to Urban Liberalism: Federal-City Relations During World War II*, pp. 52–55, 72–75, 234–242.

55. Claus Offe, *Contradictions of the Welfare State*, pp. 179–206.

56. John H. Mollenkopf, *The Contested City*, p. 3.

57. Ibid., pp. 44–48, 61–71. Mollenkopf's choices of San Francisco and Boston are open to question, given his intent of studying the anti-party logic of federal programs and its impact on the building of the modern urban Democratic party. Neither city had a strong Democratic machine in the 1930s and 1940s for federal programs to challenge. San Francisco, today's liberal bastion, was firmly in the grip of the Republican party from the Progressive era to the New Frontier. Boston's Democratic politics were faction-ridden, not centralized. In neither city did federal urban programs from the New Deal onward produce postwar reform coalitions. San Francisco's reform politics predate the New Deal, going back to the Progressive era. Boston's reform politics were a reaction to local forces—Curleyism—rather than to federal urban programs. Democratic cities like Chicago, Pittsburgh, Jersey City, and Albany with strong New Deal–era machines are more appropriate test cases for his thesis.

58. Greenstone and Peterson, "Reformers," pp. 267–292.

59. Mollenkopf, *Contested City*, pp. 267–268, 292–297.

60. Chubb, "Social Bases," pp. 123–124.
61. Paul Peterson, *City Limits,* pp. 150–166.
62. Ira Katznelson, *City Trenches,* pp. 1–72.

Chapter Seven

1. James Bryce, *The American Commonwealth,* pp. 3–167, 254–256, 302–303, 370–371; M. Ostrogorski, *Democracy and the American Party System,* pp. 225–281, 364–456.

2. Frederick C. Howe, *The City: The Hope of Democracy,* pp. 61–98, 116–118; Lincoln Steffens, *The Shame of the Cities,* pp. 4–5, 16–18. For early defenses of boss rule, see Henry Jones Ford, "Municipal Corruption," pp. 673–686; and William L. Riordan, comp., *Plunkitt of Tammany Hall.*

3. Reformer Albert Stickney, quoted in C. K. Yearley, *The Money Machines: The Breakdown and Reform of Governmental and Party Finance in the North, 1860–1920,* p. 17.

4. Regarding the treatment of the machine in the black power debate, see n. 13 in Chapter 1, above. The machine model also figured prominently in the Kerner Commission report; see U.S. National Advisory Commission on Civil Disorders, *Report,* ch. 9, "Comparing the Immigrant and Negro Experience," pp. 278–282.

5. William Foote Whyte, "Social Organization in the Slums," pp. 34–39; William Foote Whyte, *Street Corner Society: The Social Structure of an Italian Slum,* pp. 194–252; Robert K. Merton, *Social Theory and Social Structure,* pp. 125–136; Daniel Bell, "Crime as an American Way of Life," pp. 131–154; Jerome K. Myers, "Assimilation in the Political Community," pp. 175–182.

6. Fred I. Greenstein, "The Changing Pattern of Urban Party Politics," pp. 1–13; Elmer E. Cornwell, "Party Absorption of Ethnic Groups: The Case of Providence, Rhode Island," pp. 87–98; Elmer E. Cornwell, "Bosses, Machines, and Ethnic Groups," pp. 27–39; Edgar Litt, *Beyond Pluralism: Ethnic Politics in America,* esp. pp. 60–74, 155–168.

7. Robert A. Dahl, *Who Governs? Democracy and Power in an American City,* pp. 2–86.

8. Ibid., pp. 11–31. In support of his "springboard" thesis, Dahl cites a 1933 sample survey of 1,600 New Haven families conducted by Yale's Institute of Human Relations. Constituting 13 percent of the sample, Irish-Americans held nearly half of the public service jobs. Yet the city's public sector constituted only 5 percent of the local economy and employed only 15 percent of the Irish-stock workforce. The 1930 census reports that blue-collar jobs accounted for nearly half of all public em-

ployment. See John W. McConnell, *The Evolution of Social Classes,* pp. 84–85; and U.S. Bureau of the Census, *Fifteenth Census of the United States, 1930,* vol. 4, Table 12, pp. 280–283.

9. Dahl, *Who Governs?* pp. 40–44; Eric L. McKitrick, "The Study of Corruption," pp. 502–514; Steven P. Erie, "Two Faces of Ethnic Power," pp. 262–263.

10. U.S. Census Office, *Ninth Census, 1870,* vol. 1, Tables 29, 32; U.S. Bureau of the Census, *Special Reports: Occupations at the Twelfth Census,* Tables 41, 43; Andrew Greeley, *That Most Distressful Nation: The Taming of the American Irish,* pp. 122–128; Andrew Greeley, *Ethnicity, Denomination, and Inequality,* pp. 54–55.

11. Stephan Thernstrom, *The Other Bostonians,* pp. 132–133, 232.

12. Greeley, *That Most Distressful Nation,* pp. 122–128; Greeley, *Ethnicity,* pp. 54–55.

13. Dennis P. Ryan, *Beyond the Ballot Box: A Social History of the Boston Irish, 1845–1917,* pp. 106, 149.

14. Dahl, *Who Governs?* pp. 33–34, 40–41. Oscar Handlin argues that the acculturated second-generation Irish, not the transplanted first generation, saw politics as a route of personal and group advancement; see Handlin, *The Uprooted,* pp. 201–216.

15. Daniel Patrick Moynihan, "The Irish," in Nathan Glazer and Daniel Patrick Moynihan, *Beyond the Melting Pot,* pp. 229, 259–260.

16. Edward M. Levine, *The Irish and Irish Politicians: A Study of Cultural and Social Alienation,* pp. 134–138.

17. Cornwell, "Bosses."

18. Raymond E. Wolfinger, "The Development and Persistence of Ethnic Voting," pp. 896–908; Raymond E. Wolfinger, *The Politics of Progress,* pp. 30–73.

19. Wolfinger, *Politics of Progress,* p. 49; Stanley Lieberson, *A Piece of the Pie: Blacks and White Immigrants Since 1880,* pp. 77–119. For a test of the middle-class thesis, see Leo E. Carroll, "Irish and Italians in Providence, Rhode Island, 1880–1960," pp. 67–74.

20. Wolfinger, *Politics of Progress,* pp. 47–51. For a similar argument regarding the party system's role in politicizing ethnicity, see Michael Parenti, "Ethnic Politics and the Persistence of Ethnic Identification," pp. 717–726.

21. Raymond E. Wolfinger, "Some Consequences of Ethnic Politics," in M. Kent Jennings and L. Harmon Zeigler, eds., *The Electoral Process,* pp. 44–50; Handlin, *The Uprooted,* pp. 201–226.

22. Wolfinger, "Some Consequences," p. 50.

23. Dahl, *Who Governs?* pp. 52–59. In the Dahlian model, divisible material benefits represented the primary way the system muted class

conflict in the pre–New Deal era. Dahl also mentions the facilitating role of symbolic politics such as ethnic nomination to public office and, in the post–New Deal era, the role of collective benefits—redevelopment, neighborhood renewal, education, and recreation. Ibid., pp. 60–62.

24. Michael Rogin, "Nonpartisanship and the Group Interest," in Philip Green and Sanford Levenson, eds., *Power and Community: Dissenting Essays in Political Science*, pp. 112–141; Michael Rogin, *The Intellectuals and McCarthy: The Radical Specter*, pp. 193, 205.

25. Ira Katznelson, *City Trenches: Urban Politics and the Patterning of Class in the United States*, pp. 1–72. For an incisive analysis of the rise of "artisan insurgency" in the antebellum period, see Sean Wilentz, *Chants Democratic: New York City and the Rise of the Working Class, 1788–1850.*

26. Katznelson, *City Trenches.*

27. Gwendolyn Mink, *Old Labor and New Immigrants in American Political Development*, pp. 45–68, 113–157.

28. For a pioneering analysis of the forging of union-Democratic party ties, see Marc Karson, *American Labor Unions and Politics, 1900–1918*. Regarding the Irish-American role in the craft union movement, see David Montgomery, "The Irish and the American Labor Movement," in David Noel Doyle and Owen Dudley Edwards, eds., *America and Ireland, 1776–1976*, pp. 205–217.

29. Wolfinger, "Some Consequences," pp. 45–51.

30. Paul Peterson, *City Limits*, pp. 3–38, 150–166.

31. Theodore J. Lowi, "American Business, Public Policy, Case Studies, and Political Theory," pp. 677–715.

32. Peterson, *City Limits*, pp. 41–65.

33. Ibid., pp. 131–183.

34. Ibid., pp. 150–166, esp. pp. 156–158.

35. Ibid., pp. 152–156.

36. Robert Goodman, *The Last Entrepreneurs: America's Regional Wars for Jobs and Dollars*, pp. 1–31, 76–115.

37. Amy Bridges, *A City in the Republic*, pp. 24–29, 61–82, 131–137, 146–161.

38. Barry Bluestone and Bennett Harrison, *The Deindustrialization of America*, pp. 15–19.

39. Peterson, *City Limits*, pp. 17–38, 131–149. For a penetrating analysis of the "political juggling act" required of urban governance, see Martin Shefter, *Political Crisis/Fiscal Crisis: The Collapse and Revival of New York City*, esp. pp. 3–12.

40. Viewing federalism from this perspective, one questions Peterson's

assertion that "the federal system which limits the policies and politics of local governments in the United States is not an inevitable part of a capitalist system" (*City Limits*, p. 218). In a cross-national sense, the "aberration" may not be inevitable, but it is difficult to imagine the American political economy developing as it has without it.

41. Regarding urban black politics, see Leonard A. Cole, *Blacks in Power: A Comparative Study of Black and White Elected Officials;* William E. Nelson, Jr., and Philip J. Meranto, *Electing Black Mayors: Political Action in the Black Community;* John R. Howard and Robert C. Smith, eds., "Urban Black Politics," pp. 1–150; Peter K. Eisinger, *The Politics of Displacement: Racial and Ethnic Transition in Three American Cities;* Albert Karnig and Susan Welch, *Black Representation and Urban Policy;* and Michael B. Preston et al., eds., *The New Black Politics: The Search for Political Power.*

42. On Hispanic and Asian-American politics, see F. Chris Garcia and Rudolpho de la Garza, *The Chicano Political Experience: Three Perspectives;* Raymond A. Mohl, "Miami: The Ethnic Cauldron," in Richard M. Bernard and Bradley R. Rice, eds., *Sunbelt Cities: Politics and Growth Since World War Two,* pp. 58–99; David L. Clark, "Los Angeles: Improbable Los Angeles," in Bernard and Rice, eds., *Sunbelt Cities,* pp. 268–308; Joan Moore and Harry Pachon, *Hispanics in the United States;* Bruce E. Cain and D. Roderick Kiewiet, *Minorities in California;* and Judy Tachibana, "California's Asians: Power from a Growing Population," pp. 534–543.

43. Martin Kilson, "Political Change in the Negro Ghetto, 1900–1940s," in Nathan Huggins et al., eds., *Key Issues in the Afro-American Experience,* pp. 182–189; Hanes Walton, Jr., *Black Politics: A Theoretical and Structural Analysis,* pp. 56–69.

44. Roger E. Alcaly and David Mermelstein, eds., *The Fiscal Crisis of American Cities;* George Sternlieb and James W. Hughes, "The Uncertain Future of the Center City," pp. 455–572; Marilyn Gittell, "Public Employment and the Public Service," in Alan Gartner et al., eds., *Public Service Employment: An Analysis of Its History, Problems, and Prospects,* pp. 121–142.

45. Leonard Sloan, "Good Government and the Politics of Race," pp. 171–174; Albert Karnig, "Black Representation on City Councils: The Impact of District Elections and Socioeconomic Factors," pp. 223–242; Theodore P. Robinson and Thomas R. Dye, "Reformism and Black Representation on City Councils," pp. 133–142; Richard L. Engstrom and Michael D. McDonald, "The Election of Blacks to City Councils: Clarifying the Impact of Electoral Arrangements on the Seats/Popula-

tion Relationship," pp. 344–354; Peggy Heilig and Robert J. Mundt, "Changes in Representational Equity: The Effect of Adopting Districts," pp. 393–397.

46. Joyce Gelb, "Blacks, Blocs, and Ballots: The Relevance of Party Politics to the Negro," pp. 44–69; Charles V. Hamilton, "Blacks and the Crisis of Political Participation," pp. 191–193; Robert C. Smith, "The Changing Shape of Urban Black Politics: 1960–1970," pp. 16–28.

47. Linda M. Watkins, "Pittsburgh Blacks' Paucity of Political Clout Stirs Struggle over the City's At-Large Election System," p. 58; Marty Willis, "Jan. 6 Demonstration to Greet All-White City Council," pp. A–1, A–4; Gilbert Price, "Skirmish Begins 'At Large' Battle" [Cincinnati], p. H–8; Larry Green, "Chicago's Mayor Finally Grasps Power and Spoils," pp. 1, 18; Chinta Strausberg, "Mayor Seizes Control of Park Board," pp. 1, 18; Robert Davis and Joseph Tybor, "Mayor Wins Election Ruling," pp. 1, 10.

48. Daniel Patrick Moynihan, "Foreword" to Greeley, *That Most Distressful Nation,* p. xi.

49. Ira Katznelson, "The Crisis of the Capitalist City: Urban Politics and Social Control," in Willis D. Hawley et al., eds., *Theoretical Perspectives on Urban Politics,* pp. 223–226.

50. Peter K. Eisinger, "Black Employment in Municipal Jobs: The Impact of Black Political Power," pp. 380–392; Peter K. Eisinger, "The Economic Conditions of Black Employment in Municipal Bureaucracy," pp. 754–771; Peter K. Eisinger, "Black Mayors and the Politics of Racial Economic Advancement," in William C. McReady, ed., *Culture, Ethnicity, and Identity,* pp. 95–109; John J. Harrigan, *Political Change in the Metropolis,* pp. 129–139. For evidence that minority gains in elective office have not been translated into significant minority policy payoffs, see Susan Welch and Albert Karnig, "The Impact of Black Elected Officials on Urban Social Expenditures," pp. 707–714; and Edmond J. Keller, "The Impact of Black Mayors on Urban Policy," pp. 40–52.

51. Clarence N. Stone, *Economic Growth and Neighborhood Discontent: System Bias in the Urban Renewal Program of Atlanta,* pp. 90–185; Clarence N. Stone, "Atlanta: Protest and Elections Are Not Enough," in Rufus P. Browning and Dale Rogers Marshall, eds., "Black and Hispanic Power in City Politics: A Forum," pp. 618–625; Dennis R. Judd, *The Politics of American Cities: Private Power and Public Policy,* pp. 373–407; John Helyar and Robert Johnson, "Tale of Two Cities: Chicago's Busy Center Masks a Loss of Jobs in Its Outlying Areas," pp. 1, 22.

52. Rufus P. Browning et al., *Protest Is Not Enough: The Struggle of Blacks and Hispanics for Equality in Urban Politics,* pp. 207–238 (quote at p. 214).

53. Michael K. Brown and Steven P. Erie, "Blacks and the Legacy of the Great Society: The Economic and Political Impact of Federal Social Policy," pp. 302–309, esp. Table 3, p. 308; U.S. Equal Employment Opportunity Commission, *Minorities and Women in State and Local Government, 1977*, vol. 1; U.S. Civil Service Commission, *Minority Group Employment in the Federal Government, 1975.*

54. Steven P. Erie, "Public Policy and Black Economic Polarization," pp. 311–315, esp. Table 1, p. 313.

55. Charles V. Hamilton, "Public Policy and Some Political Consequences," in Marguerite R. Barnett and James A. Hefner, eds., *Public Policy for the Black Community*, p. 245; and Charles V. Hamilton, "The Patron-Recipient Relationship and Minority Politics in New York City," p. 224.

56. U.S. Bureau of the Census, *Voter Participation in the National Election, November, 1964*, pp. 11–13, 21–22; U.S. Bureau of the Census, *Voting and Registration in the Election of November, 1976*, pp. 14–23, 61–62.

Bibliography

Aaron, Henry. "Nondefense Programs." In *Setting National Priorities: The 1983 Budget,* edited by Joseph A. Pechman, pp. 101–150. Washington, D.C.: Brookings Institution, 1982.

Abbott, Richard H. "Massachusetts: Maintaining Hegemony." In *Radical Republicans in the North: State Politics During Reconstruction,* edited by James C. Mohr, pp. 1–25. Baltimore: Johns Hopkins University Press, 1976.

Abrams, Richard M. *Conservatism in a Progressive Era: Massachusetts Politics, 1900–1912.* Cambridge, Mass.: Harvard University Press, 1964.

Adler, Norman Martin. "Ethnics in Politics: Access to Office in New York City." Ph.D. dissertation, University of Wisconsin, 1971.

Akenson, Donald H. *The Irish Educational Experiment: The National System of Education in the Nineteenth Century.* London: Routledge and Kegan Paul, 1970.

Alcaly, Roger E., and David Mermelstein, eds. *The Fiscal Crisis of American Cities.* New York: Vintage Books, 1977.

Allswang, John M. *A House for All Peoples: Ethnic Politics in Chicago, 1890–1936.* Lexington: University Press of Kentucky, 1971.

Andersen, Kristi. *The Creation of a Democratic Majority, 1928–1936.* Chicago: University of Chicago Press, 1979.

Angoff, Charles. *The Tone of the Twenties and Other Essays.* New York: A. S. Barnes, 1966.

Bain, Henry. "Five Kinds of Politics: A Historical and Comparative Study of the Making of Legislators in Five Maryland Constituencies." Ph.D. dissertation, Harvard University, 1970.

Banfield, Edward C. *Political Influence: A New Theory of Urban Politics.* New York: Free Press, 1961.

Banfield, Edward C., and Martha Derthick. *A Report on the Politics of Boston.* Cambridge, Mass.: Joint Center for Urban Studies, MIT and Harvard, 1960.

Banfield, Edward C., and James Q. Wilson. *City Politics.* New York: Vintage, 1963.

———. "Political Ethos Revisited." *American Political Science Review* 65, no. 4 (December 1971): 1048–1062.

Bart, Max. "The Political Machine and Its Importance in the Irish Republic." *Political Anthropology* 1, no. 1 (March 1975): 6–20.

Bass, Herbert. *"I Am a Democrat": The Political Career of David Bennett Hill.* Syracuse, N.Y.: Syracuse University Press, 1961.

———. "The Politics of Ballot Reform in New York State, 1888–1890." *New York History* 42, no. 3 (July 1961): 253–272.

Bayor, Ronald H. *Neighbors in Conflict: The Irish, Germans, Jews, and Italians of New York City, 1929–1941.* Baltimore: Johns Hopkins University Press, 1978.

Bean, Walton E. *Boss Reuf's San Francisco: The Story of the Union Labor Party, Big Business, and the Graft Prosecution.* Berkeley and Los Angeles: University of California Press, 1952.

Beer, Paul B. *Pennsylvania Politics Today and Yesterday: The Tolerable Accommodation.* University Park: Pennsylvania State University Press, 1980.

Beer, Samuel. "The Adoption of General Revenue Sharing: A Case Study in Public Sector Politics." *Public Policy* 24, no. 2 (Spring 1976): 127–195.

———. "Political Overload and Federalism." *Polity* 10, no. 1 (Fall 1977): 5–17.

Belenchia, Joanne. "Latinos and Chicago Politics." In *After Daley: Chicago Politics in Transition,* edited by Samuel K. Gove and Louis H. Masotti, pp. 118–145. Urbana: University of Illinois Press, 1982.

Bell, Daniel. "Crime as an American Way of Life." *Antioch Review* 13 (Summer 1953): 131–154.

———. *Marxian Socialism in the United States.* Princeton: Princeton University Press, 1967.

Black, Chris. "City, Unions Not the Best of Friends." *Boston Globe,* October 4, 1979.

Blau, Peter. *Exchange and Power in Social Life.* New York: John Wiley, 1964.

Blodgett, Geoffrey. *The Gentle Reformers: Massachusetts Democrats in the Cleveland Era.* Cambridge, Mass.: Harvard University Press, 1966.

Bluestone, Barry, and Bennett Harrison. *The Deindustrialization of America: Plant Closings, Community Abandonment, and the Dismantling of Basic Industry.* New York: Basic Books, 1982.

Blumberg, Barbara. *The New Deal and the Unemployed: The View from New York City.* Lewisburg, Pa.: Bucknell University Press, 1979.

Bobcock, John Paul. "The Irish Conquest of Our Cities." *Forum* 17 (April 1894): 186–195.

Bolotin, Frederic N., and David L. Cingranelli. "Equity and Urban Policy: The Underclass Hypothesis Revisited." *Journal of Politics* 45, no. 1 (February 1983): 209–219.

Boston Finance Commission. *Reports and Communications.* Boston: Boston Printing Department, 1909.

"Boston: White ex machina." *The Economist,* December 18, 1978, p. 28.

Boulay, Harvey, and Alan DiGaetano. "Why Did Political Machines Disappear?" *Journal of Urban History* 12, no. 1 (November 1985): 25–50.

Bridges, Amy. *A City in the Republic.* Cambridge: Cambridge University Press, 1984.

———. "Rethinking the Origins of Machine Politics." In *Power, Structure, and Place,* edited by John Mollenkopf, Thomas Bender, and Ira Katznelson. Beverly Hills, Ca.: Sage Publications, 1988.

Brogan, D. W. *Politics in America.* Garden City, N.Y.: Doubleday, 1960.

Brooks, Robert C. *Political Parties and Electoral Problems.* 3d ed. New York: Harper and Brothers, 1933.

Brown, A. Theodore. *The Politics of Reform: Kansas City's Municipal Government, 1925–1950.* Kansas City, Mo.: Community Studies, Inc., 1958.

Brown, Michael K. "Gutting the Great Society: Black Economic Progress and the Budget Cuts." *Urban League Review* 7 (1982): 11–24.

———. "The Segmented Welfare State: The Political Origins and Consequences of U.S. Social Policy, 1938–1980." Paper presented at the meeting of the Western Political Science Association, Las Vegas, Nevada, March 28–31, 1985.

Brown, Michael K., and Steven P. Erie. "Blacks and the Legacy of the Great Society: The Economic and Political Impact of Federal Social Policy." *Public Policy* 29, no. 3 (Summer 1981): 299–330.

Brown, Thomas N. "The Political Irish: Politicians and Rebels." In *America and Ireland, 1776–1976,* edited by David Noel Doyle and Owen Dudley Edwards, pp. 130–150. Westport, Conn.: Greenwood Press, 1980.

Browning, Rufus P., Dale Rogers Marshall, and David H. Tabb. *Protest Is Not Enough: The Struggle of Blacks and Hispanics for Equality in Urban Politics.* Berkeley and Los Angeles: University of California Press, 1984.

Bryce, James. *The American Commonwealth.* Rev. ed. vol. 2. New York: Macmillan, 1921.

Buenker, John D. "The Mahatma and Progressive Reform: Martin Lomasney as Lawmaker, 1911–1917." *New England Quarterly* (September 1971): 397–419.

Bullough, William A. *The Blind Boss and His City: Christopher Augustine Buckley and Nineteenth-Century San Francisco.* Berkeley and Los Angeles: University of California Press, 1979.

Burchell, R. A. *The San Francisco Irish, 1848–1880.* Manchester, England: Manchester University Press, 1979.

Burner, David. *The Politics of Provincialism: The Democratic Party in Transition, 1918–1932.* New York: Alfred A. Knopf, 1968.

Burnham, Walter Dean. "The Changing Shape of the American Political Universe." *American Political Science Review* 59, no. 1 (March 1965): 7–28.

———. *Critical Elections and the Mainsprings of American Politics.* New York: W. W. Norton, 1970.

———. "Theory and Voting Research." *American Political Science Review* 68, no. 3 (September 1974): 1002–1023.

Bushee, Frederick A. *Ethnic Factors in the Population of Boston.* New York: Macmillan, 1903.

Butterfield, Fox. "Signs of Change Appearing in Boston Electorate." *New York Times,* October 13, 1983.

Butterfield, Roger. "Revolt in Philadelphia." *Saturday Evening Post* 225 (November 1, 1952): 19ff.; (November 15, 1952): 40ff.; (November 22, 1952): 36ff.

Caciagli, Mario, and Frank Belloni. "The 'New' Clientelism in Southern Italy: The Christian Democratic Party in Catania." In *Political Clientelism, Patronage, and Development,* edited by S. N. Eisenstadt and René Lemarchand, pp. 35–55. Beverly Hills, Ca.: Sage Publications, 1981.

Cain, Bruce E., and D. Roderick Kiewiet. *Minorities in California.* Pasadena, Ca.: California Institute of Technology, 1986.

Cameron, David R. "Toward a Theory of Political Mobilization." *Journal of Politics* 36, no. 1 (February 1974): 138–171.

Caro, Robert A. *The Power Broker: Robert Moses and the Fall of New York.* New York: Vintage Books, 1975.

Carroll, Leo E. "Irish and Italians in Providence, Rhode Island, 1880–1960." *Rhode Island History* 28 (August 1969): 67–74.

Cavanagh, Thomas E. *The Reagan Referendum: The Black Vote in the 1982 Elections.* Washington, D.C.: Joint Center for Political Studies, April 1983.

Charles, Searle F. *Minister of Relief: Harry Hopkins and the Depression.* Syracuse, N.Y.: Syracuse University Press, 1963.

Chicago Daily News. *Almanac.* Chicago: Daily News, 1891–1930.

Childs, Richard S. *Civic Victories: The Story of an Unfinished Revolution.* New York: Harper and Brothers, 1952.

Chubb, Judith. "The Social Bases of an Urban Political Machine: The Case of Palermo." *Political Science Quarterly* 96, no. 1 (Spring 1981): 107–125.

———. *Patronage, Power, and Poverty in Southern Italy.* Cambridge: Cambridge University Press, 1982.

———. "The Social Bases of an Urban Political Machine: The Christian Democratic Party in Palermo." In *Political Clientelism, Patronage, and Development,* edited by S. N. Eisenstadt and René Lemarchand, pp. 57–89. Beverly Hills, Ca.: Sage Publications, 1986.

Cingranelli, David L. "Race, Politics, and Elites: Testing Alternative Models of Municipal Service Distribution." *American Journal of Political Science* 25, no. 4 (November 1981): 664–692.

"The City That Survives." *The Economist,* March 29, 1980, pp. 5–28.

Clark, David L. "Los Angeles: Improbable Los Angeles." In *Sunbelt Cities: Politics and Growth Since World War Two,* edited by Richard M. Bernard and Bradley R. Rice, pp. 268–308. Austin: University of Texas Press, 1983.

Clark, Dennis. *The Irish in Philadelphia: Ten Generations of Urban Experience.* Philadelphia: Temple University Press, 1973.

Clark, Peter B., and James Q. Wilson. "Incentive Systems: A Theory of Organizations." *Administrative Science Quarterly* 6 (September 1961): 129–166.

Clark, Terry Nichols. "The Irish Ethic and the Spirit of Patronage." *Ethnicity* 2 (1975): 327–343.

Clubb, Jerome M., and Howard W. Allen. "The Cities and the Election of 1928: Partisan Realignment?" *American Historical Review* 64, no. 4 (April 1969): 1205–1220.

Cole, Leonard A. *Blacks in Power: A Comparative Study of Black and White Elected Officials.* Princeton: Princeton University Press, 1976.

Comer, James P. "The Social Power of the Negro." In *The Black Power Revolt,* edited by Floyd B. Barbour, pp. 72–84. Boston: Extending Horizons, 1968.

Connable, Alfred, and Edward Silberfarb. *Tigers of Tammany: Nine Men Who Ran New York.* New York: Holt, Rinehart and Winston, 1967.

Connors, Richard J. *A Cycle of Power: The Career of Jersey City Mayor Frank Hague.* Metuchen, N.J.: Scarecrow Press, 1971.

Converse, Philip E. "Comment on Burnham's 'Theory and Voting Research.'" *American Political Science Review* 68, no. 3 (September 1974): 1024–1027.

Coode, Thomas H., and John F. Bauman. "Democratic Politics and Pennsylvania, 1932–1938." In *People, Poverty and Politics: Pennsylvanians During the Great Depression,* edited by Thomas H. Coode and John F. Bauman, pp. 224–250. Lewisburg, Pa.: Bucknell University Press, 1981.

Cornwell, Elmer E. "Party Absorption of Ethnic Groups: The Case of Providence, Rhode Island." *Social Forces* 38 (March 1960): 205–210.

———. "Some Occupational Patterns in Party Committee Membership." *Rhode Island History* 20 (July 1961): 87–98.

———. "Bosses, Machines, and Ethnic Groups." *Annals* 353 (May 1964): 27–39.

Cowan, Peter. "1600 Facing Hub Layoffs." *Boston Globe,* November 11, 1979.

Cox, Gary W., and Morgan Kousser. "Turnout and Rural Corruption: New York as a Test Case." *American Journal of Political Science* 25, no. 4 (November 1981): 646–663.

Cox, Gary W., and Matt McCubbins. "Electoral Politics as a Redistributive Game." *Journal of Politics* 48, no. 2 (May 1986): 370–389.

Crenson, Matthew A. *The Federal Machine: Beginnings of Bureaucracy in Jacksonian America.* Baltimore: Johns Hopkins University Press, 1975.

Crooks, James B. *Politics and Progress: The Rise of Urban Progressivism in Baltimore, 1895 to 1911.* Baton Rouge: Louisiana State University Press, 1968.

Crupi, Joann. "Corning: Last of the Traditional Bosses." *Albany Times Union and Knickerbocker News,* June 3, 1983, pp. 12–13.

Cruse, Harold. *The Crisis of the Negro Intellectual: From Its Origins to the Present.* New York: Morrow, 1967.

Cunningham, Constance A. "Homer S. Brown: First Black Political Leader in Pittsburgh." *Journal of Negro History* 66 (Winter 1981–82): 304–317.

Curry, R. L., and L. L. Wade. *A Theory of Political Exchange.* Englewood Cliffs, N.J.: Prentice-Hall, 1968.

Dahl, Robert A. *Who Governs? Democracy and Power in an American City.* New Haven: Yale University Press, 1961.

Daughen, Joseph R., and Peter Binzen. *The Cop Who Would Be King.* Boston: Little, Brown, 1977.

Davis, Robert, and Joseph Tybor. "Mayor Wins Election Ruling." *Chicago Tribune,* September 3, 1986, pp. 1, 10.

Degler, Carl N. "American Political Parties and the Rise of the City: An Interpretation." In *American Urban History,* edited by Alexander B. Callow, Jr., pp. 465–479. New York: Oxford University Press, 1969.

DeMarco, William M. *Ethnics and Enclaves: Boston's Italian North End*. Ann Arbor, Mich.: UMI Research Press, 1981.

Dineen, Joseph F. *The Purple Shamrock: The Honorable James Michael Curley of Boston*. New York: W. W. Norton, 1949.

Dorsett, Lyle W. *The Pendergast Machine*. New York: Oxford University Press, 1968.

———. *Franklin D. Roosevelt and the City Bosses*. Port Washington, N.Y.: Kennikat Press, 1977.

Downs, Anthony. *Opening Up the Suburbs*. New Haven: Yale University Press, 1973.

Edsall, Thomas Byrne. *The New Politics of Inequality*. New York: W. W. Norton, 1984.

Edwards, Alba M. *A Socio-Economic Grouping of the Gainful Workers of the United States*. Washington, D.C.: Government Printing Office, 1938.

Eisenstadt, S. N., and René Lemarchand, eds. *Political Clientelism, Patronage, and Development*. Beverly Hills, Ca.: Sage Publications, 1981.

Eisinger, Peter K. *The Politics of Displacement: Racial and Ethnic Transition in Three American Cities*. New York: Academic Press, 1980.

———. "Black Employment in Municipal Jobs: The Impact of Black Political Power." *American Political Science Review* 76, no. 2 (June 1982): 380–392.

———. "The Economic Conditions of Black Employment in Municipal Bureaucracy." *American Journal of Political Science* 26, no. 4 (November 1982): 754–771.

———. "Black Mayors and the Politics of Racial Economic Advancement." In *Culture, Ethnicity, and Identity*, edited by William C. McReady, pp. 95–109. New York: Academic Press, 1983.

Eldersveld, Samuel J. "The Influence of Metropolitan Party Pluralities in Presidential Elections Since 1920: A Study of Twelve Cities." *American Political Science Review* 43, no. 6 (December 1949): 1189–1209.

Ely, Richard T. *Taxation in American States and Cities*. New York: Thomas Crowell, 1888.

Emerson, Richard M. "Power-Dependence Relations." *American Sociological Review* 27 (February 1962): 31–40.

Engstrom, Richard L., and Michael D. McDonald. "The Election of Blacks to City Councils: Clarifying the Impact of Electoral Arrangements on the Seats/Population Relationship." *American Political Science Review* 75, no. 2 (June 1981): 344–354.

Erie, Steven P. "The Development of Class and Ethnic Politics in San Francisco, 1870–1910: A Critique of the Pluralist Interpretation." Ph.D. dissertation, University of California, Los Angeles, 1975.

————. "Progressivism and San Francisco Labor, 1899–1917." Unpublished manuscript, University of Southern California, 1977.

————. "Politics, the Public Sector and Irish Social Mobility: San Francisco, 1870–1900." *Western Political Quarterly* 31, no. 2 (June 1978): 274–289.

————. "Public Policy and Black Economic Polarization." *Policy Analysis* 6, no. 3 (Summer 1980): 305–317.

————. "Two Faces of Ethnic Power: Comparing the Irish and Black Experiences." *Polity* 13, no. 2 (Winter 1980): 261–284.

————. "Rainbow's End: From the Old to the New Urban Ethnic Politics." In *Urban Ethnicity in the United States,* edited by Joan W. Moore and Lionel Maldonado, pp. 249–275. Beverly Hills, Ca.: Sage Publications, 1985.

Faulkner, Harold U. *Politics, Reform and Expansion, 1890–1900.* New York: Harper Torchbooks, 1959.

Fenno, Richard F., Jr. *Home Style: House Members in Their Districts.* Boston: Little, Brown, 1978.

Finegold, Kenneth. "Progressivism, Electoral Change, and Public Policy in New York City, 1900–1917." Center for American Political Studies, Harvard University, October 1983.

Fogelson, Robert M. *Violence as Protest.* New York: Doubleday, 1971.

Foley, John W. "Community Structure and Public Policy Outputs in 300 Eastern American Communities: Toward a Sociology of the Public Sector." *Ethnicity* 6 (September 1979): 222–234.

Foner, Eric. "Radicalism in the Gilded Age: The Land League and Irish-America." *Marxist Perspectives* 1 (Summer 1978): 6–54.

Ford, Henry Jones. "Municipal Corruption." *Political Science Quarterly* 19 (1904): 673–686.

Foster, Mark S. "Frank Hague of Jersey City: The Boss as Reformer." *New Jersey History* 86 (Summer 1968): 106–116.

Fuchs, Ester R., and Robert Y. Shapiro. "Government Performance as a Basis for Machine Support." *Urban Affairs Quarterly* 18, no. 4 (June 1983): 537–550.

Fuchs, Lawrence H. *The Political Behavior of American Jews.* Glencoe, Ill.: Free Press, 1956.

Funchion, Michael F. *Chicago's Irish Nationalists, 1881–1890.* New York: Arno Press, 1976.

Funigiello, Philip. *The Challenge to Urban Liberalism: Federal-City Relations During World War II.* Knoxville: University of Tennessee Press, 1978.

Gans, Herbert J. *The Urban Villagers: Group and Class in the Life of Italian-Americans.* New York: Free Press, 1962.

Garcia, F. Chris, and Rudolpho de la Garza. *The Chicano Political Experience: Three Perspectives.* North Scituate, Mass.: Duxbury Press, 1977.

Garrett, Charles. *The La Guardia Years: Machine and Reform Politics in New York City.* New Brunswick, N.J.: Rutgers University Press, 1961.

Gavit, John Palmer. *Americans by Choice.* Montclair, N.J.: Patterson Smith, 1971. Originally published in 1922.

Gelb, Joyce. "Blacks, Blocs, and Ballots: The Relevance of Party Politics to the Negro." *Polity* 3, no. 1 (Fall 1970): 44–69.

Genen, Arthur. "John Kelly: New York's First Irish Boss." Ph.D. dissertation, New York University, 1971.

George, Henry. "The Kearney Agitation in California." *Popular Science Monthly* 17 (August 1880): 433–453.

Gibson, Florence E. *The Attitudes of the New York Irish Toward State and National Affairs, 1848–1892.* New York: Columbia University Press, 1951.

Ginger, Ray. *Altgeld's America: The Lincoln Ideal Versus Changing Realities.* Chicago: Quadrangle, 1965.

Gittell, Marilyn. "Public Employment and the Public Service." In *Public Service Employment: An Analysis of Its History, Problems, and Prospects,* edited by Alan Gartner et al., pp. 121–142. New York: Praeger, 1973.

Glazer, Nathan, and Daniel Patrick Moynihan. *Beyond the Melting Pot.* Cambridge, Mass.: MIT Press, 1964.

Godkin, E. L. "Criminal Politics." *North American Review* 151 (1890): 706–723.

Goodman, Robert. *The Last Entrepreneurs: America's Regional Wars for Jobs and Dollars.* New York: Simon and Schuster, 1980.

Gorvine, Harold. "The New Deal in Massachusetts." In *The New Deal: The State and Local Levels,* edited by John Braeman, Robert H. Bremner, and David Brody, pp. 3–44. Columbus: Ohio State University Press, 1975.

Gosnell, Harold F. *Machine Politics: Chicago Model.* 2d ed. Chicago: University of Chicago Press, 1968. Originally published in 1937.

Gottfried, Alex. *Boss Cermak of Chicago: A Study of Political Leadership.* Seattle: University of Washington Press, 1962.

———. "Political Machines." In *International Encyclopedia of the Social Sciences.* Vol. 12. Edited by David L. Sills. New York: Crowell, Collier, and Macmillan, 1968.

Gove, Samuel K. "State Impact: The Daley Legacy." In *After Daley: Chicago Politics in Transition,* edited by Samuel K. Gove and Louis H. Masotti, pp. 203–216. Urbana: University of Illinois Press, 1982.

Gove, Samuel K., and Louis H. Masotti, eds. *After Daley: Chicago Politics in Transition.* Urbana: University of Illinois Press, 1982.

Greeley, Andrew. *That Most Distressful Nation: The Taming of the American Irish.* Chicago: Quadrangle, 1972.

―――. *Ethnicity, Denomination, and Inequality.* Beverly Hills, Ca.: Sage Publications, 1976.

Green, Larry. "Chicago's Mayor Finally Grasps Power and Spoils." *Los Angeles Times,* August 2, 1986, pt. 1, pp. 1, 18.

Green, Paul Michael. "The Chicago Democratic Party, 1840–1920: From Factionalism to Political Organization." Ph.D. dissertation, University of Chicago, 1975.

Greenfield, Jeff. "Payoffs Still Define Politics in Some Cities." *Los Angeles Times,* April 13, 1986.

Greenstein, Fred I. "The Changing Pattern of Urban Party Politics." *Annals* 353 (May 1964): 1–13.

Greenstone, J. David. *Labor in American Politics.* New York: Vintage Books, 1970.

Greenstone, J. David, and Paul E. Peterson. "Reformers, Machines, and the War on Poverty." In *City Politics and Public Policy,* edited by James Q. Wilson, pp. 267–292. New York: John Wiley, 1971.

Grimshaw, William J. "The Daley Legacy: A Declining Politics of Party, Race, and Public Unions." In *After Daley: Chicago Politics in Transition,* edited by Samuel K. Gove and Louis H. Masotti, pp. 57–87. Urbana: University of Illinois Press, 1982.

Gump, W. Robert. "The Functions of Patronage in American Party Politics: An Empirical Reappraisal." *Midwest Journal of Political Science* 15, no. 1 (February 1971): 87–107.

Guterbock, Thomas M. *Machine Politics in Transition: Party and Community in Chicago.* Chicago: University of Chicago Press, 1980.

Haas, Edward F. *DeLesseps S. Morrison and the Image of Reform: New Orleans Politics, 1946–1961.* Baton Rouge: Louisiana State University Press, 1974.

Haider, Donald H. "Capital Budgeting and Planning in the Post-Daley Era." In *After Daley: Chicago Politics in Transition,* edited by Samuel K. Gove and Louis H. Masotti, pp. 159–174. Urbana: University of Illinois Press, 1982.

Hamilton, Charles V. "Blacks and the Crisis of Political Participation." *Public Interest* 34 (Winter 1974): 185–210.

―――. "Public Policy and Some Political Consequences." In *Public Policy for the Black Community,* edited by Marguerite R. Barnett and James A. Hefner, pp. 239–255. New York: Alfred Publishing, 1976.

———. "The Patron-Recipient Relationship and Minority Politics in New York City." *Political Science Quarterly* 95 (Summer 1979): 211–227.

Hamilton, Fred. *Rizzo*. New York: Viking Press, 1973.

Handlin, Oscar. *The Uprooted*. New York: Grosset and Dunlap, 1951.

———. *Boston's Immigrants: A Study in Acculturation*. Rev. ed. New York: Atheneum, 1970. Originally published in 1941.

Hansen, Lawrence N. "Suburban Politics and the Decline of the One-City Party." In *After Daley: Chicago Politics in Transition*, edited by Samuel K. Gove and Louis H. Masotti, pp. 175–202. Urbana: University of Illinois Press, 1982.

Harmond, Richard. "The 'Beast' in Boston: Benjamin F. Butler as Governor of Massachusetts." *Journal of American History* 55 (September 1968): 266–280.

Harrigan, John J. *Political Change in the Metropolis*. Boston: Little, Brown, 1985.

Harrison, Bennett. *Urban Economic Development*. Washington, D.C.: Urban Institute, 1974.

Harrison, Bennett, and Paul Osterman. "Public Employment and Urban Poverty: Some New Facts and a Policy Analysis." *Urban Affairs Quarterly* 9 (March 1974): 305–313, 363–366.

Harrison, Carter H., Jr. *Stormy Years*. Indianapolis, Ind.: Bobbs-Merrill, 1935.

Hawkins, Frank. "Lawrence of Pittsburgh: Boss of the Mellon Patch." *Harper's Magazine* 213 (August 1956): 57–61.

Heidenheimer, Arnold J., ed. *Political Corruption: Readings in Comparative Analysis*. New York: Holt, Rinehart and Winston, 1970.

Heilig, Peggy, and Robert J. Mundt. "Change in Representational Equity: The Effect of Adopting Districts." *Social Science Quarterly* 64, no. 1 (June 1983): 393–397.

Helyar, John, and Robert Johnson. "Tale of Two Cities: Chicago's Busy Center Masks a Loss of Jobs in Its Outlying Areas." *Wall Street Journal*, April 16, 1986, pp. 1, 22.

Henderson, Thomas M. *Tammany Hall and the New Immigrants: The Progressive Years*. New York: Arno Press, 1976.

Hennessy, Timothy E. "Problems in Concept Formation: The Ethos 'Theory' and the Comparative Study of Urban Politics." *Midwest Journal of Political Science* 14, no. 4 (November 1970): 537–564.

Hentoff, Nat. "Profile: The Mayor [Lindsay]." *New Yorker* 45, no. 3 (May 3, 1969): 44ff.; (May 10, 1969): 42ff.

Heymann, Philip B., and Martha Wagner Weinberg. "The Paradox of Power: Mayoral Leadership on Charter Reform in Boston." In *Ameri-*

can Politics and Public Policy, edited by Walter Dean Burnham and Martha Wagner Weinberg, pp. 280–303. Cambridge, Mass.: MIT Press, 1978.

Higgins, George V. *Style Versus Substance: Boston, Kevin White, and the Politics of Illusion.* New York: Macmillan, 1984.

Hirsch, Arnold R. *Making the Second Ghetto: Race and Housing in Chicago, 1940–1960.* New York: Cambridge University Press, 1983.

Hirschman, Albert O. *Exit, Voice, and Loyalty.* Cambridge, Mass.: Harvard University Press, 1970.

Hofstadter, Richard. *The Age of Reform.* New York: Alfred A. Knopf, 1955.

Holli, Melvin G. *Reform in Detroit: Hazen S. Pingree and Urban Politics.* New York: Oxford University Press, 1969.

Holli, Melvin G., and Peter d'A Jones, eds. *Biographical Dictionary of American Mayors, 1820–1980: Big City Mayors.* Westport, Conn.: Greenwood Press, 1981.

Hollingsworth, J. Rogers, and Ellen Jane Hollingsworth. "Expenditures in American Cities." In *The Dimensions of Quantitative Research in History,* edited by William O. Aydelotte, Allan G. Bogue, and Robert William Fogel, pp. 347–389. Princeton: Princeton University Press, 1972.

Homans, George C. "Social Behavior as Exchange." *Journal of Sociology* 63 (May 1958): 597–606.

Howard, Donald S. *The WPA and Federal Relief Policy.* New York: Russell Sage, 1943.

Howard, John R., and Robert C. Smith, eds. "Urban Black Politics." *Annals* 439 (September 1978): 1–150.

Howe, Frederick C. *The City: The Hope of Democracy.* Seattle: University of Washington Press, 1967. Originally published in 1905.

Howe, Irving. *World of Our Fathers.* New York: Simon and Schuster, 1976.

Huthmacher, J. Joseph. *Massachusetts People and Politics, 1919–1933.* Cambridge, Mass.: Belknap Press, 1959.

———. "Urban Liberalism and the Age of Reform." *Mississippi Valley Historical Review* 49 (September 1962): 231–241.

Ingalls, Robert P. *Herbert H. Lehman and New York's Little New Deal.* New York: New York University Press, 1975.

Ingram, James Warren, III. "The 'Old Boy' Triggers the 'Fire Alarm': Boss Cox, Governor Foraker, and Machine Building in Cincinnati, 1885–1915." Senior honors thesis, Department of Political Science, University of California, San Diego, April 1986.

International City Managers' Association. *Municipal Year Book.* Chicago: International City Managers' Association, 1933–1941.

Jackson, Joy J. *New Orleans in the Gilded Age: Politics and Urban Progress, 1880–1896.* Baton Rouge: Louisiana State University Press, 1969.

Jacobs, Joanne. "Asian-American Political Muscle." *Wall Street Journal,* December 27, 1985.

Johnson, William M. "On the Outside Looking In: Irish, Italian, and Black Ethnic Politics in an American City." Ph.D. dissertation, Yale University, 1977.

Johnston, Michael. "Patrons and Clients, Jobs and Machines: A Case Study of the Uses of Patronage." *American Political Science Review* 73, no. 2 (June 1979): 385–398.

Jones, Bryan. "Party and Bureaucracy: The Influence of Intermediate Groups on Urban Public Service Delivery." *American Political Science Review* 75, no. 3 (September 1981): 688–700.

Josephson, Matthew. *The Politicos, 1865–1896.* New York: Harcourt, Brace and World, 1963. Originally published in 1938.

Judd, Dennis R. *The Politics of American Cities: Private Power and Public Policy.* 2d ed. Boston: Little, Brown, 1984.

Kain, John F. "Housing Segregation, Negro Employment, and Metropolitan Decentralization." *Quarterly Journal of Economics* 82 (May 1968): 175–197.

———. "The Distribution of Jobs and Industry." In *The Metropolitan Enigma,* edited by James Q. Wilson, pp. 23–30. Garden City, N.J.: Anchor Books, 1970.

Karnig, Albert. "Black Representation on City Councils: The Impact of District Elections and Socioeconomic Factors." *Urban Affairs Quarterly* 12, no. 2 (December 1976): 223–242.

Karnig, Albert, and Susan Welch. *Black Representation and Urban Policy.* Chicago: University of Chicago Press, 1980.

Karson, Marc. *American Labor Unions and Politics, 1900–1918.* Carbondale: Southern Illinois University Press, 1958.

Kasperson, Roger E. "Toward a Geography of Urban Politics: Chicago, a Case Study." *Economic Geography* 11, no. 2 (April 1965): 95–107.

Katznelson, Ira. "The Crisis of the Capitalist City: Urban Politics and Social Control." In *Theoretical Perspectives on Urban Politics,* edited by Willis D. Hawley et al., pp. 214–229. Englewood Cliffs, N.J.: Prentice-Hall, 1976.

———. *City Trenches: Urban Politics and the Patterning of Class in the United States.* Chicago: University of Chicago Press, 1982.

Kehl, James A. *Boss Rule in the Gilded Age: Matt Quay of Pennsylvania.* Pittsburgh: University of Pittsburgh Press, 1981.

Keller, Edmond J. "The Impact of Black Mayors on Urban Policy." *Annals* 439 (September 1979): 40–52.

Keller, Morton. *Affairs of State.* Cambridge, Mass.: Harvard University Press, 1977.

Keller, Richard C. "Pennsylvania's Little New Deal." In *The New Deal: The State and Local Levels,* edited by John Braeman, Robert H. Bremner, and David Brody, pp. 45–76. Columbus: Ohio State University Press, 1975.

Kelley, Robert. *The Cultural Patterns in American Politics.* New York: Alfred A. Knopf, 1974.

"The Kelly-Nash Political Machine." *Fortune* 14, no. 1 (August 1936): 47–126.

Kemp, John R., ed. *Martin Behrman of New Orleans: Memoirs of a City Boss.* Baton Rouge: Louisiana State University Press, 1977.

Kemp, Kathleen A., and Robert L. Lineberry. "The Last of the Great Urban Machines and the Last of the Great Urban Mayors? Chicago Politics, 1955–1977." In *After Daley: Chicago Politics in Transition,* edited by Samuel K. Gove and Louis H. Masotti, pp. 1–26. Urbana: University of Illinois Press, 1982.

Kennedy, Robert E., Jr. *The Irish: Emigration, Marriage, and Fertility.* Berkeley and Los Angeles: University of California Press, 1973.

Kennedy, William. *O Albany!* New York: Viking, 1983.

Kessner, Thomas. *The Golden Door: Italian and Jewish Immigrant Mobility in New York City, 1880–1915.* New York: Oxford University Press, 1977.

Kilson, Martin. "Political Change in the Negro Ghetto, 1900–1940s." In *Key Issues in the Afro-American Experience,* edited by Nathan I. Huggins, Martin Kilson, and Daniel M. Fox, pp. 182–189. New York: Harcourt Brace Jovanovich, 1971.

Kincaid, John. "Political Success and Policy Failure: The Persistence of Machine Politics in Jersey City." Ph.D. dissertation, Temple University, 1981.

King, Willford I. *The National Income and Its Purchasing Power.* New York: National Bureau of Economic Research, 1930.

Kleppner, Paul. *Chicago Divided: The Making of a Black Mayor.* DeKalb: Northern Illinois University Press, 1985.

Koch, Edward. *Mayor.* New York: Simon and Schuster, 1984.

Kurtzman, David Harold. *Methods of Controlling Votes in Philadelphia.* Philadelphia: Privately printed, 1935.

Kuznets, Simon. *National Income and Its Composition, 1919–1938.* New York: National Bureau of Economic Research, 1941.

Lancaster, Lance W. "State Limitations on Local Indebtedness." In *Municipal Year Book, 1936,* pp. 313–327. Chicago: International City Managers' Association, 1936.

Larkin, Emmet. "Church, State, and Nation in Modern Ireland." *American Historical Review* 80, no. 5 (December 1975): 1244–1276.

Lemarchand, René. "Comparative Political Clientelism: Structure, Process and Optic." In *Political Clientelism, Patronage, and Development,* edited by S. N. Eisenstadt and René Lemarchand, pp. 7–31. Beverly Hills, Ca.: Sage Publications, 1981.

Levin, Murray B. *The Compleat Politician: Political Strategy in Massachusetts.* New York: Bobbs-Merrill, 1962.

Levine, Edward M. *The Irish and Irish Politicians: A Study of Cultural and Social Alienation.* Notre Dame, Ind.: University of Notre Dame Press, 1966.

Lichtman, Allan J. *Prejudice and the Old Politics: The Presidential Election of 1928.* Chapel Hill: University of North Carolina Press, 1979.

Lieberson, Stanley. *A Piece of the Pie: Blacks and White Immigrants Since 1880.* Berkeley and Los Angeles: University of California Press, 1980.

Lineberry, Robert L., and Edmund P. Fowler. "Reformism and Public Policies in American Cities." *American Political Science Review* 61, no. 3 (September 1967): 701–716.

Litt, Edgar. *Beyond Pluralism: Ethnic Politics in America.* Glenview, Ill.: Scott, Foresman, 1970.

Lotchin, Roger W. "Power and Policy: American City Politics Between the Two World Wars." In *Ethnics, Machines, and the American Urban Future,* edited by Scott Greer, pp. 30–37. Cambridge, Mass.: Schenkman, 1981.

Lowi, Theodore J. "American Business, Public Policy, Case Studies, and Political Theory." *World Politics* 16 (July 1964): 677–715.

———. *At the Pleasure of the Mayor: Patronage and Power in New York City, 1898–1958.* New York: Free Press, 1964.

———. "Machine Politics—Old and New." *Public Interest* (Fall 1967): 83–92.

Lubell, Samuel. *The Future of American Politics.* 3d ed. New York: Harper and Row, 1965. Originally published in 1951.

Lucas, J. Anthony. *Common Ground: A Turbulent Decade in the Lives of Three American Families.* New York: Alfred A. Knopf, 1985.

Luebke, Frederick C. *Immigrants and Politics: The Germans of Nebraska, 1880–1900.* Lincoln: University of Nebraska Press, 1974.

Lupo, Alan. *Liberty's Chosen Home: The Politics of Violence in Boston.* Boston: Little, Brown, 1977.

Lynch, Jeremiah. *Buckleyism: The Government of a State.* San Francisco: N.p., 1889.

McCaffrey, Lawrence J. *The Irish Diaspora in America.* Bloomington: Indiana University Press, 1976.

McConnell, John W. *The Evolution of Social Classes.* Washington, D.C.: American Council on Public Affairs, 1942.

McCormick, Richard L. "The Party Period and Public Policy: An Exploratory Hypothesis." *Journal of American History* 66, no. 2 (September 1979): 279–298.

———. *From Realignment to Reform: Political Change in New York State, 1893–1910.* Ithaca: Cornell University Press, 1981.

MacDonaugh, Oliver. "The Irish Famine Emigration to the United States." *Perspectives in American History* 10 (1976): 357–448.

McKean, Dayton David. *The Boss: The Hague Machine in Action.* New York: Russell and Russell, 1967. Originally published in 1940.

McKitrick, Eric L. "The Study of Corruption." *Political Science Quarterly* 72 (December 1957): 502–514.

MacMahon, Arthur W., John D. Millett, and Gladys Ogden. *The Administration of Federal Work Relief.* New York: De Capo Press, 1971. Originally published in 1941.

McManus, R. L., Jr. "Corning Dead: Last of the Traditional Political Machine Bosses." *Albany Times Union,* May 29, 1983, p. A–5.

———. "The Mayor's Stormy Pond." *Albany Times Union,* May 29, 1983, p. A–5.

McSeveney, Samuel T. *The Politics of Depression: Political Behavior in the Northeast, 1893–1896.* New York: Oxford University Press, 1972.

Mann, Arthur. *La Guardia Comes to Power, 1933.* New York: J. B. Lippincott, 1965.

Marable, Manning. "How Washington Won: The Political Economy of Race in Chicago." *Intergroup Relations* 11, no. 2 (Summer 1983): 56–81.

Marcus, Robert D. *Grand Old Party: Political Structure in the Gilded Age.* New York: Oxford University Press, 1971.

Mayhew, David R. *Placing Parties in American Politics.* Princeton: Princeton University Press, 1986.

Merriam, Charles. *The American Party System.* New York: Macmillan, 1922.

Merriam, Charles E., and Harold F. Gosnell. *Non-Voting: Causes and Methods of Control.* Chicago: University of Chicago Press, 1924.

Merton, Robert K. *Social Theory and Social Structure*. Rev. ed. New York: Free Press, 1968. Originally published in 1949.

Miller, Alan C. "Corning: From the Shadow to 'Absolute King.'" *Albany Times Union*, October 21, 1979, p. A–19.

———. "His Honor, the Boss." *Albany Times Union*, October 25, 1979, p. 14.

Miller, William D. *Mr. Crump of Memphis*. Baton Rouge: Louisiana State University Press, 1964.

Miller, Zane L. *Boss Cox's Cincinnati: Urban Politics in the Progressive Era*. New York: Oxford University Press, 1968.

Mink, Gwendolyn. *Old Labor and New Immigrants in American Political Development*. Ithaca: Cornell University Press, 1986.

Mladenka, Kenneth R. "The Urban Bureaucracy and the Chicago Political Machine: Who Gets What and the Limits to Political Control." *American Political Science Review* 74, no. 4 (December 1980): 991–998.

———. "Citizen Demands and Urban Services: The Distribution of Bureaucratic Response in Chicago and Houston." *American Journal of Political Science* 25, no. 4 (November 1981): 693–714.

Mohl, Raymond A. "Miami: The Ethnic Cauldron." In *Sunbelt Cities: Politics and Growth Since World War Two*, edited by Richard M. Bernard and Bradley R. Rice, pp. 58–99. Austin: University of Texas Press, 1983.

Mohr, James C. *The Radical Republicans and Reform in New York During Reconstruction*. Ithaca: Cornell University Press, 1973.

Mollenkopf, John H. *The Contested City*. Princeton: Princeton University Press, 1983.

Montgomery, David. "The Irish and the American Labor Movement." In *America and Ireland, 1776–1976*, edited by David Nocl Doyle and Owen Dudley Edwards, pp. 205–217. Westport, Conn.: Greenwood Press, 1980.

Moore, Joan, and Harry Pachon. *Hispanics in the United States*. Englewood Cliffs, N.J.: Prentice-Hall, 1985.

Morris, Charles R. *The Cost of Good Intentions: New York City and the Liberal Experiment, 1960–1975*. New York: McGraw-Hill, 1981.

Moscow, Warren. *Politics in the Empire State*. New York: Alfred A. Knopf, 1948.

———. *The Last of the Big-Time Bosses: The Life and Times of Carmine De Sapio and the Rise and Fall of Tammany Hall*. New York: Stein and Day, 1971.

Mosher, William E., and Sophie Polah. "Public Employment in the United States." *National Municipal Review* 21, no. 1 (January 1932): 51–72.

Mowry, George. *The California Progressives.* Chicago: Quadrangle, 1963.

Moynihan, Daniel Patrick. "The Irish." In *Beyond the Melting Pot,* by Nathan Glazer and Daniel Patrick Moynihan, pp. 217–287. Cambridge, Mass.: MIT Press, 1964.

Munro, William Bennett. *The Government of American Cities.* 3d ed. New York: Macmillan, 1920.

Mushkat, Jerome. *Tammany: The Evolution of a Political Machine, 1789–1865.* Syracuse, N.Y.: Syracuse University Press, 1971.

———. *The Reconstruction of the New York Democracy, 1861–1874.* Rutherford, N.J.: Fairleigh Dickinson University Press, 1981.

Myers, Gustavus. *History of Tammany Hall.* New York: Dover, 1971. Originally published in 1917.

Myers, Jerome K. "Assimilation in the Political Community." *Sociology and Social Research* 35 (January-February 1951): 175–182.

Nelli, Humbert S. "John Powers and the Italians: Politics in a Chicago Ward, 1896–1921." *Journal of American History* 57 (June 1970): 67–84.

Nelson, William E., Jr., and Philip J. Meranto. *Electing Black Mayors: Political Action in the Black Community.* Columbus: Ohio State University Press, 1977.

New York State Legislature. *Red Book, State of New York.* Albany: New York State Legislature, 1887–1897.

New York Tribune. *Tribune Almanac and Political Register.* New York: G. Dearborn, 1855–1886.

New York World. *World Almanac.* New York: New York World, 1893–1941.

O'Connor, Edwin. *The Last Hurrah.* New York: Bantam Books, 1956.

O'Connor, James. *The Fiscal Crisis of the State.* New York: St. Martin's Press, 1973.

O'Connor, Len. *Clout: Mayor Daley and His City.* Chicago: Henry Regnery, 1975.

———. *Requiem: The Decline and Demise of Mayor Daley and His Era.* Chicago: Contemporary Books, 1977.

Offe, Claus. *Contradictions of the Welfare State.* Cambridge, Mass.: MIT Press, 1984.

Olin, Spencer. *California's Prodigal Sons: Hiram Johnson and the Progressive Movement, 1911–1917.* Berkeley and Los Angeles: University of California Press, 1968.

Ostrogorski, M. *Democracy and the American Party System.* New York: Macmillan, 1921.

Parenti, Michael. "Ethnic Politics and the Persistence of Ethnic Identification." *American Political Science Review* 61, no. 3 (September 1967): 717–726.

Patterson, James T. *The New Deal and the States: Federalism in Transition*. Princeton: Princeton University Press, 1969.

Peterson, Lorin. *The Day of the Mugwump*. New York: Random House, 1961.

Peterson, Paul. *City Limits*. Chicago: University of Chicago Press, 1981.

Petrocik, John. "Voting in a Machine City: Chicago, 1975." *Ethnicity* 8 (1981): 320–340.

"Philadelphia: Man or Machine?" *The Economist*, August 8, 1981.

Phillips, Kevin. "New Americans for the Next America." *Los Angeles Times*, May 11, 1986.

Piven, Frances Fox, and Richard A. Cloward. *Regulating the Poor: The Functions of Public Welfare*. New York: Vintage Books, 1971.

Pratt, John W. "Boss Tweed's Public Welfare Program." *New York Historical Society Quarterly* 45, no. 4 (October 1961): 396–411.

Preston, Michael B. "Black Politics and Public Policy in Chicago: Self-Interest Versus Constituent Representation." In *The New Black Politics: The Search for Political Power*, edited by Michael B. Preston, Lenneal J. Henderson, Jr., and Paul Puryear, pp. 159–186. New York: Longman, 1982.

———. "Black Politics in the Post-Daley Era." In *After Daley: Chicago Politics in Transition*, edited by Samuel K. Gove and Louis H. Masotti, pp. 88–117. Urbana: University of Illinois Press, 1982.

Preston, Michael B., Lenneal J. Henderson, Jr., and Paul Puryear, eds. *The New Black Politics: The Search for Political Power*. New York: Longman, 1982.

Price, Gilbert. "Skirmish Begins 'At Large' Battle." *Cleveland Call and Post*, February 13, 1986, p. H–8.

Prince, Carl E. *The Federalists and the Origins of the U.S. Civil Service*. New York: New York University Press, 1977.

Protess, David L. "Banfield's Chicago Revisited: The Conditions for and Social Policy Implications of the Transformation of a Political Machine." *Social Service Review* 48, no. 2 (June 1974): 184–202.

Quint, Howard H. *The Forging of American Socialism*. Indianapolis, Ind.: Bobbs-Merrill, 1953.

Rakove, Milton L. *Don't Make No Waves, Don't Back No Losers: An Insider's Analysis of the Daley Machine*. Bloomington: Indiana University Press, 1975.

———. "Jane Byrne and the New Chicago Politics." In *After Daley: Chicago Politics in Transition*, edited by Samuel K. Gove and Louis H. Masotti, pp. 217–236. Urbana: University of Illinois Press, 1982.

Rakove, Milton L., ed. *We Don't Want Nobody Nobody Sent: An Oral History of the Daley Years.* Bloomington: Indiana University Press, 1979.

Rawls, Wendell, Jr. "Pittsburgh Nears End of Era as Flaherty Prepares to Move." *New York Times,* February 26, 1977.

Reddig, William. *Tom's Town: Kansas City and the Pendergast Legend.* New York: J. B. Lippincott, 1947.

Reed, Adolph L., Jr. *The Jesse Jackson Phenomenon.* New Haven: Yale University Press, 1986.

Reichley, James. *The Art of Government: Reform and Organization Politics in Philadelphia.* New York: Fund for the Republic, 1959.

Reynolds, George M. *Machine Politics in New Orleans, 1897–1926.* New York: Columbia University Press, 1936.

Rieder, Jonathan. *Canarsie: The Jews and Italians of Brooklyn Against Liberalism.* Cambridge, Mass.: Harvard University Press, 1985.

Riordan, William L., comp. *Plunkitt of Tammany Hall.* New York: E. P. Dutton, 1963. Originally published in 1905.

"Rizzo's Town." *The Economist,* November 4, 1978.

Robinson, Frank S. *Machine Politics: A Study of Albany's O'Connells.* New Brunswick, N.J.: Transaction Books, 1977.

Robinson, Theodore P., and Thomas R. Dye. "Reformism and Black Representation on City Councils." *Social Science Quarterly* 59, no. 1 (June 1978): 133–142.

Rogin, Michael. *The Intellectuals and McCarthy: The Radical Specter.* Cambridge, Mass.: MIT Press, 1967.

———. "Progressivism and the California Electorate." *Journal of American History* 55 (September 1968): 297–314.

———. "Nonpartisanship and the Group Interest." In *Power and Community: Dissenting Essays in Political Science,* edited by Philip Green and Sanford Levenson, pp. 112–141. New York: Vintage Books, 1970.

Rothman, Edwin. "Factional Machine-Politics: William Curran and the Baltimore City Democratic Party Organization, 1929–1946." Ph.D. dissertation, Johns Hopkins University, 1949.

Royko, Mike. *Boss: Richard J. Daley of Chicago.* New York: Signet, 1971.

Rusk, Jerrold G. "Comment: The American Electoral Universe: Speculation and Evidence." *American Political Science Review* 68, no. 3 (September 1974): 1028–1049.

Ryan, Dennis P. *Beyond the Ballot Box: A Social History of the Boston Irish, 1845–1917.* Rutherford, N.J.: Fairleigh Dickinson University Press, 1983.

Sacks, Paul Martin. *The Donegal Mafia: An Irish Political Machine.* New Haven: Yale University Press, 1976.

Salter, J. T. *Boss Rule: Portraits in City Politics*. New York: McGraw-Hill, 1935.

San Francisco Board of Supervisors. *San Francisco Municipal Reports*. San Francisco: W. H. Hinton, 1870–1915.

San Francisco Recorder. *General List of Citizens of the United States Registered in the Great Register, 1867*. San Francisco: County Recorder, 1867.

Saxton, Alexander. "San Francisco Labor and the Populist and Progressive Insurgencies." *Pacific Historical Review* 34 (September 1965): 421–438.

———. *The Indispensable Enemy: Labor and the Anti-Chinese Movement in California*. Berkeley and Los Angeles: University of California Press, 1971.

Sayre, Wallace S., and Herbert Kaufman. *Governing New York City: Politics in the Metropolis*. New York: Russell Sage, 1960.

Scott, James C. "Corruption, Machine Politics, and Political Change." *American Political Science Review* 63, no. 4 (December 1969): 1142–1158.

———. "Political Clientelism: A Bibliographic Essay." In *Friends, Followers, and Factions: A Reader in Political Clientelism*, edited by Steffen W. Schmidt, Laura Guasti, Carl H. Landé, and James C. Scott, pp. 483–505. Berkeley and Los Angeles: University of California Press, 1977.

Scott, James C., and Benedict J. Kerkvliet. "How Traditional Rural Patrons Lose Legitimacy." In *Friends, Followers, and Factions: A Reader in Political Clientelism*, edited by Steffen W. Schmidt, Laura Guasti, Carl H. Landé, and James C. Scott, pp. 439–458. Berkeley and Los Angeles: University of California Press, 1977.

Secrist, Horace. *An Economic Analysis of the Constitutional Restrictions upon Public Indebtedness in the United States*. Madison: University of Wisconsin, 1914.

Shaw, Douglas V. *The Making of an Immigrant City: Ethnic and Cultural Conflict in Jersey City, New Jersey, 1850–1877*. New York: Arno Press, 1976.

Shefter, Martin. "The Emergence of the Political Machine: An Alternative View." In *Theoretical Perspectives on Urban Politics*, edited by Willis D. Hawley et al., pp. 14–44. Englewood Cliffs, N.J.: Prentice-Hall, 1976.

———. "New York City's Fiscal Crisis: The Politics of Inflation and Retrenchment." *Public Interest* 48 (Summer 1977): 98–127.

———. "The Electoral Foundations of the Political Machine: New York City, 1884–1897." In *The History of American Electoral Behavior*, edited by Joel H. Silbey, Allan A. Bogue, and William H. Flanigan, pp. 263–298. Princeton: Princeton University Press, 1978.

———. "Economic Crises, Social Coalitions, and Political Institutions: New York City's Little New Deal." Paper presented at the annual meeting of the American Political Science Association, New York, September 3–6, 1981.

———. *Political Crisis/Fiscal Crisis: The Collapse and Revival of New York City.* New York: Basic Books, 1985.

Shover, John L. "The Progressives and the Working-Class Vote in California." *Labor History* 10 (Fall 1969): 584–601.

———. "The Emergence of a Two-Party System in Republican Philadelphia, 1924–1936." *Journal of American History* 60, no. 4 (March 1974): 985–1002.

Skowronek, Stephen. *Building a New American State.* Cambridge: Cambridge University Press, 1982.

Sloan, Leonard. "Good Government and the Politics of Race." *Social Problems* 17 (Fall 1969): 171–174.

Smith, Reed M. *State Government in Transition: Reforms of the Leader Administration, 1955–1959.* Philadelphia: University of Pennsylvania Press, 1959.

Smith, Robert C. "The Changing Shape of Urban Black Politics: 1960–1970." *Annals* 439 (September 1978): 16–28.

Smith, Thomas F. X. *The Powerticians.* Secaucus, N.J.: Lyle Stuart, 1980.

Snowiss, Leo M. "Congressional Recruitment and Representation." *American Political Science Review* 60, no. 3 (September 1966): 627–639.

Sorauf, Frank. "State Patronage in a Rural County." *American Political Science Review* 50, no. 4 (December 1956): 1046–1056.

———. "The Silent Revolution in Patronage." *Public Administration Review* 20, no. 1 (Winter 1960): 28–34.

Speed, John Gilmer. "The Purchase of Votes in New York City." *Harper's Weekly* 49 (1905): 386–387.

Stack, John F., Jr. *International Conflict in an American City.* Westport, Conn.: Greenwood Press, 1979.

Starr, Roger. "John V. Lindsay: A Political Portrait." *Commentary,* February 1970, pp. 25–46.

Stave, Bruce M. *The New Deal and the Last Hurrah: Pittsburgh Machine Politics.* Pittsburgh: University of Pittsburgh Press, 1970.

Steffens, Lincoln. *The Shame of the Cities.* New York: Hill and Wang, 1966. Originally published in 1903.

Steinberg, Alfred. *The Bosses.* New York: Macmillan, 1972.

Sternlieb, George, and James W. Hughes. "The Uncertain Future of the

Center City." *Urban Affairs Quarterly* 18, no. 4 (June 1983): 455–472.

Stewart, Frank M. *A Half Century of Municipal Reform*. Berkeley and Los Angeles: University of California Press, 1950.

Stone, Chuck. *Black Political Power in America*. Indianapolis, Ind.: Bobbs-Merrill, 1968.

Stone, Clarence N. *Economic Growth and Neighborhood Discontent: System Bias in the Urban Renewal Program of Atlanta*. Chapel Hill: University of North Carolina Press, 1976.

———. "Atlanta: Protest and Elections Are Not Enough." In "Black and Hispanic Power in City Politics: A Forum," edited by Rufus P. Browning and Dale Rogers Marshall. *PS* 19, no. 3 (Summer 1986): 618–625.

Stone, Harold A., Don K. Price, and Kathryn H. Stone. *City Manager Government in the United States: A Review After Twenty-Five Years*. Chicago: Public Administration Service, 1940.

Strausberg, Chinta. "Wallace Won't Quit." *Chicago Defender,* April 3, 1986.

———. "Mayor Asks Illinois' Cities to Battle Feds." *Chicago Defender,* May 24, 1986.

———. "Hutch, Humes Answer Critics." *Chicago Defender,* June 2, 1986.

———. "Humes, Stroger Trade Blows." *Chicago Defender,* June 3, 1986.

———. "Mayor Seizes Control of Park Board." *Chicago Defender,* June 17, 1986, pp. 1, 18.

Suiter, William O. "State Limits on Local Property Taxes." In *Municipal Year Book, 1936*, pp. 328–339. Chicago: International City Managers' Association, 1936.

Tachibana, Judy. "California's Asians: Power from a Growing Population." *California Journal* 17, no. 11 (November 1986): 534–543.

Tarr, Joel A. *A Study in Boss Politics: William Lorimer of Chicago*. Urbana: University of Illinois Press, 1971.

Teaford, Jon C. *City and Suburb: The Political Fragmentation of Metropolitan America, 1850–1970*. Baltimore: Johns Hopkins University Press, 1979.

Thernstrom, Stephan. *The Other Bostonians: Poverty and Progress in the American Metropolis, 1880–1970*. Cambridge, Mass.: Harvard University Press, 1973.

Thompson, Edward, III. "Race and the Chicago Election." *Journal of Ethnic Studies* 11, no. 4 (Winter 1984): 1–10.

Trout, Charles H. *Boston, the Great Depression, and the New Deal*. New York: Oxford University Press, 1977.

Tucker, D. *Lieutenant Lee of Beale Street*. Nashville: Vanderbilt University Press, 1971.

Tucker, David M. *Memphis Since Crump: Bossism, Blacks, and Civic Reformers, 1948–1968*. Knoxville: University of Tennessee Press, 1980.

Tugwell, Rexford. *The Brains Trust*. New York: Viking, 1968.

U.S. Bureau of the Census. *Special Reports: Statistics of Cities, 1902*. Washington, D.C.: Government Printing Office, 1902.

———. *Special Reports: Occupations at the Twelfth Census*. Washington, D.C.: Government Printing Office, 1904.

———. *Census of Population, 1920*. Washington, D.C.: Government Printing Office, 1922–1923.

———. *Fifteenth Census of the United States, 1930*. Washington, D.C.: Government Printing Office, 1933.

———. *Financial Statistics of Cities Having a Population over 100,000, 1932*. Washington, D.C.: Government Printing Office, 1934.

———. *Statistical Abstract of the United States, 1938*. Washington, D.C.: Government Printing Office, 1938.

———. *Sixteenth Census of the United States, 1940*. Washington, D.C.: Government Printing Office, 1943.

———. *State and Local Government Special Studies: Historical Review of State and Local Government Finances*. Washington, D.C.: Government Printing Office, 1948.

———. *Statistical Abstract of the United States, 1950*. Washington, D.C.: Government Printing Office, 1950.

———. *Historical Statistics of the United States: Colonial Times to 1957*. Washington, D.C.: Government Printing Office, 1960.

———. *Census of Population: 1960*. Washington, D.C.: Government Printing Office, 1963.

———. *Voter Participation in the National Election, November, 1964*. Washington, D.C.: Government Printing Office, 1965.

———. *Local Government Employment in Selected Metropolitan Areas and Large Counties, 1970*. Washington, D.C.: Government Printing Office, 1971.

———. *1970 Census of Population*. Washington, D.C.: Government Printing Office, 1973.

———. *Voting and Registration in the Election of November, 1976*. Washington, D.C.: Government Printing Office, 1977.

———. *Statistical Abstract, 1981*. Washington, D.C.: Government Printing Office, 1981.

———. *Census of Housing, 1980*. Washington, D.C.: Government Printing Office, 1982.

———. *Local Government Employment in Selected Metropolitan Areas and Large Counties, 1981.* Washington, D.C.: Government Printing Office, 1983.

———. *1980 Census of Population.* Washington, D.C.: Government Printing Office, 1983.

U.S. Bureau of Labor Statistics. *Manpower Impact of Federal Government Programs: Selected Grants-in-Aid to State and Local Governments.* Washington, D.C.: Government Printing Office, 1973.

U.S. Census Office. *Ninth Census, 1870.* Washington, D.C.: Government Printing Office, 1872.

———. *Report on Valuation, Taxation, and Public Indebtedness: 1880.* Washington, D.C.: Government Printing Office, 1884.

———. *Eleventh Census of the United States, 1890.* Washington, D.C.: Government Printing Office, 1895.

———. *Twelfth Census of the United States, 1900.* Washington, D.C.: Government Printing Office, 1901.

———. *Special Reports: Wealth, Debt, and Taxation.* Washington, D.C.: Government Printing Office, 1907.

U.S. Civil Service Commission. *Minority Group Employment in the Federal Government, 1975.* Washington, D.C.: Government Printing Office, 1977.

U.S. Equal Employment Opportunity Commission. *Minorities and Women in State and Local Government, 1977.* Washington, D.C.: Government Printing Office, 1977.

U.S. National Advisory Commission on Civil Disorders. *Report.* Washington, D.C.: Government Printing Office, 1968.

U.S. Social Security Board. "Relief in Urban Areas." In *Municipal Year Book, 1939,* pp. 460–465. Chicago: International City Managers' Association, 1939.

U.S. Works Progress Administration. *Family Unemployment.* Washington, D.C.: Government Printing Office, 1940.

———. *Summary of Relief and Federal Work Program Statistics, 1933–1940.* Washington, D.C.: Government Printing Office, 1941.

Vanecko, James J., and Jennie Kronenfeld. "Preferences for Public Expenditures and Ethno-Racial Group Membership: A Test of the Theory of Political Ethos." *Ethnicity* 4 (December 1977): 311–336.

Wald, Kenneth D. "The Electoral Base of Political Machines: A Deviant Case Analysis." *Urban Affairs Quarterly* 16, no. 1 (September 1980): 3–29.

Waldman, Sidney. *Foundations of Political Analysis.* Englewood Cliffs, N.J.: Prentice-Hall, 1972.

Walton, Hanes, Jr. *Black Politics: A Theoretical and Structural Analysis.* Philadelphia: J. B. Lippincott, 1972.

Warner, Sam Bass, Jr. *Streetcar Suburbs: The Process of Growth in Boston, 1870–1900.* Cambridge, Mass.: Harvard University Press, 1962.

Watkins, Linda M. "Pittsburgh Blacks' Paucity of Political Clout Stirs Struggle over the City's At-Large Election System." *Wall Street Journal,* April 1, 1986, p. 58.

Watson, Donald S. "Financing Relief and Recovery: [The] Reconstruction Finance Corporation." In *Municipal Year Book, 1937,* pp. 375–381. Chicago: International City Managers' Association, 1937.

Watson, Tom. "All Powerful Machine of Yore Endures in New York's Nassau." *Congressional Quarterly Weekly Report,* April 17, 1985, pp. 1623–1625.

Weinberg, Martha Wagner. "Boston's Kevin White: A Mayor Who Survives." *Political Science Quarterly* 96, no. 1 (Spring 1981): 87–106.

Weingrod, Alex. "Patrons, Patronage, and Political Parties." *Comparative Studies in Society and History* 10, no. 4 (July 1968): 377–400.

Weiss, Nancy Joan. *Charles Francis Murphy, 1858–1924: Respectability and Responsibility in Tammany Politics.* Northampton, Mass.: Smith College, 1968.

Welch, Susan, and Albert Karnig. "The Impact of Black Elected Officials on Urban Social Expenditures." *Policy Studies Journal* 7 (Summer 1979): 707–714.

Wendt, Lloyd, and Herman Kogan. *Bosses in Lusty Chicago: The Story of Bathhouse John and Hinky Dink.* Bloomington: Indiana University Press, 1967. Originally published in 1943 as *Lords of the Levee.*

Werner, M. R. *Tammany Hall.* Garden City, N.Y.: Doubleday, Doran and Co., 1928.

Whitehead, Ralph, Jr. "The Organization Man." *American Scholar* 46 (Summer 1977): 351–357.

———. "The Chicago Story: Two Dailies, a Campaign—and an Earthquake." *Columbia Journalism Review* (July–August 1983): 25–31.

Whyte, William. *Financing New York City.* New York: Annals of the Academy of Political and Social Science, 1935.

Whyte, William Foote. "Social Organization in the Slums." *American Sociological Review* 8, no. 1 (February 1943): 34–39.

———. *Street Corner Society: The Social Structure of an Italian Slum.* Chicago: University of Chicago Press, 1955. Originally published in 1943.

Wilentz, Sean. *Chants Democratic: New York City and the Rise of the Working Class, 1788–1850.* New York: Oxford University Press, 1984.

Williams, R. Hal. *The Democratic Party and California Politics, 1880–1896.* Stanford: Stanford University Press, 1973.

Willis, Marty. "Jan. 6 Demonstration to Greet All-White City Council." *Pittsburgh Courier,* January 11, 1986, pp. A–1, A–4.

Wilson, James Q. "The Economy of Patronage." *Journal of Political Economy* 69, no. 4 (August 1961): 369–380.

———. *The Amateur Democrat: Club Politics in Three Cities.* Chicago: University of Chicago Press, 1966.

Wilson, James Q. and Edward C. Banfield. "Public-Regardingness as a Value Premise in Voting Behavior." *American Political Science Review* 58, no. 4 (December 1964): 876–887.

Wittke, Carl. *Refugees of Revolution.* Philadelphia: University of Pennsylvania Press, 1952.

———. *The Irish in America.* Baton Rouge: Louisiana State University Press, 1956.

Wolfinger, Raymond E. "The Development and Persistence of Ethnic Voting." *American Political Science Review* 59, no. 4 (December 1965): 896–908.

———. "Some Consequences of Ethnic Politics." In *The Electoral Process,* edited by M. Kent Jennings and L. Harmon Zeigler, pp. 42–54. Englewood Cliffs, N.J.: Prentice-Hall, 1966.

———. "Why Political Machines Have Not Withered Away and Other Revisionist Thoughts." *Journal of Politics* 34, no. 2 (May 1972): 365–398.

———. *The Politics of Progress.* Englewood Cliffs, N.J.: Prentice-Hall, 1974.

Wolfinger, Raymond E., and John Osgood Field. "Political Ethos and the Structure of City Government." *American Political Science Review* 60, no. 2 (June 1966): 306–326.

Woods, Robert A., ed. *Americans in Process.* Boston: Houghton Mifflin, 1903.

Wright, Gavin. "The Political Economy of New Deal Spending: An Econometric Analysis." *Review of Economics and Statistics* 56, no. 1 (February 1974): 30–38.

Yearley, C. K. *The Money Machines: The Breakdown and Reform of Governmental and Party Finance in the North, 1860–1920.* Albany: State University of New York Press, 1970.

Zink, Harold. *City Bosses in the United States.* Durham, N.C.: Duke University Press, 1930.

Index

Aaron, Henry, 184

AFDC (Aid to Families with Dependent Children): and co-optation of black service providers, 168, 265; demobilizing impact of, on welfare recipients, 168, 265; exploited by Daley machine, 225; politicization of, 167; used to placate urban blacks, 166

Affirmative action, 141; in Chicago, 152

Albany: Barnes machine in, 68; homeownership in, 84; McCabe machine in, 84; new immigrant voters in, 10, 123–124; redevelopment in, 158–160; state government interference in, 38; War on Poverty in, 169. *See also* O'Connell machine

Altgeld, John P. (governor of Illinois), 44, 204

American Labor party, 138, 173

Andersen, Kristi, 123

Annexation: as double-edged sword, 57; and New York Consolidation Act of 1897, 56; as resource-enhancement strategy, 13, 213; and suburban incorporation, 81

Asian-Americans, 259, 263. *See also* Minorities, contemporary

Banfield, Edward C., and mass theory of machine, 8, 196, 209, 226

Barnes, William E. (Republican boss of Albany), 68, 74

Beer, Samuel, 232

Bell, Daniel, 239

Belloni, Frank, 230

Black-Irish comparisons, 6, 237–238, 260–265. *See also* Rainbow theory of machine

Black mayors, 258–262. *See also names of individual mayors*

Blacks: activism of, during 1960s, 166; in Boston, 178, 187; critical to Daley mayoral victories, 152, 154, 165; declining turnout in Chicago among (1964–1976), 169; disenchanted with Daley machine, 185; migration of, to northern cities, 146; political remobilization among, and rainbow coalition, 184–186, 260–262; and sub-machines in Chicago and Pittsburgh, 3, 165–166, 168; and welfare state dependence, 168–170. *See also* Minorities, contemporary

Bobcock, John Paul, 2

Border and Southern states, political culture and machine building in, 195, 228–229. *See also* Sunbelt cities

Boston: blacks in postwar, 178, 187; factional ward politics in, 19, 42, 70; impact of Depression in, 117; Irish population in, 9, 177; new immigrants in, 128; postwar reform and redevelopment in, 143, 176–177; White's personal organization in, 177–179, 182. *See also* Curley, James Michael

Brains Trust, The (Tugwell), 16

Brennan, George, and Hopkins-Sullivan faction, 12, 78, 102

Bridges, Amy, 257

Broderick, David, 27

Brooks, Robert, 62

Brown, Homer, 3, 165

Browning, Rufus, 264

Bryce, James, 19, 49, 236

Buckley, Christopher (boss of San Francisco): fall of, 228; fiscal conservatism of, 47–48

333

Compositor:	G & S Typesetters, Inc.
Printer:	Maple-Vail Book Mfg. Group
Binder:	Maple-Vail Book Mfg. Group
Text:	11/13 Sabon
Display:	Sabon